A Humanities Press Book

We are pleased to send you a
complimentary copy of

Logical Investigations.
by Edmund Husserl
Vol. 1

. . . for review

We would appreciate two copies of
your review.

Publication date . 1970

Price $30. per set

HUMANITIES PRESS, Inc.
Publishers & Importers of Scholarly Books
303 PARK AVE. SOUTH NEW YORK 10, N. Y.

LOGICAL INVESTIGATIONS

International Library of Philosophy and Scientific Method

EDITOR: TED HONDERICH
ADVISORY EDITOR: BERNARD WILLIAMS

A Catalogue of books already published in the
International Library of Philosophy and Scientific Method
will be found at the end of this volume

LOGICAL
INVESTIGATIONS

EDMUND HUSSERL

Translated by

J. N. FINDLAY

from the Second German Edition
of *Logische Untersuchungen*

VOLUME ONE

PROLEGOMENA TO PURE LOGIC

(Volume One of the German Edition)

EXPRESSION AND MEANING

(Investigation I, Volume II of the German Edition)

THE IDEAL UNITY OF THE SPECIES

(Investigation II, Volume II of the German Edition)

NEW YORK
HUMANITIES PRESS

'*Logische Untersuchungen*' first published
by M. Niemeyer, Halle, *1900*

Second German edition Vol. I *and*
Vol. II *Part* I *published* *1913*

This edition first published in the United States
of America *1970*
by Humanities Press Inc., 303 Park Avenue South
New York, N.Y. 10010

© *This translation J. N. Findlay, 1970*

SBN 391 00053 5

Printed in Great Britain

Dedicated to
CARL STUMPF
with Honour
and
in Friendship

CONTENTS

CONTENTS

CHAPTER TWO

Theoretical Disciplines as the Foundation of Normative Disciplines

CHAPTER THREE

*Psychologism, its Arguments and its Attitude to the Usual
Counter-Arguments*

CHAPTER FOUR

Empiricistic Consequences of Psychologism

CONTENTS

CHAPTER FIVE

Psychological Interpretations of Basic Logical Principles

CHAPTER SIX

*Syllogistic Inferences Psychologistically Considered. Syllogistic and
Chemical Formulae*

CHAPTER SEVEN

Psychologism as a Sceptical Relativism

CONTENTS

CHAPTER EIGHT

The Psychologistic Prejudices

CHAPTER NINE

Logic and the Principle of the Economy of Thought

CONTENTS

CHAPTER TEN
End of our Critical Treatments

CHAPTER ELEVEN
The Idea of Pure Logic

VOLUME II OF THE GERMAN EDITION

INTRODUCTION

INVESTIGATION I
EXPRESSION AND MEANING

CHAPTER ONE
Essential Distinctions

CHAPTER TWO

Towards a Characterization of the Acts which Confer Meaning

CHAPTER THREE

Fluctuation in Meaning and the Ideality of Unities of Meaning

CONTENTS

CHAPTER FOUR

The Phenomenological and Ideal Content of the Experiences of Meaning

INVESTIGATION II
THE IDEAL UNITY OF THE SPECIES AND
MODERN THEORIES OF ABSTRACTION

CHAPTER ONE

Universal Objects and the Consciousness of Universality

CHAPTER TWO

The Psychological Hypostatization of the Universal

CHAPTER THREE

Abstraction and Attention

CONTENTS

CHAPTER SIX

Separation of Varying Concepts of Abstraction and Abstract

TRANSLATOR'S INTRODUCTION

THE *Logical Investigations* which is here translated is the work through which Edmund Husserl first established his reputation: it is also, in the opinion of many, including this translator, his greatest and most important philosophical work. First published in 1900–1, when Husserl was teaching at Halle, it was preceded by his *Philosophy of Arithmetic* (Volume 1 alone published, Halle, 1891), a surpassingly excellent but almost entirely forgotten work on the foundation of mathematics, and succeeded by a long series of brilliant works, some only published since Husserl's death in the series known as *Husserliana* (Nijhoff, The Hague), which expound a systematic position known as 'phenomenology', and of which the best known is the *Ideas towards a pure Phenomenology and phenomenological Philosophy*, first published in 1913, and translated into English by W. Boyce-Gibson (Muirhead Library, Allen and Unwin). The *Logical Investigations* occupies a position midway between the *Philosophy of Arithmetic* and the later, full-blown phenomenology, and while the word 'phenomenology' quite often occurs in its text, it is used in a somewhat different, simpler sense than that of the later system. It means only 'descriptive psychology': the study of what enters into the 'description', the clarificatory analysis, of conscious experience and its various sub-species, rather than what may be involved in the actuality of consciousness in the world, and its causal and other relations to the body and to mundane existences generally.

The text of the *Logical Investigations* underwent a few excisions, modifications and additions in the Second Edition of 1913 (The Prolegomena and Investigations I–V) and 1921 (Investigation VI), and they were mainly such as to bring it more into line with the later phenomenology. Fatigue and change of interest, however, prevented Husserl from carrying out the thorough revision of the text that he contemplated, and the Second and Third Editions of the *Logical Investigations* are not importantly different from the First. It was only in works like *Formal and transcendental Logic* (1929) that Husserl substantially developed the treatments of

Logic which occur in the *Logical Investigations*. We may be glad that this is so. For the *Logical Investigations* has merits quite independent of its interesting relations to the phenomenological system, or to the subsequent development of German philosophy. It is, despite much that is dated, and much that is drearily detailed and technical, a surpassingly good piece of philosophical work, and one that has a permanent interest for Anglo-Saxon philosophers, owing to its close relations, at many points, to traditional British empiricism, and to the analytic concerns which perturbed Russell and Moore. But it may also claim, particularly in its last two studies, 'On Intentional Experiences and their "Contents"' and 'Elements of a phenomenological Elucidation of Knowledge', to have reached an Aristotelian level of many-sided profundity, and to have sketched the basic grammar of conscious experience in a manner never before or since surpassed, or even equalled. Brentano may have led up to this remarkable consummation, and Husserl's later phenomenological writings may have developed it richly and variously, but it is here in its least controversial, best-argued form, free from the extraneous trappings of a 'system', and its dubious methodological and covertly metaphysical pretensions, and simply one of the prime achievements of philosophy. Husserl, a Jew or of Jewish origin, died dishonoured in 1938, forbidden to enter the university where he had taught, and forbidden entry (no doubt owing to political exigencies) by his own most famous pupil. It will not, however, be doubtful to anyone who carefully reads the *Logical Investigations* and many of the later works, that we have in him one of the small number of supreme contributors to philosophy, not unworthy of being spoken of in the same breath with Kant and Hegel, or with Plato and Aristotle.

It is because I have found the writings of Husserl so superlatively valuable, and so deeply stimulating even when I rejected their detail, and because I so deeply regretted his inadequate accessibility in English – particularly when infinitely less important works were both translated and much discussed – that I undertook the present translation, which has occupied me during spells of reduced academic pressure over many years. It has proved very difficult, since I was determined that the result should be English, even if inevitably it had to be a somewhat heavy, Teutonic English, such as Husserl himself might have written, had he felt himself, authentically if extraneously, into the world of Anglo-Saxon culture. The task of teasing Husserl's richly redundant, serpentine style, with its multitude of higher-order expressions having no equivalent in our own linguistic stock-in-trade, into something that would flow, and have conciseness and clarity of form, even when its content was very difficult, has agitated me immensely, and I have no doubt that I have fallen short of perfect faithfulness or perfect English at many points. I do not, however, regard a translation, however good, as a substitute for the original, and believe that the attempt to make it such a substitute makes it less good as a translation than it could be. If I have made Husserl accessible to many who will make a profitable use of his ideas, instead of ranging them in a dreary chronological museum, leading up to a final show-case which enshrines pure Nothingness or pure Being – it scarcely matters which – I shall have achieved my purpose.

Personal explanations and panegyric should not, however, extend beyond the first paragraphs of an Introduction. I must try to say, in general terms, why I think Husserl's *Logical Investigations* such an important work. It is important not because it can now count as a valuable contribution to the logical syntax of our language, but because it uses its investigations of logic to illuminate much more fundamental topics: the nature of meaning, the ontology which meaningful discourse presupposes, and, infinitely most important, the nature of those conscious acts in virtue of which alone our words point beyond themselves to things in the world, and in virtue of which alone there *is* a world for us and any fellows with whom we can communicate. Husserl's polemics in favour of an adequate theory of meaning, of an 'objective' view of logical categories and of an 'intentional' analysis of consciousness, are directed against the contemporary idols of the theatre, the naturalisms and psychologisms of the time, which he thoroughly demolishes. They could, however, with equal point, have been directed against our own more elaborate naturalisms, which, intoxicated with new-found behaviouristic categories, and employing a sophistry of models rather than a sophistry of arguments – my reference here is to certain famous 'language-games' – manage to divert attention from that central conscious subjectivity, and from its varied 'constitutive' activities, which not only *can* be rendered intelligible, whether in ourselves or in others, but in ignorance of which nothing whatever can be rendered intelligible at all.

As regards Husserl's view of meaning, he is the first to attempt a study of its phenomenology, of the queer manner in which words, whether spoken or written or heard or seen, and so 'given in intuition', yet bow themselves off the stage as prime terms of our references, and merely serve to introduce, or to help introduce, objects and connections other than themselves. And he is also the first to stress how words so used seem to *clothe* the objects to which they make reference possible, how they are phenomenologically inscribed upon the whole world around us and to what an extent knowing or cognizing an object consists in putting the right name to it, seeing it as *called* this or that. All this has many points of affinity with recent linguistic philosophy, but it is also profoundly different. For recent linguistic philosophy is a third-person, observer's analysis, which sees meaning only in the varied use made of words and combinations of words in many natural and social situations. This observer's analysis is of course both valuable and necessary, for the phenomenology of meaning would not be complete without a study of its behavioural working out, and its detailed exhibition in the conduct of persons in their environment. A life of meaningful references that had no 'fulfilment' in responsiveness to what environs the person, would, in fact, be not merely not actual, but intrinsically impossible. But this does not affect the fact that a personal appropriation of meaning, a lived-through understanding of what it is that words are naming or communicating, is a central feature of the meaningful use of words, and that, in default of it, there could be no more genuine semiosis than there is in the case of a computer or a tape-recorder. Beings who faultlessly used the right words in the right circumstances, and who got about the world and helped other similar beings to get about it, but to whom the rationale, the sense of their proceedings was never a lived experience, totally embraced in each present and not spread out over tracts of time, nor referred hypothetically to the future – we shall not say that such a sense must *always* be so experienced – would not deserve to be called speakers or users of a language at all. Of them it would be right to say: Words they are moved by, but they hear not, words they utter, but they speak not, neither do they understand. The phenomenology of meaning has, of course, been

4

carried much further than we find it in Husserl, particularly by phenomenologists like Roman Ingarden, but the all-important beginnings are there. As regards Husserl's contributions to ontology, the *Logical Investigations* introduces us to a richness of categorial distinctions such as we find in Aristotle, and such as only his great contemporary Meinong carried further. We have none of the misplaced economy, suitable in natural science, where it is all-important to have only a few explanatory ultimates or laws, carried over into the realm of thought-distinctions, where it encourages one to massacre some valuable concept, or to warp the expression of some well-understood principle, in order to satisfy the exigencies of a cheese-paring behest not to multiply entities, and which so fears the 'jungle' of ramifying things of reason that it is prepared to sink into the Serbonian bog of enforced simplification. Obviously one does not lose, but gain, by noting all the iridescent variety which confronts one even at the categorial level, and which is indefeasibly part of the world as we deal with it through word and thought. There is the distinction between the thing and its parts, and between its separable parts and its inseparable 'sides' or 'moments', there is the distinction between the patterns instantiated in things and the detached patterns which they exemplify, there is the distinction between things and states of affairs concerning things, and among the many varied sorts of such states of affairs, and there is the distinction between the forms of things and states of affairs and the matter, the items bound together by those forms. A philosopher sensitive enough to point to the semantic and ontological difference between the passing postman and the fact that the postman is passing, is obviously sensitive to differences which a training of the economizing, reductive sort only serves to blunt. In the *Logical Investigations* one sees the beginnings of the doctrine that all the categorial distinctions recognized by logic extend beyond the limits of language and symbolism and are implicit in our unverbalized experience. This was afterwards to be carried further in such works as *Erfahrung und Urteil*, where a whole world of pre-predicative negations, modalities etc., was recognized in the primitive texture of human, and even of animal experience. The heresy of 'pre-linguistic meanings', so much condemned by certain linguistic philosophers, is thus made the basis of an illuminating analysis. Husserl's ontology, further, is not uniform-ist and monolithic, as in those modern ontologies where *any* case of quantification commits one to a whole range of 'entities', which all, however, have being in precisely the same sense and manner. Like Aristotle, Husserl too has his analogy of being, where some things are there in a more foundational, primitive sense, while other entities have an essentially 'founded', secon-dary, derivative status. The developments of Husserl's ontology, and the changes induced in it by the idealistic positions of the later phenomenology, are not, however, matters that can be further discussed here.

In Husserl's phenomenology, understood as a purely descrip-tive, internal analysis of consciousness and its varieties, we have, however, the supreme contribution of the *Logical Investigations*, as of the later, specifically so-styled, phenomenological writings. What Husserl clearly saw, and what later analysts of language have failed to see, is that the interpretation of speech always proceeds in two necessarily correlated, but in many respects deeply different, and often disparate dimensions: the interpreta-tion of speech as referring to entities and situations in the world, or to ideal abstractions from these latter, and the interpretation of speech as revealing the 'references' that it thus embodies, the so-called 'acts' or 'conscious appearances' in which such entities and situations display themselves before us, are given separately or together, as making up or at least 'framing' our world, whether as possibilities or as limiting impossibilities. To talk of objects 'out there', and their actual or possible predicates and relations, may not be to talk of our conscious awareness of such matters, but it is always to imply it, and to imply it in no vague, general fashion, but in one precisely proportioned and accom-modated to the objective matters of which we are talking. There is nothing mysterious, puzzling in all this, or in the regular, natural swing-over from an external to an internal reference, in the passage from a situation as we think of it or perceive it, to the situation of our thought or perception of it: we are not suddenly translated from a world of limpid natural objects to the murky contents of the 'queer medium of the mind'. We have merely passed from the obverse to the reverse side of the same coin, and any limpidity which attaches to the objects and situations referred to, attaches also to our conscious, significant references to them.

People are wont to speak as if there were some close-wrapped mystery about the inner, private side of things which does not apply to their outer, public side, as if one could be wholly clear about the latter and deeply confused or in doubt about the former. This is not the case at all. To perceive that the soap in one's bathroom is exhausted, or to understand what it is for one's bathroom soap to be exhausted, is to be able to perceive or understand what one's own perception or understanding of the exhaustion of one's bathroom soap is like, and to understand, further, what *anyone*'s understanding of the same matter must be like. We are not unclear as to what happens in a man's experience when he knows his bathroom soap to be exhausted, at least not in the respects in which that experience is directed to the domestic situation in question.

There are of course *other* respects in which our understanding of the 'inner' situation presents difficulties which our understanding of the 'outer' situation does not, difficulties which we perfectly understand in the light of the fact that it *is* an inner situation. There are mental pictures and feelings and attenuations of mental pictures and feelings, which have to be approached, if at all, through people's hesitant, analogical accounts of what they picture and feel, and it is clear that there are difficulties, if not ones of principle, in our access to such things. There are also philosophical puzzles connected with the manner into which our experience packs or reduces to unity what can only be spelt out or unpacked in a lengthy exegesis, difficulties which have led certain philosophers to explain our packed inner state as one of *readiness* to say or do certain things, or of readiness to behave in certain ways, all explanations which reduce the packed concentration of conscious life to the content or process of its unpacking. All such solutions spring from a peculiar inability to see that consciousness just is, or at least is, the bringing into a focus of indivisible contemporaneity of what, from another point of view may be successive and dispersed, and that a world in which, perhaps per impossibile, there were only mutually external happenings in space and time, would be a world of which we could not be conscious, in which there could be no such thing as conscious experience at all. There are, therefore, and must be, corresponding to any well-formed, articulate tract of fully significant speech – and speech is of course not always fully

significant – mental stances or appearances complete and consummated in the moment, and only spread over time in the sense
of lasting and changing throughout that time, in which objects
and situations are set before us in various definite or indefinite
lights, which change and develop as we consider those objects
and situations. It is to the analysis and classification and law-
governed interconnection of these mental stances or appearances
that phenomenology must be directed, and through which it must
illuminate the mind and language and the world. The use of a
language of *acts*, of things done, is in this context traditional, but
Husserl makes clear, like Brentano and Meinong, that his use of
the term has no special connection with *activity*. The mere
presence of something to mind, its entry into consciousness in
whatever unheralded manner, its mere turning up or appearance
or *Erscheinung*, constitutes an 'act' in the sense relevant to
Husserl's analysis.

What it then becomes important to note are the wide variety of
alternative species into which the one invariant thing, consciousness, differentiates itself, and in fact only *is* the one invariant thing
consciousness because it can be thus differentiated. Of these
differences of manner, the most fundamental is the difference
between the *empty* manner in which things can be there for mere
thought, for meaning-intention, and the *fulfilled* or *seeing* manner
in which they can be there for illustrative intuition (*Anschauung*).
Husserl is infinitely skilled in showing the vast number of
differing manners and proportions in which the intuitive and
emptily cogitative can be combined, and in stressing the fact that,
except in the ideal limit, they are always so combined in our
perception of physical objects, a physical object being always
something that could be further and more richly seen and
explored, however much of it is or has been present to our senses.
Husserl also dwells by analogy on the intuitive grasp, the full
givenness of ideal characters and states of affairs, as opposed to
their imperfect presence to mind by way of symbols whose
meaning or valid combination is only partially felt. And he
stresses the case of 'fulfilment' by way of internal images and by
way of external physical models or diagrams or pictures, which
is only a surrogate for the more complete fulfilment when what
we have before us is given as 'the thing itself'. Nowhere in the
literature of philosophy are these matters more subtly treated

8

and more full of an evident clearness and rightness: it is only a pity that they have been so infrequently and so superficially studied.

Husserl's analysis of consciousness derives, of course, from Brentano's concept of intentionality, but is in several respects superior. Husserl we may say was the first to stress a property of intentional reference which Brentano also stated in the first appendix to the 1911 edition of his *Psychology*, that conscious reference is not strictly speaking a real relation, since the object or state of affairs referred to need not exist at all. The God Jupiter, Husserl says in chapter 2 of the Fifth Investigation, is not a real constituent, is not really present, in my conscious reference to him: to think that he need be, or could be, is to misunderstand the nature of conscious reference altogether. This point was never understood by Meinong, who had to give a certain *Vorhandenheit* even to non-existent or absurd objects. It is not unlikely that Brentano got the first idea for his 1911 Appendix from the 1901 discussion of the God Jupiter in the *Logische Untersuchungen*, together, of course, with much that also infuriated him: certainly the example of the God Jupiter is cited by Kraus in his exposition of Brentano's doctrine.

Husserl, however, did not fall into the prime error of making the possible non-existence of a thought-object the criterion of mentality, a mistake persisted in by Chisholm. For he is clearly aware, in the second place, that references that fail of a target imply the existence of references where the target is in the nature of things hit, is itself intuited or given – the meaning of intuition is simply that of an ultimate, perfect self-givenness – and given as it in itself is. Unless there was this limiting form of intentionality, there would be no meaning in saying that certain intentions fail of their mark, that they present their objects in an inadequate or distorted light, and not as they are, or not as they wholly are. Consciousness can only give sense to its inadequacies by contrasting them with an ultimate, inerrant adequacy or self-givenness. The notion of the self-evident or inwardly evident which in Brentano is no more than an internal index of our title to judge or believe something, is therefore for Husserl no more than the limiting state where doubt becomes senseless, irrelevant, since the standard of self-givenness has been reached. For Husserl therefore it is part of the notion of intentionality that there is a

9

limiting state (ideal in the case of physical objects) in which the object as it is thought of or given simply fades out in, or achieves coincidence with, the object as it in and for itself is. The difficulties of this account of self-evidence, the many cases of seeming self-evidence which later require revision, is finely dealt with in the 1929 *Formal and transcendental Logic* which must certainly be studied if we are fully to evaluate the *Logical Investigations*.

It is to be regretted that Husserl did not allow the implications of his own views on self-givenness to guide him away from the methodological ἐποχή or suspension of conviction which is preached in the later *Ideas* (§§31, 32 *et seq.*). For there is arguably no clear sense to be given to a total suspension of belief in the entire world: it is only in the context of a limiting, if unattainable, complete givenness of all sides of physical realities that the notion of their doubtful, distorted, merely intended presence to consciousness can be significantly entertained, a point since made by many analytic philosophers. Husserl sees that we cannot accord a merely phenomenal, intentional status to the *acts* of consciousness in which physical objects are given, a point clear to Descartes as it was not clear to Kant, and he is also unwilling to accord a merely intended status to the experiences of others: he thinks, however, that he can significantly 'bracket' the reality of all natural things, and even passes on from this to the idealistic conviction that physical things have, despite their transcendent status for consciousness, no more than a merely intended, phenomenal being, while consciousness itself exists in an 'absolute' manner (*Ideas*, §§41–6). To the extent that Husserl makes this move, he transforms his brilliant, original analysis of consciousness into one of those ordinary subjectivisms which comfort the shattered ego by assuring it, quite baselessly, that in some secret manner it has manufactured its own shattering world. Of this form of subjectivism, respectable only on a theistic background like Berkeley's, there is not a trace in the *Logical Investigations*. The examination of consciousness, and of how things are given to consciousness, goes with no implication that such things have no being other than their givenness to consciousness: the contrary implication is in fact without reservation taken to be part and parcel of consciousness itself. Room is of course left for metaphysical reversals, but a proper suspension of conviction and assertion is maintained on such possibilities. It is only in the

Ideas, with its pretended methodological suspension of all conviction, that such a suspension is, in fact, not truly practised.

A third respect in which Husserl's treatment of consciousness is greatly superior, lies in its acknowledgement of lived-through experiences or lived-through moments of experience which are not intentional at all, which present nothing to consciousness, not even themselves. Our sensations, treated as modifications of our own interior selfhood, are experienced moments of this type, and they are utterly to be distinguished from the properties of physical objects which appear in corresponding perceptions. There is, Husserl thinks, as Meinong does also, a redwise mode of interior experience which corresponds to the redness we perceive, whether validly or illusorily, out there in objects: this redwiseness we feel rather than perceive (in normal experience), but *in* feeling we can also pass to perceiving the objective redness which is as it were its 'other side'. This use of interior experience to mediate objective reference is misleadingly described in a language of *beseelende Auffassungen*, animating conceptions or interpretations, which suggests the traditional theory, infinitely repugnant to Husserl, of causal inferences from immediate sense-data to unperceived physical objects. For Husserl the sensation (though sometimes called a 'datum') is not normally given at all, and its *Auffassung* or interpretation is a primary act of mind's self-transcendence and not therefore, properly speaking, an interpretation or an inference at all. What it reveals is also not any remote function of physics but the redness that is authentically perceived. The theory of 'inner felt sides' to the sensible properties of things has of course been adversely criticized by the few who have understood it properly, among whom G. E. Moore is to be reckoned: it is arguable that, though dubious on a first analysis, it becomes ever more acceptable on further examination. Husserl uses the same notion of representing contents which are not themselves presented, in his theory of categorial intuition. Through the mind's various acts of synthetic combination it can come to set before itself various forms of *objective* synthesis, e.g. the synthesis of properties in a thing, of items in a group, of identity in varying contexts etc. It is a pity that there have been so few people to understand and discuss these interesting doctrines.

From the general consideration of the merits of Husserl's *Logical Investigations*, we pass to consider the separate studies into which it is divided. Here we have first to deal with the celebrated 'Prolegomena to Pure Logic' which is the published form, Husserl tells us, of two lively sets of lectures given at the University of Göttingen in the summer and autumn of 1896. These 'Prolegomena' were immensely influential, but they are also highly misleading. They contain a polemic against psychologism, which suggests that Husserl was against any and every psychological 'grounding' of logic and significant discourse in a study of the mind and its 'acts'. This is not the case at all, as a study of the *Logical Investigations* from I to VI abundantly proves. The psychologism that Husserl thinks is worthless as a foundation for logic and the study of significant discourse is the psychologism which reposes on psychology as an *empirical causal science*, given to establishing, through observation, experiment and induction, a theory of the workings of the mind as bound down to animal bodies in time and space, and subject to laws which must be established empirically or not at all. Empirical psychology had received an immense fillip through the new laboratory psychology-without-a-soul of Wundt at Leipzig, and had been rashly appealed to, and applied as a talisman, in all fields of philosophy, and it was *this* psychology that Husserl thought shed absolutely no light on the notions and principles of logic. Descriptive or analytic psychology, which considered what mental states intrinsically were, and what objects they presented and in what manners, and how, being what they were, they were combined in the unity of the 'ego' or 'mind', quite regardless of the empirical contingencies responsible for their origin and continuance, or of the reality of their objects, *this* was not shown, nor intended to be shown, as irrelevant for the foundations of Logic, and the whole set of studies in the Investigations after the Prolegomena is in fact concerned with it.

The full explanation of the polemical tone of the Prolegomena is, however, to be found in the fact that the Husserl of an earlier date, the Husserl who had published the *Philosophy of Arithmetic* in 1891, had been himself a psychologistic philosopher, and that he was in the Prolegomena repudiating the errors of his previous position with exaggerated emphasis. To understand what these errors were, we must dwell a little on the content of the *Philosophy of Arithmetic*. In this work Husserl was concerned to illuminate the concepts of number and the numbers, and to relate them to other cognate concepts such as unity, plurality, identity, equality etc. His concern was not like that of his great contemporary Frege, whom he trenchantly criticizes, to establish watertight definitions and axioms for arithmetic, and build them all into a watertight, embracing, deductive whole, without the slightest regard to what people actually understood by the notions in question, and whether they really operated with them in the manner followed. Husserl rather tries to develop a rational genealogy of our arithmetical notions and methods out of primitive mental acts and confrontations: his Philosophy of Arithmetic is an early essay in phenomenology. Husserl takes the Kantian view that arithmetical concepts somehow reflect the subjective form rather than the empirical content of our references, a truth witnessed by the fact that it is quite indifferent what items we assemble together and regard collectively as exemplifying this or that number. Not only do arithmetical assessments presuppose no community of character or concept among the items assessed – a point on which he criticizes Frege – but they presuppose no contentful relations among the items in question. It is not necessary that what we enumerate should form a heap or a swarm. All that is necessary is that they should be items picked out one by one by consciousness, and that they should be collected by consciousness into aggregates or pluralities having no further bond or cement than the fact that they are all referred to *together*. Such joint reference is normally mediated by a common concept, and must be so mediated if the number of the items exceeds the limits of memory or intuition, but in the foundational cases to which the whole system points back such characterization is inessential, and any item could be replaced by any other. There are three sorts of act involved in the emergence of numerical concepts. The first is the act which abstracts from the concrete nature or character of an item to be numbered, and treats it merely as an item present to consciousness: this act is expressed by the use of the word *Etwas*, 'something'. Everything is something, no matter what its specific nature may be. The second is the act which collects items together in one consciousness, which is expressed by talking of something *and* something *and* something etc. And there is, thirdly, the higher-order act which reflects on the abstractive and collective work thus performed, and sees before it a case of something mentally associated with something, or mentally associated with something and with something etc. The numbers arise as the progeny of an abstract process of collecting somethings: something and something is two, something and something and something is three etc. etc. How the system is extended to include the numbers One, Nought and Infinity need not here be considered, nor need we point out that Husserl has not considered what may be involved in the necessary *diversity* of the abstract somethings collected, since something and something and something is not three if the somethings are one and the same. Fundamentally Husserl's analysis of an arithmetical statement like $2 + 2 = 4$ does not differ greatly from the analysis given in the second volume of *Principia Mathematica*, but its philosophical foundation is plainly quite different.

It is not to our purpose, in the present Introduction, to go further in exposition or criticism of the *Philosophy of Arithmetic*. Plainly it has very many flaws. It is our belief, however, that it would not be impossible to purge it of confusions and errors, to supplement it at certain points and to carry it up to the level of the later phenomenology, and that, as so improved, it would be a better, profounder account of the basic ideas and principles of mathematics than is to be found in the work of Russell or Frege, let alone of Hilbert, Brouwer and others. One fault in its approaches must, however, be emphasized, since its correction led Husserl to develop his thought: its importing of psychological notions into the *analysis* of arithmetical notions, so that we cannot have any ideas of aggregates, numbers, equality etc., without also having ideas of mental acts of abstraction and collection. Husserl says that 'an aggregate arises in so far as a unitary interest, and in and with it a unitary observation makes different contents stand out and embraces them. The collective connection can therefore only be apprehended *through reflection* on the mental act, through which the aggregate comes into being' (*Ph. of Ar.* p. 79). He likewise remarks: 'The concept of "something" can naturally not be attained by any thinkable comparison of the content of objects whether physical or mental . . . It obviously owes its genesis *to reflection* on the psychic act of presentation, as whose content every definite object is given' (op. cit. p. 86). In other words, in judging that $2 + 1 = 3$, we have first to conceive abstractly of objects as being *merely* objects of presentation, in which all are alike, and we have to conceive of them further as held together in or by someone's regard, it does not matter whose. Now it is plain that no such references to mental doings are involved in our abstract or concrete arithmetical assertions: mental doings may help to make them possible, may help to 'constitute' their sense or their objects, as the mature doctrine of Husserl abundantly recognizes, but they plainly form no part of their 'content'. And if they did, as Husserl says in the Foreword to the First Edition of the *Logical Investigations*, it would more and more raise doubts of principle as to how mathematics, and logic too – for it had become plain to Husserl that logic and mathematics were alike branches of a single formal discipline – could have an objective, scientifically validated application to the world. That logic, or a great deal of it could be made a study of objective *Sätze an sich*, propositions in themselves, and their components, and that, as so purged, it could become exactly the same sort of non-psychological study as mathematics, had meanwhile become clear to Husserl from his reading of the early nineteenth-century *Wissenschaftslehre* of Bolzano, his generous references to which were a prime cause for its rescue from oblivion.

The Prolegomena is therefore a systematic attempt to expel psychology from the analysis of logical notions and principles (e.g. from the law of contradiction), and to expel psychology, *as an empirical, natural science*, from the philosophical explanation of logical notions and principles. It is not an attempt to exclude psychology, in the sense of a transcendental, phenomenological description of possible patterns of consciousness, from the logical field, even though in one footnote reference to Kant (ch. 5, §28) Husserl *does* say that transcendental psychology is after all *also* a psychology. It would not be profitable to outline all the moves of Husserl's argument, nor to comment on his many mistakes. His notions of value and normativity as developed in his second chapter are obviously inadequate, but the conclusion that every normative science presupposes a non-normative science which merely describes its objects, and comments on their production, has more substance, even though it might still seem open to some question. The theory favoured by the late nineteenth-century, Humean age in Germany was to the effect that the non-normative basis of logical norms was to be found in psychology: this alone would explain our pursuit of certain patterns of logical thought, and would also tell us how we might best achieve them. Husserl points out that, since psychology is an empirical, inductive science, containing not one single irrefragable law, this would compel us to give a wavering empirical account of logical procedures and principles. We should have to find out in what circumstances men were cogitatively appeased in this or that logical manner, and principles thus based could have no absolute certainty and validity: they would in fact not even resemble the principles and procedures of pure logic in the way in which we normally talk of them. Mill and Heymans, Lange and Sigwart are all given a long cross-examination, but it is obvious from the start that a necessary principle like the law of contradiction cannot be based on some doubtful psychological principle, such as that 'judgements recognized as contradictory cannot coexist in a single consciousness'. That syllogistic formulae can be profitably likened to chains of chemical equations receives a refutation scarcely merited by its arguability, and the same applies to the logical doctrines of the 'thought-economists' who added a fashionable, evolutionistic note to their misleading or irrelevant contentions. The relativism which associates logic with a particular 'mental constitution', and believes that it could be altered by a change in that constitution, receives the exposure that it deserves, though at far too great a length. In general, Husserl concludes that logical laws are ideal laws connecting certain highly general and therefore formal notions such as Proposition, Truth, Subject, Predicate, Object, Ground and Consequent etc. etc. They are laws essential to the possibility of science, no matter what its subject-matter may be. That they are *ideal* laws puts them for ever apart from the *real* laws which have their foundation in contingent matters of fact. But their being ideal does not render them subjective, not even normatively subjective: they state how things stand in a detached ether of pure meanings or 'ideal unities', which wholly transcend the acts through which they come before us or are constituted objects for us. The norms and principles of a logical technology are (to some extent) mere practical restatements, consequential prescriptive reformulations of the way we must think of things *if* we desire to think of them as they in truth ideally are. This theory of ideal irreality is somewhat obscure, as Husserl does not wish it to be confused with Platonic realism, and yet plainly does not think that his ideal entities and principles have a merely 'intentional' status or being-for-consciousness.

The last chapter of the Prolegomena develops the Idea of Pure Logic as a Theory of Science, as a *mathesis universalis* which studies the possible make-up and possible constituents of an ordered, deductive system, an enquiry which has, of course, since been carried much further than was possible in Husserl's time. The notions of this chapter are not taken up in the rest of the *Logical Investigations*, but the First Section of the *Formal and transcendental Logic* of 1929 carries them further. One point perhaps remains open to criticism in the whole Prolegomena: the great gulf set by Husserl between ideal and real objectivity, and his refusal to believe that the principles of the former can have *any* connection with the principles of the latter. But if it involves a grotesque naturalistic confusion to suppose that one can found the ideal principles and norms of logic on matters of contingent fact, it also seems absurd to hold that they can be without some bearing on matters of fact, even if only to the extent that conscious beings are in some sense influenced or moved by them. Even the most trivial of logical principles has this much of 'real significance' that it is possible to contravene it in thought, and that it is *also* possible to be moved to correct this contravention *because one sees* its trivial truth. There is a touch of the insightful *a priori* in this last statement of conscious tendency, and it has its roots in the notion of conscious insight and not, e.g. in that of a mechanical computer or suchlike. But such criticisms of Husserl are prefigured by what he himself later says in other writings.

From the Prolegomena we pass on to 'Expression and Meaning', the First Investigation of the series. Here there is at the outset an elaborate attempt to distinguish the sign, which merely indicates something else, conveys our thought to it, from the expression which means it. Thus a brand-mark indicates that someone is a slave without actually meaning this, whereas the sentence 'He is a slave' actually means it. All our meaningful expressions have, however, an indicative use when employed in communication in so far as they *intimate* to others certain experiences we are having, but such intimation is of course quite different from their meaning. Meaning for Husserl involves the carrying out of certain meaning-conferring acts or meaning-intentions, and the performance of such acts, phenomenologically speaking, is equivalent to the fact, that two intentions, one directed intuitively to the word, and another, perhaps non-intuitively, to some object (in a wide sense of the word 'object') are so fused into a single intention that there is also something like an identification of their objects (despite their disparity). There is, however, a difference in the degree to which we consciously *live* in each component intention, and since we live preferentially in the act directed to the *object* rather than in the act directed to the word-phenomenon, the latter, the word-phenomenon, appears, as it were, lost in the former, the object, or seems as it were to have the former superimposed more strongly upon it. Meaningful experience is as it were a palimpsest in which the phenomenal words, though intuitively given, show dimly through the objects, perhaps not intuitively given, that they 'stand for'. The meaningful word seems to *be* the meant thing and to have the meant thing's properties, while the meant thing, similarly, appears more dimly 'clothed' with the words which name and describe it. Primitive name- and word-magic, and the difficulty with which students learn to be scrupulous about quotation-marks in the study of semantics, point to the accuracy of Husserl's general conception, though we may note that it *presupposes* the intentional activity of the mind rather than explains it, being in fact merely a complex instance of it.

Husserl's conception of meaning involves a distinction between (*a*) the *act* of meaning which confers meaning (in a different sense of 'meaning') on words or symbols or expressions, and thereby enables them to mean, to refer to objects (in a wide sense of objects); (*b*) the objects meant, or as we should now say, referred to, by the meaningful use of the expression, (these need not, in order to render the expression meaningful, have actual existence); (*c*) the meaning in the sense of an ideal content, which is objective in the sense of being distinct from the act of meaning, but is not to be confused with the object of the meaningful use in question. Any object that we mean, refer to, can be meant by way of a vast number of distinct meanings: thus the meaningful expressions 'the victor of Jena' and 'the vanquished at Waterloo' have quite different meaningful contents though they mean an identical object. Meanings in the sense of ideal contents *can* be made objects of definite acts of meaning, as when we contemplate what is covered semantically by the two expressions in question. When this occurs however, they become the foci of a new set of meanings, the contents of a new set of higher-order intentions, and the same meaning can be differently meant: e.g. we can mean the meaning of the expression 'the victor of Jena' by describing it as the meaning contrasted on the present page with the meaning of 'the vanquished at Waterloo'. But meanings in their ordinary occurrence are not themselves objects or things meant, but help us to mean objects properly speaking, to decide *as what*, or in what capacity, we mean them. Husserl further distinguishes between fulfilling meaning and mere meaning or meaning-intention. The former is meaning fully carried out and illustrated by intuitive confrontation, as when I *see* what I mean before me and see it *as* I mean it, the latter is present when I make an intelligent reference *without* having its object before me, or not *as* I am meaning it. It will be plain that Husserl is, in all these doctrines, drawing distinctions parallel to Frege's distinction between 'sense' and 'meaning', without however making any special use of the term 'sense', the sense or meaning of which term does not for him differ from that of the term 'meaning', and that he is also for the most part, using the verb to 'mean' in the sense in which contemporary logicians use the verb to 'refer'. Confusion will not result unless we imagine that *what* we mean by a meaningful expression is its meaning, and not rather the *object* meant by it. Husserl has obviously studied the treatments of Frege and makes comments on them, but he approaches matters independently and prefers to talk of them in his own way. One is tempted to ask whether Husserl's ideal entities should not simply be identified with meanings treated as objects. Husserl tends, however, to see meanings as paralleling ideal entities, or as being also a sub-class among them, but the reasons he gives for holding this are not strong: that an ideal entity, e.g. the number 4, can be approached via different meanings.

It may be noted that Husserl is not unaware that there is a purely syntactical meaning which symbols have in so far as there are rules for manipulating them in conjunction with other symbols, and that the meaningfulness of mathematical symbols consists largely in such rule-governed manipulability rather than in a correlation with intuition. Only he believes that there is a certain inauthenticity in such a merely 'games-meaning', and that fulfilment by intuitive data, even if only for an ideal experience, is essential to full meaningfulness. Husserl also has an interesting theory of 'essentially occasional expressions' such as 'I', 'this', 'now' etc., which amounts to attributing to them a double meaning, one unindividuated and general, and one fully individuated by the actual occasion. On this we shall not comment, as he himself looks on it as a somewhat doubtful *tour de force*.

The second study in the *Logical Investigations* is entitled 'The Ideal Unity of the Species and Modern Theories of Abstraction'. It is an attempt to argue that we not only can distinguish various non-separable 'moments' or 'sides' in concrete real objects – the red of this flower, the closeness of this body to that etc. – but that we can also rise by 'ideation' to a corresponding set of universal Species – Redness as such, what it is for a body to be close to another body etc. – which are not parts of the real objects in question, and are not 'in time' at all. Husserl, like Plato, has a place *both* for Form-copies and Ideal Forms, and he differentiates between the *as*-such-and-such which is part of what is concretely there and open to perception, and the *being*-such-and-such which is neither. He is on weak ground when he justifies this view by appealing to cases in which an abstract substantive is the *verbal* subject of an assertion, e.g. Four is a number, Red is a colour etc., since forms of words may be differently analysed, but he is on strong, in fact on impregnable ground, when he stresses the authenticity of the experiences in which such abstracted patterns or meanings are dwelt on in detachment, and are made the subjects of assertions that primarily concern them and not their instances. Even if detached universals are no more than intentional objects, Husserl's statements concerning them may none the less be phenomenologically true: there may be acts of great clarity in which we consider just what it is to be equal or close or grotesque, whether or not there, in any further sense, *are* objects such as what we then consider. It is further arguable that there not only are such experiences in which detached universals are dwelt upon, but that they play an indispensable role even in the knowledge of particulars: we should not, e.g. rise to the understanding of certain modal truths concerning particulars of certain sorts, unless we had first clearly and intelligently grasped and dwelt on what it is to be of such sorts, e.g. purple in colour, an object of anger, etc. etc. The ideal being of Husserl's Species depends for him, in the present study, on the fact that there are important truths concerning them. Their ideal being is not taken to be tantamount to the merely intentional status which applies to fictitious, absurd or ill-formed objects, nor will Husserl equate it with the being of Platonic Forms, which he takes to be some confused simulacrum of spatiotemporal reality.

To the theory of Ideal Species which he thus seeks to justify on phenomenological and epistemological grounds, Husserl opposes the theories of abstraction of classical empiricism, the treatments of abstract and general ideas to be found in Locke, Berkeley, Hume, Mill and many Humeans of Husserl's own age. Theories which base the semblance of abstraction on one-sided attention to concreta, on the similarities which sort objects into 'circles', on the associative readiness to pass from one similar object to another, on substitutionary representations of which a perfectly clear account is never given, are all carefully examined and found wanting, and the treatment will interest Anglo-Saxon readers though some of the argument will have a certain wearisome familiarity. Husserl's whole system, rather than the arguments of the present study, have shown the immense fruitfulness of the hypostatization which turns the non-independent semantic scope of a word or phrase into a new, higher-order thought-object, a fruitfulness even at the lower levels of discourse. Nominalists have regarded the multiplication of abstracta as an impediment to thought: the reverse is the case. No thought is more trammelled in its powers of expression, and more involved in exhausting arbitrary complications than the thought which tries to make all true predications directly concern lowest-level particulars and their adventures. Whether universals have a merely intended or another, quasi-real status, they are an important part of the 'phenomena' for all educated intelligences.

Investigation III, the next study, is 'On the Theory of Wholes and Parts'. This is an interesting study, carried to much detailed exactness, of the distinction between the separable part or 'piece' (*Stück*) and the inseparable part or 'moment'. The separable part or piece is the part that can, in some sense, exist independently, though the notion of independent existence is far from clear and requires careful definition: the hand is, in this piece-sense part of the body, and stretches of space or time are parts of more embracing stretches. The distinction between parts sharply defined as against one another, and parts which fade gradually into one another, is carefully examined. As opposed to these parts into which wholes are genuinely fragmented, we have the 'moments', the Hegelian parts, which are *unselbständig* (non-independent) in relation to one another and to the whole. Colour, shape and extent are typical cases of such 'moments'. Husserl does not consider the possibility that it may be an ontological mistake to apply the notion of part to a non-independent moment, since a true part must arguably belong to the same category as the whole it helps to form (a page and a book) whereas a 'moment', in virtue of its non-independence, is arguably not of the same category as the whole into which it enters. There is something highly misleading about treating the shape of a book as a part of it, and many of the most confused arguments of G. E. Moore and other analysts would seem to stem from this error. Husserl's treatment can, however, be defended on analogical grounds: 'moments' are not parts, but in certain respects they behave like parts, and the identities and differences of their logical behaviour is what the Investigation attempts to determine.

Husserl goes on to point out that where we have non-independent parts, we also have *a priori* laws which require one sort of such parts to be associated with another sort or with a certain sort of whole: if this law connects sorts of part which involve 'content', as well as logical form, then we have a case of a synthetic *a priori* law, e.g. the one connecting colour with extension. The belief in, and ready use of synthetic *a priori* connections, and the belief that every field is constituted a field in virtue of them, is characteristic of Husserl's phenomenology, and is one of its most valuable features. The illumination of his approaches, as opposed to those of our native analyst, is that he thinks far more things are necessary than we do, and that we can only learn from experience in a framework not learnt from experience, which makes learning from experience possible. Such a framework is, if one likes, the object of a general or categorial experience, arising out of conceptual experiment, and Husserl's doctrine of the *a priori* has therefore none of the problematic overtones of Kant's: there is no question as to the 'possibility' of knowing things in advance of experience, in the sense of detailed encounter, since learning from experience in this sense presupposes *a priori* knowledge. The puzzle would be if we could learn things from experience, in the sense of detailed encounter, without *a priori* knowledge of the 'field' in which such encounter was to occur. Towards the end of the study Husserl deals with the *a priori* foundations of the concept of nature in general, which form the background of all empirical natural science. This phenomenology or ontology of nature is carried further in the Second Book of the *Ideas*.

The next Investigation, 'On the Distinction between Independent and Non-independent Meanings and the Idea of Pure Grammar', is one of the most illuminating in the whole work. It deals brilliantly with the related issues of complete (categorematic) and incomplete (syncategorematic) expressions, with the import of what are now called the logical laws of formation, with the distinction between senselessness (*Unsinn*) and absurdity (*Widersinn*) and lastly with the systematic modification undergone by meanings in varying contexts. As regards the first, Husserl rightly refuses to make the incomplete–complete distinction a mere distinction of symbols: it applies to meanings, ideally grasped unities, as well. The symbols 'and', 'the ... who ...', 'If ... then ...' etc., have a definite meaning for us even if they occur in isolation: their incompleteness lies in the fact that they clamour for other meanings to complete them in a rounded total of meaning, quite unlike the verbal fragment 'fu-' which may occur in both 'futile' and 'infuse', but which conveys absolutely nothing in isolation. Russell's theory of incomplete symbols assimilates 'The king of France', that highly significant fragment, with the meaningless morsel 'fu-'. Incomplete, syncategorematic expressions correspond to authentic, but supplement-requiring meanings, atoms with hooks, if one likes, which precisely foreshadow what sort of supplement they will permit. It is here that the logical laws of formation come into play, laws which govern our symbols only because they govern the meanings which inform those symbols. Each incomplete meaning limits the field of the other incomplete meanings in association with which it will form a viable total meaning. If these laws of formation are ignored one gets the senselessness (*Unsinn*) projected by a set of words like 'every all but', which is quite different from the well-formed absurdity (*Widersinn*) of 'round square'. Being both round and square is a definite and well-formed meaning, whose absurdity consists in the evident impossibility of its 'fulfilment', its carrying out in the concrete stuff of intuition, whereas 'every

23

all but' does not correspond to a definite, well-formed meaning, but at best to a mere effort after meaning. It is a pity that Husserl's valuable distinctions have not been considered by many of those who, in recent years, have written of the senselessness of a self-contradiction. As Husserl points out, the logic of the true and the false, of the necessary, the possible and the impossible, points back to a far more fundamental logic as to what can be a single, well-formed, viable meaning-content at all. There is, in the traditional logic, no adequate study of these laws of meaning-formation, and modern symbolism has been content with the mere husk of the matter. Husserl gives good reason for believing in something like the *grammaire générale raisonnée* to which the eighteenth century accorded such faith, a belief that would welcome the empirical differences of actual languages as making more clear what was genuinely categorial, and what merely empirical. Husserl points out interestingly how completeness of meaning is not incompatible with incompleteness of what is objectively meant: a character, e.g. has on most views an onto-logical incompleteness which an abstract meaning, connected with such a character, does not have, e.g. the meaning Whiteness is in every way complete. So, we may note, is the meaning of the phrase 'being the meaning of the definite article', which means an incomplete meaning. This leads Husserl on to an interesting doctrine of the way in which meanings, while remaining in some sense the same, yet undergo modification in changed contexts. Thus the meaning of the sentence 'The war is over' suffers systematic modification if it is nominalized ('The war's being over'), if it occurs in indirect or thought-reporting speech, if its tense is changed etc. One wishes that all this flexibility had penetrated to many who write copiously on these matters.

The next Investigation 'On Intentional Experiences and their "Contents"', may be held to be the crowning statement of what it is to be conscious, an analysis founded on those of Brentano, but greatly surpassing these in coherence and depth. Husserl begins by distinguishing three concepts of consciousness, con-sciousness as the total stream of lived experience, as the self-awareness or self-perception which attends certain portions of that stream, and as the 'directedness to objects' which is present at all points in the stream, and which makes it worthy to be called a mental or 'psychic' stream at all. It is the third of these conceptions that is to be the theme of his investigations, and it has obviously been involved in the analysis, up to this point, of meaning-acts, meaningful contents and meant objects. Another meaning of consciousness, as standing for the subject, the ego, which is the point of intersection of all conscious references, is identified by Husserl in this study, in so far as he thinks it a legitimate notion, with the first meaning of consciousness, that of the whole stream of conscious acts and experiences. Husserl in 1901 says that he is as unable as Hume to detect an abiding subjective centre involved in all his conscious references, and he is unable to make anything of Natorp's conception of the ego, as something presupposed in all consciousness, but of which we cannot and need not make an object. As he rightly observes, if Natorp can thus talk of the ego, he must in some manner, even if only discursively, have made it his theme or object. This denial of the ego, an echo of the empiricistic, Humean psychology then current, was abandoned by Husserl in his later phenomenology, and is only preserved in the Second Edition of the *Logical Investigations*, because it led to an interchange with Natorp. We may agree with Husserl that any trace of the deplorable 'bundle-theory' of Hume, so founded on false logic, and so much belied by Hume's own statements about the progress of 'the thought' through its ideas, is fitly to be eliminated from phenomenology. In all conscious life, we may argue, we have a paradigmatic case of identity, which is not only capable of being cogitatively envisaged, as when we stress the necessary togetherness and continuity of our experiences as against their frequently disjoined objects, but which is also at all times *lived through* or *experienced* when, as we say, we do or undergo or pass from this to that. Egology, however, as Husserl himself observes, is a side of phenomenology not very relevant to the logical investigations of the present work, and may therefore be left aside.

Husserl goes on to emphasize the valid point, to be made against all who stress the 'diaphaneity' or elusiveness-to-self of consciousness, that consciousness reveals itself in plain variations which are not variations in what we are conscious of: the floating presentedness, e.g. of an imagined object, differs from the impact of an object we believe in etc. Husserl makes plain, as said before, that though it is convenient to use a language of 'act' in this connection, the act need have nothing to do with activity. A conscious act is simply what Natorp calls a being-there-of-something-for-me, and variations of conscious acts are merely variations in this peculiar 'being-there-for-me', in 'appearance' as opposed to 'what appears'. There is also a contrast in our lived experience between cases of mere content, of sensation, feeling etc., in which – as such – there is *nothing* there for me, and cases where such contents are made use of to sustain interpretative conceptions in which objects *do* come before consciousness. Husserl thereby gives a clearer meaning to consciousness than do theories that make it a characteristic of *all* lived experience.

The main stress of the second chapter of this Investigation is, however, in an attack on the 'immanent-object' theory of consciousness, as if what we are conscious of were a real element in our consciousness of it, to which another element, our ego or a conscious act, stands in a real relation, a theory complicated by the belief in *another* transcendent object to which our immanent object may or may not correspond. It is obvious that, in so far as I am conscious of anything, what I am conscious of need not and cannot be a real part of my consciousness of it (except, perhaps, in some difficult cases of adequate self-awareness); consciousness is not less a consciousness of what it is conscious of, because it does not involve an impossible form of containment. The phenomenological or 'descriptive' analysis of consciousness will not therefore only involve an account of the varying 'manners' of consciousness, the ways in which it is 'of' objects: it will also involve an account of its specific objective direction, and this gives Husserl the notion of intentional *matter* or *material*, with which the rest of the study is mainly concerned. The notion of intentional material is what is missing in the early attempts of Russell and Moore to deal with the problems of intentional objectivity. Either, they held, the object or situation we intend must be a genuine, unitary object *somewhere*, or we must analyse our references to it into complex references to other objects. They could not rise to the notion of a mental directedness, categorially peculiar to the mental sphere, which was just such that it could be to what had being nowise and nowhere. Husserl, stresses, on Fregean lines, that objective direction involves more than direction to a precise object: the same object may be intended in different capacities, as this or as that. And in our total conscious direction or intentional 'matter' – the terms are interchangeable –

there may be many subsidiary directions to this or that contextual or component object, which help to build up the total objective direction, and there may also be a presiding direction in which we preferentially live, and whose object is central, thematic for our concern. Husserl rightly criticizes those theories of attention which make it a singling out of objects strewn about some interior conscious box: it is rather a preferred conscious living in one object-directed orientation, while others are lived in subordinately.

Husserl further points out that *if* our conscious intentionality is valid, if things really are as it conceives them as being, then there is no distinction, save one of aspect, between the object as I conceive it and the object as it is. I am not concerned with a subjective image which merely happens to resemble a reality. 'It need only be said to be acknowledged', Husserl says, 'that the intentional object of a presentation is the same as its actual object, and on occasion as its external object, and that it is absurd to distinguish between them. The transcendent object would not be the object of *this* presentation if it was not *its* intentional object ... If I represent God to myself, or an angel, or an intelligible thing-in-itself, or a physical thing or a round square etc., I mean the transcendent object named in each case, in other words my intentional object. It makes no difference whether this object exists or is imaginary or absurd ... If the intentional object exists, the intention, the reference does not exist alone, but the thing referred to exists also' (Appendix to chapter 2). The 'conscious image' theory, moreover, attributes a complex representational pattern to consciousness, which presupposes simpler, more direct patterns: we may indeed refer to something *through* a representation of it, but this implies that we have direct intentions to both objects, and so explains nothing.

In chapter 3 of Investigation v Husserl rejects one interpretation of Brentano's well-known teaching that mental acts which are not themselves presentations, e.g. judgements, desires, always presuppose and are founded on presentations. If this means that the *mere* presentation of some content, devoid of either acceptance or rejection, is present as a *real* element in every judgement or belief, the analysis is false: the suspended note of mere presentation would quarrel with the thetic note of judgement. But if it is taken to mean that both entertaining and believing something may agree in their matter, their common objective directedness, then it is of course true, but much less striking. Husserl's tortuous argument is enlivened by a vivid example taken from a deceptive waxwork charmer.

In chapter 4, however, yet another interpretation is given to Brentano's principle. Husserl dwells on the extraordinary manner in which consciousness perpetually 'collapses' its long drawn-out syntheses of postures into a single embracing stance, passes from what he vividly calls a 'many-rayed' to a 'one-rayed' reference. The most noteworthy case of this is that of *nominalization*, when, e.g. we pass from supposing or judging that the Reichstag has been opened to referring simply to the opening of the Reichstag, or to the fact that the Reichstag has been opened etc. Such a passage from spread-out to condensed reference, leads to an endless generation of new, often profitable and interesting, higher-order objectivity. Husserl does not here mention, what he afterwards studied in detail in works like *Erfahrung und Urteil*, the converse passage from a one-rayed to a many-rayed reference. This occurs, e.g. when we pass from a pre-predicative awareness of a blue flower, to a predicative awareness that this is a blue flower, or that this flower is blue. It is, however, clear, Husserl thinks, that all many-rayed references must be founded upon single-rayed references, which may be further explicable, and he further supposes, like Wittgenstein in the *Tractatus*, that there must be certain ultimate, single-rayed reference, not permitting explication into anything many-rayed, to which all many-rayed references point back. However this may be, we seem to have here a sense in which judgements can be held to be built upon presentations, if, that is, judgements are identified with many-rayed, predicative references, and presentations with the single-rayed ones, whether explicable or not, which enter into them. It seems, however, unfortunate to connect this interesting and valid distinction, with discussions of judgement and the manner of consciousness, since the distinction is plainly one of 'matter', not of manner, and since the belief-presentation antithesis is as much present in the one-rayed as in the many-rayed realm of cases. There are, as Husserl points out, uses of names which imply existence, e.g. 'Cologne', and uses of names which do not, e.g. 'Bucephalus'. The whole discussion, though brilliant, is out of place, and creates a confusing impression. Would that Brentano and his principle had not been dragged in here at all.

The last Investigation in Husserl's work, 'Elements of a phenomenological Elucidation of Knowledge', is by far the most valuable of the whole series. In the first of its three sections the central notion of *fulfilment*, mentioned by us above, is expounded. Intentionality is essentially twofold: it can occur in a merely unfulfilled, cogitative, significative (or signitive) form, and it can also occur in a fulfilled or intuitive or 'seeing' form. In both forms of intentionality an object is present to consciousness, is truly intended by it, but in the fulfilled modus the presence is presence in a truly pregnant sense. We are not merely reaching out towards the object cogitatively, but have it actually before us, it is *itself* there in all its illustrative richness, it is seen, intuited and not merely gestured at. The two forms of consciousness presuppose one another: the intuitive, fulfilled form is essentially *the* fulfilment of a corresponding 'empty' reference, because it refers back to, perfects and, in a metaphorical sense, contains the former, whereas the former only is a genuine intention, only has an objective direction, because it *could* be fulfilled in a certain manner, ideally if not in reality.

The depth and novelty of Husserl's conception will be apparent if we contrast it with some of its antecedents or parallels, e.g. Doxa and Episteme in Plato, imagination and intellection in Descartes, intuition and understanding in Kant, and, we may add, ostension and use in certain modern treatments. In these other approaches one has two disparate conscious approaches, which are either directed to quite different objects, of which one alone has a genuine object, whereas the other only has one derivatively or by courtesy, or a full reference to objects is only achieved by both together. It is conceived, on the one hand, that thought alone can touch true being, while sense has no genuine objects or merely half-formed semblances of such, or, on the other hand, that sensory confrontations alone truly bring objects before us, whereas so-called thoughts merely weave symbols in a void, and there are also, in the third place, opinions which make thought empty and intuition blind, and see genuine reference only in their mutual interplay. None of these approaches is Husserl's, to whose point of view it is essential that these two modes of consciousness, the empty and the fulfilled, however much mutually complementary, both genuinely present objects, and may, moreover, present exactly the same object and from the same point of view.

I may, e.g. perceive the Schloss in Berlin, have it actually present to my senses with much of its detailed structure, and such 'presence' is not to be resolved into any complex of subjective sensations, but a genuine intentional reaching out: I may also merely think of the Schloss in Berlin, merely make a significant reference to it, nod at it verbally: in such an act I am not merely manipulating words or mental pictures, not merely getting ready for illustrative experiences, but I have the Schloss itself before me in consciousness. I can say, if I like, that the Schloss *itself* is not given to me, but such a phrase refers merely to the manner of my consciousness of the Schloss, and does not imply that I am dealing with no object or with some different object. In other words, thought without intuition is not empty, at least not in Kant's sense of 'empty', but may have a perfectly definite object, and the same object as intuition has, and intuition, likewise cannot be blind, since it has thought, intentional reference within it, and is in fact the perfected form of the latter. There can therefore for Husserl be no problem as to the mutual adjustment of thought and sense, no tortured schisms and schematisms: they are to each other as an outline sketch is to a perfected picture, except that the sketch contains, as it were, more or less precise instructions as to how it should be filled in.

It is interesting, further, to note the affinity, and also the disparity, of Husserl's use of the notion of fulfilment with the recently fashionable verificationistic theory of meaning. Both believe that meaning has an essential relation to a carrying out, an effective showing of what a thing is or would be like etc. etc. The main difference is that for Husserl the showing has no unique prerogative, and the meaning is not merely parasitic upon it. It is as essential for a showing to fulfil a meaning, as for a meaning to be able to fulfil itself in a showing. For Husserl, further, the counters of language are not so indispensable as they are in the case of verificationism, and can sometimes fall away. Husserl further allows that a fulfilment is, in some cases, no more than an ideal limit, which cannot actually be achieved: for the verificationist this would readily provoke a charge of meaninglessness. Husserl also differs from the verificationist in allowing a plurality of forms of fulfilment, going beyond the use of sense-experience: the introspective, the categorial etc. He also holds to a less close connection with truth, or the establishment of truth, than does the verificationistic analysis. We can illustrate a meaning, imperfectly no doubt but still genuinely, in manners like the imaginative which involve nothing like verification, and we can also 'verify' things in an external, probabilistic manner which is in no sense an exhibition of meaning.

In the course of the first Section of Investigation VI, Husserl dwells on many fascinating sides of the consciousness of fulfilment. He distinguishes the static form of fulfilment, where we merely recognize a perceived object as embodying a meaning, e.g. being my inkpot, and the dynamic form in which an object that was previously thought only in symbol is now presented in intuition. Both forms of consciousness involve an *identification*, at least in the form of an *experienced* sameness of objective reference: this is *indeed* my inkpot, this is the *very* inkpot I was meaning or have meant on other occasions, this is my own inkpot *itself*. The identification is of course more vivid in the dynamic than in the static case. The identification here dealt with is to be distinguished from an explicit reference to identity, though no doubt it explains the possibility of the latter. It was a meritorious thing to have stressed the extremely primitive, foundational character of our consciousness of identity: it is something lived through, experienced, both in ourselves and in objects, long before we learn to talk of it or to have logical difficulties about it.

Husserl stresses that meaning-fulfilment has parallels in other fields of intentionality, that, e.g. of the resolution or the wish or the expectation, and is not merely confined to the field of meaning: it exemplifies a contrast which pervades the whole of conscious life. He emphasizes that this contrast is shown even where no words or symbols are involved: a familiar melody stirs up unfulfilled intentions, which are fulfilled as the melody unfolds itself. Husserl distinguishes the imaginative from the perceptual form of fulfilment, and he points to the analogy between the use of interior phantasms and the use of external physical models and diagrams. He analyses the differing intentional use of intuitive materials by the sign and the representative likeness, and he considers the curious quasi-fulfilment of signs by signs, as when we explicate the meaning of 5^3 by declaring it to be $5 \times 5 \times 5$. He dwells on the regular *mixture* of the intuitive and the signitive in almost all conscious references, which none the less have a pervasive character of the fulfilled or the unfulfilled according to the side of them in which we preferentially live, though there are cases of balance in which we are as ready to say that we are perceiving as that we are thinking and vice versa. Husserl comments on the infinitely varied proportions of the mixture, some intentions having far more of what they intend intuitively illustrated than others. And he dwells on the regular processes in which the distribution of fulfilment and non-fulfilment *changes*, sometimes involving a nice balance of gain and loss, sometimes involving a steady progress in fulfilment, sometimes a turning away from fulfilment towards symbolic emptiness. The explorations of objects through the senses or of notions and issues by the imagining and conceiving mind are sketched in some detail, and the vague 'syntheses' of Kant are for the first time given concrete flesh and blood. Husserl frames the special concept of *fulness* (*Fülle*) to indicate the precise degree of the illustrativeness or pictoriality of a meaning-intention, to the extent, of course that this is relevant to the intention and not merely adventitious: he connects this *Fülle* with the existence of representative contents, not invariably sensuous, which, without intending them, we directly live through. All this leads to distinctions of bewildering complexity (see §§26–9), of whose exegesis we cannot be confident.

Husserl then goes on, in chapter 4, to consider the genesis of the notions of possibility and impossibility in our experience of the joint fulfilment of certain intentions, and in a kind of objectively grounded resistance to such joint fulfilment which is not experienced by us as a mere case of personal impotence. Modal distinctions play a central part in phenomenological theory, and Husserl is now contributing importantly to their own phenomenology. From this he passes on in chapter 5 to consider the necessarily formed ideal of adequation or complete fulfilment, in which meaning and fulfilment match themselves at every point. Such an adequation can be actually achieved by limiting our cogitative reference to what can intuitively be set forth, and is ideally to be achieved in an extension of experience, perhaps involving the paradigmatic conception of a God, in which *all* that pertains to intended things will be intuitively carried out. Adequate fulfilment involves for Husserl the character of the evident or inwardly evident: this is not to be conceived as some adventitious subjective feeling, but as the limiting selfgivenness of the object, which is presupposed in all cases of imperfect givenness, and which it does not therefore make sense to doubt. This limiting self-givenness is responsible for our Ideas of Truth and of Real Being, which are really the same Idea, but applied to different zones of objects, Truth being for States of Affairs what Being is for what are more narrowly Things. Of such Being or Truth we have a direct experience only in the narrow sphere of the inwardly evident, but from this it is extended, in unfulfilled fashion, to cases where it surpasses experience. We must not pretend that we ourselves have achieved adequacy in this account of Husserl's fifth chapter. For while his own writing is immensely suggestive and inspiring, it is also too sketchy to be fully expounded and criticized.

In the Second Section of the Sixth Investigation Husserl passes on to consider the form taken by intuition in the categorial realm of those logical meanings which seem given through the form of our conscious references rather than through anything in the material which conditions their application. Here the problem is that there are aspects of form which are in some sense part and parcel of what we know, which we yet cannot readily suppose to be embodied in anything given in straightforward encounter. As Husserl puts it: 'The form-giving flexion *being*, whether in its attributive or predicative function, is not fulfilled, as we said, in any percept.' We here remember Kant's dictum: "Being is not a real predicate" . . . I can see colour, but not *being* coloured. I can feel smoothness, but not being smooth. Being is nothing in the object, no part of it, no moment tenanting it, no quality or intensity of it, no figure of it or no internal form whatsoever, no constitutive feature of it, however conceived.' And further: 'What holds of "being" is plainly true of the remaining categorial forms in our statements, whether these bind the constituents of terms together, or bind terms together in the unity of the proposition. The "a" and the "the", the "and" and "or", the "if" and the "then", the "all" and the "none", the "something" and the "nothing", the forms of quantity and the determinations of number etc., all these are meaningful propositional elements, but we should look in vain for their objective correlates (if such may be ascribed to them at all) in the sphere of *real* objects, which is in fact none other than the sphere of objects of possible sense-perception' (Inv. v, §43).

One can imagine how diverting the above passages would be to those schooled in modern semantic commonplaces, how Husserl's puzzlement would seem to be a typical case of pseudo-perplexity, based on ignorance of the fact that not every word is a name, that the logical constants do not represent etc. etc. The notion of Husserl spending over seventy pages in a vain search for the 'objective correlates' of 'if' and 'and', and the 'acts' in which these are 'given' to us, would seem to cast the most unfavourable light on the whole intentionalist approach to meaning. We, however, cannot laugh at Husserl's enterprise, since we live in no happy world of first-order simplicity, where people disport themselves among objects and their fellows, and use simple words simply in relation to both: for us, as for Husserl, it is not possible to banish the shadows of logical operations from the warp and woof of phenomena, or to deal with things wholly free from disjunctivity, conditionality, generality, probability, and the like. Even incomplete symbols have, on our view, an accomplished sense: their incompleteness consists in their inbuilt requirement of other senses that will supplement theirs in an embracing total, not in having no distinct contribution to make to that total. We who have *seen* high-order categorial characters such as 'uniformity' or 'variegation' illustrated in, say, the dresses in a ballroom, are not able to evade questions regarding what the logical constants 'stand for'. We might even be prepared to say that we straightforwardly perceived them, rather than that they were introduced to us through some other, higher form of intuition.

Husserl's problem is carried a stage further by bringing in the notions of fulness and fulfilment, and of the 'representative contents' which go with these last in the field of external perception. We perceive external, physical objects by some sort of passage, not inferential, and not in the *proper* sense 'interpretative', from our unnoticed experiential contents to what are in some sense their 'objective correlates', the properties of things that they, and only they, are fitted to 'present'. Is there anything analogous to this in our understanding and knowing use of categorial meanings, such as the disjunctive, the universal, the negative, the identical etc.? Husserl decides that there is and must be: there must be something we actually live through, an actual moment of our experience, which enables us to give an authentic fulfilment, a validating intuition, to our various categorial meanings.

One thing is, however, obvious from the start: that the representative content in question cannot lie in the sphere of sense, since the categories and their applications have an essentially secondary, 'founded' character. They appear as *built upon* straightforwardly given perceptual objects and their constituent parts, attributes and moments, and are not at the same ontological level as these last. They will not show themselves as long as we merely *look* at a perceptual object before us, though there may be sense in saying that they are then *implicit* in that object's make-up. But they become explicit when we start dismembering the object into parts or sides which we set over against one another and the object as a whole, and when we then proceed to reintegrate them in our total view of the object and let each make an appropriate contribution to it, and so on. The procedures thus carried out do not, in an important sense, truly change or affect the object before us, or they change it only in an ideal but not in a real way. As Husserl puts it in §61: 'Categorial forms do not glue, tie or put parts together, so that a real sensuously perceivable whole emerges. They do not form in the sense in which the potter forms. Categorial forms leave primary objects untouched: they can do nothing to them, cannot change them in their own being, since the result would otherwise be a new object in the primary, real sense'.

With the non-reality of such changes, goes, however, a certain looseness of fit between them and the straightforwardly given things on which they are imposed, and also a certain arbitrary freedom in such imposition. It is we, to a large extent, who determine the categorial *Fassung*, conception, in which things shall be taken. 'With real contents, none of the categorial forms which fit them is necessarily given: there is abundant freedom to connect and relate, to generalize and subsume etc. There are many arbitrary ways to divide up a sensuously unified group into part-groups . . . Many possibilities of categorial shaping therefore arise on the basis of the same sensuous stuff' (§62). But the freedom and arbitrariness just indicated are not unlimited: we can impose categories or not, as we choose, but *if* we decide to impose them, then the real contents before us make certain impositions necessary, others unfeasible. 'The very fact that categorial forms constitute themselves in founded characters of acts, and in these alone, involves a certain necessity of connection. For how else could we speak of categorial *perception* and *intuition* if any conceivable matter could be put into any conceivable form, and the underlying straightforward intuitions therefore permitted themselves to be arbitrarily combined with categorial characters ... We can no doubt "think" any relation between any set of terms, and any form whatever on the basis of any matter – think them, that is, in the sense of merely meaning them. But we cannot really carry out "foundings" on every foundation: we cannot *see* sensuous stuff in any categorial form we like, let alone *perceive* it thus, and above all not perceive it adequately' (§62).

The answer to the question of categorial representatives is now at hand: that the experienced moment in ourselves which enables us to mean and know categorial forms in objects which transcend ourselves, is to be found, not in some single, subjective modification, but in the *manner* or *manners* in which single subjective modifications, and the acts using these, are *synthetically united*, whether arbitrarily and emptily, or in the fulfilled manner which depends on the character of the objects standing perceptually or imaginatively before us. The categories of whole and part, subject and predicate etc., are implicit in straightforward percepts and their objects, but they become part of our meaning when we perform certain analyses and syntheses upon objects, and they become matters of categorial intuition when these analyses and syntheses have their necessary foundation in the intuitions of the objects before us. It is by *performing* acts whose pattern, though our own, is in some sense founded upon and conditioned by the intuited things on which we perform them, that we can be said, in a higher-order manner, to intuit the categorial relations corresponding to those activities. Husserl's theory, though immensely tangled, seems to raise the syntheses of Kant to a higher level of clarity, and to reconcile their subjective and objective sides: they become a binding by ourselves which the natures of the bound things also prescribe or at least limit, and we are free from the associations of an original manifold, of spontaneous synthesis, and so forth. Husserl in his Foreword of 1913 tells us that he later abandoned the theory of categorial presentation here set forth in the *Logical Investigations*. Probably he had come to a more 'straightforward' view of our perception of categories in the world. But his theory remains a good theory all the same, even if at times unbearably complex.

The Third Section of the Sixth Investigation deals with the meaning of optative, interrogative, imperative and other not purely declarative sentence-forms. Husserl considers, but rejects, the view that our acts of wishing, wanting, asking etc., are among the 'meaning-conferring acts' which these sentences imply: he considers that only presentations and judgements are 'objectifying acts' which, in conjunction with expressions, can be properly held to contribute to meaning. Acts of wishing, deciding etc., can only contribute to meaning as part of the *object* of such meaning-lending acts, and we have the unplausible, if ancient, view recommended that to say 'Oh for a breath of fresh air!' is to *declare* that we need fresh air. There can then be no such things as emotive or prescriptive meaning etc., only declarative meaning which may include emotions, prescriptions etc., in its subject-matter. Husserl defends this view by the argument that it accounts for our ability to understand optative and imperative sentences etc., without experiencing corresponding wishes and feelings: this power may, however, be as well explained by Meinong's doctrine of non-serious attitudes, which seems much more acceptable. There is of course no reason why declarative meaning should not at times supplement, at other times replace, what we suppose to be emotive-conative meaning: all this has been fully argued in the literature inspired by Stevenson. It is not, in any case, clear why Husserl should be willing to ascribe a meaning-conferring role to judgements *despite* their note of reality-affirmation which is not purely presentative, and to deny a similar role to desires, emotions etc., on account of their note of dynamism etc. If a judgement can present a state of affairs assertively, it is not clear why feelings and desires should not present it feelingly or urgently. Husserl, however, tells us that he abandoned the analysis of the *Logical Investigations* on this point shortly after the work was published. Later he certainly came to believe, as Meinong also did, that emotions and desires could help to constitute peculiar objects or objective moments, notes of value or obligation, and that these could be acknowledged in rational judgements having their own, not very clearly expounded, mode of fulfilment.

37

It is not possible, in an Introduction of this length, to do more than touch on some of the many questions of interpretation raised by Husserl's *Logical Investigations*. And it is not at all possible to trace the relations of the position of that work to those of the later phenomenology. The interpretation, criticism and evaluation of Husserl's vast, immensely hard, supremely rewarding corpus of writings is barely in its beginnings. What remains for me to do, however, is to give some account as to how I have rendered some of the key-terms of Husserl, an account which the use of the Index will improve. I have been largely, but not absolutely uniform, in my translation of these key-terms, since my aim has been to render their sense, which demands adaptation to their German or English context, rather than to provide a code from which the German can be uniformly inferred from the English. The German text is, after all, again available, even if, regrettably it was long out of print. And Husserl, despite his prolixity and technicality, conforms to the Keynesian description of a Cambridge philosopher as 'a prose writer, hoping to be understood'; he is not a hierophant, requiring a word-for-word translation of his dark locutions in the hope that some of their doubtful sense will be preserved. I have translated *Vorstellung* almost uniformly by 'presentation', recognizing that the latter is not really an English word: the concept expressed by Husserl's (and Brentano's) term is not an English concept either. 'Idea' is required for other purposes, and is in any case ambiguous, and 'representation', if anyone can tolerate it, is required for the cases where Husserl uses *Repräsentation, Darstellung* etc. *Anschauung* (*anschaulich* etc.) I have rendered by 'intuition' ('intuitive' etc.) since this is the traditional rendering of the term in translations of Kant, and since the word has no proper equivalent in English. I have occasionally varied this use by substituting or adding such terms as 'envisage', 'illustrate', 'picture', 'see', and their derivatives. *Einsicht* etc., which more properly means 'intuition' as understood in English, I have translated by 'insight' etc., though sometimes I have talked of 'perspicuity' etc. I have translated *Idee* by 'Idea' and *Spezies* by 'Species', capitalizing both terms where ideal entities are in question. I have sometimes capitalized terms, e.g. 'Perception', where ideal notions were intended, but in general I have been inconsistently sparing with capitals, as I believe that they readily become tyrannous and obfuscate sense. I have translated *Erlebnis* (*erleben* etc.) by 'experience', though I have sometimes substituted 'lived experience', 'live through' etc.; I have not devised a separate word for *Erfahrung*, since Husserl often uses the words interchangeably, and since the English word is used in two ways, clear in the context, and is in fact practically two words. 'Having an experience' and 'learning by experience' obviously involve two distinct, though cognate, uses of the word 'experience'. I have translated *psychisch* by 'mental' in informal contexts like the Prolegomena where 'psychical' would be strained, but I have used 'psychical' where Brentano's technical use, and its contrast with *physisch*, was in question. I have indicated the difference between *real* and *reell* (meaning 'in the world of natural things' and 'actually part of' respectively) by putting the German word in brackets after an English use of 'real'. I am not convinced that Husserl meant much by his solemn distinction of these two terms, and I regret the necessity of translating *wirklich* by 'actual', when 'real' is often more suitable. It is curious that Husserl should have used the word *real* of a thing-like status which need not involve 'reality' in the sense of genuine existence, and which he came afterwards to hold *never* involved 'reality' in the English sense. I have translated *schlicht* by 'straightforward', and *eigentlich* (in technical contexts) by 'authentic', and I have translated *unselbständig* by 'non-independent', since the English word 'dependent' has less negativity and more relativity than *unselbständig*. Sometimes I have also had traffic with 'self-sufficient' for *selbständig*, instead of 'independent'. *Inhalt* I have, of course, translated by 'content', but this makes difficulties in the case of other words for which 'content' alone seems suitable: *Gehalt*, e.g. has been badly translated by 'substance'. *Fundieren, fundierte* etc., are of course 'found', 'founded' (though sometimes I have yielded to the charms of 'basing', 'based' etc.) but *fundierend* has varied from 'foundational' to 'underlying' according to context or euphony. *Moment* I have usually translated as 'moment', but sometimes, in less technical contexts, as 'side' or 'aspect'. *Bedeutung* in the sense of significant content I have translated by 'meaning', less commonly by 'sense': Husserl does not follow Frege in keeping the two words distinct, and neither ever means the *object* of a reference. The word *bedeuten* I have translated by 'act of meaning' or simply by the verb 'to mean', though I have sometimes used 'refer', 'reference' as an equivalent. Husserl in the main tends to say that we mean *objects, not meanings, by way of the meanings* which words *have* rather than *mean*, and I have followed his usage in English, with which it on the whole agrees, rather than trying to introduce distinctions into my translation which have only recently been thought necessary. *Wahrnehmen, Wahrnehmung* etc., I have translated by 'perceive', 'perception', the established equivalents, though when a *Wahrnehmung* means an individual act, I have, for the sake of shortness, translated it by 'percept'. *Innere Wahrnehmung* has been translated by 'inner', 'inward' or 'internal perception' quite without principle, and the same holds *mutatis mutandis* of *äussere Wahrnehmung. Erkennen, Erkenntnis* I have generally translated by 'know', 'knowledge', though there are contexts, particularly in the Sixth Investigation where 'cognize', 'cognition', 'recognize', 'recognition' seemed more suitable. *Evidenz* and its derivatives I have rendered by 'self-evidence', 'inward evidence' according to context: there are cases of *Evidenz*, e.g. those of *innere Wahrnehmung*, which have no *self*-evidence in the English sense. The adjective *evident* I have sometimes translated by 'evident', but in general I have found that the forensic and documentary associations of the English word 'evidence' are fatal to understanding. Many students are permanently bewildered by these associations. That a similar thing holds of 'reflection', 'reflective' etc., used to translate the German word where it has to do with introspection, and not with 'reflection' as we ordinarily understand it, has not led me to depart from the use in question. After all, Locke's similar use of 'reflection' has misled, and always will mislead, countless incautious and forgetful students. I have translated *begründen, Begründung* etc., by 'grounding' etc., also by 'prove' ('proof'), 'demonstrate' ('demonstration'), 'validate' ('validation'). It expresses a reversed view of argument more usual to Continental than to British intellectuals. With these explanations, it is to be hoped that Husserl can speak for himself.

J. N. FINDLAY

Yale University

FOREWORD

(First Edition)

THE *Logical Investigations* whose publication begins with these Prolegomena, have arisen out of unavoidable problems which have constantly hindered, and finally interrupted, the progress of my efforts, spread over many years, at achieving a philosophical clarification of pure mathematics. Together with questions regarding the origin of the basic concepts and insights of mathematics, these efforts were especially concerned with difficult questions of mathematical theory and method. The expositions of the traditional logic, so often reformulated, should have succeeded in providing us with an intelligible and perspicuous account of the rational essence of deductive science, with its formal unity and symbolic methodology. A study of the actually given deductive sciences, however, left all these things problematic and obscure. The deeper that my analyses penetrated, the more conscious I became that the logic of our time was not adequate to that actual science which it was none the less its function to elucidate.

I was plunged into peculiar difficulties by my logical researches into formal arithmetic and the theory of manifolds, a discipline and method which stretches far beyond all peculiarities of the special forms of number and extension. They forced me into discussions of a very general sort, which lifted me above the narrow sphere of mathematics, and pushed me towards a universal theory of formal deductive systems. There were many sets of problems that then bore down upon me, of which I shall here mention only a single one.

There were evidently possibilities of generalizing (transforming) formal arithmetic, so that, without essential alteration of its theoretical character and methods of calculation, it could be taken beyond the field of quantity, and this made me see that quantity did not at all belong to the most universal essence of the mathematical or the 'formal', or to the method of calculation which has its roots in this essence. I then came to see in 'mathematicizing logic' a mathematics which was indeed free from quantity, while remaining none the less an indefeasible discipline having mathematical form and method, which in part dealt with the old syllogisms, in part with new forms of inference quite alien to tradition. Important problems then loomed before me regarding the universal essence of the mathematical as such, and the natural connection, or the possible boundaries, between systems of quantitative and non-quantitative mathematics, and especially, e.g., regarding arithmetical and logical formality. Naturally, I also had to go on from this point to more fundamental questions regarding the essence of the form of knowledge in contradistinction to its matter, and the sense of the distinction between formal (pure) and material properties, truths and laws.

But in another quite different direction I also found myself involved in problems of general logic and epistemology. I began work on the prevailing assumption that psychology was the science from which logic in general, and the logic of the deductive sciences, had to hope for philosophical clarification. For this reason psychological researches occupy a very large place in the first (the only published) volume of my *Philosophy of Arithmetic*. There were, however, connections in which such a psychological foundation never came to satisfy me. Where one was concerned with questions as to the origin of mathematical presentations, or with the elaboration of those practical methods which are indeed psychologically determined, psychological analyses seemed to me to promote clearness and instruction. But once one had passed from the psychological connections of thinking, to the logical unity of the thought-content (the unity of theory), no true continuity and unity could be established. I became more and more disquieted by doubts of principle, as to how to reconcile the objectivity of mathematics, and of all science in general, with a psychological foundation for logic. In this manner my whole method, which I had taken over from the convictions of the reigning logic, that sought to illuminate the given science through psychological analyses, became shaken, and I felt myself more and more pushed towards general critical reflections on the essence of logic, and on the relationship, in particular, between the subjectivity of knowing and the objectivity of the content known. Logic left me in the lurch wherever I hoped it would give me definite answers to the definite questions I put to it, and I was eventually compelled to lay aside my philosophical-mathematical investigations, until I had succeeded in reaching a certain clearness on the basic questions of epistemology and in the critical understanding of logic as a science.

If I now publish these essays, the product of many years of work, *on a new foundation of pure logic and epistemology*, I do so in the conviction that I shall not be misunderstood for independently choosing a path remote from that of prevailing logical trends, in view of the grave, factually based motives that have inspired me. The course of my development has led to my drawing apart, as regards basic logical convictions, from men and writings to whom I owe most of my philosophical education, and to my drawing rather closer to a group of thinkers whose writings I was not able to estimate rightly, and whom I consulted all too little in the course of my labours. I have had, however, unfortunately to abstain from any subsequent insertion of comprehensive literary and critical references to researches having an affinity with my own. As regards my frank critique of the psychologistic logic and epistemology, I have but to recall Goethe's saying: There is nothing to which one is more severe than the errors that one has just abandoned.

Halle a. d. S. May 21st 1900

(Second Edition)

THE question as to the form in which I should undertake to republish the present work, out of print for some years, has caused me no little concern. My *Logical Investigations* were my 'break-through', not an end but rather a beginning. When the work had been printed, my studies continued forthwith. I tried to give a fuller account of the meaning, the method and the philosophical scope of phenomenology, to pursue the woven threads of my problems further in every direction, and to track down and tackle parallel problems in all ontic and phenomenological fields. Understandably, as the horizon of my research widened, and as I became better acquainted with the intentional 'modifications' so perplexingly built on one another, with the multiply interlacing structures of consciousness, there came a shift in many of the conceptions formed in my first penetration of the new territory. Remaining obscurities were cleared up, ambiguities removed, isolated observations to which at the start no special importance could be given, gained fundamental meaning as one passed over into larger contexts. Everywhere, in brief, there were not merely supplementations but transvaluations in one's original field of research, and from the point of view of one's widened, deepened knowledge, even the arrangement of one's treatments no longer seemed quite adequate. The sense and the extent of these forward steps, and their widening effect on one's field of research comes out in the recently published First Book of my *Ideas towards a pure Phenomenology and Phenomenological Philosophy*, printed in the first volume of the *Jahrbuch für Philosophie und phänomenologische Forschung* (1913), and the publication of the two remaining Books, which will follow immediately, will show this still better.

I originally cherished the hope that, after discovering and exploring the radical problems of pure phenomenology and phenomenological philosophy, I should be able to present a series of systematic expositions that would render a reprinting of the old work unnecessary, in so far as its content, not at all jettisoned, but purged and divided according to subject, would come into its own in association with the new work. But when execution began, a serious objection at once raised itself. Many years would be needed for the carrying out of the extensive, difficult task of imposing literary unity on our Investigations: though they stood there complete and concrete, they would have for the most part to be expounded anew and to have their difficulties ironed out. I therefore decided first of all to plan my *Ideas*. They were to give a universal, yet contentful presentation of the new phenomenology, based throughout on actually executed work, a presentation of its method, of its systematic field of problems, of its function in making possible a strictly scientific philosophy, as well as a reduction to rational theory of empirical psychology. After all this, the *Logical Investigations* would be republished, and that in a better form, adapted to the standpoint of the *Ideas*, and so helping to introduce the reader to the nature of genuinely phenomenological and epistemological *work*. For if these Investigations are to prove helpful to those interested in phenomenology, this will be because they do not offer us a mere programme (certainly not one of the high-flying sort which so encumber philosophy) but that they are attempts at genuinely executed fundamental work on the immediately envisaged and seized things themselves. Even where they proceed critically, they do not lose themselves in discussions of standpoint, but rather leave the last word to the things themselves, and to one's work upon such things. The *Ideas* ought in effect to rest on the work of the *Logical Investigations*. If, through the latter, the reader has been brought openly to investigate and concern himself with a group of fundamental questions, then the *Ideas*, with their policy of illuminating method from ultimate sources by putting a sketch of the main structures of pure consciousness before one, by systematically locating one's work-problems in the latter, could assist him to a further, independent advance.

The carrying out of the first part of my plan was relatively easy, though the unexpected length of the first two Books of the *Ideas*, essential for my purposes and undertaken by me in one piece, forced me to divide their publication, so that the First Book alone had to suffice provisionally. But the fulfilment of my second aim was far harder. Anyone who knows the old work, will see the impossibility of lifting it entirely on to the level of the *Ideas*. That would mean a complete recasting of the work, and a postponement to the Greek kalends. It seemed to me, on the other hand, to be a comfortable rather than a conscientious decision, in view of the aims justifying a new edition, to abandon all revision and merely reprint the work mechanically. Was I entitled to mislead the reader once more, through all my omissions, waverings and self-misunderstandings, which, however unavoidable and pardonable in the first edition of such a work, would yet put unnecessary difficulties in the way of a clear grasp of essentials?

All that remained possible was to attempt a middle course, and in a manner to let myself go in attempting it. It meant leaving untouched certain unclarities, and even errors, which were part and parcel of the unified style of the work. The following maxims guided my revision:

1. To allow nothing into the new edition regarding which I was not fully persuaded that it deserved thorough study. In this respect single errors could be left standing, since I could allow them to count as natural steps towards a truth that would trans-

form their good intentions. I could say to myself in all this: Readers who stem from general philosophical drifts of the present – which are in essence the same as those in the decade of this work's origin – can, like the work's author, only at first gain access to what are mere steps towards certain phenomenological (logical) positions. Only when they have gained sure mastery over the style of phenomenological research, do they see the fundamental meaning of certain distinctions which appeared previously to be insignificant nuances.

2. To improve all that could be improved, without altering the course and style of the old work, and, above all, to bring to most definite expression the new thought-motives that had their 'break-through' in the old work, but which had, in the first edition, been at times sharply stressed, at times blurred, by the hesitant and timid author.

3. To lift the reader gradually, in the course of the expositions, to a relatively rising total level of insight, following in this the original peculiarity of the work. We must here voice the reminder that the work was a systematically bound *chain of investigations* but not, properly speaking, *one* book or work in a literary sense. There is in it a regular ascent from a lower to a higher level, and a working of oneself into ever new logical and phenomenological insights, which never leave the previously achieved ones quite untouched. Ever new phenomenological strata swim into our view and add determination to our conceptions of the earlier ones. This character of the old work made a kind of revision seem possible, which consciously leads the reader onward and upward, in such a way that, in the final Investigation, the level of the *Ideas* is in essentials reached, so that the previous unclearnesses and half-truths, that we had to put up with, appear perspicuously clarified.

I went ahead in the sense of these maxims, and have the impression as regards both provisionally published pieces (the Prolegomena and the first part of the Second Volume) that the big efforts I made have not been wasted. I have naturally had to add here, and strike out there, at times to rewrite single sentences, and at times whole paragraphs and chapters. The thought-content has become more packed and full in extent: the total extent of the work, more specifically that of the Second Volume, has grown unavoidably, despite all suppression of critical supplementation, so that this volume has had to be divided.

Regarding the individual Investigations and their reconstructed form, the following should be said. The *Prolegomena to Pure Logic* is, in its essential content, a mere reworking of two complementary series of lectures given at Halle in the summer and autumn of 1896. To this the greater liveliness of the exposition is due, which has assisted its influence. The piece is, moreover, written in one cast of thought, and I therefore thought I ought not to revise it radically. But I found I could, on the other hand, from about the middle on, carry out many quite large improvements in presentation, could expunge slips and put main points into sharper light. Some very essential, if partial, insufficiencies – such as the concept of a 'truth in itself' which is too one-sidedly oriented to *vérités de raison* – had to be left, since they were part of the unified level of the piece. The Sixth Investigation (now the Second Part of the Second Volume) brings in necessary clarification in this respect.

To burden the polemic on psychologism with new criticisms and counter-criticisms (which would not have introduced the least new thought-motive) did not seem very appropriate to me. I must emphasize the relation of this piece to 1899, the precise date at which I merely rewrote it. (The printing of the Prolegomena, minus the Foreword, was already complete in November 1899. See my self-reference in the *Vierteljahrschr. f. wiss. Philosophie*, 1900, p. 512 f.) Since its appearance, some authors that I looked on as representing logical psychologism have essentially changed their position. Th. Lipps, e.g., in his extremely significant, original writings, has since 1902 not at all been the man that is here quoted. Other authors have, in the meantime, sought different foundations for their psychologistic position, a point not to be ignored, since my presentation takes no account of it.

As regards the Second Volume of the new edition, the hesitant Introduction, so little true to the essential sense and method of the actually written Investigations, was radically revised. I felt its defects immediately after its appearance, and also found immediate occasion (in a review in the *Archiv f. system. Philos.* XI (1903), p. 397 ff.) to object to my misleading account of phenomenology as descriptive psychology. Some of the main points of principle are there briefly but sharply characterized. The psychological description performed in inner experience appears as put on a level with the description of external events in nature performed in external description, but it is, on the other hand *opposed* to phenomenological description, from which all transcendent interpretations of immanent data, even those of psychical acts and states of a real ego, are entirely excluded. The descriptions of phenomenology are said (p. 399) 'to deal neither with lived experiences nor classes of lived experiences of empirical persons . . . phenomenology knows nothing of persons, of my experiences or those of others, and surmises nothing regarding them: it raises no questions in regard to such matters, attempts no determinations, constructs no hypotheses'. The complete reflective clarity that I had achieved in these and following years regarding the essence of phenomenology, which led gradually to the systematic doctrine of 'phenomenological reduction' (cf. *Ideas*, 1, Section 2), was of use in the rewriting of this Introduction, and also in the text of all the following Investigations, thereby raising the whole work to an essentially higher level of clarity.

Of the five Investigations which occupy the First Part of the Second Volume, the first, *Expression and Meaning*, retains its merely preparatory character in the new edition. It stimulates thought, it directs the gaze of the phenomenological beginner to the initial, already most difficult problems of the consciousness of meaning, without doing full justice to them. The manner in which it deals with occasional meanings (to which, however, in strictness, all empirical predications belong) is a tour de force – the enforced consequence of the imperfect conception of the essence of 'truth in itself' in the Prolegomena.

As a further defect of this Investigation, only understood and corrected at the end of the volume, we must note that it has no regard to the distinction and parallelism between the 'noetic' and the 'noematic': the fundamental role of this distinction in *all* fields of consciousness is first fully laid bare in the *Ideas*, but comes through in many individual arguments in the last Investigation of the old work. For this reason, the essential ambiguity of 'meaning' as an Idea is not emphasized. The noetic concept of meaning is one-sidedly stressed, though in many important passages the noematic concept is principally dealt with.

The Second Investigation concerning *The Ideal Unity of the Species and Modern Theories of Abstraction*, had a style and limitation of theme, a certain completeness, which made a few detailed amendments, but no thoroughgoing reconstructions, desirable.

As before, there is no discussion of the various types of Ideas, with their demand for a deep separation of essence, to which naturally Ideations, as deeply and essentially separate, correspond. All that this Investigation is concerned with, is the fact that one can learn to see Ideas, represented, e.g. by the Idea Red, and that one can become clear as to the essence of such 'seeing'.

The Third Investigation *On the Doctrine of Wholes and Parts* has undergone very thorough revision, though in its case no unsatisfactory compromises needed to be made, and no subsequent corrections or deepenings were necessary. All that was here needed was to assist the inner sense of the Investigation, and what I thought were its important results, to better operation and to remove numerous imperfections of statement. I have the impression that this Investigation is all too little read. I myself derived great help from it: it is also an essential presupposition for the full understanding of the Investigations which follow.

The position of the Fourth Investigation, *On the Distinction between independent and non-independent Meanings and the Idea of Pure Grammar*, is similar to that of the Third. My position in this case is also unaltered. I not only amended, but also in many places enriched, the content of the text, changes which point to future publications from my lectures on logic.

The Fifth Investigation, *On intentional Experiences and their Contents*, had to undergo deep-going revision. In it cardinal problems of phenomenology (those in particular of the phenomenological doctrine of judgement) were tackled: in these it was possible to achieve a considerably higher level of clarity and insight without needing to alter the structure and essential content of the Investigation. I no longer approve of the rejection of the pure ego, but left the arguments in question in a shortened and formally improved form, as being the basis of P. Natorp's interesting polemic in his new *Allgemeine Psychologie*, volume i, 1913. I have completely excised the much cited, very unclear, and, in the context, quite dispensable §7, 'Reciprocal Demarcation of Psychology and Natural Science'. I was perhaps all too conservative in retaining the quite unsuitable term 'nominal presentation': I was afraid in general of tampering with the terminology of the old work.

The revised version of the Sixth Investigation, now in the press, is designed as the Second Part of the Second Volume: it is the most important Investigation from a phenomenological point of view. In this case I soon persuaded myself that it would not be enough to revise the old content, following the original content paragraph by paragraph. Its fund of problems still were my pace-setter, but I had advanced considerably in regard to them, and the sense of my 'maxims' would not permit a further use of compromises in regard to them. I accordingly went along quite freely, and, in order to give scientific treatment to the great themes so imperfectly dealt with in the first edition, I added whole series of new chapters, which increased the bulk of this Investigation very considerably.

As in the Prolegomena I did not, in my second volume (my Fourth Investigation made a small exception) go into the many criticisms which rest, I am sorry to say, almost exclusively on misunderstandings of the *sense* of my positions. I therefore thought it more useful to discuss in universal form, and in their historical position, the *typical* misunderstandings of my philosophical endeavours, and that at the end of the Second Volume, in an epilogue, so to say. It will be a good thing if the reader has a look at this Appendix immediately after reading the Prolegomena, so as to guard himself in time against such apparently natural misunderstandings.

A full index will be added to the work, prepared with great care by my doctoral candidate Rudolf Clemens. I must express my heartfelt thanks for much friendly assistance, and, in the first place, to the Privatdozent Dr Adolf Reinach, who helped me with his zeal and knowledge when, two years ago, I first went thoroughly into deliberations concerning the possibilities of revision. The labours of correction were greatly lightened by the help of Dr Hans Lipps and by the doctoral candidate Jean Hering.

E. HUSSERL

Göttingen October 1913

PROLEGOMENA TO
PURE LOGIC

INTRODUCTION

§1 *The controversy regarding the definition of Logic and the essential content of its doctrines*

'THERE is accordingly as much difference of opinion in regard to the definition of logic as there is in the treatment of the science itself. This was only to be expected in the case of a subject, in regard to which most writers have only employed the same words to express different thoughts' (John Stuart Mill, *Logic*, Introduction, §1). Many decades have passed since John Stuart Mill introduced his valuable work on logic with these sentences, and important thinkers here and beyond the Channel have devoted their best powers to logic and have enriched its literature with ever new presentations. But even today these sentences could serve as a suitable expression of the state of logical science, even today we are very far from complete agreement as to the definition of logic and the content of its essential doctrines. Contemporary logic, of course, wears quite a different face from the logic of the mid-century. Owing particularly to the influence of the distinguished thinker just mentioned, the first of the three main tendencies that we find in logic, the psychological, has definitely come to prevail over the formal and the metaphysical tendencies, both as regards the number and the importance of its exponents. But the other two tendencies are still carried on, and the disputed questions of principle, reflected in different definitions of logic, are still disputed, while it is still true, and perhaps more true than ever, that different writers merely employ the same words to express different thoughts. This is not merely true of expositions stemming from different philosophical 'camps'. The side on which most life is to be found, that of psychological logic, manifests unity of conviction only in regard to the demarcation of the discipline, its essential aims and methods. But one could scarcely be blamed for exaggerating if one applied the phrase *bellum omnium contra omnes* to the doctrines put forth, and, in particular, to the opposed interpretations of traditional formulae and doctrines. It would be vain to seek to delimit a sum total of substantial propositions or theories in which one might see the hard core of our epoch's logical science and the heritage bequeathed by it to the future.

§2 *Necessity of a renewed discussion of questions of principle*

In this state of the science, which does not permit one to separate individual conviction from universally binding truth, a reversion to questions of principle remains a task that must ever be tackled anew. This holds particularly as regards the questions which play a decisive role in the dispute among logical 'tendencies' and, together with this, in the dispute as to the correct demarcation of the science. The interest in just these questions has certainly cooled off in the last decades. After Mill's brilliant attacks on the logic of Hamilton, and the no less famous, but not so fruitful, logical investigations of Trendelenburg, these questions seemed to have been fully dealt with. But with the great resurgence of psychological studies, the psychologistic tendency in logic also gained dominance, and all effort centred in the systematic building up of the discipline upon principles presumed valid. The fact, however, that so many attempts made by such important thinkers to put logic on the sure path of a science, have not led to any shattering success, suggests that the ends in view have perhaps not been sufficiently clarified to allow successful investigation.

One's conception of the aims of a science find expression in its definition. We naturally do not think that successful work on a discipline demands a prior conceptual demarcation of its field. The definitions of a science mirror the stages of that science's development; knowledge of the conceptual character of a science's objects, of the boundaries and place of its field, follow the science and progress with it. None the less, the degree of adequacy of such definitions, or of the views of the field they express, react on the progress of the science itself, and, according to the direction in which such definitions depart from truth, such a reaction can have a slight, or a very important influence on the development of the science. The field of a science is an objectively closed unity: we cannot arbitrarily delimit fields where and as we like. The realm of truth is objectively articulated into fields:

researches must orient themselves to these objective unities and must assemble themselves into sciences. There is a science of numbers, a science of spatial figures, of animal species etc., but there are no special sciences of prime numbers, of trapezia, or of lions, nor of all three taken together. Where a group of discoveries and problems impresses us as 'belonging together', and leads to the setting up of a science, inadequate demarcation can consist merely in the fact that the field-concept is at first too narrow for what is given, and that concatenations of grounding connections stretch beyond the delimited field, and only draw together in a closed unity over a much wider field. Such limitations of horizon need not be prejudicial to the flourishing progress of the science. It may be that theoretical interest finds its first satisfaction in the narrower field, and that work that can be done without regard to deeper and wider logical ramifications, is what is needed in the first instance.

There is another, much more dangerous fault in field-delimitation: the confusion of fields, the mixture of heterogeneous things in a putative field-unity, especially when this rests on a complete misreading of the objects whose investigation is to be the essential aim of the proposed science. Such an unnoticed μετάβασις εἰς ἄλλο γένος can have the most damaging consequences: the setting up of invalid aims, the employment of methods wrong in principle, not commensurate with the discipline's true objects, the confounding of logical levels so that the genuinely basic propositions and theories are shoved, often in extraordinary disguises, among wholly alien lines of thought, and appear as side-issues or incidental consequences etc. These dangers are considerable in the philosophical sciences. Questions as to range and boundaries have, therefore, much more importance in the fruitful building up of these sciences than in the much favoured sciences of external nature, where the course of our experiences forces territorial separations upon us, within which successful research can at least be provisionally established. It was Kant who uttered the famous special words on logic which we here make our own: 'We do not augment, but rather subvert the sciences, if we allow their boundaries to run together.' The following Investigation hopes to make plain that all previous logic, and our contemporary, psychologically based logic in particular, is subject, almost without exception, to the above-mentioned dangers:

through its misinterpretation of theoretical principles, and the consequent confusion of fields, progress in logical knowledge has been gravely hindered.

§3 *Disputed questions. The path to be entered*

The traditionally disputed questions which concern the demarcation of logic are the following:

1. Is logic a theoretical or a practical discipline (a 'technology')?

2. Is it independent of other sciences, and, in particular, of psychology and metaphysics?

3. Is it a formal discipline? Has it merely to do as usually conceived, with the 'form of knowledge', or should it also take account of its matter?

4. Has it the character of an *a priori*, a demonstrative discipline or of an empirical, inductive one?

All these disputed questions are so intimately bound up together, that to take up a stance on one of them, is to some extent at least to be determined, or factually influenced, in the stance one takes up on the others. There are really only two parties. Logic is a theoretical discipline, formal and demonstrative, and independent of psychology: that is one view. For the other it counts as a technology dependent on psychology, which of course excludes the possibility of its being a formal, demonstrative discipline like the other side's paradigm arithmetic.

Since we do not really mean to become involved in these traditional disputes, but rather to clarify the differences of principle at work in them, and to work towards a clarification of the essential aims of a pure logic, we shall proceed as follows: we shall start from the almost universally accepted contemporary treatment of logic as a technology, and shall pin down its sense and its justification. This will naturally lead on to the question of the theoretical foundations of this discipline, and of its relations, in particular, to psychology. This question coincides in essence, in the main if not entirely, with the cardinal question of epistemology, that of the objectivity of knowledge. The outcome of our investigation of this point will be the delineation of a new, purely theoretical science, the all-important foundation for any technology of scientific knowledge, and itself having the character of an *a priori*, purely demonstrative science. This is the science intended by Kant and the other proponents of a 'formal' or 'pure' logic, but not rightly conceived and defined by them as regards its content and scope. The final outcome of these discussions is a clearly circumscribed idea of the disputed discipline's essential content, through which a clear position in regard to the previous mentioned controversies will have been gained.

CHAPTER ONE

Logic as a Normative and, in particular, as a Practical Discipline

§4 *The theoretical incompleteness of the separate sciences*

IT is a common experience that the excellence of an artist's mastery over his material, and the decisive certainty with which he judges and assesses works in his art, is only quite exceptionally based on a theoretical knowledge of the rules which prescribe direction and order to his practice, and determine the standards of value on which the perfection or imperfection of the complete work must be assessed. Normally the practising artist is not the man who can inform us rightly regarding the principles of his art. He follows principles neither in his creation nor his evaluation. In his creation he follows the inner activity of his harmoniously trained powers, in his judgement his finely formed artistic taste and feeling. This is not merely so in the case of fine art, of which one may first have thought, but in that of the arts generally, in the widest sense of the word. It therefore holds for the activities of scientific creation and the theoretical evaluation of their results, for the scientific demonstrations of facts, laws, theories. Even the mathematician, the physicist and the astronomer need not understand the ultimate grounds of their activities in order to carry through even the most important scientific performances. Although their results have a power of rational persuasion for themselves and others, yet they cannot claim to have demonstrated all the last premisses in their syllogisms, nor to have explored the principles on which the success of their methods reposes. The incomplete state of all sciences depends on this fact. We do not here mean the mere incompleteness with which the truths in a field have been charted, but the lack of inner clarity and rationality, which is a need independently of the expansion of the science. Even mathematics, the most advanced of all sciences, can in this respect claim no special position. Though often still treated as the ideal of all science as such, how little it really is such is shown by the old, yet never finally composed disputes as to the foundations of geometry, or as to the justification of the method of imaginaries. The same thinkers who sustain marvellous mathematical methods with such incomparable mastery, and who add new methods to them, often show themselves incapable of accounting satisfactorily for their logical validity and for the limits of their right use. Though the sciences have grown great despite these defects, and have helped us to a formerly undreamt of mastery over nature, they cannot satisfy us theoretically. They are, as theories, not crystal-clear: the function of all their concepts and propositions is not fully intelligible, not all of their presuppositions have been exactly analysed, they are not in their entirety raised above all theoretical doubt.

§ 5 The theoretical completion of the separate sciences by metaphysics and epistemology

To reach this theoretical goal we first need, as is fairly generally admitted, a type of investigation which belongs to the metaphysical realm.

Its task is to pin down and to test the untested, for the most part not even noticed, yet very significant metaphysical presuppositions that underlie at least all those sciences that are concerned with actual reality. Such presuppositions are, e.g., that an external world exists, that it is spread out in space and time, its space being, as regards its mathematical character, three-dimensional and Euclidean, and its time a one-dimensional rectilinear manifold; that all process is subject to the causal principle etc. These presuppositions, all to be found in the framework of Aristotle's First Philosophy, are at present ranked under the quite unsuitable rubric of 'epistemology'.

Such a metaphysical foundation is not, however, sufficient to provide the desired theoretical completion of the separate sciences. It concerns, moreover, only such sciences as have to do with actual reality, which does not include all sciences, certainly not the purely mathematical sciences whose objects are numbers, manifolds etc., things thought of as mere bearers of ideal properties independent of real being or non-being. The case is different in regard to another class of investigations whose theoretical completion is plainly an indispensable postulate in our quest for knowledge, investigations which concern all sciences equally, since they concern, in brief, whatever makes sciences into sciences. This names the field of a new, and, as we shall see, complex discipline, whose peculiarity it is to be the science of science, and which could therefore be most pointedly called *Wissenschaftslehre* or theory of science.

§6 *The possibility and justification of logic as theory of science*

The possibility and justification of such a discipline – a normative and practical discipline relating to the Idea of science – can be shown by the following considerations.

Science is concerned, as its name indicates, with knowing, but this does not mean that it itself consists of a tissue of acts of knowing. Science exists objectively only in its literature, only in written work has it a rich relational being limited to men and their intellectual activities: in this form it is propagated down the millennia, and survives individuals, generations and nations. It therefore represents a set of external arrangements, which, just as they arose out of the knowledge-acts of many individuals, can again pass over into just such acts of countless individuals, in a readily understandable manner, whose exact description would require much circumlocution. For us it is here sufficient that science provides, or should provide, certain more immediate preconditions of acts of knowing, real possibilities of knowing, whose realization by the 'normal' or 'suitably endowed' individual in well-known, 'normal' circumstances can be looked on as an attainable goal of his endeavour. In this sense, therefore, science aims at knowledge.

In knowledge, however, we possess truth. In actual knowledge, to which we see ourselves ultimately referred back, we possess truth as the object of a correct judgement. But this alone is not enough, since not every correct judgement, every affirmation or rejection of a state of affairs that accords with truth, represents *knowledge* of the being or non-being of this state of affairs. Rather we may say that, if it is to be called 'knowledge' in the narrowest, strictest sense, it requires to be evident, to have the luminous certainty that what we have acknowledged *is*, that what we have rejected *is not*, a certainty distinguished in familiar fashion from blind belief, from vague opining, however firm and decided, if we are not to be shattered on the rocks of extreme scepticism. Common talk does not, however, stay put in this strict concept. We also speak, e.g. of an act of knowing where the judgement we pass is associated with a clear memory that we previously passed a judgement of precisely the same content accompanied with inner evidence. This happens particularly where our memory also concerns a demonstrative thought-process out of which this inner evidence grew, and that we are sure we can reproduce *with* such evidence. ('I know that the Pythagorean theorem is true – I can prove it': instead of the second half, one can of course also say 'but I have forgotten the proof'.)

We therefore conceive 'knowledge' in a wider, but not wholly loose sense: we separate it off from baseless opinion, by pointing to some 'mark' of the presumed state of affairs or for the correctness of the judgement passed by us. The most perfect 'mark' of correctness is inward evidence, it counts as an immediate intimation of truth itself. In the vast majority of cases we lack such absolute knowledge of truth, in whose place we make use – one need *only* think how memory functions in the above examples – of the inner evidence for a higher or lower degree of probability for our state of affairs, with which, if probability-levels become high enough, a firm judgement is usually associated. The inward evidence of the probability of a state of affairs A will not serve to ground the inward evidence of its truth, but it will serve to ground those comparative, inwardly evident value-assessments, through which, in accordance with positive or negative probability-values, we can distinguish the reasonable from the unreasonable, the better-founded from the worse-founded assumptions, opinions and surmises. Ultimately, therefore, all genuine, and, in particular, all scientific knowledge, rests on inner evidence: as far as such evidence extends, the concept of knowledge extends also.

There is none the less a remaining duality in the concept of knowing or knowledge. Knowledge in the narrowest sense of the word is the being inwardly evident that a certain state of affairs is or is not, e.g. that S is P or that it is not P. If it is evident that a certain state of affairs is probable to this or that degree, then we have knowledge in the strictest sense of such a probability, but, in regard to the being of the state of affairs itself, and not of its probability, we only have knowledge in a wider, modified sense. It is in this latter sense, with an eye to degrees of probability, that one speaks of a greater or lesser degree of knowledge. Knowledge in the pregnant sense – its being quite evident that S is P – then counts as the absolutely fixed, ideal limit which the graded probabilities for the being-P of S approach asymptotically.

But the concept and task of science covers more than mere knowledge. If we live through and recognize the presence of inner percepts, singly or in groups, we have knowledge, but are far removed from science: the same applies generally to all incoherent groups of acts of knowing. A group of isolated bits of chemical knowledge would certainly not justify talk of a science of chemistry. More is plainly required, i.e. *systematic coherence in the theoretical sense*, which means finding grounds for one's knowing, and suitably combining and arranging the sequence of such groundings.

The essence of science therefore involves unity in the whole system of grounded validation: not only isolated pieces of knowledge, but their grounded validations themselves, and together with these, the higher interweavings of such validations that we call theories, must achieve systematic unity. The aim is not merely to arrive at knowledge, but knowledge in such degree and form as would correspond to our highest theoretical aims as perfectly as possible.

That we look upon, and practically strive after, systematic form as the purest embodiment of the Idea of science, does not evince some merely aesthetic trait in our nature. Science neither wishes nor dares to become a field for architectonic play. The system peculiar to science, i.e. to true and correct science, is not our own invention, but is present in things, where we simply find or discover it. Science seeks to be a means towards the greatest possible conquest of the realm of truth by our knowledge. The realm of truth is, however, no disordered chaos, but is dominated and unified by law. The investigation and setting forth of truths must, therefore, likewise be systematic, it must reflect the systematic connections of those truths, and must use the latter as a ladder to progress and penetrate from the knowledge given to, or already gained by us to ever higher regions of the realm of truth.

Science can never do without this helpful ladder. The inward evidence on which all knowledge ultimately reposes, is no gift of nature, appearing together with the mere idea of states of affairs without any methodically artful set-up. People would otherwise never have thought of building up sciences. The longueurs of method would lose their sense if to intend meant to succeed. Why should one search into relations of entailment or construct proofs, if one shared in truth through immediate intimation? The inward evidence, moreover, which stamps one presented state of affairs as having real being, or the absurdity which stamps it as having no being at all (and the same, likewise, in regard to probability and improbability) is, in fact, only immediately felt in the case of a relatively quite limited group of primitive facts. Countless true propositions are only grasped by us as true when we methodically validate them. In their case, a mere regard to our propositional thought, will not induce inward evidence, even if it does induce judgemental decision. Both are, however, induced, certain circumstances being normal, where we set forth from certain known truths, and tread a certain path in thought to our intended proposition. There may be many ways of establishing the same proposition, starting from these or those bits of knowledge. It is, however, a characteristic and essential circumstance that there are infinitely many truths which could never be transformed into knowledge without such methodical procedures.

That this is the case, that we need grounded validations in order to pass beyond what, in knowledge, is immediately and therefore trivially evident, not only makes the sciences possible and necessary, but with these also a *theory of science*, a *logic*. All sciences proceed methodically in the pursuit of truth, employ more or less artificial aids in order to bring to knowledge truths or probabilities that would otherwise remain hidden, and in order to use the obvious or the already established as a lever for achieving what is remote and only mediately attainable. The comparative treatment of these methodical aids, in which the insights and experiences of countless generations of thinkers are stored up, should provide the means for setting up general norms for such procedures and likewise rules for their inventive construction in various classes of cases.

§7 *Continuation. The three most noteworthy peculiarities of grounded validations*

Let us penetrate somewhat more deeply into this matter, and reflect on the most noteworthy peculiarities of the remarkable thought-sequences called by us 'validations'.

They have in the *first* place the character of a fixed structure in relation to their content. We cannot, in order to reach a given piece of knowledge, that, e.g. of the Pythagorean theorem, choose our starting point at random among the pieces of knowledge immediately given to us, nor can we add or subtract any thought-items at will, if the evidence of the proposition to be validated is to burst forth genuinely, the validation to be a genuine validation.

A *second* point is at once evident. It might seem thinkable *a priori*, i.e. before we glance at, and compare instances of validation streaming in on us abundantly from every quarter, that each validation should be unique both in content and in form. A whim of nature – this might at first seem a tenable thought – might have framed our psychic constitution so wantonly that our familiar talk of a multiplicity of modes of validating matters might have lacked all sense. The only thing that could be pronounced common to any validations that we might compare would be that a proposition S, itself lacking inner evidence, achieves an evident character if it appears in combination with certain known truths P_1, P_2 ... truths whose relevance to it is a non-recurrent matter not subject to a rational rule. This is not how the matter stands, however. A blind caprice has not bundled any set of truths P_1, P_2 ... S together and then so instituted the human mind that it must necessarily (or in 'normal' circumstances) connect the knowledge of S with the knowledge of P_1, P_2 ... In no single case is this so. Connections of validation are not governed by caprice or chance, but by reason and order, i.e. by regulative laws. We hardly need an example to illuminate the point. If in a mathematical problem relating to a certain triangle *ABC*, we apply the proposition *An equilateral triangle is equiangular*, we carry out a validation which, made explicit, runs: Every equilateral triangle is equiangular; the triangle *ABC* is equilateral, and is therefore equiangular. If we set beside this the arithmetical argument: Every decimal number with an even last digit is an even number, 364 is a decimal number with an even last digit, and is therefore an even number, we note at once that the 'establishments' have something in common, an inner constitution of like type, which is intelligibly expressed in the syllogistic form 'Every A is B, X is A, so X is B'. Not only have these two arguments this same form, but countless others have it as well. Our syllogistic form further represents a class-concept, under which falls an infinite multitude of sentence-combinations all with the constitution that this form pointedly expresses. There is also an *a priori* law, making any putative validation that follows this form, also actually a correct one, provided, that is, that it proceeds from correct premisses.

This holds in general. Wherever we ascend by an establishing argument from given pieces of knowledge to new ones, a certain form resides in our modes of validation, which is common to countless other validating arguments, and which stands in a certain relation to a general law that allows us to justify all these single validations at one 'go'. No validating procedure – such is the quite remarkable fact – stands in isolation. None ties bits of knowledge up with other bits of knowledge, unless in their external mode of association, or in this together with the inner structure of the separate propositions, a definite type is brought out, a type which, if conceptually generalized, at once leads to a general law applying to an infinity of possible cases of validation.

A *third* remarkable feature deserves emphasis. *A priori*, i.e. before one compares validating arguments in *different* sciences, one might think it a possible thought that forms of validation should be bound up with territories of knowledge. Though the appropriate validations do not vary with types of object, it might still be the case that they divide sharply along certain highly general class-lines, the lines perhaps that demarcate varying scientific fields. Is it not the case that there is no pattern of validation common to two sciences, to mathematics, e.g. and chemistry? But this too is plainly not so, as our above example shows. There is no science where laws are not applicable to individual cases, where we do not therefore have syllogisms of the form illustrated above. The same holds of many other types of syllogism. We may in fact say of all other types of syllogism that they may be so generalized, so purely conceived, as to be free of all essential relation to some conceivably limited field of knowledge.

65

§8 *The relation of these peculiarities to the possibility of science and the theory of science*

These peculiarities of our validations, whose remarkable character escapes us since we are all too little disposed to turn everyday matters into problems, are visibly related to the *possibility of a science* and, further, of *a theory of science*.

That there are validating arguments is not in this connection enough. If they were formless and lawless, if it were not a fundamental truth that all validating arguments have certain indwelling 'forms', not peculiar to the simple or indefinitely complex arguments set before us here and now, but typical of a whole class of arguments, and that the correctness of this whole class of arguments is guaranteed just by their form – if the contrary of all this were true, there would be no science. Talk about a method, about a systematically regulated progress from one bit of knowledge to another, would be senseless, and all progress would be fortuitous. The propositions P_1, P_2 . . . which were fitted to confer evident truth on the proposition S, might fortuitously come up together in our consciousness, and this evident truth would then become duly luminous. It would no longer be possible to learn anything at all from a validating argument for future use on new validating arguments with novel material. No validating argument could serve as a paradigm for any other, none could embody a type, and no set of judgements, conceived as a system of premises, could have anything typical about it which could (without conceptual high-lighting or recourse to explicit 'inference-forms') crop up, on the occasion of a new case with quite novel materials, and help us on to a fresh gain in knowledge. It would be senseless to look for a proof of a given proposition. How indeed could one attempt it? Should one try out all possible sets of propositions to see if they could be employed as premises for the proposition in question? The cleverest man would here have no advantage over the stupidest, and it may be questioned whether he would have any essential advantage over him at all. A rich imagination, a comprehensive memory, a capacity for close attention etc., are fine things, but they have intellectual meaning only in the case of a *thinking* being, whose validation and invention falls under laws and forms.

It is generally true, in fact, that in all mental compounding, combinatory forms as well as mere elements have their associative or reproductive effect. The form, therefore, of our theoretical thoughts and thought-combinations may well prove useful. As, e.g., the form of certain premisses makes the emergence of appropriate conclusions much easier, since former inferences of like form have succeeded, so the form of some proposition to be proved may recall certain validating forms that have formerly yielded conclusions of the same form. If this is no clear, genuine case of memory, it is none the less analogous to the latter, a to some extent latent memory, an 'unconscious excitation' (in the sense of B. Erdmann). It is in any case something that greatly promotes proofs (and this not only in fields like mathematics that are dominated by arguments in form). The trained thinker finds proofs more readily than the untrained one. Why is this so? Because types of proof have been ever more deeply engraved on his mind through a varied experience, and so must operate more readily for him and determine the direction of his thought. To a certain extent any sort of scientific thought gives us practice in scientific thinking, but it is true also that to a peculiar degree and extent mathematical thought predisposes to what is mathematical, physical thought to what is physical etc. The former rests on the existence of typical forms common to all sciences, the latter on the existence of other forms, perhaps to be characterized as peculiarly structured complexes of the former – which are peculiarly related to what is peculiar to the separate sciences. The unique features of scientific flair, of anticipatory intuition and divination, hang together with this. We speak of a philological, of a mathematical flair and eye etc., and who possesses them? The trained philologist, mathematician etc., with his many years of practice. In the general nature of the objects of each realm certain forms of factual connection are rooted; these in their turn determine typical peculiarities of forms of validation that predominate in this realm. Herein we have the foundation for the pioneering hunches of science. All testing, invention and discovery therefore rests on regularities of form.

If all this shows that it is *regular form* that makes possible the existence of sciences, so, on the other hand, it is the wide degree of *independence of form from a field of knowledge* that makes possible a *theory of science*. Were there no such independence, there would only be coordinated logics separately corresponding to the separate sciences, but no general logic. In fact both are needed: investigations into the theory of science concerning all sciences equally, and, supplementary to these, particular investigations concerning the theory and method of the separate sciences which endeavour to search into what is peculiar to them.

To stress the peculiarities revealed by the comparative treatment of validating arguments, is not therefore without use in casting light on our discipline itself, on logic in the sense of a theory of science.

§9 *Methodical modes of procedure in the sciences are in part validatory, in part auxiliary devices towards validations*

Certain points must still be added, first in regard to the restriction of our treatment to validations, which plainly do not exhaust the notion of methodical procedure. Validations have, however, a central significance that will justify our provisional restriction.

One can in fact say that all scientific methods which do not themselves have the character of actual validating arguments (whether simple or of any degree of complexity) are, on the one hand, *abbreviations* and *substitutes* for such validating arguments, used to economize thought, since, having themselves once and for all received sense and value from such validation, their application now in practice does the work of validation without its charge of cogitative insight. They may, on the other hand, represent more or less complex *auxiliary devices*, which serve to prepare for, to facilitate, to ensure or to render possible future processes of validation without themselves being able to claim a significance which is of like value with, or independent of, these basic scientific processes.

To take up the latter group of methods, it is, e.g. an important prerequisite for securing one's validations that one's thoughts are adequately expressed by readily distinguishable, unambiguous signs. Language offers the investigator a widely applicable sign-system to express his thoughts, but, though no one can do without it, it represents a most imperfect aid towards strict research. The pernicious influences of ambiguities on the validity of syllogistic inferences are familiar. The careful thinker will not therefore use language without artificial precautions; to the extent that the terms he uses are not unambiguous and lack sharp meaning, he must define them. The definition of names we therefore see as a methodical auxiliary procedure towards ensuring validations, the latter being one's primary, truly theoretical procedures.

The same is true of *nomenclature*. Brief, characteristic symbols for the more important, recurrent concepts are – to mention only one point – indispensable wherever the expression of such concepts, by means of one's original stock of defined expressions would be unduly circumstantial. Involved expressions with such inbuilt Chinese-box complexity impede validatory operations or render them unperformable.

The method of *classification* can be treated from similar points of view etc.

Examples of the first group of methods are provided by the extraordinarily fruitful *algorithmic methods*, whose peculiar function is to save us as much genuine deductive mental work as possible by artificially arranged mechanical operations on sensible signs. Whatever marvels these methods may achieve, their sense and justification depends on validatory thought. Here also belong what are literally mechanical methods – one may think of the apparatus for mechanical integration, calculating machines etc. – as well as the methodical procedures for establishing objectively valid empirical judgements, such as the various methods of determining the position of a star, electrical resistance, inert mass, refractive index, the gravitational constant etc. Each such method represents a set of provisions whose choice and arrangement is fixed by a validatory context, which shows, in general, that such a procedure, even when blindly performed, must necessarily lead to an objectively valid individual judgement.

But enough of examples. It is plain that each actual advance in science is performed in an act of validation: to this all those methodical precautions and devices relate, which logic considers in addition to processes of validation. To this relation their typical character is likewise due, which is essentially involved in the Idea of method. On account of this typical character they too have a place in the discussions of the previous paragraph.

§ 10 *The Ideas of Theory and Science as problems of the theory of science*

Something more must be added. The theory of science, as here shown up, is not merely concerned to investigate the forms and laws of isolated validations, and the auxiliary devices which go with these. Isolated validations also occur beyond the boundaries of science: clearly, therefore, isolated validations – and loosely piled heaps of such validations – do not make up science. Science requires, as said above, a certain unity of validatory interconnection, a certain unity in the stepwise ascent of its validatory arguments, and this form of unity has itself a lofty teleological meaning in the attainment of the highest goal of knowledge for which all science strives: to advance as far as possible in the research into truth, i.e. not in the research into separate truths, but into the realm of truth or its natural provinces.

The task of the theory of science will therefore also be to deal with the sciences as *systematic unities of this or that sort* in other words, with the formal features that stamp them as sciences, with the features that determine their mutual boundaries and their inner articulation into fields, into relatively closed theories, with the features which fix their essentially different species or forms etc.

This systematic tissue of validatory arguments can in fact be subordinated to the concept of method, so that science's task is not merely to deal with the methods of knowledge in the sciences, but also with such methods as are themselves styled sciences. Its task is not merely to separate off valid from invalid demonstrations, but also valid from invalid theories and sciences. The task thus assigned it is plainly not independent of the one previously mentioned, but to a considerable extent presupposes a prior carrying out of the former. Research into the sciences as systematic unities is unthinkable without prior research into their validatory procedures. Both at least enter into the notion of a science of science as such.

§ 11 *Logic or theory of science as normative discipline and as technology*

From our discussions up to this point logic – in the sense of the theory of science here in question – emerges as a *normative discipline*. Sciences are mental creations which are directed to a certain end, and which are for that reason to be judged in accordance with that end. The same holds of theories, validations and in short of everything that we call a 'method'. Whether a science is truly a science, or a method a method, depends on whether it accords with the aims that it strives for. Logic seeks to search into what pertains to genuine, valid science as such, what constitutes the Idea of Science, so as to be able to use the latter to measure the empirically given sciences as to their agreement with their Idea, the degree to which they approach it, and where they offend against it. In this logic shows itself to be a normative science, and separates itself off from the comparative mode of treatment which tries to conceive of the sciences, according to their *typical* communities and peculiarities, as concrete cultural products of their era, and to explain them through the relationships which obtain in their time. For it is of the essence of a normative science that it establishes general propositions in which, with an eye to a normative standard, an Idea or highest goal, certain features are mentioned whose possession guarantees conformity to that standard, or sets forth an indispensable condition of the latter. A normative science also establishes cognate propositions in which the case of non-conformity is considered or the absence of such states of affairs is pronounced. Not as if one had to state general marks in order to say what an object should be to conform to its basic norm: a normative discipline never sets forth universal criteria, any more than a therapy states universal symptoms. Special criteria are what the theory of science particularly gives us, and what it alone can give us. If it maintains that, having regard to the supreme aim of the sciences and the human mind's actual constitution, and whatever else may be invoked, such and such methods M_1, M_2 . . . arise, it states general propositions of the form: 'Every group of mental activities of the sorts AB . . . which realize the combinatory form M_1 (or M_2 . . .) yield a case of correct method', or, what amounts to the same 'Every (soi-disant) methodical procedure of the form M_1 (or M_2 . . .) is a correct one.' If one could really formulate all intrinsically possible valid propositions of this and like sort, our normative science would certainly possess a measuring rod for every pretended method, but then also only in the form of special criteria.

Where the basic norm is an end or can become an end, the normative discipline by a ready extension of its task gives rise to a technology. This occurs in this case too. If the theory of science sets itself the further task of investigating such conditions as are subject to our power, on which the realization of valid methods depends, and if it draws up rules for our procedure in the methodical tracking down of truth, in the valid demarcation and construction of the sciences, in the discovery and use, in particular, of the many methods that advance such sciences, and in the avoidance of errors in all of these concerns, then it has become a *technology of science*. This last plainly includes the whole normative theory of science, and it is therefore wholly appropriate, in view of the unquestionable value of such a technology, that the concept of logic should be correspondingly widened, and should be defined in its sense.

§12 *Relevant definitions of logic*

The definition of logic as a technology was much favoured by tradition, but closer determinations of it left much to be desired. Definitions such as 'technology of judgement, of reasoning, of knowing, of thinking' (*l'art de penser*) are misleading, and in any case too narrow. If we restrict the vague meaning of the word 'thinking' in the last-mentioned definition (in use to this day) to the concept of correct judgement, our definition reads: 'the technology of correct judgement'. But that this definition is too narrow is plain from the fact that the aim of scientific knowledge does not follow from it. If one says that 'the aim of thinking is first perfectly fulfilled in science', this is without doubt right, but it concedes that not thought or knowledge is really the end of the technology in question, but that towards which thought itself is a means.

Other definitions are open to similar objections. They are open to the objection recently revived by Bergmann that the technology of an activity, e.g. painting, singing, riding, would be expected above all 'to show what one must do to perform the relevant activity correctly, e.g. how one must hold and wield the brush in painting, how one must use the chest, throat and mouth in singing, how one must pull and relax the reins in riding and press with one's legs'. This would admit into the field of logic doctrines wholly alien to it.[1]

[1] Bergmann, *Die Grundlagen der Logik* (1895), p. 78. Cf. also Bolzano's *Wissenschaftslehre* (Sulzbach 1837), I, p. 24: 'Is the question whether coriander helps to strengthen memory a logical question? It surely should be if logic is an *ars rationis formandae* in the complete meaning of the words'.

Schleiermacher's definition of logic as the technology of scientific knowledge certainly comes closer to the truth. For obviously in a discipline so defined one would have to consider only what is peculiar to scientific knowledge, and to probe its possible demands: the further preconditions which in general favour the emergence of knowledge would be left to pedagogy, hygiene etc. But Schleiermacher's definition does not plainly say that this technology should also set up rules for the demarcation and construction of the sciences, whereas this aim, on the other hand, includes the aim of scientific knowledge. Excellent thoughts towards the circumscription of our discipline are to be found in Bolzano's *Wissenschaftslehre*, but rather in his preliminary critical searchings than in the definition he himself espouses. This last sounds oddly enough: the theory of science (or logic) is 'the science which shows us how to present the sciences in convenient textbooks'.[1]

[1] Bolzano, *Wissenschaftslehre*, I, p. 7. The fourth volume of the *Wissenschaftslehre* is indeed specially devoted to the task which the definition expresses. But it strikes one as strange that the incomparably more important disciplines which the first three volumes treat of, should be represented merely as aids to a technology of scientific textbooks. Naturally, too, the value of this by no means as yet sufficiently valued work, which is, in fact, almost unused, rests on the researches of these earlier volumes.

CHAPTER TWO

Theoretical Disciplines as the Foundation of Normative Disciplines

§13 The controversy regarding the practical character of logic

OUR last discussions have given so obvious a justification to the view of logic as a technology, that it might seem remarkable that there should ever have been controversy on this point. A practically oriented logic is an indispensable postulate of all the sciences, and this corresponds to the historical fact that logic arose out of practical motives connected with the business of science. This we know happened in those thought-stirring times when the young, budding science of the Greeks was in danger of succumbing to the attacks of sophists and subjectivists, when all its future success depended on finding objective criteria of truth, which might destroy the cheating illusions of the sophistical dialectic.

In modern times, mainly under the influence of Kant, there have been repeated denials that logic is a technology, though such a characterization has, on the other hand, been held to have some value: this dispute cannot have turned on the mere question whether it is possible to give logic practical aims, and so to conceive of it as a practical discipline. Kant himself spoke of an applied logic which should have as its task the regulation of the use of the understanding 'under the contingent conditions of the subject, which might hinder or assist it', (*Crit. of Pure Reason*: Intro. to Trans. Logic, I, last paragraph), and from which we might learn 'what promotes the correct use of the understanding, what assists it and what cures it from logical mistakes and errors' (Kant's *Logik*, Introduction II, Hartenstein's edition 1867, VIII, p. 18). Though he is not willing to let it rank, with *pure* logic, as an authentic science, though he even thinks that 'it should not properly be called logic' (*Crit. of Pure Reason*, Intro. to Trans. Log. III, p. 83), everyone is none the less at liberty to extend the

74

aim of logic so as to include applied, practical logic.[1] It may in any case be disputed, as has in fact frequently happened, whether great gain can be hoped for from logic as a practical theory of science, whether, e.g. one could really hope for such great revolutions and advances from an extension of the old logic (which could only serve to test given knowledge) into an *ars inventiva*, a 'logic of discovery', as Leibniz is known to have believed etc. This dispute, however, concerns no point important in principle, and it is settled by the clear maxim that even the moderate probability of a future advance in the sciences justifies us in working on a normative discipline pledged to this end, without regard to the fact that the rules we deduce represent a valuable enrichment of knowledge.

The genuinely disputed question of important principle, to which neither side has given precision, lies in quite a different direction: whether the definition of logic as a technology really touches its *essential character*. We ask, in other words, if it is only a practical standpoint that establishes the right of logic to count as a peculiar scientific discipline, while, from a theoretical standpoint, all the findings accumulated by logic consist, on the one hand, in purely theoretical propositions having their original home in otherwise known theoretical sciences, and mainly in psychology, and, on the other hand in rules based on these theoretical propositions.

The essence of Kant's conception of logic does not, in fact, lie in the fact that he disputes the practical character of logic, but that he believes in the possibility and the epistemologically basic character of a certain delimitation or restriction of logic, which would make of it a wholly independent science, one which, in comparison with the otherwise known sciences, is wholly new

---

[1] Kant thinks there is a *contradictio in adjecto* in a general logic with a practical part, and therefore rejects the division of logic into theoretical and practical logic (*Logik*, Introduction II). This does not, however, prevent us from regarding as practical logic what he calls 'applied logic'. A 'practical logic', spoken of as we ordinarily use the expression, by no means necessarily presupposes 'the knowledge of a certain sort of objects to which it is applied', but the knowledge of a mind whose efforts after knowledge it will promote. Application can occur in two directions. Logical rules can help us in a particular field of knowledge: this pertains to a particular science and the methodology connected with it. But it is also thinkable that, with the aid of laws of pure logic, independent of the peculiarities of the human mind (if such laws there be) we might deduce rules having peculiar regard to the nature of man (*in specie*). In that case we should have a universal and yet practical logic.

and entirely theoretical, and which, like mathematics, stands outside of any thought of possible application, in being an *a priori*, purely demonstrative discipline.

The restriction of logic to its theoretic knowledge-content leads, on the prevailing form of the doctrine opposed to Kant's, to psychological and perhaps also grammatical and other propositions, i.e. to small excerpts from otherwise delimited, and, let us add, empirical sciences. Whereas, on Kant's view, we rather dig down to an internally closed, independent and, let us add, *a priori* field of theoretical knowledge, to pure logic.

It is apparent that other weighty oppositions are at work in these doctrines; whether logic should count as an *a priori* or an empirical science, as an independent or dependent science, as a demonstrative or non-demonstrative science. If we drop these questions as remote from our immediate interests, only the above mentioned point of dispute remains: on one side we abstract the assertion that under every logic thought of as a technology lies a *peculiar* theoretical discipline, a pure logic, whereas, on the other view, all theoretical doctrines admitted into the logical technology are held to be classifiable in otherwise known theoretical sciences.

The second point of view was stoutly defended by Beneke,[1] and J. Stuart Mill stated it clearly in his *Logic* which has also been influential in this respect.[2] Sigwart's *Logik*, the leading contribution to recent logical work in Germany, also stands on similar ground. Clearly and decisively it is there said: 'The highest task of logic, and the one which constitutes its real essence, is to be a technical discipline'.[3]

On the other side we have, in addition to Kant, principally Herbart, and a large number of their disciples.

How easily the most extreme empiricism accords in *this* respect with Kant's conception is seen from Bain's *Logic* which, constructed as a technology, expressly acknowledges, and claims to include, a logic which is a peculiar, abstract, theoretical discipline

---

[1] The belief in the essentially practical character of logic is even expressed in the titles of Beneke's expositions of Logic – *Textbook of Logic as Technology of Thinking* (1832), *System of Logic as Technology of Thinking* (1842). See with reference to this matter the Foreword, Introduction and particularly the polemic against Herbart in the *System*, p. 21 *f*.

[2] For the present question Mill's polemic against Hamilton is more relevant than his principal work on logic. Necessary references follow below.

[3] Sigwart, *Logik*, ed. 3, p. 10.

– a science of the same sort as mathematics. This theoretical discipline is held by Bain to rest on psychology; it is not thought of, as by Kant, to precede all other sciences as an absolutely independent science. But it remains a science on its *own* account: it is not, as Mill would have it, a mere assemblage of psychological chapters, offered with the intention to regulate knowledge practically.[1]

In the many treatments which logic has received this century, the point of difference here in question has hardly ever been clearly emphasized and carefully considered. Since the practical treatment of logic accords with either standpoint, and is generally admitted to be useful on either, the whole dispute as to the essentially practical or theoretical character of logic has seemed meaningless to many. They have never in fact been clear as to how the standpoints differ.

We are not required by our purposes to go critically into the disputes of older logicians as to whether logic is an art or a science or both, and whether, in the second case, it is a practical or speculative science or both. On these questions, and on the value of these questions, Sir William Hamilton has pronounced as follows:

> The controversy . . . is perhaps one of the most futile in the history of speculation. In so far as Logic is concerned, the decision of the question is not of the very smallest import. It was not in consequence of any diversity of opinion in regard to the scope and nature of this doctrine, that philosophers disputed by what name it should be called. The controversy was, in fact, only about what was properly an art, and what was properly a science; and as men attached one meaning or another to these terms, so did they affirm Logic to be an art, or a science, or both, or neither (*Lectures on Logic*, ed. III, vol. I (1884), pp. 9–10).

One must note, however, that Hamilton himself did not dig very deeply into the content and value of the distinctions and controversies in question. If there were appropriate agreement as to the way to treat logic, and the content of the doctrines to be attributed to it, the question if and how the concepts *art* and *science* entered into its definition, would be of minor importance, though by no means a mere question of labelling. But the dispute over the definition (as we have already maintained) is really a

---

[1] Cf. Bain, *Logic*, I (1879), 50, p. 34 *f.*

dispute regarding the science itself, and one not regarding the completed science but the provisionally pretended one, the one still in progress, whose methods, doctrines, in short everything, are still in doubt. Even in Hamilton's day, and long before, men differed considerably as to the essential content, the scope and the manner of treatment of logic. One need only compare the works of Hamilton, Bolzano, Mill and Beneke. And how the differences have grown since then. Put together Erdmann and Drobisch, Wundt and Bermann, Schuppe and Brentano, Sigwart and Überweg, and ask whether one then has a single science, or only a single name. One might settle for the latter, if there were not occasionally some more comprehensive groups of common themes, though in respect of the doctrine, and even the problems, no two logicians reach a tolerable understanding among themselves. If we associate with this the point stressed in the Introduction, that definitions of logic merely express beliefs as to its essential tasks and methodical character, and that errors and prejudices on these points can help to mislead so retarded a science on to wrong paths of research. We shall certainly not agree with Hamilton in saying that 'the decision of the question is not of the very smallest import'.

Confusion has not a little been promoted by the fact that even distinguished protagonists of the autonomy of a *pure* logic, such as Drobisch and Bergmann, have put the normative character of the discipline among the features essential to its notion. Their opponents saw in this a patent inconsequence, even a contradiction. Has not the concept of normativity got an inherent relation to a guiding aim, and to activities devoted to it? Does not a normative science mean exactly the same as a technology?

The manner in which Drobisch introduces and conceives his determinations merely confirms these impressions. In his ever valuable *Logic* we read: 'There are two angles from which thought can be made the object of a scientific investigation: as an activity of mind whose conditions and laws may be looked into, and as a tool for acquiring mediate knowledge, permitting both of a correct and a faulty use, and leading in the one case to true, in the other to false results. There are therefore both *natural* and *normal* *laws* for thinking, and the latter are *prescriptions* (norms) to which one must *direct* oneself to reach these results. The investigation of the natural laws of thinking is a task for psychology, whereas the establishment of its normal rules is the task of logic' (*Neue Darstellung der Logik*, §2, p. 3). And to this the further more than sufficient explanation is added: 'Normal rules always regulate an activity in conformity with a certain end.'

On the other hand one might say: here nothing is said to which Beneke or Mill could not subscribe, and which they could not adapt to their own advantage. If we grant the identity of the concepts 'normative discipline' and 'technology', it is obvious that, as in the case of technologies in general, it is not the mutual connectedness of matters but our guiding aim which serves to bind and unite logical truths into a discipline. It is then plainly wrong to set logic bounds as narrow as those of the traditional Aristotelian logic, since 'pure' logic certainly goes beyond these. It is absurd to set logic a goal, and then to exclude from it classes of norms and normative investigations that pertain to this goal. The exponents of pure logic still live under the spell of tradition; the marvellous magic distilled by the hollow formularies hawked about by the school logic down the ages, still works powerfully in them.

Such is the list of obvious objections likely to turn modern interest from a closer discussion of the objective reasons which have weighed with great, independent thinkers in favour of an autonomous science of pure logic, and which still call for serious probing. The worthy Drobisch may have gone wrong in his statement, but this does not prove that his position, or that of his master Herbart, or that ultimately of his prime inspirer Kant,[1] was in essence misguided. It does not even rule out the possibility that a valuable thought, that has not achieved conceptually clear expression, may lie hidden under his imperfect statement. Let us dwell on the coordination of logic with pure mathematics, of which the champions of pure logic are so fond. The mathematical disciplines also yield a basis for technologies. To arithmetic

---

[1] Kant himself, though he opposes logical laws, as 'necessary rules' which say 'how the understanding should proceed in thought', to psychological laws which say 'what the understanding is like and how it thinks' (cf. *Vorlesungen über Logik*, Hart. ed. VIII, p. 14), did not ultimately wish to regard logic as a normative discipline (in the sense of one that measures adequacy in relation to set ends). This is decisively shown by his coordination of logic and aesthetic to accord with the two 'basic sources of the mind', the latter being the (rational) 'science of the rules of sensibility in general', the former the correlative 'science of the rules of the understanding in general'. Logic in this Kantian sense can, no more than Aesthetics, count as a regulative discipline guided by goals. (Cf. *Critique of Pure Reason*, Introduction to the Transcendental Logic I, end of paragraph 2.)

corresponds the practical art of calculation, to geometry the art of land-surveying. Technologies are similarly connected, though somewhat differently, with the abstract theoretical natural sciences, physical technologies with physics, chemical technologies with chemistry. This readily suggests the view that it is the true sense of our supposed pure logic to be an abstract theoretical discipline providing a basis for a technology just as the previously mentioned disciplines do, its technology being logic in the ordinary, practical sense. And just as technologies sometimes have one main, basic, theoretical discipline from which their norms flow, sometimes several such basic disciplines, so logic, taken as a technology, might depend on a plurality of such disciplines, and have pure logic merely as one, though perhaps the most important one, of its basic disciplines. Possibly it could be further shown that logical laws and forms, in the pregnant sense of these words, belong to a theoretically closed round of abstract truth, that cannot in any way be fitted into previously delimited theoretical disciplines and so must themselves be regarded as the pure logic in question. We should then be led to suppose that defects in the conceptual definition of this discipline, and the inability to present it in its purity, and clearly state its relation to logic as a technology, have favoured its confusion with this technology, and have made possible the dispute as to whether logic should be defined as being essentially a theoretical or a practical discipline. While the one party trained its sights on purely theoretical propositions that were logical in the pregnant sense, the other party stuck to the vulnerable *definitions* of the pretended theoretical science, and the manner in which it was actually carried out.

To object that we are attempting to restore the Aristotelian-scholastic logic, on whose worthlessness history has pronounced judgement, will not perturb us. Possibly it may yet appear that the discipline in question is by no means so narrow in scope, and so poor in profound problems, as it is here reproached with being. Possibly traditional logic was merely a highly imperfect, distorted realization of the Idea of Pure Logic, but none the less sound and respectable as a first onslaught and initiative. One may also ask whether our scorn for the traditional logic is not perhaps an unjustifiable after-effect of renaissance attitudes, whose motives no longer touch us. It is understandable that the historically justified, but in reality often foolish battle, against scholastic science, should be above all directed against its logic, its characteristic doctrine of method. But that formal logic should, in the hands of scholasticism, particularly decadent scholasticism, have taken on the character of a false methodology, perhaps only shows the lack of a correct philosophical understanding of logical theory, as so far developed. The practical use of this logic therefore entered mistaken pathways, and methodological achievements were attributed to it for which it is in essence unqualified. In the same way, number-mysticism proves nothing against arithmetic. The logical polemics of the renaissance are well known to have been void of substance or effect: they are the utterances of passion, not of insight. Why should we still yield ourselves to the guidance of such scornful utterances? A theoretically creative mind like Leibniz, in whom the enthusiastic reformatory zeal of the renaissance went together with a sober, scientific, modern spirit, would hear nothing of a baiting or harrying of scholasticism. With warm words he took the despised Aristotelian logic to his bosom, however much he thought it needed extension and improvement. We can in any case quietly leave aside the reproach that pure logic represents a revival of 'hollow, formal, scholastic truck', while we have not yet become clear as to the sense and content of the discipline in question, nor as to the justification of the surmises that have suggested themselves to us.

In order to test these surmises, we do not intend to assemble and to subject to a critical analysis any and every argument historically advanced for this or that conception of logic. This would not be a way to give new interest to an old dispute. The oppositions of principle which were not properly sorted out in this dispute, have, however, their own interest, and this interest rises above the empirical limitations of the disputants. It is these oppositions that we have to track down.

§14 The concept of a normative science. The basic standard or principle that gives it unity

We begin by concentrating on a proposition that is of decisive importance for our further investigation: that every normative and likewise every practical discipline rests on one or more theoretical disciplines, inasmuch as its rules must have a theoretical content separable from the notion of normativity (of the 'shall' or 'should'), whose scientific investigation is the duty of these theoretical disciplines.

To clear up this point, let us first discuss the concept of a normative science in its relation to that of a theoretical science. The laws of the former tell us (it is usually held) what shall or should be, though perhaps, under the actual circumstances, it neither is nor can be. The laws of the latter, contrariwise, merely tell us what is. We must now ask what is meant by such a 'shall be' or 'should be' as opposed to what is.

The original sense of 'shall' or 'should', which relates to a certain wish or will, a certain demand or command, is plainly too narrow, e.g. You shall listen to me, X shall come to me. As we speak in a wider sense of a demand, where there is no one who demands, and perhaps no one on whom demand is made, so we frequently speak of a 'shall' or a 'should' which is independent of anyone's wishing or willing. If we say 'A soldier should be brave', this does not mean that we or anyone else are wishing or willing, commanding or requiring this. One might rather suppose that a corresponding wishing and requiring would be generally justified, i.e. in relation to every soldier, though even this is not quite right, since it is surely not necessary that we should here be really evaluating a wish or a demand. 'A soldier should be brave' rather means that only a brave soldier is a 'good' soldier, which implies (since the predicates 'good' and 'bad' divide up the extension of the concept 'soldier') that a soldier who is not brave is a 'bad' soldier. *Since* this value-judgement holds, everyone is entitled to demand of a soldier that he should be brave, the same ground ensures that it is desirable, praiseworthy etc., that he should be brave. The same holds in other instances. 'A man should practise neighbourly love', i.e. one who omits this is no longer a 'good' man, and therefore *eo ipso* is (in this respect) a 'bad' man. 'A drama should not break up into episodes' – otherwise it is not a 'good' drama, not a 'true' work of art. In all these cases we make our positive evaluation, the attribution of a positive value-predicate, depend on a condition to be fulfilled, whose non-fulfilment entails the corresponding negative predicate. We may in general, take as identical or at least as equivalent the forms 'An A should be B' and 'An A that is not B is a bad A', or 'Only an A which is a B is a good A'.

The term 'good' naturally functions in the widest sense of what is in any way valuable: in the concrete propositions ranged under our formula it is to be understood in the specific sense of the valuations it presupposes, e.g. as useful, beautiful, moral etc. There are as many ways of speaking of a 'should' as there are different species of valuations, as there are, in consequence, actual or presumed values.

Negative statements of what should not be are not to be taken as negations of the corresponding affirmative statements, as, too, in the ordinary sense, the denial of a demand does not amount to a prohibition. 'A soldier should not be cowardly' does not mean that it is false that a soldier should be cowardly, but that a cowardly soldier also is a bad one. The following forms are therefore equivalent: 'An A should not be B', and 'An A which is B is in general a bad A' or 'Only an A which is not B is a good A'.

That 'should' and 'should not' are mutually exclusive follows formally from their interpretations, and the same holds of the proposition that judgements regarding what should be entail no assertion regarding what correspondingly is.

The just clarified judgements of normative form are plainly not the only ones that one would allow to count as such, even if the word 'should' or 'shall' does not occur in their expression. It is inessential if, instead of saying 'A should (or should not) be B' we also are able to say 'A must (or may not) be B'. We touch more substance if we point to the two new formulae 'A need not be B' and 'A may be B', which are in contradictory opposition to the above forms. 'May not' is therefore the negation of 'should', or, what is the same, of 'must'; 'may' the negation of 'should not' or, what is the same, of 'may not', as can readily be seen from the interpreting value-judgements: 'An A need not be B' = 'An A that is not B is not therefore a bad A'; 'An A may be B' = 'An A that is B is not therefore a bad A'.

There are yet other propositions that must be reckoned with here, e.g. 'For an A to be a good A it suffices (or does not suffice) that it is B'. Whereas our former propositions are about certain *necessary* conditions for attributing or denying positive or negative value-predicates, our concern in the present proposition is with *sufficient* conditions. Other further propositions aim at stating what are at once necessary and sufficient conditions.

We have thus run through the essential forms of general

normative propositions. To them of course correspond forms of particular and singular value-judgement which contribute nothing of importance to our analysis, and of which the latter at least do not count for our purposes. They have always a nearer or remoter relation to certain normative generalities: in abstract normative disciplines, they can only occur in relation to their governing generalities. Such disciplines are as such located beyond all individual existence, their generalities are 'purely conceptual', they have a lawlike character in the strict sense of the word 'law'.

We see from these analyses that each normative proposition presupposes a certain sort of valuation or approval through which the concept of a 'good' or 'bad' (a value or a disvalue) arises in connection with a certain class of objects: in conformity with this, objects divide into good and bad ones. To be able to pass the normative judgement 'A soldier should be brave', I must have some conception of a 'good' soldier, and this concept cannot be founded on an arbitrary nominal definition, but on a general valuation, which permits us to value soldiers as good or bad according to these or those properties. Whether or not this valuation is in any sense 'objectively valid', whether we can draw any distinction between the subjectively and objectively 'good', does not enter into our determination of the sense of should-propositions. It is sufficient that something is held valuable, that an *intention* is effected having the content that something is valuable or good.

If, conversely, a pair of value-predicates has been laid down for an appropriate class, following upon a certain general valuation, then the possibility of normative judgements is given: all forms of normative proposition have then definite sense. Every constitutive property B of the 'good' A yields, e.g. a proposition of the form 'An A should be B', every property incompatible with B, a proposition 'An A may not (should not) be B' etc.

Finally, as regards the *concept of the normative judgement* we can, following our analysis, describe it as follows: In relation to a general underlying valuation, and the content of the corresponding pair of value-predicates determined by it, every proposition is said to be 'normative' that states a necessary, or a sufficient, or a necessary and sufficient condition for having such a predicate. If we have once drawn a distinction between 'good' and 'bad' in our valuations in a particular sense, and so in a particular sphere, we are naturally concerned to decide the circumstances, the inner or outer properties that are or are not guarantees that a thing is good or bad in this sense: what properties may not be lacking if an object from that sphere is to be accorded the value of 'good'.

Where we speak of good and bad, we also usually make comparative valuational distinctions between *better* and best or between *worse* and worst. If pleasure is our good, then the more intense, and again the more enduring, pleasure is better. If knowledge counts as our good, not every piece of knowledge will therefore count as 'equally good'. We value the knowledge of laws more highly than the knowledge of singular facts: the knowledge of more general laws, e.g. 'Every equation of the nth degree has n roots', more highly than the knowledge of the special laws that fall under them – 'Every equation of the fourth degree has four roots'. There are therefore normative questions relating to relative value-predicates just as there are in the case of absolute value-predicates. If the constitutive content of what is to be esteemed good or bad is fixed, one must ask what, in comparative valuation, will count constitutively as better or worse, and, further, what are the nearer and the more remote, the necessary and the sufficient conditions for the relative predicates, laying down the content of the better and worse, and ultimately of the relatively best. The constitutive contents of positive and relative value-predicates are, so to say, the metric units in terms of which objects of the relevant sphere are measured.

The sum total of these norms plainly forms a closed group, determined by our fundamental valuation. The normative proposition which demands generally of the objects of a sphere that they should measure up to the constitutive features of the positive value-predicate to the greatest extent possible, has a central place in each group of mutually coherent norms, and can be called their *basic norm*. This role is, e.g., played by the categorical imperative in the group of normative propositions which make up Kant's Ethics, as by the principle of the 'greatest possible happiness of the greatest possible number' in the Ethics of the Utilitarians.

The basic norm is the correlate of the definition of 'good' and 'bad' in the sense in question. It tells us on what basic standard or basic value all normativization must be conducted, and does not therefore represent a normative proposition in the strict sense. The relationship of the basic norm to what are, properly speaking, normative propositions, is like the relation between so-called definitions of the number-series and the arithmetical theorems about the relations of numbers which are always referred back to these. The basic norm could also be called a 'definition' of the standard conception of good – e.g. of the morally good – but this would mean departing from the ordinary logical concept of definition.

If, in relation to such a 'definition', or fundamental and universal valuation, we make it our aim to conduct scientific researches into a sum total of mutually relevant normative propositions, we come upon the Idea of a Normative Discipline. Each such discipline is therefore unambiguously characterized by its basic norm, or by the definition of what shall count as 'good' in such a discipline. If, e.g. the production, maintenance, increase and intensification of pleasure counts as our good, we shall ask by what objects, or in what subjective and objective circumstances, pleasure is excited. We shall enquire generally into the necessary and sufficient conditions for the emergence, maintenance, increase etc., of pleasure. These questions taken as targets for our scientific discipline yield a *hedonic*: this hedonic is normative ethics in the sense of the hedonists. The valuation directed to the arousal of pleasure yields the basic norm which determines the unity of the discipline and distinguishes it from every other normative discipline. Every normative discipline therefore has its own basic norm which is in each case its unifying principle. *Theoretical disciplines* do not have this central reference of all researches to a fundamental valuation as the source of a dominant normative interest. The unity of their researches, and the co-ordination of what they know, is determined exclusively by a theoretical interest directed to investigating matters that really belong together theoretically, in virtue of the inner laws of things, and which must therefore be investigated together in their mutual coherence.

§15 *Normative disciplines and technologies*

A normative interest is naturally dominant in the case of *real* (*realen*) objects, as the objects of *practical* valuations. Hence the undeniable tendency to identify the notion of a normative discipline with that of a practical discipline or a *technology*. It is easy to see, however, that such an identification cannot be sustained. Schopenhauer, e.g., who is led by his doctrine of inborn character to reject in principle all practical moralizing, has an ethics in the sense of a normative science, which he himself works out. For he does not at all abandon distinctions in moral value. A technology represents a particular case of a normative discipline which arises when the basic norm consists in achieving a universal practical aim. Plainly, therefore, every technology includes in itself an entire normative discipline, which is not itself a practical discipline. For its task presupposes that, altogether apart from everything relating to practical attainment, the narrower task of fixing norms has first been carried out, norms by which we can assess the adequacy to the general notion of the end to be achieved, or the possession of the properties characteristic of the class of values in question. Every normative discipline, conversely, whose fundamental valuation is transformed into a corresponding teleological prescription, widens out into a technology.

§ 16 *Theoretical disciplines as the foundation of normative disciplines*

It is now easy to see that each normative, and, *a fortiori*, each practical discipline, presupposes one or more theoretical disciplines as its foundations, in the sense, namely, that it must have a theoretical content free from all normativity, which as such has its natural location in certain theoretical sciences, whether these are already marked off or yet to be constituted.

The basic norm (or basic value, or ultimate end) determines, we saw, the unity of the discipline: it also is what imports the thought of normativity into all its normative propositions. But alongside of this general thought of measurement in terms of a basic norm, these propositions have their own theoretical content, which differs from one case to another. Each expresses the thought of a measuring relation between norm and what it is a norm for, but this relation is itself objectively characterized – if we abstract from valuational interest – as a relation between condition and conditioned, which relation is set down as existent or non-existent in the relevant normative propositions. Every normative proposition of, e.g., the form 'An A should be B' implies the theoretical proposition 'Only an A which is B has the properties C', in which 'C' serves to indicate the constitutive content of the standard-setting predicate 'good' (e.g. pleasure, knowledge, whatever, in short, is marked down as good by the valuation fundamental to our given sphere). The new proposition is purely theoretical: it contains no trace of the thought of normativity. If, conversely, a proposition of the latter form is true, and thereupon a novel valuation of a C as such emerges, and makes a normative relation to the proposition seem requisite, the theoretical proposition assumes the normative form 'Only an A which is B is a good A', i.e. 'An A should be B'. Normative propositions can therefore make an appearance even in theoretical contexts: our theoretical interest in such contexts attaches value to the being of a state of affairs of a sort – to the equilateral form, e.g., of a triangle about to be determined – and then assesses other states of affairs, e.g. one of equiangularity, in relation to this: If the triangle is *to be* equilateral, it must be equiangular. Such a modification is, however, merely passing and secondary in theoretical sciences, since our last intention is here directed to the theoretical coherence of the things themselves. Enduring results are not therefore stated in normative form, but in the forms of this objective coherence, in the form, that is, of a general proposition.

It is now clear that the theoretical relations which our discussion has shown to lie hidden in the propositions of normative sciences, must have their logical place in certain theoretical sciences. If the normative science is to deserve its name, if it is to do scientific work on the relations of the facts to be normatively considered to their basic norms, it must study the content of the theoretical nucleus of these relations, and this means entering the spheres of the relevant theoretical sciences. In other words: Every normative discipline demands that we know certain non-normative truths: these it takes from certain theoretical sciences, or gets by applying propositions so taken to the constellation of cases determined by its normative interest. This naturally holds, likewise, in the more special case of a technology, and plainly to a greater extent. The theoretical knowledge is there added which will provide a basis for a fruitful realization of ends and means.

One point should be noted in the interest of what follows.

Naturally these theoretical sciences may share in very different degrees in the scientific foundation and elaboration of the normative discipline in question. Their significance for it can also be greater or less. It may become plain that, to satisfy the interests of a normative discipline, the knowledge of certain sorts of theoretical connection has a prime urgency, and that the development and bringing closer of the theoretical field of knowledge to which they belong therefore plays a decisive part in making such a normative discipline possible. In building up such a discipline, it may be that certain sorts of theoretical knowledge play a useful and perhaps very weighty role, but none the less are of secondary significance, since their removal would only narrow, but not wholly destroy, the field of the discipline. One may think, e.g., of the relation between merely normative and practical ethics (see above, §15). All the propositions which have to do with making practical realization possible, do not affect the sphere of the pure norms of ethical valuation. If these norms, or the theoretical knowledge underlying them, were to fall away, ethics would vanish altogether. If the former propositions were to drop out, there would be no possibility of ethical practice (or no possibility of a technology of ethical conduct).

It is in relation to such distinctions that talk of the *essential* foundations of a normative science must be understood. We mean thereby the theoretical sciences that are absolutely essential to its construction, perhaps also the relevant groups of theoretical propositions which are of decisive importance in making the normative discipline possible.

CHAPTER THREE

Psychologism, its Arguments and its Attitude to the Usual Counter-Arguments

§17 The disputed question as to whether the essential theoretical foundations of normative logic lie in psychology

IF we now apply the general results arrived at in the last chapter to logic as a normative discipline, a first, very weighty question arises: Which theoretical sciences provide the essential foundations of the theory of science? And to this we forthwith add the further question: Is it correct that the theoretical truths we find dealt with in the framework of traditional and modern logic, and above all those belonging to its essential foundations, have their theoretical place in the sciences that have been already marked off and independently developed?

Here we encounter the disputed question as to the relation between psychology and logic, since one dominant tendency of our time has a ready answer to the questions raised: The essential theoretical foundations of logic lie in psychology, in whose field those propositions belong – as far as their theoretical content is concerned – which give logic its characteristic pattern. Logic is related to psychology just as any branch of chemical technology is related to chemistry, as land-surveying is to geometry etc. This tendency sees no need to mark off a new theoretical discipline, and, in particular, not one that would deserve the name of logic in a narrower and more pointed sense. Often people talk as if psychology provided the sole, sufficient, theoretical foundation for logical technology. So we read in Mill's polemic against Hamilton: 'Logic is not a science separate from and coordinate with psychology. To the extent that it is a science at all, it is a part or branch of psychology, distinguished from it on the one hand as the part is from the whole, and on the other hand as the art is from the science. It owes all its theoretical foundations to psychology, and includes as much of that science as is necessary to establish the rules of the art' (*An Examination of Sir William Hamilton's Philosophy*, p. 461). According to Lipps it even seems that logic is to be ranked as a mere constituent of psychology for he says: 'The fact that logic is a specific discipline of psychology distinguishes them satisfactorily from one another' (Lipps, *Grundzüge der Logik* (1893), §3).

§18 *The line of proof of the psychologistic thinkers*

If we ask for the justification of such views, a most plausible line of argument is offered, which seems to cut off all further dispute *ab initio*. However one may define logic as a technology – as a technology of thinking, judging, inferring, knowing, proving, of the courses followed by the understanding in the pursuit of truth, in the evaluation of grounds of proof etc. – we find invariably that mental activities or products are the objects of practical regulation. And just as, in general, the artificial working over of a material presupposes the knowledge of its properties, so this will be the case here too, where we are specially concerned with psychological material. The scientific investigation of the rules according to which this stuff should be worked over, naturally leads back to the scientific investigation of these properties. Psychology therefore provides the theoretical basis for constructing a logical technology, and, more particularly, the psychology of cognition.[1]

Any glance at the contents of logical literature will confirm this. What is being talked of throughout? Concepts, judgements, syllogisms, deductions, inductions, definitions, classifications etc. – all psychology, except that they are selected and arranged from normative and practical points of view. Draw the bounds of pure logic as tightly as one likes, it will not be possible to keep out what is psychological. This is implicit in the concepts constitutive for logical laws: truth and falsehood, affirmation and negation, universality and particularity, ground and consequent etc.

[1] 'Logic is a psychological discipline just as surely as knowing only arises in the mind, and as thinking which terminates in knowledge is a mental happening.' Lipps, op. cit.

§19 *The usual arguments of the opposition and the psychologistic rejoinder*

Remarkably enough, the opposition believes that it can base a sharp separation of the two disciplines on precisely the normative character of logic. Psychology, it is said, deals with thinking as it is, logic with thinking as it should be. The former has to do with the natural laws, the latter with the normative laws of thinking. It reads in this sense in Jäsche's version of Kant's Lectures on Logic: 'Some logicians presuppose psychological principles for logic, but to introduce such principles into logic, is as absurd as to derive morality from Life. If we take principles from psychology, i.e. from observations of our understanding, we shall only see how thought proceeds, and what happens under manifold subjective hindrances and conditions. Those would only lead to a knowledge of merely *contingent* laws. Logic does not however ask after *contingent*, but after *necessary* laws – not how we think but how we ought to think. The rules of logic must therefore be taken, not from the *contingent*, but from the *necessary* use of reason, which one finds in oneself apart from all psychology. In logic we do not wish to know what the understanding is like and how it thinks, nor how it has hitherto proceeded in its thinking, but how it ought to proceed in its thinking. It should teach us the correct use of the understanding, the use in which it is consistent with itself' (Introduction, 1. Concept of Logic. Kant's *Werke*, ed. Hartenstein, 1867, VIII, p. 15). Herbart takes up a similar position when he objects to the logic of his time and 'the would be psychological stories about understanding and reason with which it starts', by saying that this is as badly in error as a moral theory which tried to begin with the natural history of human tendencies, urges and weaknesses, and by pointing to the normative character of logic as of ethics (Herbart, *Psychologie als Wissenschaft*, II, §119, original ed. II, p. 173).

Such arguments do not dismay the psychologistic logicians. They answer: A necessary use of the understanding is none the less a use of the understanding, and belongs, with the understanding itself, to psychology. Thinking as it should be, is merely a special case of thinking as it is. Psychology must certainly investigate the natural laws of thinking, the laws which hold for all judgements whatever, whether correct or false. It would, however, be absurd to interpret this proposition as if such laws only were psychological as applied with the most embracing generality to *all* judgements whatever, whereas special laws of judgement, like the laws of correct judgement, were shut out from its purview. (Cf., e.g. Mill, *An Examination*, p. 459 *f.*) Or does one hold a different opinion? Can one deny that the normative laws of thinking have the character of such special laws? This also will not do. Normative laws of thought, it is said, only try to say how one must proceed *provided* one wants to think *correctly*. 'We think correctly, in the material sense, when we think of things as they are. But for us to say, certainly and indubitably, that things are like this or like that, means that the nature of our mind prevents us from thinking of them otherwise. For one need not repeat what has been so often uttered, that one can obviously not think of a thing as it is, without regard to the way in which one must think of it, nor can one make of it so isolated an object of knowledge. The man, therefore, who compares his thought of things with the things themselves can in fact only measure his contingent thinking, influenced by custom, tradition, inclination and aversion, against a thinking that is free from such influences, and that heeds no voice but that of its own inherent lawfulness.'

'The rules, therefore, on which one must proceed in order to think rightly are merely rules on which one must proceed in order to think as the nature of thought, its specific lawfulness, demands. They are, in short, identical with the natural laws of thinking itself. Logic is a physics of thinking or it is nothing at all.' (Lipps, 'Die Aufgabe der Erkenntnistheorie', *Philos. Monatshefte*, XVI (1880), p. 530 *f.*)

It may perhaps be said from the antipsychologistic side:[1] Of course the various kinds of presentations, judgements, syllogisms etc., also have a place in psychology as mental phenomena and dispositions, but psychology has a different task in regard to them than logic. Both investigate the laws of these activities, but 'law' means something quite different in the two cases. The task of psychology is to investigate the laws governing the real connections of mental events with one another, as well as with related mental dispositions and corresponding events in the bodily

[1] Cf., e.g. W. Hamilton's Lectures III, p. 78, Drobisch, *Neue Darstellung der Logik*, ed. IV, §2; cf. also B. Erdmann, *Logik* I, p. 18.

93

organism. 'Law' here means a comprehensive formula covering coexistent and successive connections that are without exception and necessary. Such connections are causal. The task of logic is quite different. It does not enquire into the causal origins or consequences of intellectual activities, but into their truth-content: it enquires what such activities *should* be like, or how they *should* proceed, in order that the resultant judgements should be true. Correct judgements and false ones, evident ones and blind ones, come and go according to natural laws, they have causal antecedents and consequences like all mental phenomena. Such natural connections do not, however, interest the logician; he looks rather for ideal connections that he does not always find realized, in fact only exceptionally finds realized in the actual course of thoughts. He aims not at a physics, but an ethics of thinking. Sigwart therefore rightly stresses the point that, in the psychological treatment of thought, 'the opposition of true and false has as little part to play as the opposition of good or bad in human conduct is a psychological matter.'[1]

We cannot be content – such will be the psychologistic rejoinder – with such half-truths. The task of logic is of course quite different from that of psychology: who would deny it? It is a technology of knowledge, but how could such a technology ignore questions of causal connection, how could it look for ideal connections without studying natural ones? 'As if every "ought" did not rest on an "is", every ethics did not also have to show itself a physics.' (Lipps, 'Die Aufgabe der Erkenntnistheorie', op. cit. p. 529.) 'A question as to what should be done always reduces to a question as to what must be done if a definite goal is to be reached, and this question in its turn is equivalent to a question as to how this goal is *in fact reached*' (Lipps, *Grundzüge der Logik*, §1). That psychology, as distinct from logic, does not deal with the opposition of true and false 'does not mean that psychology treats these different mental conditions on a like footing, but that it renders both intelligible in a like manner' (Lipps, op. cit. §2, p. 2). Theoretically regarded, Logic therefore is related to psychology as a part to a whole. Its main aim is, in particular, to set up propositions of the form: Our intellectual activities must, either generally, or in specifically characterized circumstances,

---

[1] *Logik*, vol. I, p. 10. Sigwart's own way of treating logic (as we shall see in Ch. VIII) is altogether on psychologistic lines.

have such and such a form, such and such an arrangement, such and such combinations and no others, if the resultant judgements are to have the character of evidence, are to achieve knowledge in the pointed sense of the word. Here we have an obvious causal relation. The psychological character of evidence is a causal consequence of certain antecedents. What sort of antecedents? This is just what we have to explore.[1]

The following often repeated argument is no more successful in shaking the psychologistic ranks: Logic, it is said, can as little rest on psychology as on any other science; since each science is only a science in virtue of its harmony with logical rules, it presupposes the validity of these rules. It would therefore be circular to try to give logic a first foundation in psychology.[2]

The opposition will reply: That this argument cannot be right, is shown by the fact that it would prove the impossibility of all logic. Since logic itself must proceed logically, it would itself commit the same circle, would itself have to establish the validity of rules that it presupposes.

Let us, however, consider more closely what such a circle could consist in. Could it mean that psychology presupposes the validity of logical laws? Here one must notice the equivocation in the notion of 'presupposing'. That a science presupposes the validity of certain rules may mean that they serve as premisses in its proofs: it may also mean that they are rules in accordance with which the science must proceed in order to be a science at all. Both are confounded in our argument for which reasoning *according* to logical rules, and reasoning *from* logical rules, count as identical. There would only be a circle if the reasoning were *from* such rules. But, as many an artist creates beautiful works without the slightest knowledge of aesthetics, so an investigation may construct proofs without ever having recourse to logic. Logical laws cannot therefore have been premisses in such proofs. And what is true of single proofs is likewise true of whole sciences.

[1] This point of view is expressed with increasing clearness in the works of Mill, Sigwart, Wundt, and Höfler-Meinong. Cf. on this the quotations and criticisms in Ch. VIII, §49 f.

[2] Cf. Lotze's *Logik*, ed. II, §332, pp. 543–4; Natorp 'Über objektive und subjektive Begründungen der Erkenntnis', *Philos. Monatshefte* XXIII, p. 264; Erdmann's *Logik*, vol. I, p. 18. As against this cf. Stumpf 'Psychologie und Erkenntnistheorie', p. 5 (*Proceedings of Kais. Bay. Akad. d. Wiss.*, I Kl., vol. XIX, Section II, p. 469). That Stumpf is discussing epistemology, not logic, obviously makes no essential difference.

§20 *A gap in the psychologistic line of proof*

In these and similar arguments the anti-psychologistic party seem undoubtedly to have got the worst of it. Many think the battle quite at an end, they regard the rejoinders of the psychologistic party as completely victorious. One thing only might arouse our philosophical wonder, that there was and is such a battle at all, that the same arguments have repeatedly been adduced while their refutations have not been acknowledged as cogent. If everything really were so plain and clear as the psychologistic trend assures us, the matter would not be readily understandable, since there are unprejudiced, serious and penetrating thinkers on the opposite side as well. Is this not again a case where the truth lies in the middle? Has each of the parties not recognized a valid portion of the truth, and only shown incapacity for its sharp conceptual circumscription, and not even seen that they only had part of the whole? Is there not perhaps an unresolved residuum in the arguments of the anti-psychologists – despite much unclearness and error in detail which has made refutation easy; are they not informed by a true power, which always re-emerges in unbiased discussion? I for my part would answer 'Yes'. It seems to me that the greater weight of truth lies on the anti-psychologistic side, but that its key-thoughts have not been properly worked out, and are blemished by many mistakes.

Let us go back to the question we raised above regarding the essential foundations of normative logic. Have the arguments of psychologistic thinkers really settled this? Here a weak point at once appears. The argument only proves one thing, that psychology *helps* in the foundation of logic, not that it has the only or the main part in this, not that it provides logic's *essential foundation* in the sense above defined (§16). The possibility remains open that another science contributes to its foundation, perhaps in a much more important fashion. Here may be the place for the 'pure logic' which on the other party's view, has an existence independent of all psychology, and is a naturally bounded, internally closed-off science. We readily grant that what Kantians and Herbartians have produced under this rubric does not quite accord with the character that our suggested supposition would give it. For they always talk of normative laws of thinking and particularly of concept-formation, judgement-framing etc.

Proof enough, one might say, that their subject-matter is neither theoretical nor wholly unpsychological. But this objection would lose weight if closer investigation confirmed the surmise suggested to us above in §13, that these schools were unlucky in defining and building up the intended discipline, yet none the less approached it closely, in so far as they discerned an abundance of interconnected theoretical truths in traditional logic, which did not fit into psychology, nor into any other separate science, and so permitted one to divine the existence of a peculiar realm of truth. And if these were the truths to which all logical regulation in the last resort related, truths mainly to be thought of when 'logical truths' were in question, one could readily come to see in them what was essential to the whole of logic, and to give the name of 'pure logic' to their theoretical unity. That this hits off the true state of things I hope actually to prove.

CHAPTER FOUR

Empiricistic Consequences of Psychologism

§21 *Two empiricistic consequences of the psychologistic standpoint,
and their refutation*

LET us place ourselves for the moment on the ground of the
psychologistic logic, and let us assume therefore that the essential
theoretical foundations of the prescriptions of logic lie in psychology. However the latter discipline may be defined – as the
science of psychic phenomena, of the facts of consciousness, of
the facts of internal experience, of experiences in their dependence
on the experiencing individual, or whatever – it is universally
agreed that psychology is a factual and therefore an empirical
science. We shall also not be controverted if we add that psychology has so far lacked genuine and therefore exact laws, and
that the propositions in it which are dignified with the name of
laws, are merely vague,[1] even if valuable, generalizations from
experience. They are statements about approximate regularities
of coexistence and succession, which make no claim to determine,
with infallible, unambiguous definiteness, what will go together
or will follow in exactly described relationships. One may look
to the laws of the association of ideas, to which association-
psychology wished to accord the position and importance of basic
psychological laws. As soon as one takes the trouble adequately
to formulate their empirically justified sense, they at once lose
the pretended character of laws. This being granted, most serious
consequences arise for the psychologistic logicians.

The first is that only vague rules could be based on vague
theoretical foundations. If psychological laws lack exactness, the

---

[1] I employ the term 'vague' in contrast to 'exact'. I do not in the least mean to
express any depreciation of psychology by it; to pick holes in psychology is remote
from my intention. Even natural science has vague 'laws' in many disciplines,
particularly in such as are concrete. Meteorological laws, e.g., are vague yet very
valuable.

same must be true of the prescriptions of logic. It cannot be doubted that many of these prescriptions are infected with empirical vaguenesses. But precisely the laws which are pointedly called 'logical', which as laws of proof make up the real core of all logic – the logical 'principles', the laws of syllogism, the laws of many other kinds of inference, as, e.g. equational inferences, the Bernoullian argument from n to $n+1$, the principles of probability-inferences etc. – are of absolute exactness. Every interpretation that would base them on empirical indefinitenesses, make them depend for their validity on vague 'circumstances', would fundamentally alter their true sense. Plainly they are genuine laws, and not 'merely empirical', i.e. approximate, laws.

If, as Lotze thought, pure mathematics is merely an independently developed branch of logic, the above-mentioned sphere of exact logical laws will also cover the inexhaustible wealth of the laws of pure mathematics. In all further objections we must keep our eye on the sphere of pure mathematics together with our sphere of logic.

In the second place, were one to seek to counter our first objection by denying the thoroughgoing inexactness of psychological laws, and try to found norms of the above-mentioned type on supposedly exact natural laws, little would have been gained.

No natural laws can be known *a priori*, nor established by sheer insight. The only way in which a natural law can be established and justified, is by induction from the singular facts of experience. Induction does not establish the holding of the law, only the greater or lesser probability of its holding; the probability, and not the law, is justified by insight. Logical laws must, accordingly, without exception, rank as mere probabilities. Nothing, however, seems plainer than that the laws of 'pure logic' all have *a priori* validity. They are established and justified, not by induction, but by apodeictic inner evidence. Insight justifies no mere probabilities of their holding, but their holding or truth itself.

The Law of Contradiction does not tell us that one must *surmise* that one of two contradictory judgements is true, one false, the mood *Barbara* does not tell us that when two propositions of the form 'All A's are B's' and 'All B's are C's' are true, it is to be *surmised* that a corresponding proposition of the form 'All A's are C's' is true. And so generally, and in the field of mathematics as well. Otherwise we should have to treat it as an open *possibility* that such a surmise would fail to be confirmed by an extension of our ever limited horizon of experience. Perhaps our logical laws are mere 'approximations' to genuinely valid laws of thought that are beyond our reach. Such possibilities are seriously and rightly weighed in the case of natural laws. Though the law of gravitation is recommended by the most comprehensive inductions and verifications, no investigator of nature would now look on it as an absolutely valid law. New gravitational formulae are occasionally tried out: it was shown, e.g. that Weber's basic law for electrical phenomena could quite well function as the basic law of gravity. The differentiating factor in both formulae conditions differences in calculated values not exceeding the field of unavoidable observational error. Innumerable factors of this sort are, however, thinkable; hence we know *a priori* that endlessly many laws could and must do the same work as the Newtonian law of gravitation, recommended only by its peculiar simplicity. We know that, in view of ineliminable observational imprecision, it would be foolish to look for a uniquely true law. Such is the situation in the exact factual sciences, but by no means in logic. The justified possibility of the former becomes the open absurdity of the latter. We have insight into, not merely the probability, but the truth of the logical laws. We see the truth of the principles of the syllogism, of Bernoullian induction, of arguments in probability, of general arithmetic etc. We grasp their very truth, so that talk of zones of inexactness, of mere approximations etc., loses all possible sense. But if what follows from a demand for a psychological validation of logic is absurd, this validation is itself absurd.

Against the truth that is itself grasped with insight, the strongest psychologistic argument cannot avail: probability cannot wrestle with truth, nor surmise with insight. If anyone likes to stay in a sphere of general discussions, he may allow the psychologistic arguments to deceive him. But a mere glance at any logical principle, at its real meaning and the full insight with which it is seen as true in itself, must abolish such deceit.

How plausible the ready suggestions of psychologistic reflection sound. Logical laws are laws for validations, proofs. What are validations but peculiar human trains of thought, in which, in normal circumstances, the finally emergent judgements seem endowed with a necessarily consequential character. This character is itself a mental one, a peculiar mode of mindedness and no more. And, obviously, none of these mental phenomena is isolated, but is a single thread in the tangled web of mental phenomena, of mental disposition and organic process, called human life. How could anything beyond empirical generalities result in such circumstances? Where has psychology yielded more?

We reply: Psychology certainly does not yield more, and cannot for this reason yield the apodeictically evident, and so metempirical and absolutely exact laws which form the core of all logic.

§ 22 *The laws of thought as supposed laws of nature which operate in isolation as causes of rational thought*

Here is also the place to take up an attitude towards a widely held conception of logical law, which characterizes correct thought by its conformity with certain laws of thought (however we may formulate them), but is disposed at the same time to interpret such conformity in the following psychologistic manner: The laws of thought count as natural laws characterizing the peculiarity of our mind *qua* thinking, and the essence of the conformity, as definitory of correct thinking, lies in the *pure* operation of these laws, their non-disturbance by alien mental influences (such as custom, inclination, tradition). (Cf. the citations above in § 19 from Lipps' article on the task of epistemology.)

We need only instance one of the grave consequences of this doctrine. Laws of thought, as causal laws governing acts of knowledge in their mental interweaving, could only be stated in the form of probabilities. On this basis, no assertion could be *certainly* judged correct, since probabilities, taken as the standard of all certainty, must impress a merely probabilistic stamp on all knowledge. We should stand confronted by the most extreme probabilism. Even the assertion that all knowledge was merely probable would itself only hold probably: this would hold of this latter assertion, and so on *in infinitum*. Since each successive step reduces the probability level of the previous one a bit, we should become gravely concerned about the worth of all knowledge. One may hope, however, that, with some luck, the probability-levels of these infinite series may always have the character of a Cantorian 'fundamental series', of such a sort that the final limiting value or the probability of the knowledge to be judged is a real number > 0. Sceptical awkwardnesses would of course vanish if one looked on the laws of thought as matters of direct insight. But how should one have insight into causal laws?

Even if this difficulty were removed, we could still ask: Where on earth is the proof that the pure operation of these laws (or any other laws) would yield correct laws of thinking? Where are the descriptive and genetic analyses which entitle us to explain the phenomena of thought by two sorts of natural law, one exclusively determining such causal sequences as allow logical thought to emerge, whereas others help to determine alogical thought? Does the assessment of thoughts by logical laws amount to a proof of their causal origin in these same laws as laws of nature?

It seems that certain ready confusions have here opened the way to psychologistic errors. Logical laws have first been confused with the judgements, in the sense of acts of judgement, in which we may know them: the laws, as '*contents of judgement*' have been confused with the *judgements themselves*. The latter are real events, having causes and effects. Judgements whose contents are laws are, in particular, frequently operative as *thought-motives*, directing the course of our thought-experience, as those contents, the laws of thinking, prescribe. In such cases the real order and connection of our thought-experiences conforms to that which we think generally in our governing knowledge of the law: it is a concrete individual instance of that general law. If, however, the law is confused with the judgement or knowledge of the law, the ideal with the real, the law appears as a *governing power* in our train of thought. With understandable ease a second confusion is added to the first: we confuse a law as a *term in causation with a law as the rule of causation*. In other fields, too, we familiarly employ mythic talk of natural laws as presiding powers in natural events – as if the rules of causal connection could themselves once more significantly function as causes, i.e. as terms in just such connections. The serious confusion of things so essentially dissimilar has plainly been favoured in the case before us by the previous confusion of a law with the knowledge of a law. Logical laws already appeared as motive powers in thinking. They presided causally, it was imagined, over the course of our thoughts – they were accordingly causal laws of thinking. They expressed how we must think in consequence of the nature of *our* mind, they characterized the human mind as a thinking mind in the pointed sense. If at times we think otherwise than these laws require, we are not, properly speaking, 'thinking' at all, we are not judging as the natural laws of thinking, or the *nature of our mind qua* thinking, requires, but as other laws determine (once more causally). We are following the disturbing leads of custom, passion etc.

Other motives of course may have suggested the same conception. The empirical fact that persons performing normally in a given sphere, e.g. scientists in their fields, usually judge in a logically correct manner, seems to demand, as a natural explanation, that the logical laws by means of which the correctness of thinking is assessed, also determine the course of thinking, in the manner of causal laws, while isolated deviations from the norm may readily be put to the account of the troubling influences stemming from other psychological sources.

Against this the following argument should suffice. Let us imagine an ideal person, in whom *all* thinking proceeds as logical laws require. Naturally the fact that this occurs must have its explanatory ground in certain psychological laws, which govern the course of the mental experiences of this being, starting from certain initial 'collocations'. I now ask: Would the natural laws and the logical laws in this assumed situation be one and the same? Obviously the answer is 'No'. Causal laws, according to which thought must proceed in a manner which the ideal norms of logic might justify, are by no means identical with those norms. If a being were so constituted as never to be able to frame contradictory judgements in a unified train of thought, as never to be able to perform inferences which defy the syllogistic moods, this would not mean that the law of contradiction, the *Modus Barbara* etc., were laws of nature explanatory of this being's constitution. The example of a computer makes the difference quite clear. The arrangement and connection of the figures which spring forth is regulated by natural laws which accord with the demands of the arithmetical propositions which fix their meanings. No one, however, who wants to give a physical explanation of the machine's procedures, will appeal to arithmetical instead of mechanical laws. The machine is no thought-machine, it understands neither itself nor the meaning of its performances. But our own thought-machine might very well function similarly, except that the real course of one kind of thought would always have to be recognized as correct by the insight brought forward in another. This latter thinking could be the product of the same or other thought-machines, but ideal evaluation and causal explanation would none the less remain disparate. The 'initial collocations' should also not be forgotten: indispensable in causal explanation, they are senseless for ideal evaluation.

The psychologistic logicians ignore the fundamental, essential, never-to-be-bridged gulf between ideal and real laws, between normative and causal regulation, between logical and real necessity, between logical and real grounds. No conceivable gradation could mediate between the ideal and the real. It is characteristic of the low state of logical insights in our time, that a thinker of Sigwart's stature should dare, in connection with the fiction of an intellectually ideal being like that discussed above, to maintain that, for such a being, 'logical necessity would also be a real necessity that engenders real thinking', or that he should make use of the concept of thought-compulsion to elucidate the notion of 'logical ground' (Sigwart, *Logik*, I, ed. ii, p. 259 *f.*). The same holds of Wundt when he sees in the law of sufficient reason the 'basic law of the dependence of our thought-acts on one another' (Wundt, *Logik*, I, ed. ii, p. 573). That one is really concerned in these connections with basic errors in logic will, one hopes, become a certainty, even to the prejudiced, in the course of further investigations.

§23 *A third consequence of psychologism, and its refutation*

A third consequence for the psychologistic logician is that, if the laws of logic have their epistemological source in psychological matter of fact, if, e.g., as our opponents generally say, they are normative transformations of such facts, they must themselves be psychological in content, both by being laws for mental states, and also by presupposing or implying the existence of such states. This is palpably false. No logical law implies a 'matter of fact', not even the existence of presentations or judgements or other phenomena of knowledge. No logical law, properly understood, is a law for the facticities of mental life, and so not a law for presentations (as experiences), nor for judgements (experiences of judging), nor for our other mental experiences.

Most psychologistic thinkers are too deeply enthralled by their general prejudice even to try to verify it in the case of the definitely acknowledged logical laws. If such laws *must* be psychological, why try to show in detail that they really are so? No one sees that a consistent psychologism would force one to interpret logical laws in a manner quite alien to their true sense. One fails to see that these laws, naturally understood, presuppose nothing mental, no facts of psychic life, whether in their establishment or their content. They do so no more than the laws of pure mathematics do so.

If psychologism were on the right track, one should, in treating of syllogisms, expect only rules of the following type: It is an empirical fact that, in circumstances X, conclusions of the form C, stamped with apodeictically necessary consequence, attend upon premises of the form P. To syllogize 'correctly', i.e. to achieve judgements of this distinctive stamp through syllogizing, one must proceed in this manner, one must see that the circumstances really are X, and the premises P. Mental matters of fact would then be the matters regulated, the existence of such matters would be presupposed in the grounding of such laws, and would be part of their content. But no single syllogistic rule is of such a type. What, e.g., does the mood *Barbara* tell us? Only this: that, if in the case of any class-terms A, B, C all A's are B's and all B's C's, then all A's will be C's. The *Modus Ponens*, likewise, written out in full, reads: It is a valid law for any propositions P, Q, that if P is the case, and it also is the case that if P is the case Q is so, then Q also is the case. These and all similar laws are as little psychological as they are empirical. They were of course set up by traditional logic to serve as norms for our judging activities. But do they implicitly say anything about a single actual judgement, or about any other mental phenomenon? If anyone thinks they do let him prove it. Whatever a proposition implicitly asserts can be inferred from it in a valid syllogism. But what forms of syllogism permit us to deduce facts from a pure law?

It is irrelevant to object that talk of logical laws never could have arisen had we not actually experienced presentations and judgements, and abstracted the relevant, basic logical concepts from them, or that, wherever we understand and assert such laws, the existence of presentations and judgements is implied, and can therefore be inferred. We need hardly observe that this does not follow from our law, but from the fact that we understand and assert such a law, and that a like consequence could be inferred from every assertion. One ought not, further, to confuse the psychological presuppositions or components of the *assertion* of a law, with the logical 'moments' of its *content*.

'Empirical laws' have, *eo ipso*, a factual content. Not being true laws, they merely say, roughly speaking, that certain coexistences or successions obtain generally in certain circumstances, or may be expected, with varying probability, in varying circumstances. But even the strict laws of the natural sciences are not without factual content. They do not merely concern facts, but also imply their existence.

We must, however, be more precise. Exact laws, as normally formulated, are pure laws: they exclude all factual content. But, if we consider the proofs to which they owe their scientific justification, it is at once clear that we cannot justify them as pure laws, in their normal formulation. The law of gravitation, as formulated in astronomy, has never really been proved. What has been proved is a proposition of the form: Our knowledge up to date serves to found a probability of the highest theoretical dignity to the effect that, in so far as experience yields to the instruments on hand, either Newton's law, or one of the endlessly many conceivable mathematical laws whose differences from Newton's law lie within the limits of unavoidable experimental error is true. This truth carries its big load of factual content, and is not at all a law in the strict sense of the word. It also plainly includes several vaguely delimited concepts.

All laws of fact in the exact sciences are accordingly genuine laws, but, epistemologically considered, no more than idealizing fictions with a *fundamentum in re*. They fulfil the task of rendering those theoretical sciences possible, which bring the ideal of science as near as may be to actuality, and so realize, to the extent that this can be within the unsurmountable limits of human knowledge, the ideal of explanatory theory, of law-governed unity, the highest theoretical aim of all scientific research into facts. Instead of the absolute knowledge that is denied us, we use our insight on individual and general facts of experience, and from these first work out those apodeictic probabilities (so to speak) in which all attainable knowledge of the real is comprehended. We then reduce these probabilities to certain exact thoughts having the genuine form of laws, and so succeed in building up formally perfect systems of explanatory theory. Such systems as theoretical mechanics, theoretical acoustics, theoretical optics, theoretical astronomy etc., really only hold as ideal possibilities with a *fundamentum in re*; they do not exclude countless other possibilities, but even include these within limits. This, however, concerns us no further, nor are we concerned to discuss the practical functions in knowledge of these ideal theories, their feats of successfully predicting future facts or reconstructing past ones, and their technical feats of enabling us to master nature practically. We return to the case we were considering.

If, as we have shown, pure law remains a mere ideal in the realm of factual knowledge, it is realized in the realm of 'purely conceptual' knowledge. In this sphere our purely logical laws belong, as well as the laws of *mathesis pura*. Their origin, or, rather, their justifying proof, is not an inductive one, and so they are free from that existential content which attaches to all probabilities as such, even to such as are the highest and most valuable. What they say has entire validity: they themselves in their absolute exactness are evident and proven, and not, in their stead, certain other assertions of probability of obviously vague constitution. The law we have is not one of countless theoretical possibilities within a certain factually delimited sphere. It is the single, sole truth which excludes all other possibilities and which, being established by *insight*, is kept pure from fact in its content and mode of proof.

The above considerations show how intimately the two halves of the psychologistic case hang together: that logical laws do not merely entail existential assertions of mental facts, but are also laws *for* such facts. We have just refuted the first half of their case. But the following argument suggests that our refutation also covers the second half. For just as each law established empirically and inductively from singular facts, is a law *for* such facts, so, conversely, each law *for* facts is a law established empirically and inductively, and from such a law, as has been shown, assertions with existential content are inseparable.

We ought of course to exclude from factual laws such general assertions as merely apply pure conceptual propositions – which state universally valid relations on a basis of pure concepts – to matters of fact. If 3 > 2, then the three books on this table also exceed the two books in this cupboard, and so for any things whatever. But our pure proposition of number does not refer to things, but to numbers in their pure generality – it is *the* number 3 that is greater than *the* number 2 – and it applies not merely to individual, but to 'general' objects, e.g. to species of colour or sound, to types of geometrical figure and to suchlike timeless generalities.

If all this is admitted, it is of course impossible to regard logical laws (considered in their purity) as the laws either of mental activities or of mental products.

§24 *Continuation*

Many would perhaps try to evade our conclusion by objecting: Not every law for facts has an empirico-inductive origin. We should rather draw a distinction. All knowledge of law rests on experience, but not all such knowledge arises out of experience inductively, by the well-known logical process which goes from singular facts, or empirical generalities of lower level, to general laws. The laws of logic are, in particular, empirical, but not inductive laws. The basic notions of logic are abstracted from psychological experience together with the purely conceptual relations given with them. What we find true in the individual case, we recognize at a glance to be true universally, since based upon abstracted contents. Experience accordingly yields an immediate awareness of the law-governed character of our mind. And since we have no need of induction, our conclusion is likewise free from inductive imperfection: it has no mere character of probability, but one of apodeictic certainty. It is not vague, but precise in sense, it in no way includes assertions having existential content.

What is here objected will not, however, do. Undoubtedly our knowledge of logical laws, considered as an act of mind, pre-supposes an experience of individuals, has its basis in concrete intuition. But one should not confuse the *psychological* 'pre-suppositions' and 'bases' of the *knowledge* of a law, with the *logical* presuppositions, the grounds and premisses, of that *law*: we should also, therefore, not confuse psychological dependence (e.g. dependence of origin) with logical demonstration and justification. The latter conforms to an insight into the objective relation of ground and consequence, whereas the former relates to mental links of coexistence and succession. No one can seriously hold that the concrete singular cases before us, on which our insight into a law is 'grounded', really function as logical grounds or premisses, as if the mere existence of such singulars entailed the universality of law. Our intuitive grasp of the law may require two psychological steps: one glance at the singulars of intuition, and a related insight into law. Logically, however, only one step is required. The content of our insight is not inferred from singulars.

All knowledge 'begins with experience', but it does not therefore 'arise' from experience. What we assert is that each law for facts arises *from* experience, which means that it can only be inductively based on individual experiences. If there are laws known by insight, these cannot (immediately) be laws for facts. Where in the past immediate self-evidence has been claimed for factual laws, it is clear that men have been confusing genuine factual laws, i.e. laws of coexistence and succession, with ideal laws to which a reference to definite times is alien, or that they have been confusing the lively persuasive force of familiar empirical generalities, with the insight only found in the realm of pure concepts.

Should such an argument not seem decisive, it can none the less serve to strengthen other arguments. Another such argument will be here added.

Hardly anyone would deny that all laws of pure logic are of one and the same character. If we can show, in the case of some of them, that they cannot possibly be regarded as laws for facts, the same must hold for all of them. Among logical laws there are, however, some which concern truths, which have truths as their regular 'objects'. It is the case, e.g., that for every truth A, its contradictory opposite is no truth. It is the case, for each pair of truths A, B, that their conjunctions and disjunctions[1] are truths, and that if three truths A, B, C are so related that A is a ground for B, B for C, that A is also a ground for C. It is, however, absurd to treat laws which hold for truths as such, as laws for facts. No truth is a fact, i.e. something determined as to time. A

---

[1] I mean by these the senses of the propositions 'A and B', i.e. both hold, and 'A or B', i.e. one holds – which does not imply that *only* one holds.

truth can indeed have as its meaning that something is, that a state exists, that a change is going on etc. The truth itself is, however, raised above time: i.e. it makes no sense to attribute temporal being to it, nor to say that it arises or perishes. This absurdity is clearest in the case of the laws of truth themselves. If they were 'real' laws, they would be rules for the coexistence and succession of facts, i.e. of such facts as are truths, and to these facts, which they govern, they themselves as truths would belong. A law would therefore ascribe a 'coming and going' to certain facts called truths, among which, as one among others, the law would itself be found. The law would arise and perish in conformity with the law, a patent absurdity. The case is similar if we treat the law of truth as a law of coexistence, as temporally singular and yet fixing a general rule for each and every existence in time. Such absurdities[1] are unavoidable if the fundamental distinction between ideal and real objects, and the corresponding distinction between ideal and real laws, is disregarded or misunderstood. We shall see repeatedly how this distinction settles the disputes which divide psychologistic logic from pure logic.

---

[1] Cf. the systematic discussions of Ch. VIII of this work regarding the sceptical-relativistic absurdity of all conceptions which make logical principles depend on facts.

CHAPTER FIVE

Psychological Interpretations of Basic Logical Principles

§ 25 *The law of contradiction in the psychologistic interpretation of Mill and Spencer*

WE have said above that a consistent carrying out of the notion of logical laws as laws which concern mental facts, must lead to essential misinterpretations of these laws. The logic which at present prevails has, however, generally been afraid of consistency, on this point as on all others. One might almost say that it is only inconsistency that keeps psychologism alive: to think it out to the end, is already to have given it up, unless extreme empiricism affords an example of the greatly superior strength of ingrained prejudices to the most certain deliverances of insight. What we have said in objection to this logical position – that on it logical truths must lose their *a priori* guarantee, and their wholly exact, purely conceptual character, and must become more or less vague probabilities resting on experience and induction, concerned with matters of fact in the mental life of man – all this, if we ignore its emphasis on vagueness, is what empiricism expressly teaches. We cannot attempt an exhaustive criticism of such an epistemological trend. But we have a special interest in the psychological interpretation of logical laws which this school has fostered, and whose bemusement has also spread beyond its borders.[1]

John Stuart Mill,[2] it is well known, held the principle of contradiction to be 'one of our earliest and most familiar generalizations from experience'. Its original foundation is taken by Mill

---

[1] A general discussion of the main defects of empiricism, carried as far as seemed likely to help our idealistic intentions in logic, is given in the Appendix to this and the following section.

[2] *Logic*, Book II, ch. VII, § 5.

to be the fact 'that belief and disbelief are two different mental states' which exclude one another. This we know – we follow him *verbatim* – by the simplest observation of our own minds. And if we carry our observation outwards, we find that here too light and darkness, sound and silence, equality and inequality, precedence and subsequence, succession and simultaneity, any positive phenomenon, in short, and its negation, are distinct phenomena, in a relation of extreme contrariety, and that one of them is always absent when the other is present. 'I consider the axiom in question', he remarks, 'to be a generalization from all these facts.'

Where the fundamental principles of his empiricistic prejudices are at stake, all the gods seem to abandon Mill's otherwise keen intelligence. Only one thing is hard to understand: how such a doctrine could have seemed persuasive. It is obviously false to say that the principle that two contradictory propositions cannot both be true, and in this sense exclude one another, is a generalization from the 'facts' cited, that light and darkness, sound and silence etc., exclude one another, since these are not contradictory propositions at all. It is quite unintelligible how Mill thinks he can connect these supposed facts of experience with the logical law. In vain one looks for light among Mill's parallel statements in his polemic against Hamilton. Here he approvingly quotes 'the absolutely constant law' on which the like-minded Spencer bases the logical principle in question, i.e. 'that the appearance of any positive mode of consciousness cannot occur without excluding a correlative negative mode: and that the negative mode cannot occur without excluding the correlative positive mode'.[1] Who can fail to see that this law is a pure tautology, since mutual exclusion enters into the *definition* of the correlative terms 'positive and negative phenomenon'? The law of contradiction, on the other hand, is by no means tautologous. We do not *define* contradictory propositions by saying that they are mutually exclusive, and, even if the principle in question makes them so, the converse does not hold: not every pair of mutually exclusive propositions is a contradictory pair – proof enough that one should not confuse our principle with the above tautology. Mill himself does not want it to be taken as a tautology, since he locates its original source in an induction from experience.

---

[1] Mill, *An Examination*, ch. XXI, p. 491. Mill slips in not noticing that Spencer's reference is not to the law of contradiction but to that of excluded middle.

The empirical sense of the principle is not illuminated by Mill's barely intelligible references to non-coexistences among the data of outer experience: more light is shed by other statements where Mill asks if the three basic logical laws should be treated as 'inherent necessities of thought', 'an original part of our mental constitution', 'laws of our thoughts by the native structure of our minds', or if they are not perhaps laws of thought merely 'because we perceive them to be universally true of observed phenomena', an issue on which Mill does not, however, care to pronounce positively. We read in regard to these laws:

> They may or may not be capable of alteration by experience, but the conditions of our existence deny to us the experience which would be required to alter them. Any assertion, therefore, which conflicts with one of these laws, any proposition, for instance, which asserts a contradiction, though it were on a subject wholly removed from the sphere of our experience, is to us unbelievable. The belief in such a proposition is, in the present constitution of nature, impossible as a mental fact.[1]

We conclude from this passage that the inconsistency expressed in the law of contradiction, the impossibility of the joint truth of contradictory propositions, is seen by Mill as an incompatibility of such propositions in our belief. In other words, he substitutes for the impossibility that the propositions should *both be true*, the *real incompatibility* of the corresponding *acts of judgement*. This also fits in with Mill's repeated assertion that acts of belief are the only things that can properly be called true and false. The principle must be interpreted as saying: *Two contradictorily opposed acts of belief cannot coexist.*

§26 *Mill's psychological interpretation of the principle yields no law, but a wholly vague, scientifically unproven empirical proposition*

All sorts of difficulties now rise up. The expression of the principle is certainly incomplete. What are the circumstances, we should have to ask, in which opposed acts of belief cannot coexist? Opposed judgements can very well coexist in different individuals. We ought therefore to be more precise, and at the same time to

---

[1] Mill, op. cit. p. 491. Cf. also p. 487: 'It is the generalization of a mental act, which is of continued occurrence, and which cannot be dispensed with in reasoning.'

set forth the sense of real coexistence, by saying that in the same individual, or rather in the same consciousness, contradictory acts of belief are incapable of lasting for any time, however short. But is this really a *law*? Can we really utter it with such boundless generality? What are the psychological inductions which justify its acceptance? May there not have been people, and may there not still be people who, deceived by fallacies, contrive at times to believe contradictories together? Has the occurrence of contradictions, even quite obvious ones, been scientifically investigated in the case of the insane? What happens in hypnotic states, in delirium tremens etc.? Does this law also hold for animals?

Possibly the empiricist will escape these objections by suitably qualifying his law, e.g. by saying that it only applies to normal individuals of the *genus homo*, having a normal mental constitution. It is sufficient to raise the insidious question of the exact definition of the concepts 'normal individual', and 'normal mental constitution' to see how imprecise and complex the content of the law, as now stated, has become.

We need not carry our discussions further, though the law's reference to time might, e.g., provide occasion to do so: they are enough to leave us with the amazing result that our familiar principle of contradiction, which has always counted as a wholly exact, self-evident, exceptionless law, is the very paradigm of a grossly imprecise, unscientific proposition, that can only be raised to the status of a plausible surmise after its seemingly exact content has been rendered quite vague by numerous corrections. This must indeed be the truth if empiricism is right in regarding the incompatibility mentioned in the principle, as the real non-coexistence of contradictory acts of judgement, if the principle is itself to be treated as a generalization of empirical psychology. Mill's brand of empiricism does not even think of scientifically delimiting and proving his extraordinarily imprecise proposition, the immediate outcome of his psychological interpretation: it takes it in all its native imprecision, as being 'one of the earliest and most familiar generalizations from experience', i.e. as being what a rough generalization from pre-scientific experience might be expected to be. At the very point where the last foundations of all science are in question, we have recourse to this naïve empiricism with its blind mechanism of association. Persuasions begotten without insight, through psychological mechanisms, and with no better justification than widespread prejudices, whose origin rules out all fixed, tenable delimitation, and which, taken literally, include manifest falsehood – these are to be the last grounds on which all strictly scientific knowledge is to be justified.

The matter need not be pursued further. It is, however, important to touch on the basic mistake in the doctrines we are attacking, by asking whether our proposition about acts of belief can, in any formulation, be the proposition we make use of in logic. It tells us: In certain subjective circumstances X (unfortunately not further investigated nor capable of being completely specified) two acts of belief having a Yes–No opposition cannot coexist in the same consciousness. Is this what logicians really mean when they say that two contradictory propositions cannot both be true? We need only look at the cases where our law serves to regulate our activities of judging to see that it means something quite different. In its normative form it plainly says one thing and one thing only: Whatever pairs of opposed acts of belief we may select, whether belonging to one or to several individuals, whether coexisting in the same time-stretch or separated by time-stretches, it holds strictly, and absolutely, and without exception, that not both members of each such pair are correct, or in accordance with truth. I do not think that even an empiricist could question the validity of this norm. Logic at all events, when it speaks of 'laws of thought', is concerned only with these second, *logical* laws, not with our former vague 'laws' of psychology, whose content is totally different, and has not even yet been formulated.

Appendix to the last two sections

On certain basic defects of empiricism

Since empiricism and psychologism are intimately linked, we may perhaps permit ourselves a small digression to expose the basic errors of empiricism. Extreme empiricism is as absurd a theory of knowledge as extreme scepticism. *It destroys the possibility of the rational justification of mediate knowledge, and so destroys its own possibility* as a scientifically proven theory.[1] It admits that there is

---

[1] In the pointed sense of 'scepticism' developed in ch. VII, empiricism is therefore called a sceptical theory. Windelband tellingly applies the Kantian term 'hopeless attempt' to empiricism – it is the hopeless attempt 'to establish by an empirical theory what is itself presupposed by every theory' (*Präludien*[1], p. 261).

mediate knowledge, the product of various validating connections, and it does not reject principles of validation. It not only admits that there is a logic, but itself helps to construct it. If, however, all proof rests on principles governing its procedure, and if its final justification involves an appeal to such principles, then we should either be involved in a *circle* or in an infinite *regress* if the principles of proof themselves required further proof, in a circle if the principles of proof used to justify the principles of proof were the same as the latter, in a regress if both sets of principles were repeatedly different. Plainly, therefore, the demand for a fundamental justification of all mediate knowledge can only have a sense if we can both see and know certain ultimate principles on which all proof in the last instance rests. All principles which justify possible proofs must therefore be deductively inferrible from certain last, immediately evident principles, so that even the principles of the deduction in question all themselves occur among such principles.

Extreme empiricism, therefore, since it only basically puts full trust in singular judgements of experience – a quite uncritical trust since it ignores the difficulties which so richly attend upon such singular judgements – *eo ipso* abandons all hope of rationally justifying mediate knowledge. It will not acknowledge as immediate insights, and as given truths, the ultimate principles on which the justification of mediate knowledge depends; it thinks it can do better by deriving them from experience and induction, i.e. by justifying them mediately. But if one asks what principles justify such a derivation, empiricism, forbidden to appeal to immediately evident universal principles, appeals rather to naïve, uncritical, everyday experience, which it thinks to dignify more highly by explaining it psychologically in Humean fashion. It therefore fails to see that, having no insightful justification for our mediate assumptions, no justification, therefore, for the relevant proof-procedures from the immediately evident general principles that they follow, its whole psychological theory, its whole mediately known doctrine of empiricism, is without rational foundation, is, in fact, a mere assumption, no more than a common prejudice.

It is extraordinary that empiricism should give a readier credence to a theory so loaded with absurdities than to the fundamental trivialities of logic and arithmetic. As a genuine psychologism, it tends always to confuse the psychological origin of certain general judgements in experience, on account of some supposed 'naturalness', with a justification of the same judgements.

It is worth noting that it goes no better with Hume's moderate empiricism which, despite bouts of psychologistic confusion, still tries to keep for the pure spheres of logic and mathematics, an *a priori* justification, and only surrenders the factual sciences to experience. Such an epistemological standpoint can likewise be shown up as untenable, even absurd, for a reason similar to that brought by us against extreme empiricism. Mediate judgements of fact – we may compress the sense of Hume's theory into this phrase – *never permit of rational justification, only of psychological explanation*. One need then but ask how this applies to the rational justification of the psychological judgements (about custom, association of ideas etc.) on which the theory itself rests, and the factual arguments that it itself employs. One then at once sees the self-evident conflict between the sense of the proposition that the theory seeks to prove, and the sense of the deductions that it employs to prove it. The psychological premisses of the theory are themselves mediate judgements of fact, and therefore lack all rational justification in the sense of the thesis to be established. In other words: the correctness of the theory presupposes the irrationality of its premisses, the correctness of the premisses the irrationality of the theory (or thesis). (Hume's doctrine is on this showing also a *sceptical* one, in the pointed sense to be defined in chapter VII.)

§27 *Analogous objections against remaining psychological interpretations of our logical principle. Ambiguities as sources of delusion*

It is easy to see that objections like those raised in our last section must touch every psychological misinterpretation of the so-called laws of thought, and all laws which depend on them. There is no route of escape from the demand for definition and proof by an appeal to the 'self-confidence of reason', or to the self-evidence which these laws have in logical thinking. Our insight into the *logical* laws is assured. But in so far as their thought-content is seen as psychological, their original sense, to which our insight into them attaches, has been wholly altered. Exact laws have, as we saw, been turned into vague, empirical generalities: if their range of indefiniteness is duly noted, they may claim validity, but they are quite removed from self-evidence. Following their natural thought-trends, though without a clear consciousness of them, psychological theorists of knowledge no doubt *at first* understand the laws in question in an objective sense – before, that is, their arts of philosophical interpretation are brought into play. They then make the mistake of thinking that they can appeal to the self-evidence attaching to the properly interpreted formulae, a self-evidence guaranteeing their absolute validity, even when subsequent reflection has imposed wholly new senses on the logical formulae in question. If there is any case where one can justifiably speak of an insight through which truth itself is directly perceived, the statement that of two contradictory statements not both are true, is a case in point, but, if we are to deny justification to such talk, we may plainly do so in regard to all psychologizing reinterpretations of the same (or of its equivalents), e.g. 'that affirmation and negation exclude one another in our thought', 'that judgements recognized to be contradictory cannot coexist in a single consciousness',[1] 'that it is impossible for us to believe an explicit contradiction',[2] that no one can take something to be and not to be at the same time, and so forth.

Let us dwell for a while, to leave no residual unclarity, on all these shimmering wordings. Regarded more closely, they at once reveal the misleading influence of *ambiguities*, as a result of which the true law, or its equivalent normative transformation, is confused with psychological assertions. Affirmation and denial exclude one another in *thought*. The term 'thought', which in its wider sense covers all intellectual activities, is in the usage of certain logicians by preference applied to rational, 'logical' thought, to correct judgement. That in *correct* judgement, Yes and No exclude one another, is plain, but this is merely an equivalent of the logical law, and not at all a psychological

---

[1] Formulations of Heymans (*Die Gesetze und Elemente des wissenschaftlichen Denkens*, I[1], §§ 19–20. Sigwart's formulation in Logik, I[2], p. 419, resembles H's second formulation: 'It is impossible consciously to affirm and deny the same proposition.'

[2] Cf. the end of our quotation from Mill's polemic against Hamilton in §25 above. On p. 484 op. cit. Mill likewise writes 'two assertions, one of which denies what the other affirms, cannot be thought together', in which 'thought' is immediately equated with 'believed'.

proposition. It tells us that no judgement is correct in which the same state of affairs is at once affirmed and denied: it says nothing regarding a possible coexistence of contradictory acts of judgement, whether in *one* consciousness, or in several. (Even Höfler and Meinong's *Logic*, 1890, p. 133, inadvertently substitutes the thought of non-coexistence for our logical principle.)

The second formula – 'that judgements recognized as contradictory cannot coexist in a single consciousness' – is likewise excluded if consciousness is interpreted as 'consciousness as such', as a timeless, *normal* consciousness. A primitive logical principle can of course not presuppose a notion like 'normality', since this cannot even be formulated without regard to such a principle. It is plain, further, that if our proposition is thus misunderstood, and is kept free from all metaphysical hypostatization, it is merely an equivalent rewriting of our logical principle, and has nothing whatever to do with psychology.

An ambiguity similar to that in our first formulation occurs in our third and fourth. No one *can* believe in a contradiction, no one *can* take something both to be and not to be – no one, that is, who is rational, to add an obvious qualification. The impossibility concerns anyone who wishes to judge rightly and no one else. It does not therefore express a psychological compulsion, but our insight that contradictory propositions are not both true, that the states of affairs corresponding to them cannot both coexist, so that, if anyone claims to judge rightly, i.e. to treat the true as the true, and the false as the false, he must judge as this law prescribes. Actual judgements may be quite different: no psychological law drives the judging subject under the yoke of logical laws. We therefore again have before us an equivalent restatement of the logical law, infinitely far from the thought of psychological laws which govern judgement-phenomena. But this thought forms the essential kernel of the psychological interpretation. This last arises when 'cannot believe' etc. is taken to mean a non-coexistence of judgements instead of the incompatibility of the corresponding propositions, i.e. a necessary non-realization of their joint truth.

The proposition: No 'reasonable' (or merely 'responsible') individual *can* believe a contradiction, permits of yet another interpretation. We call a man 'reasonable', if we credit him with an habitual tendency to judge rightly, in his own sphere, of course, and in a normal frame of mind. A man regularly capable, when normal, of hitting off 'the obvious', what 'lies to hand', is a 'responsible thinker' in the sense here in question. The avoidance of explicit contradiction is naturally included in the (quite vague) range of the 'obvious'. If we carry out this subsumption, the statement 'No responsible, reasonable person can believe in contradictions', does no more than trivially apply a general principle to a particular case. We should of course not *call* a thinker 'responsible', if the case were otherwise. Here again there is no reference to a psychological law.

But we have not reached the end of possible interpretations. There is a grave ambiguity in the word 'impossibility', which not only points to *a union excluded by objective law*, but also to a *subjective incapacity* to unify factors: this ambiguity serves to reinforce our psychologistic tendencies. I *cannot believe* that contradictories coexist: try as hard as I will, my attempt shivers itself upon an unconquerable, felt resistance. This incapacity for belief is arguably an inwardly evident experience: I see belief in contradictories to be impossible for me, as for any being that I must think of by analogy with myself. I therefore have evident insight into a psychological law of which the principle of contradiction is the expression.

To limit ourselves to the new errors in this argument, we may answer as follows: Experience shows that, once we have passed judgement on an issue, the attempt to give up the conviction now flooding us, and to embrace some opposed alternative, is vain, even if new thought-motives come up, retrospective doubts arise, old convictions at variance with our present ones haunt us, we are often assailed by an obscure 'feeling' of upsurging, embattled thought-masses. The 'vain attempt', the 'felt resistance' etc., are individual experiences, limited as to person and time, bound up with definite, if not exactly specifiable circumstances. How could they provide inner evidence for a universal *law* which transcends persons and times? One ought not to confuse the assertoric inner evidence for the existence of a single experience, with the apodeictic inner evidence for the holding of a general law. Can the evidence for the existence of a feeling which we interpreted as one of incapacity, provide the insight that what we now in fact do not bring off will be for ever denied us by law? One should note how impossible it is to specify the circumstances which play so essential a role in the situation. Often enough we make mistakes on the matter, though deep conviction as to the reality of a fact A pushes us to say: It is unthinkable that anyone should judge not-A. It is in this same sense that we are able to say: 'It is unthinkable that anyone should not accept the law of contradiction' (of which we are most firmly convinced), or 'No one can manage to believe in two contradictory propositions at the same time'. It may be that multiplied testing by examples has engendered a lively empirical judgement to this effect, but the inner evidence that this always and necessarily happens we do not possess at all.

The true situation can be set forth thus: we have apodeictic inner evidence, insight in the pointed sense, in regard to the not-both-being-true of contradictory *propositions* or the not-both-being-the-case of opposed states of affairs. This law of incompatibility is the true principle of contradiction. Apodeictic inner evidence then extends itself to a useful psychological application: we can also see that two *judgements* of contradictory content, both merely setting forth in judgement what their intuitive foundations offer, cannot coexist. We can also see that pairs of contradictory judgements having either assertoric inner evidence, or apodeictic inner evidence, can coexist neither in a single consciousness, nor dispersed among several consciousnesses. All this merely tells us that states of affairs which, as contradictory, are objectively incompatible, can also in fact never be *thought together* in the sphere of anyone's intuition or insight – which does not at all mean that he cannot *hold* them to be coexistent. We have, on the other hand, no apodeictic inner evidence in regard to contradictory judgements in general: we only *empirically* know that, within the limits of practically familiar classes of cases, sufficiently defined for practical purposes, contradictory acts of judgement in fact exclude one another.

§ 28 *The supposed two-sidedness of the principle of contradiction in virtue of which it should be taken both as a natural law of thinking, and as a normal law for its logical regulation*

In our psychologically obsessed age, few logicians have been quite able to steer clear of psychological misinterpretations of logical principles, even if they have stood out against attempts to found logic on psychology, and even if they would, on other grounds, resent the charge of 'psychologism'. What is not psychological is not accessible to psychological illumination, and each well-meant attempt to use psychological researches to throw light on the essence of 'laws of thinking', presupposes a psychological reinterpretation of those laws. If one reflects on these truths, one will have to count all German logicians who have followed the lead of Sigwart among such psychological reinterpreters, even if they have been far from expressly formulating, or characterizing, logical laws as psychological, and even if they have strongly opposed them to other psychological laws. If such conceptual shifts are not expressed in the chosen formulations of the laws, they more certainly appear in the accompanying elucidations, or in the whole expository context.

Very remarkable attempts have been made to give the principle of contradiction a *double status*, in virtue of which it is, on the one hand, a *natural law* which determines our actual judging, while, on the other hand, it is a *normal law*, serving as a foundation to all logical rules. This conception is most attractively presented by F. A. Lange in his *Logische Studien*, a brilliant work whose aim is not to contribute to a psychologistic logic à la Mill, but to lay 'new foundations for formal logic'. But if one looks more closely at these 'new foundations', one reads that the truths of logic, like those of mathematics, derive from our intuition of space (*op. cit.* (1877), p. 130), and that, 'since the simple foundations of these sciences guarantee the strict correctness of all knowledge whatsoever', they are 'the foundations of our intellectual organization', and that the 'lawfulness we admire in them, *springs from ourselves* . . . from our own unconscious foundations' (*op. cit.* p. 148). When we read this, we cannot fail to classify Lange's view as a psychologism, even if of another sort, to which Kant's formal idealism – on the prevailing interpretation – as well as all other forms of the doctrine of innate faculties and innate sources of knowledge, belong.[1]

---

[1] It is well-known that Kant's theory of knowledge has sides in which it strives and successfully gets beyond the psychologism of mental faculties as sources of knowledge. Here it is enough to stress that it also has prominent sides which fall within this psychologism, which of course does not preclude lively polemics against other forms of the psychologistic founding of knowledge. Not merely Lange, but most Kantianizing philosophers, fall in the field of psychologizing epistemologists, however little they may fancy the name. For even transcendental psychology *also* is psychology.

Lange writes on this point as follows:

The law of contradiction is the point at which the natural laws of thought come into touch with the normative laws. The ever-active psychological conditions of our idea-formation bring forth truth and error in ever burgeoning abundance in our natural, unregulated thinking, but they are supplemented, restricted, and employed towards a definite end, by the fact that we cannot combine contradictory elements in our thought, when once they have been made (as it were) to coincide. The mind swallows the grossest contradictions as long as the contradictory elements can be kept apart in different thought-compartments. Only when a statement and its contradictory relate to the same object, do we lose our power to combine them: we either become quite unsure of ourselves or one of the two assertions has to yield. Psychologically such an elimination of contradiction may be temporary, since the immediate coincidence of the contradictions is temporary. What has deep roots in different departments of thought cannot simply be destroyed, if mere inferences have shown it to be contradictory. At the point where the consequences of the two propositions are brought to immediate coincidence, this result certainly follows, but it does not filter back through the whole deductive chain to the seat of the original conflict. Doubt as to the validity of this deductive chain or as to the identity of its object often serve to protect error. And even when such error is disturbed for the moment, it springs once more from the familiar round of associated ideas, and lives on for as long as repeated assaults do not finally lay it low.

Despite this toughness of error, the psychological law which rules out the union of immediate contradictions must continue to exert great influence on our thought. It is the sharp edge by which, in the course of experience, untenable combinations of ideas are destroyed while the more tenable combinations survive. It is the destructive principle in the natural progress of human thought, which, like the progress of organisms, depends on the fact that ever new combinations of ideas are being produced, of which the main mass are continually destroyed, while the better ones survive and have further effects.

This *psychological* law of contradiction is given immediately by our organism, and operates prior to all experience, as a condition of all experience. Its mode of action is objective, and it need not first be brought to consciousness in order to act.

If we now wish to conceive of the same law as the foundation of logic, if we wish to acknowledge it as the *normative law* of all thought, as it also has been operative as a law of nature without our acknowledgement, then we certainly have need of typical intuitions to convince us, as in the case of all other axioms (*op. cit.* p. 27 *f.*).

What is the essential element in logic, when all psychological additions have been stripped away? Only the fact of the continual removal of contradictories. It is a mere pleonasm in our intuitively based schema if one denies that contradiction *can* exist, as if there were yet another necessity behind the ground of the necessary. The fact is that a contradiction *does not exist*, that each judgement which oversteps the limits of this notion, is at once superseded by an opposed, better founded judgement. But this factual supersession is for logic the ultimate ground of all rules. Psychologically regarded, it can itself again be called 'necessary', in that it is seen as a special case of a more general law of nature. With this, however, logic has nothing to do, since it originates at the same point as its law of contradiction (*op. cit.* p. 49).

These doctrines of F. A. Lange have, in particular, had a plain influence on K. Kroman (*Unsere Naturkenntnis*, trans. by Fischer-Benzon, Copenhagen, 1883) and G. Heymans (*Gesetze und Elemente des wissenschaftlichen Denkens* Leipzig, 1890, 1894). To the latter we owe a systematic attempt to base epistemology on psychology in the most thoroughgoing manner. As an almost pure thought-experiment it must be warmly welcomed: we shall have occasion to go into it more fully. Similar notions have been expressed by O. Liebmann (*Gedanken und Tatsachen*, vol. 1 (1882), pp. 25–7), to our surprise in the course of a discussion which quite correctly attributes to logical necessity an 'absolute validity for every rational, thinking being, whether or not the rest of his constitution agrees with ours or not'.

It is plain from the above what our objections to these doctrines are. We do not deny the psychological facts mentioned in Lange's penetrating exposition, but we find nothing to justify talk of a *law of nature*. If we compare the various formulations of the supposed law with the facts, they reveal themselves as very careless expressions of the latter. If Lange had tried to describe and delimit these familiar experiences in an exact conceptual manner, he must have seen that they could not qualify as particular instances of an exact law, in the sense in which logical principles are such laws. What we have before us as a 'natural law of contradiction' is, in fact, a rough, empirical generalization, which suffers from a quite unspecifiable degree of indefiniteness. It relates, moreover, merely to *normal* individual minds, for how abnormal minds behave is something on which the everyday experience here adduced has nothing to tell us. We miss, in short, the strictly scientific attitude, which is quite indispensable if pre-scientific judgements of experience are to be used for scientific purposes. We protest vigorously against the mixing up of a vague empirical generalization with an absolutely exact, purely conceptual law, which has its place in logic alone. We think it absurd to identify the one with the other, or to deduce the one from the other, or to weld both into the supposedly two-sided law of contradiction. Only sheer ignoring of the plain content of the logical law could permit us to ignore the further fact that this content is not at all relevant, directly or indirectly, to the actual elimination of contradiction in thought. This actual elimination plainly only concerns the judgement experienced by one and the same individual in one and the same time and act: it does not concern affirmation if divided among different individuals and in different times and acts. For the factual element here relevant such distinctions are essential, but they do not affect the logical law at all. For this says nothing concerning the conflict among contradictory judgements, among real, dated acts of this or that character; it only speaks of the law-based incompatibility of the timeless ideal unities we call contradictory propositions. The truth that the members of such a pair of propositions are not both true, contains no shadow of an empirical assertion about any consciousness and its acts of judgement. I think that one has only to make this quite clear to oneself, and take it seriously, to see the wrongness of the whole notion that we are now criticizing.

§ 29 *Continuation. Sigwart's doctrine*

Eminent thinkers before Lange have inclined to this disputed attribution of a double character to the basic laws of logic. Even Bergmann (*Reine Logik*, end of §2), otherwise little disposed to make concessions to psychologism, does so in one chance remark, but Sigwart above all is guilty. His wide influence over modern logic justifies a narrower discussion of the relevant passages.

On the view of this important logician

the principle of contradiction is a normative law in no other sense than it is a natural law, a law which simply establishes the meaning of negation. As a natural law, it merely says that it is impossible consciously to affirm that A is B and that A is *not* B at a given moment, but as a normative law it is applied to the whole range of standing concepts to which the unity of consciousness extends. Seen in this regard, it underlies the Principle of Contradiction ordinarily so called, which is not, however, to be coordinated with the Law of Identity (in the sense of the formula A is A) since it presupposes the fulfilment of this law, i.e. the absolute constancy of our concepts (*Logik*, I, §45.5).

Parallel things are said in the statements regarding the Law of Identity (interpreted as a principle of agreement):

> The difference between the principle of agreement treated as a natural and a normative law, does not lie in its own nature, but in the presupposition of its application. In the former case it is applied to what is present to consciousness: in the latter case to the ideal state of a persistent, unchanging presence of all ordered, presentative content to a single consciousness, a state which is empirically incapable of complete fulfilment (*Logik*, I, §45.2).

To this we object: How can a proposition which (as law of contradiction) 'establishes the meaning of negation', have the character of a law of nature? Sigwart of course does not mean that the law is a nominal definition which lays down the sense of the word 'negation', but only that it is rooted in the sense of 'negation', that it sets forth what pertains to the concept's meaning: Sigwart in other words only wants to say that to give up the law is to give up the meaning of 'negation'. This, however, can never make up the thought-content of a law of nature, and, in particular, not of that law which Sigwart formulates in the following words: 'It is impossible consciously to affirm that A is B and that A is not B at a given moment.' Propositions whose roots lie in concepts (not mere applications of such conceptually rooted propositions to facts) can say nothing as to what we can or cannot consciously do at a given moment. If, as Sigwart elsewhere teaches, they are timeless, there can be nothing in their essential content which concerns the temporal, and which therefore concerns the factual. To drag facts into propositions of this sort is always to destroy their genuine sense. All this makes it clear that the natural law which concerns matters in time, and the normative law, the true principle of contradiction, that concerns timeless matters, differ completely in kind, and that we cannot accordingly be dealing with a single law which, *with unchanged sense merely functions differently or has a different sphere of application.* If the disputed view were correct, there should further be a general formula concerning both the law concerning facts and the law concerning ideal objects. A man who believes in a single law here, must have a single, definite conception of it. We see, however, that it is quite vain to ask for this unitary conception.

To this objection I shall add another. The normative law of contradiction is thought to presuppose absolute constancy among our concepts. The law would then only hold on condition that we always used expressions with the same meaning, and where this condition was not fulfilled, it would not hold. This cannot be what the famous logician seriously believes. The *empirical* application of the law certainly presupposes that the concepts or propositions which function as the meanings of our expressions really are the same, since the law ideally extends to all possible pairs of propositions of opposed quality but *identical* subject-matter. But this of course is no condition of the law's *validity*, as if this were merely hypothetical, but conditions the possible *application* of the law to previously given instances. Just as it is a precondition for applying a numerical law, that we have, in a given case, numbers actually before us, and numbers of such a character as the law expressly refers to, so it is a precondition for applying the logical law of contradiction that propositions are before us; that they are propositions of identical subject-matter is also expressly stipulated.

It does not seem to me helpful, furthermore, to relate the law to the Consciousness in General sketched by Sigwart. In such a concept all concepts (more exactly all expressions) would be used with absolutely identical meanings: there would be no flux of meanings, no ambiguities or *quaterniones terminorum.* The laws of logic have, however, no intrinsic, essential relation to this ideal, which we rather construct to fit them. The constant reference to an ideal consciousness makes us feel disagreeably that the logical laws perhaps only strictly hold for fictitious ideal cases, and not for such as we encounter in experience. The sense in which the laws of pure logic 'presuppose' identity of concepts has just been discussed. If our conceptions are in flux, if the same expression recurs with an altered content, we no longer have the same concept in the sense of logic, but a second one, and a new one for each further alteration. But each single concept is in itself a supra-empirical unity, and falls under the logical rules which apply to its form. As the flux of empirical colour-contents and the imperfect identification of qualities do not affect colour-differentiations as *species* of qualities, as one species has ideal identity over against its manifold possible cases (which are not themselves colours, but instances of one colour), so meanings or concepts have identity in relation to the conceptions of which they are the 'contents'. Our capacity to ideate universals in singulars, to have a 'seeing' grasp of a concept in an empirical presentation, and to be assured of the identity of our conceptual intentions in repeated presentation, is presupposed by the possibility of knowledge. Just as, in the act of ideation, we intuitively lay hold of *one concept* – as the single species, whose unity over against actual instances, or instances thought of as actual, is given with *insight* – so we can apprehend the inward evidence of the logical laws as relating to concepts formed in this or that manner. Among concepts, in the sense of ideal unities, are also to be found the 'propositions' of which the principle of contradiction speaks, and so also the meanings of the algebraic signs used in the formal expression of logical principles. Wherever acts of conceptual presentation are carried out, we encounter concepts: our presentations have their 'contents', their ideal meanings, which we can lay hold of abstractively, in ideational abstraction, and this means that we can *apply* logical laws everywhere. The *validity* of these laws is, however, absolutely unrestricted, nor does it depend on our power, nor on anyone's power, to achieve acts of conceptual presentation, nor to sustain or repeat such acts in the consciousness that they have the same intention.

CHAPTER SIX

Syllogistic Inferences Psychologistically Considered. Syllogistic and Chemical Formulae

---

§30 *Attempts at interpreting syllogistic principles psychologically*

THE discussions of our last chapter have mainly been on the ground of the law of contradiction, since in its case, as in the case of all fundamental logical principles, psychologistic interpretations are very tempting. The thought-motives that push our thinking in this direction have, in fact, a strong air of obviousness. Empiricistic doctrines are less often specially applied to the *laws of the syllogism*: their reducibility to the basic logical principles makes it seem needless to take further trouble with them. If the logical axioms are psychological laws, and the syllogistic rules follow in a purely deductive manner from these axioms, these syllogistic rules must also count as psychological. It might be thought that each fallacious inference would furnish a decisive counter-example, and that the deduction here in question would provide us with an argument against any psychological interpretation of the logical axioms. It might further be thought that the care needed in laying down, whether in thought or word, the supposed psychological content of the axioms, would convince the empiricists that such interpretations can contribute nothing whatever to proving the syllogistic formulae. Wherever such a proof succeeds, its premises and conclusions alike have the status of laws, which differ *toto caelo* from what are called laws in psychology. But even the clearest refutations break upon the complacent conviction of the psychologistic doctrine. G. Heymans in his recent elaborate development of the doctrine, is so little dismayed by the existence of fallacious arguments, that he even regards his psychological view as confirmed by the possibility of pointing out such fallacies. For this pointing out does not consist in bettering our thought-habits, which do not as yet conform to the law of contradiction, but in drawing attention to an unnoticed contradiction in our wrong syllogism. One might well ask whether contradictions that pass unnoticed are not genuine contradictions, and whether our logical law merely affirms the impossibility of unifying contradictions that are noticed, while allowing unnoticed contradictions to be jointly true. Again, one need only reflect on the difference between psychological and logical incompatibility, to be quite clear that we are once more lost in the thick fog of the aforementioned ambiguities.

It would not profit us greatly to say that talk of 'unnoticed' contradictions in fallacious arguments is improper: that the contradiction first emerges as a novelty in the course of the thought-train that refutes it, that this emergence has as a further (psychological) consequence that we feel ourselves bound to reject this argument as invalid. One thought-movement has one consequence, another another: no psychological law connects a refutation with a fallacy. The fallacy makes an appearance on countless occasions without the refutation, and retains our conviction. What right has one thought-shift, which only follows the fallacy in certain psychological circumstances, to attribute absolute contradiction to the latter, and not merely to say that it is an invalidity in the circumstances, but that it is an objective, absolute invalidity? The same naturally holds in regard to the correct syllogistic forms in relation to their justifying demonstration through the logical axioms. How can the demonstrative thought-train that only arises in certain mental circumstances, rise to the claim that the syllogistic form it justifies is *absolutely* valid? The psychologistic doctrine has no acceptable answer to such questions. Here as elsewhere it lacks the capacity to make sense of the claim made by logical truths to objective validity, and therewith also their functioning as absolute norms of correct and false judgement. How often has it been observed and objected that the identification of logical with psychological law would also destroy every difference between correct and incorrect thinking, since the incorrect modes of judgement are no less governed by psychological laws than the correct ones? Or should we perhaps follow an arbitrary convention, and treat the outcome of certain laws as correct, of others as incorrect? How does the empiricist counter such objections? 'The thought that is directed to truth no doubt strives to achieve thought-combinations that are free from contradiction, but the *value* of these non-contradictory thought-combinations again plainly resides in the circumstance that the non-contradictory alone can be asserted, that the law of contradiction is therefore a natural law of thinking.'[1] Thought is here credited with an extraordinary *nisus* towards the non-contradictory, when there are, and can be, no other than non-contradictory combinations, if, indeed, there really is a law of nature to such an effect. Or is the argument any better if one says: 'We have no reason to condemn the combination of two mutually contradictory judgements as incorrect, beyond the fact that we instinctively and immediately experience it as impossible to assert two such judgements together? If one seeks to show, independently of this fact, that only the non-contradictory *may* be asserted, one finds repeatedly that the proof always presupposes what it has to prove' (*op. cit.* p. 69). One at once sees the operation of the ambiguities analysed above: our insight into the logical law that contradictory propositions are not both true, is identified with the instinctive, supposedly immediate 'sensation' of psychological inability to perform contradictory acts of judgement at the same time. Self-evidence and blind conviction, exact and empirical generality, logical incompatibility of states of affairs and psychological incompatibility of acts of belief, impossibility of joint truth and impossibility of joint belief, all run together.

§31 *Syllogistic and chemical formulae*

Heymans has tried to lend plausibility to the doctrine that syllogistic formulae express 'empirical laws of thinking' by likening them to chemical formulae.

Just as the chemical formula $2H_2 + O_2 = 2H_2O$ only expresses the general fact that, in suitable circumstances, two volumes of Hydrogen combine with one volume of Oxygen to form two volumes of water, so the logical formula

$$MaX + MaY = YiX + XiY$$

merely expresses the fact that, in suitable circumstances, two universal affirmative judgements with a common subject, produce

[1] Heymans, op. cit. 1, p. 70. F. A. Lange likewise said (cf. the last paragraph of the long citation from the *Logische Studien*, above, §28) that the *factual* elimination of contradictions in our judgements was the ultimate *ground* of logical rules.

two new particular judgements in consciousness, in which the predicate-concepts of the original judgement appear both as predicate- and as subject-concepts. Why in this case two new judgements are produced, but not in the case of the combination $Mex + MeY$, we are at present ignorant. Repeated experiment will, however, assure us of the irrefragable necessity which governs these relationships, a necessity which compels us to affirm the conclusion when we have conceded the premisses (*op. cit.* p. 62).

The institution of these experiments of course demands 'an exclusion of disturbing influences', and this consists in 'representing the premiss-judgements to oneself as clearly as possible, letting the mechanism of thought operate, and then waiting for the generation or non-generation of a new judgement'. If a new judgement really arises, one must look closely to see whether there are not any intermediate stages in consciousness beside the beginning- and end-point, and must take note of these latter as exactly and completely as possible (*op. cit.* p. 57).

What astonishes us in this conception is the assertion that, in the case of combinations excluded by logicians, no new judgements are generated. If we consider every fallacy of, e.g. the form

$$XeM + MeY = XeY$$

we shall have to say that generally, in suitable circumstances, two judgements of the forms XeM and MeY generate a new judgement in consciousness. The analogy with the chemical formulae fits just as correctly or as badly as in the other cases. Naturally one is not permitted to reply that the 'circumstances' are unlike in the two cases. They are psychologically of equal interest, and the corresponding empirical propositions of equal value. Why then do we draw such a fundamental distinction between the two classes of formulae? If the question were put to us, we should naturally reply: Because we *see* in the case of the one that what they *express* are truths, while, in the case of the other, they are falsehoods. The empiricist, however, cannot give this answer. On the interpretations he accepts, the empirical propositions corresponding to fallacious inferences are valid in the same way as are those which correspond to other inferences.

The empiricist appeals to the experience of 'irrefragable necessity', which, 'if the premisses are conceded, *compels* us also to hold the conclusion to be true.' But all syllogisms, whether logically justified or not, come about with psychological necessity, and the felt compulsion (when it is felt) is always the same. One who incurs a fallacy, and sustains it against critical objections, feels 'irrefragable necessity', the compulsion of not being able to think otherwise, in exactly the same way as the man who draws a correct conclusion and continues to recognize its correctness. Like all judgement, the drawing of conclusions is no arbitrary matter. This felt irrefragability so little proves real irrefragability that it may yield to the force of new reasons, even in the case of correctly drawn conclusions recognized as such. It should therefore not be confused with the genuine logical necessity that pertains to every syllogistic inference, which means, and can mean, nothing beyond the insightfully knowable (though not actually known by each judging person) validity of the syllogism, with its governance by ideal law. The law-governed character of this validity certainly first makes itself known in the insight with which we apprehend the syllogistic principle. In comparison with this, the insight accompanying a conclusion drawn here and now, seems to be an insight into the *necessary validity* of the particular case, i.e. a validity grounded in the law.

The empiricist thinks that 'we are as yet ignorant' why the combinations of premisses condemned by Logic 'yield no conclusion'. Does he expect to discover more as knowledge widens? One would imagine that here at least we know everything that can be known, for here we *see* that each possible form of conclusion, i.e. each conclusion falling in the framework of syllogistic combinations, will combine with the combinations of premisses in question to yield a false syllogistic law. One would think that, in such a case, even an infinitely perfect intelligence could have nothing more to know.

To such and like objections, one of another sort may be added; it is no less powerful, but seems less important for our purposes. It cannot be doubted that the analogy with chemical formulae does not reach far, not far enough, I consider, for us to treat very seriously the psychological laws that have been confused with the logical laws. In the chemical case, we know the circumstances in which the syntheses expressed in the formulae take place, they can be very precisely stated: this is why we count chemical equations as among the most valuable inductions of natural science. In the psychological case, on the other hand, our knowledge of the circumstances amounts to so little, that we have in the end nothing more to say than that people quite often think in conformity with logical laws. Circumstances which cannot be specified exactly, such as a certain 'concentration of attention', a certain 'mental freshness', a certain 'preparedness' etc., are favourable conditions for the emergence of a logical act of inference. The circumstance or conditions (in the strict sense), from which the inferential act of judgement follows with causal necessity, are entirely hidden from us. The situation being what it is, it is quite understandable that no psychologist has so far thought of introducing, one by one, into psychology, generalizations which can be connected with syllogistic formulae, and which involve the vague circumstances just mentioned. Nor has any psychologist tried to dignify such generalizations with the title of 'laws of thought'.

After all this, we may count as a 'hopeless' undertaking, in the sense of Kant, Heymans' interesting attempt – full of stimulating points that have not been mentioned here – at a 'theory of knowledge that could also be called a chemistry of judgements', and that is 'nothing more than a psychology of thinking'. It will at least not make us swerve from our rejection of psychologistic interpretations. Syllogistic formulae do not have the empirical content men attribute to them: their true sense is plainest when we state them in the equivalent form of *ideal incompatibilities*, e.g. It is universally the case that two propositions having the forms 'All M's are X' and 'No P is M' are not true unless a proposition having the form 'Some X are not P' is also true. And so in every case. Nothing is here said about a consciousness or the acts and circumstances of its judgement etc. If one keeps the true content of the syllogistic formulae in mind, one will vanquish the illusion that makes the experimental production of the insightful judgement which recognizes the syllogistic principle, into an experimental proof of that principle, or into something that can lead to such a proof.

CHAPTER SEVEN

Psychologism as a Sceptical Relativism

§32 *The ideal conditions for the possibility of a theory as such.*
The strict concept of scepticism

THE worst objection that can be made to a theory, and particularly to a theory of logic, is that it goes against *the self-evident conditions for the possibility of a theory in general.* To set up a theory whose content is explicitly or implicitly at variance with the propositions on which the sense and the claim to validity of all theory rests, is not merely wrong, but basically mistaken.

There are two respects in which one can here talk of the self-evident 'conditions of the possibility' of any theory whatever. One can talk of these in a *subjective* respect. Here one's concern is with the *a priori* conditions upon which the possibility of immediate and mediate *knowledge*[1] depends, as also the possibility of rationally *justifying* any theory. The theory which validates knowledge is itself a piece of knowledge: its possibility depends on certain conditions, rooted, in purely conceptual fashion, in knowledge and its relation to the knowing subject. It is, e.g. part of the notion of knowledge, in the strict sense, that it is a judgement that does not merely claim to state truth, but is also certain of this claim's justification, and actually possesses the justification in question. If the judging person were never in a position to have direct personal experience and apprehension of his judgement's self-justifying character, if all his judgements lacked that inner evidence which distinguishes them from blind prejudices, and yields him luminous certainties, it would be impossible to provide a rational account and a foundation for knowledge, or to discourse on theory and science. A theory therefore violates the subjective conditions of its *own* possibility as a theory, when, following our example, it in no way prefers an inwardly evident

[1] Please note that the term 'knowledge' is, in this work, not restricted, as it usually is restricted, to objects that are real.

135

judgement to a blind one. It thereby destroys the very thing that distinguishes it from an arbitrary, unwarranted assertion.

It is plain that, by the subjective conditions of possibility, we do not here mean real conditions rooted in the individual judging subject, or in the varied species of judging beings (e.g. of human beings), but ideal conditions whose roots lie in the form of subjectivity as such, and in its relation to knowledge. We shall distinguish them by speaking of *noetic* conditions.

In an *objective* respect, talk of the conditions for the possibility of any theory do not concern the theory as a subjective unity of items of knowledge, but theory as an objective unity of truths or propositions, bound together by relations of ground and consequent. The conditions here are all the *laws* whose foundation lies purely in the notion of theory, or more specifically, in the notions of truth, of proposition, of object, of property, of relation etc., the notions, i.e. which enter *essentially into the concept of theoretical unity*. To deny these laws amounts to an assertion that all such terms – theory, truth, object, property etc. – lack a *coherent sense*. A theory is self-destroying, in this logico-objective respect, if its content offends against the laws without which theory as such can have no rational, no coherent sense.

The logical offences of such a theory can lie in its *presuppositions*, in its forms of *theoretic connection*, or in the *thesis that it sets forth*. The violation of logical conditions is at its grossest when the *sense* of the theoretic thesis involves a rejection of those laws on which the rational possibility of any thesis, and the proof of any thesis, depend. The same holds of noetic conditions and of theories which violate them. We may distinguish (without attempting a classification) between false, nonsensical, logically and noetically absurd, and finally *sceptical theories*. The last cover all theories whose theses either plainly say, or analytically imply, that the logical or noetic conditions for the possibility of any theory are false.

The term 'scepticism' is thus connected with a clear concept and is clearly divided into logical and noetic scepticism. The concept of such scepticism applies to the ancient forms of scepticism with theses such as: There is no truth, no knowledge, no justification of knowledge etc. Our previous treatments have shown[1] that empiricism, whether moderate or extreme, is an

---

[1] See Ch. v, Appendix to §§25–6.

instance of our pregnant concept of scepticism. That it is of the essence of a sceptical theory to be *nonsensical*, is at once plain from its definition.

§33 *Scepticism in the metaphysical sense*

The term 'scepticism' is commonly used with some vagueness. Ignoring its popular sense, we find that philosophical theories are called 'sceptical' if they try to limit human knowledge considerably and on principle, and especially if they remove from the sphere of possible knowledge wide fields of real being, or such especially precious sciences as metaphysics, natural science, or ethics as a rational discipline.

Among such inauthentic forms of scepticism there is one which is readily confused with the purely epistemic scepticism here defined, which would limit knowledge to mental existence, and would deny the existence or knowability of 'things in themselves'. Such theories are plainly *metaphysical*, they have no connection with scepticism proper, their thesis is free from logical and noetic *absurdity*, their claim to validity is a mere question of arguments and proofs. Confusions and genuinely sceptical modifications then only arise from the paralogistic influence of tempting ambiguities or of sceptical convictions elsewhere fostered. If, e.g., a metaphysical sceptic states his view in the form 'There is no *objective* knowledge' (i.e. no knowledge of things in themselves), or 'All knowledge is *subjective*' (i.e. all factual knowledge is merely the knowledge of facts of consciousness), there is a great temptation to yield to the ambiguity of the subject-object terminology, and to transform the original sense which suits our metaphysical standpoint into a noetic-sceptical sense. The proposition 'All knowledge is subjective' becomes the totally new assertion 'All knowledge as a conscious phenomenon is subject to the laws of human consciousness: the so-called forms and laws of knowledge are merely functional forms of consciousness, or laws governing such functional forms, i.e. psychological laws.' When metaphysical scepticism thus wrongly favours epistemological scepticism, the latter, contrariwise, if taken to be self-evident, seems to provide powerful arguments for the former. People reason, e.g.:

> Logical laws, as laws for our functions of knowing, lack 'real meaning'; we can at least never know if they agree with things in

themselves. To assume a 'preformation-system' is wholly gratuitous. If the comparison of an item of knowledge with its object (needed to establish an *adaequatio rei et intellectus*) is excluded by the notion of the thing-in-itself, this applies also to the comparison of the subjective laws of our conscious functions with the objective being of things and their laws. If there are things in themselves, we can know nothing whatever about them.

Metaphysical questions do not concern us here. We have mentioned them only to have before us at an early stage, an instance of the confusion between metaphysical and logico-noetic scepticism.

§34 *The concept of relativism and its specific forms*

In order to criticize psychologism we have yet to discuss the concept of *subjectivism* or *relativism* which also is part of the above-mentioned metaphysical theory. One of its original forms is caught in the Protagorean formula: 'Man is the measure of all things', provided this last is interpreted as saying 'The individual man is the measure of all truth.' For each man that is true which seems to *him* true, one thing to one man and the opposite to another, if that is how he sees it. We can therefore also opt for the formula 'All truth (and knowledge) is relative – relative to the contingently judging subject.' If, however, instead of such a subject, we make some contingent *species* of judging beings the pivot of our relations, we achieve a new form of relativism. Man as *such* is then the measure of all human truth. Every judgement whose roots are to be found in what is *specific* to man, in the constitutive laws of man as species – is a true judgement, for us human beings. To the extent that such judgements belong to the form of common human subjectivity, the term 'subjectivism' is in place here too (in talk of the subject as the ultimate source of knowledge etc.). It is best to employ the term 'relativism', and to distinguish *individual* from *specific* relativism. The restriction of the latter to the human species, stamps it as *anthropologism*. We turn to criticism. Our interests demand that it should be very careful.

§35 *Critique of individual relativism*

Individual relativism is such a bare-faced and (one might almost say) 'cheeky' scepticism, that it has certainly not been seriously held in modern times. It is a doctrine no sooner set up than cast down, though only for one who recognizes the objectivity of all that pertains to logic. One cannot persuade the subjectivist any more than one can the open sceptic, a man simply lacking the ability to see that laws such as the law of contradiction have their roots in the mere meaning of truth, that from these it follows that talk of a subjective truth, that is one thing for one man and the opposite for another, must count as the purest nonsense. He will not bow to the ordinary objection that in setting up his theory he is making a claim to be convincing to others, a claim presupposing that very objectivity of truth which his thesis denies. He will naturally reply: My theory expresses my standpoint, what is true for me, and need be true for no one else. Even the subjective fact of his thinking, he will treat as true for himself, and not as true in itself.[1] That we should, however, be able to convince the subjectivist personally, and make him admit his error, is not important: what is important is to refute him in an objectively valid manner. Refutation presupposes the leverage of certain self-evident, universally valid convictions. Such are those trivial insights on which every scepticism must come to grief, insights which show up sceptical doctrines as in the strictest, most genuine sense nonsensical. The content of such assertions rejects what is part of the sense or content of every assertion and what accordingly cannot be significantly separated from any assertion.

§36 *Critique of specific relativism and, in particular, of anthropologism*

In the case of subjectivism, it is doubtful whether anyone seriously holds it. Modern and recent philosophy leans, however, so strongly towards specific relativism, and, in particular, towards anthropologism, that it is quite rare to encounter a thinker free

---

[1] His view should recommend itself to those who think to separate subjective from objective truths by denying an objective character to judgements of introspection. They assume that the being-for-me of a conscious content cannot at the same time be a being-in-itself, that subjectivity in the psychological sense excludes objectivity in the logical sense.

from the taint of such erroneous doctrines. But such doctrines are, however, sceptical in the sense defined above, and so suffer from the grossest absurdities conceivable in a theory: we find in them, too, slightly masked, an evident contradiction between the sense of their thesis, and that which cannot be separated from the sense of any thesis *qua* thesis. It is not hard to show this in detail:

1. Specific relativism makes the assertion: Anything is true for a given species of judging beings that, by their constitution and laws of thought, must count as true. This doctrine is absurd. For it is part of its sense that the same proposition or content of judgement can be true for a subject of the species *homo*, but may be false for another subject of a differently constituted species. The same content of judgement cannot, however, be both true and false: this follows from the mere sense of 'true' and 'false'. If the relativist gives these words their appropriate meaning, his thesis is in conflict with its own sense.

It is plainly a vain evasion to plead that the words of the adduced principle of contradiction were incomplete, but that, when we unfolded the sense of the words 'true' and 'false', it was the humanly true and false that were in question. For the ordinary subjectivist could likewise plead that talk about the true and the false was inexact, and that truth (or falsehood) for the individual were what was really meant. And one would of course answer him by saying: An evidently valid law cannot have a plainly absurd meaning, and talk of what is true *for* this one or that one is absurd. It is absurd to regard it as an open possibility that the same judged content – with dangerous ambiguity we say 'the same judgement' – should be alike true and false, as one or other judges it. There will be a corresponding answer to specific relativism: 'Truth for this or that species', e.g. for the human species, is, as here meant, an absurd mode of speech. It can no doubt be used in a good sense, but it then means something wholly different, i.e. the circle of truths to which man as such has access. What is true is absolutely, intrinsically true: truth is one and the same, whether men or non-men, angels or gods apprehend and judge it. Logical laws speak of truth in this ideal unity, set over against the real multiplicity of races, individuals and experiences, and it is of this ideal unity that we all speak when we are not confused by relativism.

2. We saw that the principles of contradiction and excluded

middle tell us what pertains to the mere sense of the words 'true' and 'false'. In this regard it is possible to restate our objection in the words: If the relativist says that there could be beings not bound by these principles – this assertion is easily seen as equivalent to the relativistic formula stated above – he *either* means that there could be propositions or truths, in the judgements of such beings, which do not conform to these principles, *or* he thinks that the course of judgement of such beings is not *psychologically* regulated by these principles. If he means the latter, his doctrine is not at all peculiar, since we ourselves are such beings. (One need only recall our objections to the psychologistic interpretation of logical principles. But if he means the former, we may simply reply: Either such beings understand the words 'true' and 'false' in our sense, in which case it is irrational to speak of logical principles not holding, since they pertain to the mere sense of these words as understood by us. We should never dream of *calling* anything true or false, that was at variance with them. Alternatively, such beings use the words 'true' and 'false' in some different sense, and the whole dispute is then one of words. If, e.g., they call those things 'trees' which we call 'propositions', then the statements in which the logical laws are expressed of course do not hold, but they will also have lost the sense in which we asserted them. It therefore comes out that the sense of the word 'truth' has been totally altered by relativism, which yet pretends to talk of truth in the sense laid down by the logical laws, which is the only sense we all employ when we talk of truth. In a single sense there is only a single truth, in an equivocal sense there are naturally as many 'truths' as there are equivocal uses.

3. The constitution of a species is a fact: from a fact it is only possible to derive other facts. To base facts relativistically on the constitution of the species therefore means to give it a factual character. This is absurd. Every fact is individually and therefore temporally determinate. In the case of truth, talk of temporal determination only makes sense in regard to a fact posited by a truth (provided, that is, that it is a truth about facts): it makes no sense in regard to the truth itself. It is absurd to think of truths as being causes or effects, as we have already indicated. If someone wished to argue from the fact that a true judgement, like any judgement, must spring from the constitution of the judging

subject in virtue of appropriate natural laws, we should warn him not to confuse the 'judgement', *qua* content of judgement, i.e. as an ideal unity, with the individual, real act of judgement. It is the former that we mean when we speak of the judgement $2 \times 2 = 4$, which is the same whoever passes it. One should likewise not confuse the true judgement, as the correct judgement in accordance with truth, with the *truth* of this judgement or with the true content of judgement. My act of judging that $2 \times 2 = 4$ is no doubt causally determined, but this is not true of the truth $2 \times 2 = 4$.

4. If, as anthropologism says, all truth has its source in our common human constitution, then, if there were no such constitution, there would be no truth. The thesis of this hypothetical assertion is absurd, since the proposition 'There is no truth' amounts in sense to the proposition 'There is a truth that there is no truth'. The absurdity of the thesis entails the absurdity of the hypothesis, but, since the hypothesis represents the negation of a valid proposition, having factual content, it admits of falsehood but not of absurdity. No one has in fact ever thought of rejecting as *absurd* those geological and physical theories which give the human race a beginning and an end in time. The stigma of absurdity therefore taints the whole hypothetical statement, since it connects an antecedent having a coherent ('logically possible') sense with an absurd ('logically impossible') consequent. The same stigma then taints anthropologism, and extends naturally, *mutatis mutandis*, to the wider form of relativism.

5. On a relativistic view the constitution of a species might yield the 'truth', valid for the species, that no such constitution existed. Must we then say that there is in reality no such constitution, or that it exists, but only for us? But what if all men, and all species of judging beings, were destroyed, with the exception of the species in question? We are obviously talking nonsense. The notion that the non-existence of a certain constitution should be based on this very constitution, is a flat contradiction: that the truth-conditioning, and therefore existent constitution should condition the truth (among other truths) of its own non-existence. The absurdity is not greatly lessened if we substitute existence for non-existence, and apply our arguments, not to an imaginary species, which from a relativistic standpoint is possible, but to our human species. Our contradiction then

vanishes, but not the absurdity associated with it. The relativity of truth means that, what we call truth, depends on the constitution of the species *homo* and the laws which govern this species. Such a dependence will and can only be thought of as causal. The truth that such a constitution and such laws subsist must then have its real explanation in the fact of this subsistence: the principles of our explanation must be identical with such laws – again mere nonsense. Our constitution would be *causa sui* in respect of laws, which would cause themselves in virtue of themselves etc.

6. The relativity of truth entails the relativity of cosmic existence. For the world is merely the unified objective totality corresponding to, and inseparable from, the ideal system of all factual truth. One cannot subjectivize truth, and allow its object (which only exists as long as truth subsists) to count as absolutely existent, or as existent 'in itself'. There would therefore be no world 'in itself', but only a world for us, or for any other chance species of being. This may suit some, but it becomes dubious once we point out that the ego and its conscious contents also pertain to the world. That I am, and that I am experiencing this or that, might be false if my specific constitution were such as to force me to deny these propositions. And there would be absolutely no world, not merely no world for this or that one, if no actual species of judging beings in the world was so constituted as to have to recognize a world (and itself in that world). If we confine ourselves to the only species actually known to us, animal species, then a change in their constitution would mean a change in the world, and that although animal species are thought to be evolutionary products of the world. We are playing a pretty game: man evolves from the world and the world from man; God creates man and man God.

The essential core of this objection lies in the self-evident conflict between relativism and the inner evidence of immediately intuited existence, i.e. with the evidence of 'inner observation' in the legitimate, indispensable sense. The inner evidence of judgements resting on intuition is rightly contested when such judgements intentionally transcend the content of the actual data of consciousness. They have true inward evidence when their intention rests on this content itself, and finds fulfilment in it, just as it is. This inner evidence is not attainted by the vagueness of all such judgements: one need only think of the ineliminable vagueness of the determination of time, and perhaps also of place, in any immediate judgement of intuition.

§37 *General observation. The concept of relativism in an extended sense*

Our two forms of relativism are special cases of relativism in the widest sense of the word, as a doctrine which somehow derives the pure principles of logic from facts. Facts are 'contingent': they might very well not have been the case, they might have been different. If the facts then differ, logical principles also will differ; they will also be contingent, with a being relative to the facts on which they are founded. I do not wish to counter this by merely bringing in the apodeictic inner evidence of logical laws, points argued for in former chapters: I wish to bring in another point which is more important in this context (cf. §32 of the present chapter). Anyone can see from my statements up to this point that for me the pure truths of logic are all the ideal laws which have their whole foundation in the 'sense', the 'essence' or the 'content', of the concepts of Truth, Proposition, Object, Property, Relation, Combination, Law, Fact etc. More generally stated, they have their whole foundation in the sense of the concepts which make up the heritage of *all* science, which represent the categories of constituents out of which science as such is essentially constituted. Laws of this sort should not be violated by any theoretical assertion, proof or theory, not because such a thing would render the latter false – so would conflict with any truth – but because it would render them inherently absurd. An assertion, e.g., whose content quarrels with the principles whose roots lie in the *sense* of truth as such, is self-cancelling. For to assert, is to maintain the truth of this or that content. A proof whose content quarrels with the principles rooted in the *sense* of the relation of ground and consequent, is self-cancelling. For to prove, is to state that there is such and such a relation of ground and consequent etc. That an assertion is 'self-cancelling', is 'logically absurd', means that its particular content (sense, meaning) contradicts the general demands of its own, pertinent meaning-categories, contradicts what has its general root in the general meaning of those categories. It is now clear that, in this pregnant sense, any theory is logically absurd which deduces logical principles from any matters of fact. To do so is at variance with the general sense of the concepts of 'logical principle' and 'fact', or, to speak more precisely and more generally, of the concepts of 'truth based on the mere content of concepts' and 'truth concerning individual existence'. It is easy to see that the objections against the above discussed relativistic theory are, in the main, objections to relativism in the most general sense.

§38 *Psychologism in all its forms is a relativism*

In our attacks on relativism, we have of course had psychologism in mind. Psychologism in all its subvarieties and individual elaborations is in fact the same as relativism, though not always recognized and expressly allowed to be such. It makes no difference whether, as a formal idealism, based on a 'transcendental psychology', it seeks to save the objectivity of knowledge, or whether, leaning on empirical psychology, it accepts relativism as its ineluctable fate.

Every doctrine is *ipso facto* relativistic, a case of specific relativism, if, with the empiricists, it treats the pure laws of logic as empirical, psychological laws. It is likewise relativistic, if, with the apriorists, it deduces these laws, in more or less mythic fashion, from certain 'original forms' or 'modes of functioning' of the (human) understanding, from consciousness as such, conceived as generic (human) reason, from the psycho-physical constitution of man, from the *intellectus ipse* which, as an innate (generically human) disposition, precedes all actual thought and experience. All the objections we have made to specific relativism also affect such doctrines. One must of course take the somewhat shifting key-words of apriorism, e.g. 'understanding', 'reason', 'consciousness', in the natural sense which gives them an essential connection with the human species. It is the curse of the theories under consideration that they at one time give these words a real, at another time an ideal sense, and so weave an inextricable tangle of true and false statements. Aprioristic theories, to the extent that they yield to relativistic motives, must be counted as relativistic. Such relativism is no doubt restricted, i.e., to the realm of mathematics and natural science, when, as in the case of some Kantian thinkers, certain logical principles are set aside as principles of 'analytic' judgements, but sceptical absurdities are not thereby avoided. For, in their narrower field, they still deduce truth from generic human nature, the ideal from the real, or, more precisely, the necessity of laws from the contingency of facts.

We are, however, more interested in the extreme, consistent psychologism which permits no such restrictions. To such a psychologism the main English empiricists, as well as the more recent German logicians, belong, i.e. thinkers such as Mill, Bain, Wundt, Sigwart, Erdmann and Lipps. To criticize all such works is neither possible nor desirable. In view, however, of the reformatory aims of these Prolegomena, I do not wish to pass over the main works of modern German logic, and especially not the important work of Sigwart, which, more than any other, has pushed logic in the last decades into psychological channels.

§39 Anthropologism in Sigwart's Logic

Isolated statements of a psychologistic tone and character are to be found, as passing misunderstandings, in thinkers whose logical works have a consciously antipsychologistic tendency. This is not so in the case of Sigwart. Psychologism is in his case not an unessential, eliminable addition, but the systematically dominant, basic conception of his work. Right at the beginning of this work, he expressly denies 'that the norms of logic (not merely technical, methodological rules, but the principles of pure logic, the law of contradiction, of sufficient ground etc.) can be otherwise known than by studying the natural powers and types of functioning that these norms are to regulate' (*Logik*, 1^2, p. 22). His whole mode of treating the discipline accords with this conception. Logic, according to Sigwart, is divided into an analytic, a law-giving and a technical part. If we ignore this last, as not concerning us here, the analytic part has as its task 'to investigate the nature of the function for which rules must be found'. On this the law-giving part is built, which has to set up the 'conditions and laws of its normal functioning' (op. cit. §4, p. 16). The 'demand that our thought should be necessarily and universally valid', if 'kept to the known functions of the judgement in all its factors and conditions', yields 'definite norms which judgement must satisfy'. These demands are concentrated in two points: '(1) that the elements of the judgement should be completely definite, conceptually fixed, and (2) that the act of judging should arise necessarily out of its presuppositions. This part therefore embraces the doctrine of concepts and syllogisms as the whole set of normative laws for the formation of perfect judgements' (*op. cit.* p. 21). In other words, this part contains all the principles and laws of pure logic (to the extent that these are envisaged by the traditional or the Sigwartian logic), and to Sigwart these principles and laws really have a psychological foundation.

His detailed statements agree with this programme. Nowhere does he remove the laws and theorems of pure logic, and the objective elements out of which they are constituted, from the flux of psychological and practical research into knowledge. Sigwart always talks of *our* thought and its *functions*, where he is trying to characterize logical necessity, with its ideal legality, as opposed to psychological contingencies. Pure laws like that of contradiction or sufficient ground, are constantly called 'laws of functioning' or 'fundamental forms of the movement of our thought' (*op. cit.* p. 184 and the whole context of pp. 184–5). We read, for instance: 'Though negation is rooted in a movement of our thought which goes beyond reality, and applies contents to one another that cannot be combined, yet there can be no doubt that Aristotle's principle only purports to touch *the nature of our thought*' (*op. cit.* p. 253). 'The absolute validity of the law of contradiction, and of the consequent laws which deny a *contradictio in adjecto*', we read in another passage, rests 'on our immediate consciousness that we always do and always will do the same thing when we deny' (*op. cit.* p. 386). The same holds, on Sigwart's view, of the law of identity (as 'principle of agreement'), and of all purely conceptual propositions and propositions of pure logic.[1] We read statements like the following:

If we reject the possibility of knowing something as it is in itself, if being is no more than one of the ideas produced by ourselves, it still remains the case that objectivity is attributed by us to such ideas as we produce with a consciousness of necessity, and that, whenever we treat anything as existent, we assert thereby that all other thinking

---

[1] Cf. *op. cit.* p. 411: 'These propositions must be *a priori* certainties in the sense that we only recognize in them *a constant and unavoidable function of our thought*'. I may quote this passage though in its context it does not refer to the laws of logic. I am justified by the whole sense of Sigwart's statements (see §48), and by the fact that, on the same page I have quoted, the law of contradiction is expressly compared with the certainties in question.

beings, even purely hypothetical ones, endowed with *the same nature as ourselves*, must produce it with the same necessity (*op. cit.* p. 8).

The same anthropological tendency pervades all the statements relative to basic logical concepts, and in the first place to the concept of truth. It is, says Sigwart, 'a fiction . . . that a judgement could be true if we abstract from the fact that some intelligence thinks such a judgement'. A philosopher who speaks in this manner has accepted a psychologistic reinterpretation of truth. On Sigwart's view, it would be a fiction to speak of truths that *hold* in themselves unknown to anyone, e.g. such truths as transcend men's capacity for knowledge. An atheist, at least, who rejects superhuman intelligences, could not speak in this fashion, nor could such as we, before we have proofs that there are such intelligences. The judgement expressed in the formula of gravitation was not true before the time of Newton, which makes it, strictly speaking, a self-contradictory and wholly false utterance, since an unrestricted validity for all times is plainly part of what it means to assert.

To go further into Sigwart's many statements which concern the notion of *truth* would involve us in an inadmissibly long treatment. But it would at least show that we were right in taking the passage we quoted literally. Sigwart resolves truth into conscious experiences: though he often talks of objective truth, he renounces its true objectivity, which depends on its supra-empirical ideality. Experiences are real particulars, temporally determinate, which come into being and pass away. Truth, however, is 'eternal', or, better put, it is an Idea, and so beyond time. It makes no sense to give truth a date in time, nor a duration which extends throughout time. Naturally one says of truth that on occasion it 'comes to mind', and is accordingly 'apprehended' or 'experienced' by us. But such 'apprehension', 'experiencing' and 'coming to consciousness', are spoken of in quite a different sense in relation to ideal being, from what they have in relation to empirical, individualized being. We do not 'apprehend' truth as we apprehend some empirical content which comes up, and again vanishes, in the stream of mental experiences: truth is not a phenomenon among phenomena, but is an experience in that totally different sense in which a universal, an Idea, is an experience. We are conscious of truth, as we are in general conscious of a Species, e.g. of 'the' Colour Red.

A red object stands before us, but this red object is not the Species Red. Nor does the concrete object contain the Species as a 'psychological' or 'metaphysical' part. The part, the non-independent moment of red, is, like the concrete whole object, something individual, something here and now, something which arises and vanishes with the concrete whole object, and which is *like*, not identical, in different red objects. Redness, however, is an ideal unity, in regard to which it is absurd to speak of coming into being or passing away. The part (moment) red is not Redness, but an instance of Redness. And, as universal objects differ from singular ones, so, too, do our acts of apprehending them. We do something wholly different if, looking at an intuited concretum, we refer to its sensed redness, the individual feature it has here and now, and if, on the other hand, we refer to the Species Redness, as when we say that Redness is a Colour. And just as, while regarding some concrete case, we refer, not to it, but to its universal, its Idea, so, while regarding several acts of such Ideation, we rise to the inwardly evident recognition of the identity of these ideal unities which are meant in our single acts. These unities have identity in the authentic, strictest sense: they are *identical* Species, or are Species of the *same* Genus, etc.

Truth now is likewise an Idea: like any other Idea it is given in an act of Ideation based upon an intuition – this last naturally is the act of insight – and we are evidently clear as to truth's unity and identity over against the dispersed multitude of concrete, compared cases of inwardly evident judgement. And just as, in other cases, the being or 'holding' of something general amounts to an *ideal* possibility – i.e. a possibility in regard to the being of empirical cases falling under the general Idea – so too in this case: the statements 'It is the truth that . . .' and 'There could have been thinking beings having insight into judgements to the effect that . . .', are equivalent. If there are no intelligent beings, if the natural order excludes them, or if they are, in a *real* sense, impossible – or if there are no beings capable of knowing certain classes of truths – then such *ideal* possibilities remain without fulfilling actuality. The apprehension, knowledge, bringing to consciousness of truth (or of certain classes of truths), is nowhere ever realized. Each truth, however, remains in itself what it is, it retains its ideal being: it does not hang somewhere in the void, but is a case of validity in the timeless realm of Ideas. It belongs to the realm of the absolutely valid, into which we fit all cases of validity into which we have *insight* or at least well-founded surmises, and in which we further locate the vaguely presented range of things indirectly and indefinitely thought valid, i.e. the cases of validity not as yet known to us, and perhaps never to be known.

In this situation, Sigwart does not seem to me to press forward to a clear position. He would like to save the objectivity of truth, and not let it sink under the tide of subjective phenomenalism. But, if we enquire just how Sigwart's psychological epistemology hopes to penetrate to the objectivity of truth, we come upon statements like the following:

> The certainty of keeping to a judgement, of the irrevocability of a synthesis, that I shall always say the same thing[1] – this certainty can only be present when I see that it does not rest on *momentary, variable, psychological motives*, but on something that *stays unalterably the same wherever I think*, and is immune from all change. This, on the one hand, is my *self-consciousness itself*, the certainty that I am and that I think, that I am I, the being who now thinks and who has thought, who thinks of this and that. On the one hand, it is what I judge about, *what I think of, in its invariant content: recognized as identical by myself:* which is quite independent of the individual states of the thinker (op. cit. §39.2, p. 310).

A psychologism consistent in its relativism will naturally here reply: Not merely individual variation, but pervasive constancies, such as the whole invariant content and the abiding functional laws that govern it, are psychological facts. If there are such traits and laws essentially common to all men, then they make up the specific nature of man. All truth in its universal validity is therefore relative to the human species, or, more generally, to some species or other of thinking beings. If species differ, so do truths and laws of thought.

We for our part would say: Universal likeness of content, and constant functional laws of nature which regulate the production of such content, do not constitute a genuine universal validity, which rather rests upon ideality. If all creatures of a genus are constitutionally compelled to judge alike, they are in empirical agreement, but, in the ideal sense demanded by a supra-empirical logic, there might as well have been disagreement as agreement.

[1] Can I ever say this with certainty? The irrevocability in question does not concern the actual, but the ideal. It is not the certainty of my judgement that is unchangeable (as Sigwart has just maintained) but its *validity* or its truth.

To define truth in terms of a community of nature is to abandon its notion. If truth were essentially related to thinking intelligences, their mental functions and modes of change, it would arise and perish with them, with the species at least, if not with the individual. With the genuine objectivity of truth, the objectivity of being, even the objectivity of subjective being or the being of the subject, would be gone. What if, e.g., no thinking being were capable of seriously postulating its own being? Then such thinking beings would be and also not be. Truth and being are 'categories' in the same sense, and plainly correlative: truth cannot be relativized, while the objectivity of being is maintained. The relativization of truth presupposes the objective being of the point to which things are relative: this is the contradiction in relativism.

Sigwart's doctrine of universality is in harmony with the rest of his psychologism: we must treat it here, since the ideality of truth presupposes the ideality of the universal, the conceptual. On occasion he says in jest that 'the universal as such is only in our heads' (*op. cit.* p. 103 Note): more seriously he remarks that it is 'something purely inward . . . depending on nothing but the inner power of our thought' (*op. cit.* §45.9, p. 388). One may undoubtedly say this of our conceptual presentation, as a subjective act having this or that psychological content. But the 'what' of such presentation, the concept, can in no sense be regarded as a real part of this psychological content, as something here and now, which comes and goes with the act. It can be meant, but not produced, in our thought.

Sigwart is consistent in practising the same relativization he uses on the notion of truth on the very closely connected concepts of *ground* and *necessity*. 'A logical ground', he says, 'that is unknown to us, is, in strictness a contradiction, for a ground only becomes a logical ground when we know it' (*op. cit.* §32.2, p. 248). The statement that mathematical theorems have their ground in mathematical axioms therefore relates, 'in strictness', to a fact of human psychology. Could we still hold this fact to be a fact whether or not anyone knew, knows or will know it? The usual manner of speaking, which gives objectivity to relations of ground and consequent, and talks of their *discovery*, must accordingly be mistaken.

Despite Sigwart's earnest attempts to distinguish essentially different notions of ground, and the acuteness he shows therein

– an acuteness only to be expected in so eminent a thinker – he is still hindered by the psychologistic tendency of his thought from making the most essential distinction of all, one which presupposes a sharp sundering of ideal from real. When he opposes the 'logical ground' or 'ground of truth' to the 'psychological ground of certainty', he finds the former merely in a certain universal alikeness, alikeness of what is presented, 'since only this, not an individual's mood etc., can be common to all'. We need not reiterate the objections raised above.

The fundamental distinction between a *purely logical ground of truth* and a *normatively logical ground of judgement* is not to be found in Sigwart. On the one hand, a truth (not a true judgement, but the ideally valid unity), has a ground, which is tantamount to saying that there is a theoretical proof which deduces the truth from this objective, theoretical ground. The principle of sufficient ground is to be taken in this sense, and in this alone. And on *this* acceptation of ground, it is not at all the case that every judgement has a ground, let alone that it 'implicitly asserts' such a ground. Every principle of inference, every genuine axiom, is in this sense groundless, as in the opposite direction likewise every judgement of fact. Only the probability of a fact can be grounded, not the fact itself, or the judgement of fact. The expression 'ground of judgement', on the other hand – if we ignore the psychological 'grounds' or causes of judging and their motivating contents[1] – means no more than our *logical right* to judge. In this sense, every judgement certainly 'claims' this right (though there are objections to saying that the right is 'implicitly asserted'). This means that we may demand of each judgement that it should declare to be true what is true. As craftsmen of knowledge, i.e. logicians in the ordinary sense, we must demand many things of our judgements with an eye to the further growth of knowledge. If these are unfulfilled, we reproach a judgement with logical imperfection, with 'groundlessness': the latter expression certainly involves a stretching of the word's ordinary meaning.

There are similar objections to Sigwart's statements about necessity. We read: 'If we are to talk intelligibly, all logical necessity ultimately presupposes the *existence* of a thinking subject whose nature it is to think in this manner' (*op. cit.* §33.7, p. 262).

---

[1] Cf. Sigwart's excellent distinction between the occasion of a connection and the ground of a decision (*op. cit.* p. 250).

Or we may follow up his statements regarding the difference between assertoric and apodeictic judgements, which Sigwart thinks unessential, 'since in every judgement uttered in full consciousness, the necessity of uttering it is also asserted' (*op. cit.* §31.1, p. 230 *ff.*). Sigwart has not given reciprocal distinctness to two totally different concepts of necessity. The subjective necessity, the compulsive conviction, which colours every judgement (or rather, appears in each such judgement when, remaining under its sway, we try to assert its contrary) is not distinguished from entirely different concepts of necessity, from apodeictic necessity, in particular, the peculiar consciousness in which we apprehend *law*, or *conformity to law*, with insight. The latter (really twofold) concept of necessity is really quite lacking in Sigwart. He quite ignores the fundamental equivocation which permits us to apply the term 'necessary', not only to our apodeictic *consciousness* of necessity, but also to its *objective correlate*, i.e. the law, or the conformity to the law, of which this consciousness represents the insight. It is only in the latter sense that the expressions 'It is necessary that . . .' and 'It is a law that . . .' gain their objective equivalence, and likewise the expressions '*S* is necessarily *P*' and '*S*'s being *P* is grounded on a law'.

It is naturally the second, *purely objective, ideal* notion, which underlies all apodeictic judgements in the objective sense of pure logic: it alone dominates and constitutes all theoretical unity, it determines the meaning of a hypothetical combination as an objectively ideal form of propositional truth, it connects the conclusion as a 'necessary' (ideally law-governed) consequence with the premisses.

How little Sigwart does justice to these differences, how deeply he is enmeshed in his psychologism, is shown by his treatments of Leibniz's fundamental distinction between *vérités de raison et celles de fait*. The 'necessity' of both sorts of truth, Sigwart thinks, is 'ultimately hypothetical', for 'from the fact that the contrary of a factual truth is not impossible *a priori*, it does not follow that it is not necessary for me to assert it, once the fact has occurred, or that the opposite assertion would be possible for one who knows the fact' (*op. cit.* §31.6, p. 239). And again: 'On the other hand, our possession of universal concepts on which propositions of identity rest, is ultimately a factual matter, which has to be there before the principle of identity can be applied to it, and so can generate a necessary judgement'. From which he thinks he can conclude that Leibniz's distinction 'in respect of necessity, breaks down' (*op. cit.* p. 240).

What is here maintained at the outset is quite correct. Every judgement, while I make it, represents a necessary assertion for me, as its denial, while I remain sure of my judgement, represents an impossibility for me. But does Leibniz intend this psychological necessity when he denies necessity, rationality to factual truths? It is likewise certain that one can know no law without possessing the universal concepts out of which it is built. This possession, certainly, like the whole knowledge of a law, is a factual matter. But did Leibniz call the knowing of a law 'necessary', and not rather the truth of the law that we know? The necessity of the *vérité de raison* surely accords quite well with the contingency of the act of judgement, to the extent that this amounts to insight and knowledge. Only through a confusion of two essentially different concepts of knowledge, a subjective, psychologistic concept and Leibniz's objective, idealistic one, can Sigwart wind up his argument by holding that Leibniz's distinction 'in respect of the character of necessity breaks down'. There is undeniably a subjective, experiential distinction which corresponds to the fundamental objective-ideal distinction between law and fact. If we never had experienced the consciousness of rationality, of apodeicticity in its characteristic distinction from the consciousness of facticity, we should not have possessed the concept of law, nor been able to distinguish fact from law. We should not have been able to distinguish generic (Ideal, law-determined) generality from universal (factual, contingent) generality, nor necessary (i.e. law-determined, generic) implication from factual (i.e. contingently universal) implication. This follows from the fact that concepts not given as combinations of known concepts (nor as combinations of known forms of combination) could only have arisen in us from an intuition of individual instances. Leibniz's *vérités de raison* are merely the laws, i.e. the ideal truths in the pure and strict sense, which are solely rooted in our concepts, which are given and known to us in pure, apodeictically evident generalizations. Leibniz's *vérités de fait* are individual truths; they form a sphere of propositions which, even if expressed in universal form, e.g. 'All southerners are hot-blooded', are, above all, assertions of existence.

§40 *Anthropologism in the Logic of B. Erdmann*

Sigwart provides us with no explicit discussion of the relativistic consequences implicit in his whole treatment of the fundamental concepts and problems of logic. The same holds of Wundt. Wundt's *Logic* gives even freer rein to psychological motives than Sigwart's: it contains long epistemological chapters, but hardly touches on ultimate doubts of principle. The same is true of Lipps, in whose *Logic* psychologism is so originally and consistently sustained, so free from compromise and so thoroughly carried out in all branches of the discipline, as has not been the case since the time of Beneke.

Erdmann is in a quite different case. At considerable length, and with instructive consistency, he decidedly comes down on the side of relativism, and points to possible changes in the laws of thought as a counter to the presumption 'which thinks that it can overleap the limits of our thought and find a standpoint for us beyond ourselves' (B. Erdmann, *Logik*, 1^1, §60, Nr. 370, p. 378 *f.*). It will be useful to consider his teaching further.

Erdmann begins by refuting the opposed standpoint. 'By a great majority', we read,

> it has been maintained, since Aristotle, that the necessity of these (logical) principles is unconditional, their validity therefore eternal ... The decisive reason for this has been sought in the impossibility of thinking judgements that contradict them. But this only proves that these principles mirror the essence of our presentation and thinking. For if they reveal this, it will not be possible to carry out their contradictories, since these seek to abolish the condition to which all our presentation and thinking, and so all our judgement, is bound (*op. cit.* Nr. 369, p. 375).

Some words on the sense of this argument, which seems to run: From the impossibility of successfully denying these principles, it follows that they mirror the essence of our presentation and thought, for, if they do so, this impossibility will necessarily follow. This cannot be the argument. For I cannot conclude from the fact that *A* follows from *B*, that *B* follows from *A*. The thought plainly is only that the impossibility of denying logical principles is explained by supposing that these principles 'mirror the essence of our presentation and thought'. By this last we mean that they are laws stating what generally pertains to human presentation and thought as such, 'that they state conditions to which all our presentation and thinking are bound'. Because they do this, judgements which contradict and deny them cannot, on Erdmann's view, be entertained.

I can, however, neither approve this inference, nor the assertions which enter into it. It seems quite possible to me that, just on account of those laws to which all a creature's (e.g. a man's) thinking is subject, individual judgements may be framed denying the validity of these laws. The denial of these laws *contradicts* their *assertion*, but the denial as a *real act* is quite compatible with the objective validity of the laws, or with the real operation of the conditions on which the laws pronounce generally. If contradiction is an ideal relation among the contents of judgements, we are here dealing with a real relation between an act of judgement and its governing conditions. If it were the case that the laws of the association of ideas basically governed human presentation and judgement, as the association-psychology actually taught, should we then, we may ask, have to reject as absurd and impossible that a *judgement* denying these laws should itself arise through their working? (Cf. §22 above.)

But even if the argument were sound, it must fail of its purpose. For the logical absolutist (*sit venia verbo*) could rightly object: The *laws of thought* of which Erdmann speaks, are either not those laws of which I and everyone else speaks, in which case my thesis is untouched, or he attributes a character to them which is quite at variance with their sense. And again he would object: The *impossibility of thinking* the negation of these laws, which those laws themselves are thought to entail, is either what I and everyone mean by such an impossibility, in which case it *supports* my conception, or it is something different, in which case I am again untouched.

As regards the *former* alternative, the principles of logic only express certain truths whose roots are to be found in the mere sense (content) of such concepts as Truth, Falsehood, Judgement (Proposition) etc. But Erdmann calls them 'laws of thought', laws which express the essence of *our human thinking*. He thinks they state the conditions by which all *human* presentation and thinking are bound, that they would change, as he thereupon explicitly says, with a change in human nature. They accordingly have, on Erdmann's view, a real content. This, however, contradicts their character as purely conceptual propositions. No proposition whose roots lie in mere concepts, which merely states what those concepts contain, and what is given with them, makes an assertion about the real. One need only consider the genuine sense of the laws of logic to see that they do not do this. Even where they speak of judgements, they do not refer to what psychological laws seek to indicate by this word, i.e. judgements as real experiences, but they mean judgements in the sense of statement-meanings *in specie*, meanings which retain their identity whether serving to found actual acts of assertion or not, and without regard as to who asserts them. If logical laws are treated as laws of the real (*Realgesetze*) which, like natural laws, govern our real presentation and judgement, their whole sense is altered, as has been discussed at length above.

One sees the danger of calling the principles of logic 'laws of thought'. They are only laws of thought, as we shall show more precisely in the next chapter, in the sense of being laws that have a part to play in the governance of our thinking, a mode of expression that shows that we are dealing with a practical function, a mode of use, and not with something that enters into their content. That they express the 'essence of thought' could be given a good sense in view of their normative function, provided the condition were fulfilled that in them lay the necessary and sufficient criteria for assessing the correctness of each judgement. Thus the matter was conceived by traditional rationalism, which never became clear that logical principles are no more than trivial generalities, with which our assertions may not clash on pain of being *absurd*, and that the harmony of thought with these norms guarantees no more than its formal consistency. On this ground it would be quite unfitting to go on speaking in this ideal sense of the 'essence of thinking', and to define it in terms of these laws[1]

---

[1] I am here thinking of all pure logical principles taken together. With the two or three 'laws of thought' in the traditional sense, the concept of formally consistent thought is not even defined, and everything traditionally said on this head I (and not only I) regard as erroneous. Each formal absurdity can be reduced to a contradiction, but only through the mediation of many other formal principles, e.g. syllogistic, arithmetical etc. Even in syllogistics there are at least a dozen principles. They can all be wonderfully proved – in sham proofs that presuppose themselves or equivalent propositions.

which, as we know, only keep us free from formal absurdity. It is a residue of rationalist prejudice that, even in our time, men speak of formal truth instead of formal consistency, a most deplorable, because misleading, play on the word 'truth'.

Let us pass, however, to our second point. The *impossibility* of denying the laws of thought is conceived by Erdmann as the impossibility of *performing* such a denial. But we logical absolutists think these two concepts so little identical, that we deny the non-performability altogether, while maintaining the impossibility. It is not the act of denial that is impossible – this would mean, since it pertains to something real, that it is a real-impossibility – but it is the negative proposition which forms its content that is impossible, and this content, being ideal, is ideally impossible, which means that it is absurd, and therefore self-evidently false. This ideal impossibility of the negative proposition does not clash with the real possibility of the negative act of judgement. The last remaining equivocation should thus be eliminated, and we should say, with complete clarity, that the proposition is absurd, but that the act of judging it is not causally ruled out.

In the actual thought of *normal* persons the actual denial of a law of thought does not usually occur, but it can scarcely be said that it cannot thus occur, since great philosophers like Epicurus and Hegel have denied the law of contradiction. Perhaps genius and madness are in this respect allied, perhaps there are also lunatic rejecters of the laws of thought: these will certainly also have to count as men. One should also reflect that it is in the same sense impossible to think the negation of the *consequences* of primitive logical principles as the negation of these principles themselves. It is well-known, however, that we can be mistaken regarding complicated syllogistic or arithmetical theorems, and this too is an unassailable argument. These are, however, disputed questions that do not touch anything essential. Logical impossibility, as absurdity of an ideal content of judgement, and psychological impossibility, as the non-performability of the corresponding act of judgement, are heterogeneous notions, even if the latter were to go with the former in all human cases, and the acceptance of absurdities were ruled out by natural laws. (Cf. the discussions of §22 in chapter IV.)

The logical absolutist makes use of the genuine logical impossibility of contradicting the laws of logic as an argument for the 'eternity' of these laws. What does such talk of eternity mean? Only that every judgement is bound by the pure laws of logic without regard to time and circumstances, or to individuals and species. This being bound is not meant psychologically in the sense of a thought-compulsion, but in the ideal sense of a norm: whoever judges differently, judges quite wrongly, no matter what species of mental creatures he may belong to. A relation to mental creatures plainly puts no restriction upon universality: norms for judgements bind judging beings, not stones. This is part of their sense, and so it would be ridiculous to treat stones and similar entities as in this respect exceptions. The logical absolutist's proof is now very simple. He will simply say: The following thought-chain is one into which *I* have insight. Such and such principles are valid, and their validity depends merely on unfolding the content of their concepts. Any proposition, i.e. any possible content of judgement in the ideal sense, is therefore absurd, if it either immediately or mediately clashes with such principles. Such a mediate clash merely means that a purely deductive chain runs from the hypothetical truth of such contents of judgement to the consequent untruth of the principles in question. If then such contents of judgement are absurd, and as such false, any *actual judgement* which has them as its contents will be incorrect, since a judgement is called 'correct' when what it judges, i.e. its content, is true, and incorrect when this content is false.

I stress the reference to every judgement, to make plain that the sense of this strict universality rules out any restriction *eo ipso*, and so also the restriction to human or other kinds of judging persons. I can compel nobody to see what I see. But I myself cannot doubt; I once more see, here where I have insight, i.e. am embracing truth itself, that all doubt would be mistaken. I therefore find myself at a point which I have either to recognize as the Archimedean point from which the world of doubt and unreason may be levered on its hinges, or which I may sacrifice at the peril of sacrificing all reason and knowledge. I see that this is the case, and that in the latter case – if it were then still reasonable to speak of reason or unreason – I should have to pack in all rational striving for truth, all assertion and all demonstration.

On all these points I find myself in conflict with our distinguished thinker who (following on the above citations) proceeds as follows:

The necessity thus established of the formal logical laws could only be an unconditional one ... if our knowledge of it were such as to guarantee that the essence of the thought we find in ourselves and expressed in them, were unchangeable, or were the only possible essence of thinking, that these conditions of *our* thinking were the conditions of any possible thinking. But we only know about our own thinking. We are not in a position to construct the picture of a thought different from our own, nor therefore that of a genus of thought for all these different sorts of thinking ... Words that *appear* to describe such a genus have no sense that we can work out which would satisfy the claims raised by such an appearance. For every attempt to work out what they describe is bound to the conditions of our presentation and thinking, moves within their limits.

If we lend to tempting expressions such as that of the 'essence of our thinking' a currency in purely logical contexts, if, following our analyses, we interpret them as the sum total of ideal laws which determine the formal consistency of our thinking, we should naturally also claim to give a strict proof of what Erdmann thinks unproveable: that the essence of thought is unchangeable, that it is unique in its possibility etc. It is clear, however, that Erdmann, in denying all this, does not stick to the only justifiable sense of 'essence of thinking', it is clear – as the quotation below will show more blatantly – that he thinks the laws of thought express the real essence of our thinking, that they are accordingly real laws, through which we have an immediate insight into the cognitive side of our common human constitution. This is unfortunately not the case. How could propositions which breathe no word regarding reality, which merely elucidate what is inseparably asserted in certain verbal or statement-meanings of great generality, guarantee important real knowledge regarding (as we read a little further on) the 'essence of mental events, and, in short, of our soul'?

If, on the other hand, such laws or others *did* give us insight into the real essence of thinking, we should come to quite other conclusions than our esteemed thinker. 'We only know about our thinking.' More precisely, as scientific psychologists we not only know about our own individual thinking, but a little about human thought in general, and a little less about animal thinking. A type of thinking which differs from ours in this real sense, and species of thinking beings that exemplify it, are at least things that we can conceive: they admit of a significant description, just as this is possible in the case of imaginary natural species. Böcklin has painted most magnificent centaurs and water-sprites with the most concrete naturalness – we believe in them, at least aesthetically. Who can say if the laws of nature allow of such? If, however, we enjoyed final insight into the law-governed ways in which organic elements could be combined to constitute the organism's living unity, if we knew what laws keep the stream of becoming in its typically formed channels, we could form scientifically exact concepts of many objectively possible species, and add these to those that *are* actual, and such possibilities could be as squarely discussed as are imaginary types of gravitation in the writings of theoretical physicists. The *logical possibility* of such fictions is at least unassailable, whether in the field of natural science or that of psychology. Only when we make a μετάβασις ἐις ἄλλο γένος, and mix up the realm of psychological laws of thought with those of pure logic, and, further, misinterpret the latter psychologistically, will there be a shadow of justification for asserting our incapacity to imagine other modes of thinking, and for denying to the words that seem to describe these any achievable sense. Quite possibly we can form 'no real idea' of such modes of thinking, quite possibly this is unachievable for us, but such unachievability in no case amounts to impossibility in the sense of what is senseless or absurd.

Possibly the following discussion will assist understanding. Theorems belonging to the theory of Abelian transcendents have no 'achievable sense' for babies in arms, or for 'babies in mathematics', as mathematicians jestingly call us laymen. As adults stand to children, as mathematicians stand to us laymen, so a higher species of thinking beings, e.g. of angels, could stand to men. Such words and concepts have no achievable sense for us, since certain peculiarities of our mental constitution stand in the way. A normal man takes about five years to understand the theory of Abelian functions or even to grasp its concepts. It might be the case that a millennium would be needed for a humanly constituted being to grasp angelic functions, though he can hardly hope to live as long as a century. But such an absolute unattainability, rooted in the natural limits of a specific constitution, would not be the one that absurdities and senseless statements offer. We are in one case concerned with propositions absolutely beyond our comprehension, though possibly consistent, and even valid in themselves. In the other case we understand propositions very well, but they are absurd, and we therefore 'cannot believe them', i.e. we see that, as absurd, they ought to be rejected.

Let us now look at the extreme consequences which Erdmann deduces from his premises. Basing ourselves on the 'empty postulate of an intuitive thought', we must, on his view, 'admit the *possible* existence of a thought differing in essence from our own', from which he draws the conclusion that

> logical laws only hold within the limits of our thinking, without our being able to guarantee that this thinking might not alter in character. For it is possible that such a transformation should occur, whether affecting all or only some of these laws, since they are not all analytically derivable from one of them. It is irrelevant that this possibility is unsupported by the deliverances of our self-consciousness regarding our thinking. Though nothing presages its actualization, it remains a possibility. We can only take our thought as it now is, and are not in a position to fetter its future character to its present one. We are, in particular, incapable of so grasping the essence of our mental states, in brief of our soul, that we can deduce therefrom the unalterability of thought as it is given to us.[1]

According to Erdmann,

> we cannot help admitting that all the propositions whose contradictories we cannot envisage in thought, are only necessary if we presuppose the character of our thought, as definitely given in our experience: they are not absolutely necessary, or necessary in all possible conditions. On this view our logical principles retain their necessity for our thinking, but this necessity *is not seen as absolute, but as hypothetical* [in our sense, as relative]. We cannot help assenting to them – such is the nature of our presentation and thinking. They are universally valid, provided our thinking remains

[1] Cf. *op. cit*. Nr. 369, sub e, pp. 377–8. Once men had accustomed themselves to the notion of a change in logical thinking, the thought of its development was not far. According to G. Ferrero, *Les lois psychologiques du Symbolisme, Paris 1895* – I read from a report by A. Larson in the *Zeitschr. f. Philos. vol. 113, p. 85* – 'Logic should become positive and should present rules of inference in connection with the period and stage of a culture, since even logic alters with the development of the brain . . . That pure logic and deductive methods were previously preferred, is due to mental laziness. Metaphysics has remained the colossal monument to this mental laziness up to this day, fortunately only operative among a few retarded thinkers.'

the same. They are necessary, since to think means for us to pre-suppose them, as long, that is, as they express the essence of our thinking (cf. *op. cit.* Nr. 370, p. 378).

I need not say, after my previous statement, how little I think these consequences are valid. It is certainly possible that there is a mental life essentially different from our own. Certainly we can only take our thinking for what it is, and it would certainly be stupid to try to deduce any permanence from 'the essence of our mental states, in brief of our soul'. But from this the totally different possibility does not follow, that changes in our specific constitution could affect all or some logical principles, and that such principles have a merely hypothetical necessity. All this is absurd, absurd in the pregnant sense which has always been employed here, a sense strictly scientific and free from emotive tincture. It is the curse of our ambiguous logical terminology that such doctrines can still come up and can deceive serious thinkers. If the primitive conceptual distinctions of elementary logic had been completed, and terminology clarified on their basis, and we no longer dragged around with the wretched equivocations that attach to all logical terms – law of thought, form of thought, real and formal truth, presentation, judgement, proposition, concept, character, property, ground, necessity etc. – it would not be possible for absurdities as gross as relativism to be theoretically represented in logic and epistemology, nor could they have the plausibility by which even eminent thinkers are blinded.

Talk of the possibility of variable 'laws of thought', as *psychological* laws of presentation and judgement differing in many respects for varying species of mental being, and even from time to time for one and the same species – all this has a good sense. For psychological 'laws' are for us 'empirical laws', approximate generalities of coexistence and succession, relating to matters of fact which may in one case be thus, in another case otherwise. We even gladly allow the possibility of varying *normative* laws of presentation and judgement. Normative laws can certainly be adapted to the specific constitution of judging beings, and so vary with them. This obviously affects the rules of practical logic as a doctrine of method, as well as the methodological prescriptions of the separate sciences. Mathematical angels may no doubt use other methods of calculation than ours – does this mean that they may have different axioms and theorems? This question carries us further. Talk of variable laws of thought only becomes absurd when we are referring to the laws of *pure logic* (to which may be added the pure laws of the theory of numbers, of ordinals, of sets etc.). The vague phrase 'normative laws of thought' by which these are likewise designated, favours the general temptation to dump them all in together with our former psychologically founded rules of thinking. They, however, are purely theoretical truths, ideal in character, rooted in their own semantic content and not straying beyond it. They can accordingly not be affected by any actual or imagined change in the world of 'matter of fact'.

We must here keep in mind a threefold opposition: not merely the opposition between *practical rule* and *theoretical law*, or that between *ideal law* and *real law*, but also the opposition between an *exact law* and an *empirical law* (i.e. a statement of for-the-most-part or average universality, governed by the principle 'No law without its exception'). If our insight extended to the *exact* laws of mental process, these too would be eternal and unchangeable, as are the laws of theoretical natural science; they would therefore hold even if there were no mental processes at all. If all gravitating masses were eliminated, the law of gravitation would not thereby be suspended: it would merely lack the possibility of factual application. For it tells us nothing regarding the existence of gravitating masses, only regarding what pertains to gravitating masses as such. (No doubt, as acknowledged above, an idealizing fiction plays its part in the setting up of exact laws of nature: here we ignore this, confining ourselves to the mere intention of such laws.) As soon as the exact character of logical principles is conceded, and they are seen in their exactness, the possibility of their being changed by changes in the collocations of what actually is, and of consequent transformations of zoological and mental species, is ruled out, and the 'eternal' validity of such principles guaranteed.

A defender of psychologism could here oppose our position by saying that the truth of logical principles, like all truth, has its seat in knowledge, and that knowledge as a mental experience is of course subject to psychological laws. But, without exhaustive discussion of the sense in which truth has its seat in knowledge, I yet point out that no change in psychological facts can turn knowledge into error, or error into knowledge. The arising and the perishing of phenomenal cases of knowledge, no doubt depends on psychological conditions, as does the arising and perishing of other mental phenomena, e.g. sensory ones. But, as no mental happenings can cause the Red I intuit not to be a Colour, but a Tone, or the lower of two tones to be the higher, or, more generally, as what rests on the general nature of an experience is elevated above all possible change, since all change affects what is individual, and makes no sense in regard to concepts, so the same holds of 'contents' of acts of knowledge. It pertains to the notion of knowledge that its content has the character of truth, a character which does not pertain to the evanescent phenomena of knowledge, but to their selfsame content, to the ideal, universal element we have in mind when we say, e.g., I know that $a+b = b+a$, and countless other persons know it too. Of course errors can develop out of cases of knowledge, e.g. through fallacious inferences, but this does not turn knowledge as such into error, for one is merely causally tied up with the other. It may likewise be the case that a species of beings capable of judgement may develop no knowledge, that what they suppose true may always be false, and what they suppose false true. This would leave truth and falsehood intrinsically unaffected: they are essentially properties of the contents of such judgements, not of judgements as acts. They pertain to such contents even if no one recognizes their presence. Colours, Tones, Triangles etc., always have the essential properties of Colours, Tones, Triangles etc., whether anyone in the world knows such a fact or not.

The possibility, therefore, that Erdmann has sought to establish, that other beings might have quite different logical principles, cannot be accepted. An absurd possibility is an impossibility. One need only try to think out what his doctrine implies: that there might be peculiar beings, logical supermen, as it were, for whom *our logical principles do not hold*, but rather quite different principles, so that every truth for us is a falsehood for them. For them it is the case that the mental phenomena they are experiencing are not experienced by them. That we and they exist may be true for us, but is false for them etc. We everyday logicians would say: Such beings are mad, they talk of truth, yet destroy its laws, they say they have their own laws of thought, but they deny those on which the possibility of any such laws depends. They make assertions, yet countenance the denial of what they assert. Yes and No, truth and error, existence and non-existence, lose all their distinctness in their thought. Only they fail to notice their absurdities, which we notice, and see to be absurd in the most luminous fashion. Someone who tolerates such possibilities is divided only by a hairsbreadth from the extremest scepticism: the subjectivity of truth is applied to the species instead of to the individual person. He is a specific relativist in the sense defined above, and is exposed to the objections we developed, which we shall not here repeat. For the rest I see no reason why we should stop at the boundaries of imaginary racial differences. Why not recognize real racial differences, differences between sanity and insanity, and all individual differences, as having an equal right?

Perhaps a relativist will object to our appeal to inner evidence, to the evidence with which we see the absurdity of the possibility here suggested, by repeating what we quoted above, 'that it is irrelevant that this possibility is unsupported by our self-observation', since it is obvious that our thought cannot be at variance with its own forms. Ignoring such psychologistic interpretation of our thought-forms, which was refuted above, we shall merely point out that such an expedient means absolute scepticism. If we have lost faith in the inwardly evident, how can we rationally make and sustain assertions? Perhaps, inasmuch as other people may be constituted as we are, and may incline to similar judgements in virtue of identical laws of thinking? But how can we know this, if we can know nothing whatever? Without insight, there can be no knowledge.

It is really odd that men are prepared to put their trust in statements so dubious as those regarding what is common to human beings, but not in those mere trivialities, which though offering us only the slenderest instruction, grant us the clearest insight into what little they say. In this we can at least find nothing which relates to thinking beings and their specific peculiarities.

The relativist cannot secure a temporarily improved position by saying that he is being treated as an extreme relativist: he is only a relativist as regards logical principles, while leaving other truths unassailed. This will not enable him to escape the general objections to specific relativism. For, if one relativizes the basic truths of logic, one relativizes all truth whatever. It is enough to consider the content of the law of contradiction and to draw some immediate consequences.

Erdmann keeps far from such half-measures: he has founded his Logic on the *relativistic concept of truth* which his doctrine demands. His definition runs: 'The truth of a judgement consists in the fact that the logical immanence is subjectively, more specifically put, objectively, certain, and that the predicative expression of this immanence represents a necessity for thought' (*op. cit*. Nr. 278, p. 275). For an object is for Erdmann what is presented to us, and this in its turn is expressly identified with our presentation. In the same way, his 'objective or universal certainty' is only apparently objective, since it is 'based on the general agreement of judging subjects' (*op. cit*. p. 274). The expression 'objective truth' is to be found in Erdmann's writing, but he identifies it with 'universal validity', i.e. validity for all. This is divided for him into certainty for all, and, if I understand him rightly, also into a necessity of thought for all. This is just what is meant by the above definition. It might seem a problem how, on this definition, we should ever rise to the justified assertion of even a single case of objective truth, and how we can escape the infinite regress that his definition demands, and of which the distinguished thinker is fully conscious. He does not, unfortunately, tell us enough on this point. The judgements in which we assert that others will agree with us are of course not, as he says, this agreement itself, but how does this help us? And how are we helped by our subjective certainty regarding such agreement? Our assertion would only be *justified* if we knew of the agreement, and this means if we perceived its truth. One might also ask how one ever came to be subjectively certain of the agreement of *everyone*, and, ignoring this difficulty, whether it is at all proper to demand such universal certainty, and whether truth may not rather be the appurtenance of a select few than possessed by everyone.

CHAPTER EIGHT

The Psychologistic Prejudices

so far our attack has been mainly upon the consequences of psychologism. We now turn against its arguments: we shall try to show that what it regards as obvious truths are in fact delusive prejudices.

§41 *First prejudice*

A first prejudice runs: Prescriptions which regulate what is mental must obviously have a mental basis. It is accordingly self-evident that the normative principles of knowledge must be grounded in the psychology of knowledge.

One's delusion vanishes as soon as one abandons general argumentation and turns to the 'things themselves'.

We must first put an end to a distorted notion which both parties share, by pointing out that logical laws, taken in and for themselves, are not normative propositions at all in the sense of prescriptions, i.e. propositions which tell us, as part of their *content*, how one *should* judge. One must always distinguish between laws that *serve as norms* for our knowledge-activities, and laws which include normativity in their thought-content, and *assert* its universal obligatoriness.

Let us take as an example the well-known syllogistic principle we expressed in the words: A mark of a mark is also a mark of the thing itself. This statement would be commendably brief if its expression were not also an obvious falsehood.[1] To express it concretely, we shall have to adjust ourselves to a few more words. 'It is true of every pair of characters A, B, that if every object which has the character A also has the character B, and if any definite object S has the character A, then it also has the character

---

[1] A mark of a mark is, generally speaking, plainly *not* a mark of the thing. If the principle meant what it literally says, we could infer: This blotting-paper is red, Red is a colour, therefore this blotting-paper is a colour.

B.' That this proposition contains the faintest thought of norm-ativity must be strongly denied. We can employ our proposition for normative purposes, but it is not therefore a norm. Anyone who judges that every *A* is also *B*, and that a certain *S* is *A*, ought also to judge that this *S* is *B*. Everyone sees, however, that this proposition is not the original proposition of logic, but one that has been derived from it by bringing in the thought of normativity.

The same obviously holds of all syllogistic laws, as of all laws of pure logic as such.[1] But not of such laws alone. A capacity for normative use is shared by the truths of other theoretical dis-ciplines, and above all by those of pure mathematics, which are usually kept separate from logic.[2] The well-known principle

$$(a+b)(a-b) = a^2 - b^2$$

tells us, e.g. that the product of the sum and the difference of any two numbers equals the difference of their squares. Here there is no reference to our judging and the manner in which it *should* be conducted; what we have before us is a theoretical law, not a practical rule. If, however, we consider the corresponding practical proposition: 'To arrive at the product of the sum and difference of two numbers, one should find the difference of their squares', we have conversely uttered a practical rule and not a theoretical law. Here, too, the transformation of law into rule involves a bringing in of the notion of normativity; the rule is the obvious, apodeictic consequence of the law, but it none the less differs from it in thought-content.

---

[1] In this view, that the normative notion of 'ought' does not form part of the content of logical laws, I am glad to find myself in agreement with Natorp, who has recently made the brief and clear remark in his *Sozialpädagogik* (Stuttgart, 1899), §4, that 'logical principles, we maintain, are as little about what people actually think in such and such circumstances, as they are about what they ought to think'. He says of the equational reasonings 'If *A* = *B* and *B* = *C*, *A* = *C*' that 'I per-ceive its truth when only the terms to be compared, and the relations given together with them, are before me, without having to think in the least of the actual or proper conduct of some corresponding act of thought' (pp. 20–1). There are certain other equally important *rapprochements* between these Prolegomena and the distinguished thinker's present work, which unhappily came too late to assist in forming and expounding these thoughts. Two previous writings of Natorp, the above quoted article from *Phil. Monatshefte*, xxiii and the *Einleitung in die Psychologie*, stimulated me, however – though other points in them provoked me to controversion.

[2] 'Pure' or 'formal' mathematics, as I use the term, includes all pure arithmetic and theory of manifolds, but not geometry. Geometry corresponds in pure mathe-matics to the theory of a three-dimensional Euclidean manifold. This manifold is the generic Idea of space, but not space itself.

We can even go further. It is clear that *any* theoretical truth belonging to *any* field of theory, can be used in a like manner as the foundation for a universal norm of correct judgement. The laws of logic are not at all peculiar in this respect. In their proper nature, they are not normative but theoretical truths, and as such we can employ them, as we can the truths of all other disciplines, as norms for our judgement.

We cannot, however, treat the general persuasion that the laws of logic are norms of thinking as quite baseless, nor the obviousness with which it impresses us as a mere delusion. These laws must have some intrinsic *prerogative* in the regulation of our thought. But does this mean that the idea of regulation, or of an 'ought', must therefore form part of the content of such laws? Can it not *follow* from that content with self-evident necessity? In other words: May not the laws of logic and pure mathematics have a distinctive meaning-content which gives them a *natural right* to regulate our thought?

This simple treatment shows us how both sides have made their mistakes.

The anti-psychologists went wrong by making the regulation of knowledge the 'essence', as it were, of the laws of logic. The purely theoretical character of formal logic, and its identity of character with formal mathematics, were thereby insufficiently recognized. It was correctly seen that the set of laws treated in traditional syllogistic theory were remote from psychology. Their natural right to regulate knowledge was recognized, for which reason they must be made the kernel of all practical logic. The difference between the proper content of these laws, and their function, their practical application, was, however, ignored. Men failed to see that so-called basic laws of logic were not in themselves norms, though they could be used normatively. Concern with this normative use had led men to speak of such laws as laws of thought, and so it appeared that these laws, too, had a psychological content, and that their only difference from what are ordinarily called psychological laws lay in this normative function, not possessed by other psychological laws.

The psychologistic thinkers, on the other hand, went wrong in putting forward a presumed axiom whose invalidity we may expose in a few words: It is entirely obvious that each general truth, whether psychological or not, serves to found a rule for correct judgement, but this not only assures us of the meaningful possibility, but even of the actual existence of rules of judgement which do not have their basis in psychology.

Not all rules which set standards for correct judgement are on that account *logical* rules. It is, however, evident that, of the genuinely logical rules which form the nucleus of a technology of scientific thinking, only one set permits and demands a psychological establishment: the technical precepts concerning the acquisition and criticism of scientific knowledge. The remaining, much more important group consists of normative transformations of laws, which belong solely to the objective or ideal content of the science. Psychological logicians, even such as are of the stature of a Mill or a Sigwart, treat science from its subjective side (as a methodology of the specifically human acquisition of knowledge), rather than from its objective side (as the Idea of the theoretical unity of truth), and therefore lay one-sided stress on the methodological tasks of logic. In doing so they ignore the *fundamental difference between the norms of pure logic and the technical rules of a specifically human art of thought*. These are totally different in character in their content, origin and function. The laws of logic, seen in their original intent, concern only what is ideal, while these methodological propositions concern only what is real. If the former spring from immediately evident axioms, the latter spring from empirical facts, belonging mainly to psychology. If the formulation of the former promotes our purely theoretical interests, and gives only subsidiary practical help, the latter, on the other hand, have an immediate practical aim, and they only give indirect help to our theoretical interests, in so far as they aim at the methodical progress of scientific knowledge.

§42 *Elucidations*

Every theoretical statement, we saw above, permits of a normative transformation. But the rules for correct judgement which thus arise, are not, in general, such as logic, considered as a technology, requires: few of them are, as it were, predestined to normativity. If such a logical technology is to be of real help in our scientific endeavours, it must not presuppose that full knowledge of the complete sciences which we hope to achieve by its means. We shall not be helped by the mechanical restatement of all given theoretical knowledge as norms: what we need are general norms, extending beyond all particular sciences to the critical evaluation of theoretical knowledge and its methods in general, as well as practical rules for its promotion.

This is exactly what logic as a technology aims at, and if it aims at this as a scientific discipline, it must itself presuppose certain items of theoretical knowledge. It is clear from the start that it must attach exceptional worth to all knowledge resting only on the notions of Truth, Proposition, Subject, Predicate, Object, Property, Ground and Consequent, Relation and Relatum etc. For all science in its objective, theoretical aspects, i.e. in respect of *what* it tells us, consists of truths, truth pertains to propositions, all propositions have subjects and predicates, and refer by way of these to things or properties, propositions are connected as grounds and consequents etc. Those truths, it is now clear, which have their roots in such *essential constituents of all science considered as an objective theoretical unity*, truths which, accordingly, cannot be thought away without thinking away all that gives science as such its objective purchase and sense, such truths obviously provide the fundamental standards by which we can decide whether anything claiming to be a science, or to belong to one, whether as premiss, conclusion, syllogism, induction, proof or theory, really lives up to its intentions, or does not rather stand in an *a priori* conflict with the ideal conditions of the possibility of theory and science as such. Men should admit that truths which have their roots in the concepts which constitute the objectively conceived Idea of Science, cannot also belong to the field of any particular science. They should see that such truths, being ideal, cannot have their home-ground in the sciences of matter of fact, and therefore not in psychology. If these facts were realized, our case would be won, and it would be impossible to dispute the existence of a peculiar science of pure logic, absolutely independent of all other scientific disciplines, which delimits the concepts constitutive of the Idea of System or of theoretical unity, and which goes on to investigate the theoretical connections whose roots lie solely in these concepts. This science would have the unique peculiarity of itself, *qua* form, underlying the content of its laws; the elements and theoretical connections of which it, as a systematic unity of truths, consists, are governed by the very laws which form part of its theoretical content.

That the science which deals with all sciences in respect of their form, should *eo ipso* deal with itself, may sound paradoxical, but involves no inner conflict. The simplest example will make this clear. The law of contradiction governs all truth, and since it is itself a truth, governs itself. To realize what such self-government means one need only apply the law of contradiction to itself: the resultant proposition is an obvious truism, having none of the marks of the remarkable or the questionable. This is invariably the case where pure logic is used to regulate itself.

This pure logic is therefore the first and most essential foundation of methodological logic. The latter, however, has other quite different foundations contributed by psychology. Every science, as we stated above, permits of a double treatment: it is, on the one hand, an aggregate of human devices for acquiring, systematically delimiting and expounding this or that territory of truth. These devices are called methods, e.g. calculation by abacus or slide-rule, by written signs on a slate, by this or that computer, by logarithmic, sine- or tangent-tables, astronomical methods involving cross-wires or telescopes, physiological methods involving microscopy, staining etc. All these methods, and also all forms of exposition, are adapted to the human constitution as it at present normally is, and are in fact in part expressive of contingent, national features. Even physiological organization has a not unimportant part to play. Would our most refined optical instruments be of much use to a being whose sense of sight was attached to an end-organ differing considerably from our own?

But all science permits of quite another treatment; it can be considered in regard to *what* it teaches, in regard to its theoretical content. What each statement states is – in the ideal case – a truth. No truth is, however, isolated in science: it occurs in combination with other truths in theoretical connections bound by relations of ground and consequent. This objective content of science, to the extent that it really lives up to its intent, is quite independent of the scientist's subjectivity, of the peculiarities of human nature in general. It is objective truth.

Pure logic aims at this ideal side of science, in respect of its form. It does not aim at the peculiar material of the various special sciences, or the peculiarity of their truths and forms of combination: it aims at what relates to truths and theoretical combinations of truths as such. For this reason *every* science must, on its objective, theoretical side, conform to the laws of logic, which are of an entirely ideal character.

In this way these ideal laws acquire a methodological significance, which they also have since mediate justification is provided by proofs whose norms are merely normative transformations of the ideal laws whose sole grounds lie in logical categories. The characteristic peculiarities of proofs mentioned in the first chapter of this work (§7) all have their origin and complete explanation in the fact that inner evidence in demonstration – whether in the syllogism, in connected, apodeictic proof, or in the unity of the most comprehensive, rational theory, or also in the unity of an argument in probabilities – is simply our consciousness of an ideal law. Purely logical reflection, whose first historic awakening occurred in the genius of Aristotle, abstracts the underlying law itself, and then brings the multiplicity of laws discoverable in this manner, and at first seen in isolation, under primitive basic laws, and so creates a scientific system which, in a purely deductive order, permits the derivation of all possible laws of pure logic, all possible forms of syllogisms, proofs etc. The forms of logic transform themselves into norms or rules telling us how we should conduct proofs, and – in relation to possible illegal formations – into rules telling us how we should not conduct them.

Norms accordingly fall into two classes. One class of norms regulates all proof and all apodeictic connection *a priori*; it is purely ideal, and only relates to our human knowledge by way of a self-evident application. The other class is empirical, and relates essentially to the specifically human side of the science. It consists of what might be called mere auxiliary devices or substitutes for proofs (above §9). It has its roots in our general human constitution, in the main, in our mental constitution, since this is more important for logical technology, but also in part in our physical constitution.[1]

---

[1] Elementary arithmetic provides good examples of this last. A being that could intuit three-dimensional arrangements (with difference of sign) as clearly and with as much practical mastery as men are able to intuit two-dimensional arrangements would possibly have quite different methods of calculation. My *Philosophie der Arithmetik* deals with such questions, and, in particular, with the influence of physical circumstances on methodical set-up, pp. 275 f., 312 ff.

§43 *A look at the opposed arguments of idealism. Their defects and their justified sense*

In the dispute over a psychological or objective foundation for logic, I, accordingly, occupy an intermediate position. The antipsychologists looked by preference on the ideal laws, called by us 'purely logical', while the psychologistic part fixed their gaze on the methodological rules that we have classed as 'anthropological'. This difference of orientation barred mutual understanding. The psychologistic party were little inclined to do justice to the worthwhile core of their opponents' arguments, but this is understandable when we reflect how psychological motives and confusions played their part in these arguments, despite all pretensions to avoid them. The actual content of works which claim to expound 'formal' or 'pure' logic, must have confirmed the psychologistic party in their negative attitude, and must have made them feel that the projected discipline really only dealt with a piece of shamefaced, and therefore arbitrarily restricted psychology of cognition, or with a set of rules for cognition founded upon this. The antipsychologistic party were not at least in a position to put stress in their argument on the fact that psychology deals with laws of nature, whereas logic deals with normative laws (cf. above §19, and the citation from Drobisch in §13). The *opposite of a law of nature*, as an empirically based rule regarding what in fact is and occurs, *is not a normative law* or a prescription, but an *ideal law*, in the sense of one based purely on concepts, Ideas, purely conceived essences, and so not empirical. To the extent that formal logicians, in their talk of normative laws, were concerned with this purely conceptual, *a priori* character, their arguments hit on a point that was undoubtedly correct. But they overlooked the theoretical character of the laws of pure logic, they failed to recognize the difference between theoretical laws destined by their content to the regulation of cognition, and normative laws which are *intrinsically* and *essentially* prescriptive.

It is not even correct to say that the opposition between truth and falsehood is irrelevant to psychology, for truth is certainly apprehended in knowledge, and the ideal thereby becomes a determination of a real experience. But the propositions, on the other hand, which treat of this determination in its conceptual purity are not laws of real psychical happenings: the psychologistic party were wrong in this regard. Ignoring the essence of the ideal in general, they also ignored the ideality of truth. This important point will require further and fuller discussion.

The final argument of the antipsychologistic party likewise combines truth with error. Since no logic, whether formal or methodological, can provide criteria by which every truth can be recognized as a truth, there is no circle in seeking a psychological basis for logic. It is, however, one thing to ask for such a psychological basis for logic (understanding 'logic' in the usual sense of a technology), and quite a different thing to seek such a basis for the theoretically closed group of logical propositions, that we styled 'purely logical'. It is in this respect quite repugnant (though only in a few circular cases) to deduce propositions rooted in the essential constituents of all theory, and so in the conceptual form of the systematic content of science as such, from the contingent content of some special science, and a factual science at that. Let one but conceive the principle of contradiction clearly, and then seek its foundation in some special science, let one conceive of a truth which rests on the sense of truth as such, and then base it on truths about numbers, stretches etc., or even about physical or mental matters of fact. The repugnance of such proceedings was at least clear to the exponents of formal logic, except that their confusion of purely logical with normative laws or criteria, obscured their good ideas and rendered them inoperative. The repugnancy consists basically in the fact that propositions relating to mere form (i.e. to the conceptual elements of scientific theory as such) were to be deduced from propositions having a wholly heterogeneous content.[1] In the case of primitive principles like the law of contradiction, the *modus ponens* etc., this repugnancy would plainly amount to a circle in so far as the deduction of these principles would involve steps that presupposed them – not in the form of premises, but in the form of deductive principles upon whose validity the sense and validity of the deduction depends. One could, in this respect, speak of a *reflective circle*, as against the usual, direct *circulus in demonstrando*, where premises and conclusions overlap.

Of all sciences only pure logic escapes such objections, since its

---

[1] The impossibility of theoretical connections between heterogeneous fields, and the nature of the heterogeneity in question, has of course not been sufficiently investigated in logic.

premisses are homogeneous in respect of their objects with the conclusions they establish. Pure logic further escapes circularity in that, in a given deduction, it never proves principles which the deduction itself presupposes, and that it never proves principles that *every* deduction presupposes, but that it simply lays them down as axioms at the summit of all its deductions. Pure logic, therefore, has the extraordinarily difficult task of analytically ascending to such axioms as are indispensable starting-points for deduction, and are also irreducible to one another without a direct or a reflective circle, and then constructing and arranging a deduction for the theorems of logic – of which the rules of the syllogism form a small part – so that at each step, not only the *premisses*, but also the *principles* of our deductive transitions, are either among our axioms, or among our previously proven theorems.

§44 *Second prejudice*

To confirm his first prejudice that rules for cognition must rest on the psychology of cognition, the psychologistic party appeals to the actual content of logic (cf. the arguments of §15 above, p. 52, par. 2). What is logic about? Everywhere it concerns itself with presentations and judgements, with syllogisms and proofs, with truth and probability, with necessity and possibility, with ground and consequent, and with other closely related or connected concepts. But what can be thought of under such headings but mental phenomena and formations? This is obvious in the case of presentations and judgements. Syllogisms, however, are proofs of judgements by means of judgements, and proof is plainly a mental activity. Talk of truth, probability, necessity, possibility etc., likewise concerns judgements: what they refer to can only be manifested or experienced in judgements. Is it not, therefore, strange that one should wish to exclude from psychology propositions and theories which relate to psychological phenomena? In this regard the distinction between purely logical and methodological propositions is pointless, the objection affects both equally. Every attempt, therefore, to extrude even a part of logic from psychology, on ground of its pretended 'purity', must count as radically mistaken.

*§45 Refutation. Pure mathematics would likewise be made
a branch of psychology*

Obvious as all this may seem, it *must* be mistaken. This is shown
by the absurd consequences which, as we know, psychologism
cannot escape. There is, however, another reason for misgiving:
the natural affinity between purely logical and mathematical
doctrine, which has often led to an assertion of their theoretical
unity.

We have already mentioned by the way that even Lotze taught
that mathematics must be regarded as 'an independently developed branch of general logic'. 'Only a practically motivated
division of teaching' can, he thinks, blind us to the fact that
mathematics 'has its whole home-ground in the general field of
logic' (*Logik*, ed. 2, §18, p. 34 and §112, p. 138). To which Riehl
adds that 'one could well say that logic coincides with the general
part of purely formal mathematics (taken in the sense of H.
Hankel)' (A. Riehl, *Der philosophische Kritizismus und seine Bedeutung
für die positive Wissenschaft*, vol. II, Part 1, p. 226). However this
may be, an argument that is correct for logic must be approved
in the case of arithmetic as well. Arithmetic sets up laws for
numbers, for their relations and combinations: numbers, however, are the products of colligation and counting, which are
mental activities. Relations arise from relating activities, combinations from acts of combination. Adding and multiplying,
subtracting and dividing – these are merely mental processes.
That they require sensuous supports makes no difference, since
this is true of any and every act of thinking. Sums, products,
differences and quotients, and whatever may be determined in
arithmetical propositions, are merely mental processes, and must
as such obey mental laws. It may be highly desirable that modern
psychology with its earnest pursuit of exactness should be
widened to include mathematical theories, but it would hardly be
much elevated by the inclusion of mathematics itself as one of its
parts. For the heterogeneity of the two sciences cannot be denied.
The mathematician, on the other hand, would merely smile if
psychological studies were pressed upon him as supposedly
providing a better and deeper grounding for his theoretical
pronouncements. He would rightly say that mathematics and
psychology belong to such different worlds, that the very thought

of interchange among them was absurd: here, if anywhere, talk of a μετάβασις εἰς ἄλλο γένος is applicable.[1]

§46 *The territory to be investigated by pure logic is, like that of mathematics, an ideal territory*

These objections may have taken our argument far afield, but, when we attend to their content, they help us to state the basic errors of our opponents' position. *The comparison of pure logic with pure mathematics*, its mature sister discipline, which no longer needs fight for its right to independent existence, provides us with a reliable *Leitmotiv*. We shall first glance at mathematics.

No one regards the theories of pure mathematics, e.g. the pure theory of numbers, as 'parts or branches of psychology', though we should have no numbers without counting, no sums without addition, no products without multiplication etc. The patterns of all arithmetical operations refer back to certain mental acts of arithmetical operation, and only in reflection upon these can we 'show' what a total, sum, product etc., is. In spite of the 'psychological origin' of arithmetical concepts, everyone sees it to be a fallacious μετάβασις to demand that mathematical laws should be psychological. How is this to be explained? Only *one* answer is possible. Counting and arithmetical operation as *facts*, as mental acts proceeding in time, are of course the concern of psychology, since it is the empirical science of mental facts in general. Arithmetic is in a totally different position. Its domain of research is known, it is completely and exhaustively determined by the familiar series of ideal species 1, 2, 3 ... In this sphere there can be no talk of individual facts, of what is temporally definite. Numbers, Sums and Products and so forth are not such casual acts of counting, adding and multiplying etc., as proceed here and there. They also differ obviously from *presentations* in which they are given. The number Five is not my own or anyone else's

[1] See in addition the fine statement of Natorp 'Über objektive und subjektive Begründung der Erkenntnis', *Philos. Monatshefte*, XXIII, p. 265 *f*. Cf. also G. Frege's stimulating work *Die Grundlagen der Arithmetik* (1884), p. vi *f*. I need hardly say that I no longer approve of my own fundamental criticisms of Frege's antipsychologistic position set forth in my *Philosophie der Arithmetik*, I, pp. 124–32. I may here take the opportunity, in relation to all of the discussions of these Prolegomena, to refer to the Preface of Frege's later work *Die Grundgesetze der Arithmetik*, vol. I (Jena, 1893).

counting of five, it is also not my presentation or anyone else's presentation of five. It is in the latter regard a possible *object* of acts of presentation, whereas, in the former, it is the ideal *species* of a form whose concrete *instances* are found in what becomes objective in certain acts of counting, in the collective whole that these constitute. In no case can it be regarded without absurdity as a *part* or *side* of a mental experience, and so not as something real. If we make clear to ourselves what the number Five truly is, if we conceive of it adequately, we shall first achieve an articulate, collective presentation of this or that set of five objects. In this act a collection is intuitively given in a certain formal articulation, and so as an instance of the number-species in question. Looking at this intuited individual, we perform an 'abstraction', i.e. we not only isolate the non-independent moment of collective form in what is before us, but we apprehend the Idea in it: the number Five as the species of the form swims into our conscious sphere of reference. What we are now meaning is not this individual instance, not the intuited object as a whole, not the form immanent in it, but still inseparable from it: what we mean is rather the *ideal form-species*, which is absolutely one in the sense of arithmetic, in whatever mental act it may be individuated for us in an intuitively constituted collective, a species which is accordingly untouched by the contingency, temporality and transience of our mental acts. Acts of counting arise and pass away and cannot be meaningfully mentioned in the same breath as numbers.

Arithmetical propositions are concerned with such ideal unities ('lowest species' in a heightened sense quite different from that of empirical classes), and this holds both of numerical propositions (arithmetical singulars) and of algebraic propositions (arithmetical generalizations). They tell us nothing about what is real, neither about the real things counted, nor about the real acts in which they are counted, in which such and such indirect numerical characteristics are constituted for us. Concrete numbers and numerical propositions belong in the scientific fields to which the relevant concrete units belong: propositions about arithmetical thought-processes belong in psychology. In strict propriety, arithmetical propositions say nothing about 'what is contained in our mere number-presentations': as little as they speak of other presentations, do they speak of ours. They are rather concerned with absolute numbers and number-combinations in their abstract purity and ideality. The propositions of universal arithmetic – the nomology of arithmetic we may call it – are laws rooted *in the ideal essence of the genus Number*. The *ultimate* singulars which come within the range of these laws, are *ideal singulars*: they are the determinate numbers, i.e. the lowest specific differences of the genus number. It is to these singulars that arithmetically singular propositions relate, propositions which belong to the arithmetic of definite numbers. These arise through the application of universal arithmetical laws to numerically specific numbers, they express what is purely part of the ideal essence of these numbers. None of these propositions reduces to one that has empirical generality, not even to the widest case of such generality, one that applies without exception to the entire real world.

What we have here said in regard to pure arithmetic carries over at all points to *pure* logic. In the latter case too, we accept as obvious the fact that logical concepts have a psychological origin, but we deny the psychologistic conclusion to which this seems to lead. In consideration of the domain that must be granted to logic in the sense of a *technology* of scientific knowledge, we naturally do not doubt that logic is to a large extent concerned with our mental states. Naturally the methodology of scientific research and proof must take full cognizance of the nature of the mental states in which research and proof take their course. Logical terms such as 'presentation', 'concept', 'judgement', 'syllogism', 'proof', 'theory', 'necessity', 'truth' etc., may therefore, and must therefore, come up as general names for psychical experiences and dispositions. We deny, however, that this ever occurs in the purely logical parts of logical technology. We deny that the theoretical discipline of pure logic, in the independent separateness proper to it, has any concern with mental facts, or with laws that might be styled 'psychological'. We saw that the laws of pure logic, e.g. the primitive 'laws of thought', or the syllogistic formulae, totally lose their basic sense, if one tries to interpret them as psychological. It is therefore clear from the start *that the concepts which constitute these and similar laws have no empirical range*. They cannot, in other words, have the character of those mere universal notions whose range is that of individual singulars, but they must be notions truly *generic*, *whose range is exclusively one of ideal singulars, genuine species*. It is clear, for the rest, that the terms in question, and all such as function in purely logical contexts, must be *equivocal*; they must, on the one hand, stand for class-concepts of mental states such as belong in psychology, but, on the other hand, for generic concepts covering ideal singulars, which belong in a sphere of pure law.

§47 *Confirmatory indications given by the basic notions of logic and the sense of logical laws*

Our view is confirmed even by a passing look over historically existent treatments of logic, if we pay especial attention to the fundamental distinction between the subjective-anthropological unity of knowledge and the objective-ideal unity of its content. Equivocations then become apparent, and explain the deceptive appearance of an internal homogeneity and pervasive psychological character in the materials dealt with under the traditional rubric of 'doctrine of terms'.

Under this rubric it is presentations that are principally discussed, for the most part in psychological fashion; the apperceptive events in which presentations arise, are plumbed as deeply as possible. As regards differences in the essential 'forms' of presentations, a gulf soon emerges in the mode of treatment, which is continued in the doctrine of judgement-forms, and yawns most widely in the doctrine of the forms of syllogisms, and of the pertinent laws of thinking. The term 'presentation' suddenly loses the character of a psychological class-concept. This becomes plain as soon as we enquire into the instances that are to fall under the concept in question. If the logician pins down differences like that between singular and general presentations, between Socrates and Man in General, or between the Number Four and Number in General, or between an attributive and a non-attributive presentation – Socrates, Whiteness, as opposed to a Man, a Colour – or if he enumerates various modes of combining presentations to form new presentations, such as the conjunctive, disjunctive or determinative combinations etc., or if he classifies essential relations of presentations such as those between intension and extension – everyone must here perceive that he is not dealing with phenomenal, but with specific singulars. Suppose someone makes use of the following sentence as a logical illustration: 'The presentation Triangle includes the presentation Figure, and the extension of the latter includes the extension of the former'. Is he talking at all about someone's subjective experiences, or about the real inclusion of phenomena in phenomena? Does the extension of what we here, and in all similar contexts, call a 'presentation' cover *as distinct members* the presentation of a triangle had now and one to be had an hour hence? Is not *the* Presentation Triangle *one* of its members, and in similar, singular fashion, *the* Presentation Socrates, *the* Presentation Lion etc.?

Throughout logic there is much talk of *judgements*, but here again such talk is equivocal. In the psychological parts of logical technology, 'judgements' are spoken of as affirmations, one is therefore speaking of definite sorts of conscious experiences. In the logical parts there is no mention of these. 'Judgement' has the same meaning as 'proposition', the latter understood, not as a grammatical, but as an *ideal meaning-unit*. This is true of all the distinctions of judgement-acts or forms, which provide the necessary bases for the laws of pure logic. Categorical, hypothetical, disjunctive or existential judgements, and however else we may call them, are not in pure logic titles for classes of judgements, but for ideal forms of propositions. The same holds of the forms of syllogism, of the existential syllogism, the categorical syllogism, etc. The relevant analyses are analyses of meaning, and not in any degree psychological ones. Not individual phenomena, but forms of intentional unities are subjected to analysis, not experiences of syllogizing, but syllogisms. If a logical analyst remarks: 'The categorical judgement *God is just* has *God* as its subject-presentation', he is certainly not speaking of the judgement as a mental experience, which he or someone else has had, nor about some included mental act which the word 'God' arouses. He is rather speaking of the proposition *God is just*, which is *one* proposition despite the multitude of possible experiences of it, and of the presentation *God* which is likewise single, as must be the case in regard to the single parts of one single whole. When the logician accordingly speaks of 'every judgement', he means, not every *act of judging*, but every *objective proposition*. The extension of the logical concept Judgement does not impartially cover the judgement $2 \times 2 = 4$ now experienced by me, and the judgement $2 \times 2 = 4$ experienced yesterday or at whatever other time or by whatever other person. None of these acts enters the extension in question, but only $2 \times 2 = 4$ and alongside of it, e.g. *The earth is a cube*, the theorem of Pythagoras etc., and each only in the singular. The same is obviously true if one says 'The judgement *S* follows from the judgement *P*', and so in all similar cases.

We can thereby pin down the true sense of logical laws, and make it such as we have said it to be in our previous analyses. The principle of contradiction, we are told, is a judgement about judgements. But, in so far as 'judgements' are taken to mean mental experiences, acts of affirmation, believing etc., this conception can have no validity. To utter the principle is to judge, but neither the principle, nor what it judges about, are judgements. If someone says: 'Of two contradictory judgements, one is true and one false', he means (if he does not misunderstand himself, as subsequent interpretation may well lead him to do) no law for acts of judgement, but a law for the *contents of judging*, in other words for the *ideal meanings* which we call 'propositions'. He would have done better to say: 'Of two contradictory propositions, one is true and the other false'.[1] It is also clear that we require nothing, in order to understand the law of contradiction, beyond conceiving the sense of opposed propositional meanings. We need not think of judgements as real acts; they are in no sense our relevant objects. One need only look in order to see that only judgements in an ideal sense fall within the range of this logical law: 'the' judgement $2 \times 2 = 5$ is one judgement, 'the' judgements *There are dragons* another, 'the' proposition about the sum of the angles etc., another, but not one of the actual or imaginary *acts* of judgement falls within it, that in their endless multiplicity, correspond to each of these ideal unities. The case of all purely logical propositions, e.g. the laws of syllogism, is exactly parallel.

The distinction between the psychological mode of treatment, whose terms function as class-terms for mental states, and the objective or ideal mode of treatment where the same terms stand for ideal genera and species, is not a subsidiary, or a merely subjective distinction. It determines the difference between

---

[1] The law of contradiction should not be confused with the normative proposition for judgements which is its evident consequence: 'Of two contradictory judgements, one is *correct*.' The concept of correctness is correlative with that of truth. A judgement is correct when it treats what is true as true, a judgement, therefore, whose 'content' is a true proposition. The logical predicates True and False, taken in their proper sense, only concern propositions in the sense of the ideal meanings of assertions. The concept of a contradictory judgement is again correlated with that of a contradictory proposition. Judgements are called 'contradictory' in the noetic sense, if their 'contents', their ideal meanings stand in the descriptively definite relation which, in the sense of formal logic, we call 'contradiction'.

essentially distinct sciences. Pure logic and arithmetic, as sciences dealing with the ideal singulars belonging to certain genera (or of what is founded *a priori* in the ideal essence of these genera) are separated from psychology, which deals with the individual singulars belonging to certain empirical classes.

§48 *The fundamental differences*

We shall conclude by stressing the fundamental differences on whose recognition or non-recognition one's total response to the psychologistic line of argument depends. These are as follows:

1. There is an essential, quite unbridgeable difference between sciences of the ideal and sciences of the real. The former are *a priori*, the latter empirical. The former set forth ideal general laws, grounded with intuitive certainty in certain general concepts: the latter establish real general laws, relating to a sphere of fact, with probabilities into which we have insight. The extension of general concepts is, in the former case, one of lowest specific differences, in the latter case one of individual, temporally determinate singulars. Ultimate objects are, in the former case, ideal species, in the latter case, empirical facts. The essential differences between natural laws and ideal laws, between universal propositions of fact (perhaps disguised as general propositions: 'All ravens are black', 'The raven is black') and genuine generalizations (such as the universal propositions of pure mathematics), between the notion of an empirical class and that of an ideal genus etc. A correct assessment of these differences presupposes the complete abandonment of the empiricistic theory of abstraction, whose present dominance renders all logical matters unintelligible. We shall have to speak in detail of this matter later on (cf. Investigation II).

2. In all knowledge, and particularly in all scientific knowledge, there are three fundamentally distinct patterns of connection:

(*a*) A pattern of connection of *cognitive experiences*, in which science is subjectively realized, a *psychological pattern of connection* among the presentations, judgements, insights, surmises, questions etc., in which research is carried out, in which a theory already discovered receives its insightful thinking out.

(*b*) A pattern of connection among the *matters* investigated and theoretically known in the science, which constitute its sphere a territory. The pattern of connection of investigation and knowing is plainly quite different from that of what is investigated and known.

(*c*) The logical pattern of connection, i.e. the specific pattern of connection of the theoretical Ideas in which the unity of the truths of a scientific discipline, and those, in particular, of a scientific theory or proof or inference, are constituted (the unity of concepts in a true proposition, of simple truths in truth-combinations etc.).

In the case, e.g., of physics we distinguish between the pattern of connection of the mental states of the physical thinker from that of the physical nature that he knows, and both from the ideal pattern of connection of the truths in physical theory, e.g. in the unity of analytical mechanics, of theoretical optics etc. Even the form of an argument in probability, which governs the connection between facts and hypotheses, is part of this logical line. The logical pattern of connection is the ideal form for the sake of which we speak *in specie* of the same truth, the same syllogism or proof, the same theory and rational discipline, by whomsoever these 'same things' may be thought. This unity of form is one of legal validity, of the validity of laws under which all these 'same things' stand, the validity, i.e. of the laws of pure logic, which accordingly overshadow all science, and do so, not in respect of the psychological or objective content of science, but in respect of its ideal meaning-load. The peculiar patterns of combination of the concepts, propositions and truths which form the ideal unity of a particular science, can of course only be called 'logical', in so far as they are *instances* falling under logic. They do not belong among the actual parts of logic.

The three patterns of combination just distinguished naturally concern logic and arithmetic like all other sciences. Only in their case, the matters investigated are not, as in physics, real matters of fact, but ideal species. The specific nature of logic involves the previously noted peculiarity that the ideal patterns of combination which make up its theoretical unity are themselves subordinate instances of the laws that it sets up. Logical laws are at once parts and rules of such patterns of combination: they belong to the *theoretical structure*, but at the same time to the *field*, of logical science.

§49 *Third prejudice. Logic as the theory of inner evidence*

We shall state a third prejudice – one particularly to the fore in the arguments of chapter II, §19 – in the following words: All truth pertains to judgement. Judgement, however, is only recognized as true when it is *inwardly evident*. The term 'inner evidence' stands, it is said, for a peculiar mental character, well-known to everyone through his inner experience, a peculiar feeling which guarantees the truth of the judgement to which it attaches. If logic is the technology which will assist us to know the truth, logical laws are obviously psychological propositions. They are, in fact, propositions which cast light on the psychological conditions on which the presence or absence of this 'feeling of inner evidence' depends. Practical prescriptions are naturally connected with such propositions, and help us to achieve judgements having this distinctive character. Such psychologically based rules of thought must surely be meant where we speak of logical laws or norms.

Mill hits on this conception when he attempts to draw a line between logic and psychology, and says: 'The properties of thought which concern logic are some of its contingent properties, those namely on the presence of which depends good thinking as distinguished from bad' (*An Examination of Sir William Hamilton's Philosophy*, p. 462). In his further statements, he repeatedly calls logic the (psychologically conceived) 'theory' or 'philosophy of evidence' (*op. cit.* pp. 473, 475–6, 478) he was of course not immediately concerned with the propositions of pure logic. In Germany this point of view occasionally crops up in Sigwart. 'Logic', he says, 'can only proceed by becoming conscious of the way this subjective feeling of necessity [the 'inner feeling' of the evident of our previous paragraph] makes its appearance, and then expressing these conditions in a general manner' (*Logik*, I, ed. 2, p. 16). Many statements of Wundt's tend in a similar direction. We read, e.g., in his *Logik* that 'the properties of self-evidence and universal validity involved in certain thought-connections, permit us to derive the logical from the psychological laws of thought'. The normative character of the former 'has its sole foundation in the fact that certain psychological thought-connections actually *do* have self-evidence and universal validity, without which it would not be possible for us to approach thought with the demand that it *should* satisfy the conditions of the self-evident and universally valid'. 'The conditions that must themselves be fulfilled if we are to have self-evidence and universal validity are called the logical laws of thought'. But Wundt emphasizes that 'psychological thinking is always the more comprehensive form of thinking'.[1]

In the logical literature at the end of last century the interpretation of logic as a practically applied psychology of the inwardly evident certainly became more penetrating and more widely entertained. The *Logik* of Höfler and Meinong here deserves special mention, since it may be regarded as the first properly carried out attempt to make a thorough, consistent use of the notion of the psychology of inward evidence over the whole field of logic. Höfler says that the main task of logic is the investigation of 'those laws, primarily psychological, which express the dependence of emergent inward evidence on the particular properties of our presentations and judgements' (*Logik*, Vienna 1890, p. 16). 'Among all actually given thought-phenomena, or even such as we can conceive possible, logic must pick out the types or forms of thinking to which inner evidence attaches directly, or which are necessary conditions for the emergence of inner evidence' (*op. cit.* p. 17). The seriousness of such psychologism is shown by the rest of the treatment. Thus the method of logic, in its concern with the theoretical groundwork of correct thinking, is said to be the same method that psychology applies to *all* mental phenomena: it must *describe* such phenomena, in this case those of correct thinking, and reduce them as far as may be to simple laws, i.e. explain more complex laws by way of simple ones (*op. cit.* p. 18). Further on, one reads that the logical doctrine of the syllogism is given the task of 'formulating the laws, which tell us what features in our premises determine whether a certain judgement can be deduced from them with inward evidence'. Etc. etc.

---

[1] Wundt, *Logik*, 1, ed. 2, p. 91. Wundt regularly couples inner evidence with universal validity in this passage. As regards the latter, he distinguishes between a subjective form of universal validity, a mere consequence of inner evidence, and an objective form, which also covers the postulate of the intelligibility of experience. But as the justification and adequate fulfilment of this postulate itself rests on inner evidence, it does not seem feasible to drag in 'universal validity' into discussions of basic principles.

§50 Transformation of logical propositions into equivalent propositions about the ideal conditions for inner evidence. The resultant propositions are not psychological

We turn to criticism. We are far from regarding as unobjectionable the nowadays commonplace, but far from clear assumption with which the argument starts, that all truth lies in our judgements. We do not of course doubt that to know truth and to utter it justifiably, presupposes the prior seeing of it. Nor do we doubt that logic as a technology must look into the psychological conditions in which inner evidence illuminates our judgements. We may even go a further step in the direction of the conception we are refuting. While we seek to preserve the distinction between purely logical and methodological propositions, we expressly concede that the former have a relation to the psychological datum of inner evidence, that they in a sense state its psychological conditions.

Such a relation must, however, be regarded as purely ideal and indirect. The pure laws of logic say absolutely nothing about inner evidence or its conditions. We can show, we hold, that they only achieve this relation through a process of application or transformation, the same sort of process, in fact, through which every purely conceptual law permits application to a generally conceived realm of empirical cases. The propositions about inner evidence which arise in this manner keep their *a priori* character, and the conditions of inner evidence that they assert bear no trace of the psychological or the real. They are purely conceptual propositions, transformable, as in every like case, into statements about *ideal* incompatibilities or possibilities.

A little reflection will make matters clear. Every law of pure logic permits of an (inwardly evident) transformation, possible *a priori*, which allows one to read off certain propositions about inward evidence, certain conditions of inward evidence, from it. The combined principles of contradiction and excluded middle are certainly equivalents to the proposition: One and only *one* of two mutually contradictory judgements *can* manifest inner evidence.[1] The mood *Barbara* is likewise certainly equivalent to

---

[1] If we really had to interpret the theory of inner evidence in the manner of Höfler on p. 133, *op. cit.*, it would have been corrected by our previous critique of empiricistic misunderstandings of logical principles (see §23). Höfler's statement

the proposition: The inner evidence of the necessary truth of a proposition of the form *All A's are C's* (more precisely, its truth as a necessary consequence), may appear in a syllogizing act whose premisses are of the forms *All A's are B's* and *All B's are C's*. The like holds of every proposition of pure logic. Understandably so, since there evidently is a general equivalence between the proposition *A is true* and *It is possible for anyone to judge A to be true in an inwardly evident manner*. The propositions, therefore, whose sense lies in stating what necessarily is involved in the notion of truth, that the truth of propositions of certain forms determines the truth of propositions of corresponding other forms, can certainly be transformed into equivalent propositions which connect the possible emergence of inner evidence with the forms of our judgements.

Our insight into such connections will, however, provide us with the means to refute the attempt to swallow up pure logic in a psychology of inner evidence. In itself, plainly, the proposition *A is true* does not state the same thing as the equivalent proposition *It is possible for anyone and everyone to judge that A is the case*. The former says nothing about anyone's judgement, not even about judgements of anyone in general. The position here resembles that of propositions of pure mathematics. The statement that $a+b = b+a$ states that the numerical value of the sum of two numbers is independent of their position in such a sum, but it says nothing about anyone's acts of counting or addition. The latter first enters the picture in an inwardly evident, equivalent transformation. It is an *a priori* truth that no number can be given *in concreto* unless we count, and no sum unless we add.

But even when we abandon the original forms of the propositions of pure logic, and turn them into corresponding equivalents regarding inward evidence, nothing results which psychology could claim as its own. Psychology is an empirical science, the

'that an affirmative and a negative judgement about the same object are incompatible', is, as an exact statement, false, and can even less count as a statement of the logical principle. A similar mistake slips into the definition of the correlatives 'ground' and 'consequence': if it were correct, it would falsify all syllogistic rules. It runs: 'A judgement *C* is the consequence of a ground *G*, if the *belief* in the falsity of *C* is incompatible with the (imagined) *belief* in the truth of *G*' (op. cit. p. 136). Note that Höfler explains incompatibility in terms of evident non-coexistence (*op. cit.* p. 129). He plainly confuses the ideal non-coexistence (i.e. lack of joint truth) of the propositions in question, with the real non-coexistence of the corresponding acts of affirmation, presentation etc.

science of mental facts, and psychological possibility is accordingly a case of real possibility. Such possibilities of inner evidence are, however, real ones, and what is psychologically impossible may very well be ideally possible. The solution of the generalized '3-body problem', or '*n*-body problem' may transcend all human cognitive capacity, but the problem *has* a solution, and the inner evidence which relates to it is therefore possible. There are decimal numbers with trillions of places, and there are truths relating to them. No one, however, can actually imagine such numbers, nor do the additions, multiplications etc., relating to them. Inward evidence is here a psychological impossible, yet, *ideally* speaking, it undoubtedly represents a possible state of mind.

The turning of the notion of truth into the notion of the possibility of evident judgement has its analogue in the relation of the concepts *Individual Being* and *Possibility of Perception*. The equivalence of these concepts, if by 'perception' we mean adequate perception, is undeniable. A perception is accordingly *possible*, in which the whole world, with the endless abundance of its bodies, is perceived at *one* glance. But this ideal possibility is of course no real possibility, we could not attribute it to any empirical subject, particularly since such a vision would be an endless continuum of vision: unitarily conceived, it would be a Kantian Idea.

Though we stress the ideality of the possibilities of evident judgement which can be derived from logical principles, and which we see to reveal their *a priori* validity in cases of apodeictic self-evidence, we do not deny their *psychological utility*. If we take the law that, out of two contradictory propositions, one is true and one is false, and deduce from it the truth that, one only out of every pair of possible contradictory judgements can have the character of inward evidence, we may note this to be a self-evidently correct deduction, if self-evidence be defined as the experience in which the correctness of his judgement is brought home to a judging subject, the new proposition utters a truth about the compatibilities or incompatibilities of certain *mental experiences*. In this manner, however, every proposition of pure mathematics tells us something about possible and impossible happenings in the mental realm. No empirical enumeration or calculation, no mental act of algebraical transformation or geometrical construction, is possible which conflicts with the ideal laws of mathematics. These laws accordingly have a psycho-logical use. We can read off from each of them *a priori* possibilities and impossibilities relating to certain sorts of mental acts, acts of counting, of additive and multiplicative combination etc. These laws are not thereby made into psychological laws. Psychology, the natural science concerned with what we mentally live through, has to look into the *natural conditions* of our experience. In its field are specifically to be found the empirically real relationships of our mathematical and logical activities, whose *ideal* relations and laws make up an independent realm. This latter realm is set up in purely universal propositions, made up out of 'concepts' which are not class-concepts of mental acts, but ideal concepts of essence, each with its concrete foundation in such mental acts or in their objective correlates. The number Three, the Truth named after Pythagoras etc., are, as our discussion showed, neither empirical singulars nor classes of singulars: they are ideal objects ideationally apprehended in the correlates of our acts of counting, of inwardly evident judging etc.

In relation to inner evidence, psychology has therefore merely the task of tracking down the *natural* conditions of the experiences which fall under this rubric, of investigating the real contexts in which, as experience shows, inward evidence arises and perishes. Such natural conditions are concentration of interest, a certain mental freshness, practice etc. Their investigation does not lead to knowledge which is exact in its content, to inwardly evident, truly lawlike generalizations, but only to vague, empirical generalizations. The inward evidence of our judgements does not merely depend on such psychological conditions, conditions that one might also call external and empirical, since they are rooted not purely in the specific form and matter of our judgement, but in its empirical context in mental life: it depends also on *ideal* conditions. Each truth stands as an ideal unit over against an endless, unbounded possibility of correct statements which have its form and its matter in common. Each actual judgement, which belongs to this ideal manifold, will fulfil, either in its mere form or in its matter, the ideal conditions for its own possible inward evidence. The laws of pure logic are truths rooted in the concept of truth, and in concepts essentially related to this concept. They state, in relation to possible acts of judgement, and on the basis of their mere form, the ideal conditions of the possibility or impossibility of their inner evidence. Of these two sorts of conditions of the inwardly evident, the former relates to the special constitution of the sorts of psychical being which the psychology of the period recognizes, psychological induction being limited by experience. The other conditions, however, have the character of ideal laws, and hold generally for every possible consciousness.

§51 *The decisive points in this dispute*

A final clearing-up of our present dispute depends likewise on a correct discernment of the most fundamental of epistemological distinctions, the distinction between the real and the ideal, or the correct discernment of all the distinctions into which this distinction can be analysed. We are here concerned with the repeatedly stressed distinctions between real and ideal truths, laws, sciences, between real and ideal (individual and specific) generalities and also singularities etc. Everyone, no doubt, has some acquaintance with these distinctions: even so extreme an empiricist as Hume draws a fundamental distinction between 'relations of ideas' and 'matters of fact', a distinction which the great idealist Leibniz drew before him, using the rubrics *vérités de raison* and *vérités de fait*. To draw an epistemologically important distinction does not, however, mean that one has as yet grasped its epistemological essence. One must clearly grasp what the ideal is, both intrinsically and in its relation to the real, how this ideal stands to the real, how it can be immanent in it and so come to knowledge. The basic question is whether ideal objects of thought are – to use the prevailing jargon – mere pointers to 'thought-economies', verbal abbreviations whose true content merely reduces to individual, singular experiences, mere presentations and judgements concerning individual facts, or whether the idealist is right in holding that such an empiricistic doctrine, nebulous in its generality, can indeed be uttered, but in no wise thought out, that all attempts to reduce ideal unities to real singulars are involved in hopeless absurdities, that its splintering of concepts into a range of singulars, without a concept to unify such a range in our thought, cannot be thought etc.

The understanding of our distinction between the real and the ideal 'theory of inner evidence' presupposes, on the other hand, correct concepts of *inner evidence* and *truth*. In the psychologistic literature of the last decades we have seen inner evidence spoken of as a casual feeling which attends on certain judgements, and is absent from others, which at best has a universally human linkage with certain judgements and not with others, a linkage in every normal human being in normal circumstances of judgement. There are certain normal circumstances in which every normal person feels self-evidence in connection with the proposition $2 + 1 = 1 + 2$, just as he feels pain when he gets burnt. One might then well ask what gives such a special feeling authority, how it manages to guarantee the truth of our judgement, 'impress the stamp of truth' on it, 'proclaim its truth', or whatever other metaphor one cares to use. One might also ask what such vague talk of normal endowment and normal circumstances precisely covers, and might point to the fact that even this recourse to normality will not make inwardly evident judgements coincide with true ones. It is in the last resort undeniable that even the normal man in normal circumstances must pass, in an un-numbered majority of cases, possible correct judgements which lack inner evidence. One would surely not wish to conceive the 'normality' in question in such a way that no actual human being, and no possible human being living in our finite natural conditions, could be called 'normal'.

Empiricism altogether misunderstands the relation between the ideal and the real: it likewise misunderstands the relation between truth and inner evidence. Inner evidence is no accessory feeling, either casually attached, or attached by natural necessity, to certain judgements. It is not the sort of mental character that simply lets itself be attached to any and every judgement of a certain class, i.e. the so-called 'true' judgements, so that the phenomenological content of such a judgement, considered in and for itself, would be the same whether or not it had this character. The situation is not at all like the way in which we like to conceive of the connec-tion between sensations and the feelings which relate to them: two persons, we think, have the same sensations, but are differ-ently affected in their feelings. Inner evidence is rather nothing but the 'experience' of truth. Truth is of course only experienced in the sense in which something ideal can be an experience in a real act. Otherwise put: *Truth is an Idea, whose particular case is an actual experience in the inwardly evident judgement.* The inwardly evident judgement is, however, an experience of primal givenness: the non-self-evident judgement stands to it much as the arbitrary positing of an object in imagination stands to its adequate perception. A thing adequately perceived is not a thing merely meant in some manner or other: it is a thing primarily given in our act, and as what we mean it, i.e. as itself given and grasped without residue. In like fashion what is self-evidently judged is not merely judged (meant in a judging, assertive, affirmative manner) but is given in the judgement-experience as itself present – present in the sense in which a state of affairs, meant in this or that manner, according to its kind, whether singular or general, empirical or ideal etc., can be 'present'. The analogy which connects all experiences of primal givenness, then leads to analogous ways of speaking, and inner evidence is called a seeing, a grasping of the self-given (true) state of affairs, or, as we say with tempting equivocation, of the truth. And, as in the realm of perception, the unseen does not at all coincide with the non-existent, so lack of inward evidence does not amount to untruth. *The experience of the agreement* between meaning and what is itself present, meant, between the actual *sense of an assertion* and the self-given *state of affairs*, is inward evidence: the *Idea* of this agreement is truth, whose ideality is also its objectivity. It is not a chance fact that a propositional thought, occurring here and now, agrees with a given state of affairs: the agreement rather holds between a self-identical propositional meaning, and a self-identical state of affairs. 'Validity' or 'objectivity', and their opposites, do not pertain to an assertion as a particular temporal experience, but to the assertion *in specie*, to the pure, self-identical assertion $2 \times 2 = 4$ etc.

This conception alone accords with the fact that it makes no difference whether we perform a judgement (a judgement with the content, the meaning *J*) insightfully, or whether we have insight into the truth, the being of *J*. We accordingly also have insight into the fact that no one's insight can be at variance with our own (to the extent that either of us really has insight). This has its source in the essential relation between the experience of truth and truth. Our conception alone escapes the doubt which the conception of inner evidence as a casually connected feeling never can escape, and which plainly amounts to a complete scepticism: the doubt whether, when we have insight that *J* is the case, another might not have the insight that J', incompatible with J, is the case, that insights in general might not clash with insights, without a hope of settlement. We understand, accordingly, why the 'feeling' of inner evidence has no other essential precondition but the truth of the judged content in question. It is obvious that where there is nothing, nothing can be seen, but it is no less obvious that where there is no truth, there can be no seeing something to be true, i.e. no inward evidence (cf. Investigation VI, chapter 5).

CHAPTER NINE

Logic and the Principle of the Economy of Thought

§52 *Introductory*

WE now turn to another empiricistic attempt to find a basis for logic and epistemology, closely related to the psychologism which we have hitherto sought to refute, and which has won wide acceptance in recent years: the attempt to provide a *biological* basis for these disciplines, either through the Principle of Least Action, as Avenarius styles it, or through the principle of the Economy of Thought, as Mach calls it. That this new tendency ends up by being a psychologism, is made very clear in the *Psychologie* of Cornelius. In that work the principle in question is expressly given the position of 'the basic law of the understanding', of 'a universal, basic law of psychology' (H. Cornelius, *Psychologie*, pp. 82, 86). Psychology – the psychology of cognitive processes in particular – when built upon this basis, will also yield us the foundations of all philosophy (*op. cit.* pp. 3–9).

It seems to me that, by these theories of thought-economy, ideas well-justified and fruitful in their due limits, are given a twist that, if universally accepted, would entail the corruption of all genuine logic and epistemology, as well as of all psychology.[1]

We shall first consider the principle of Avenarius and Mach in the teleological guise of a principle of adaptation. In this we shall see its worthwhile content, and the justified goal of the investigations that might spring from it, both in psychological anthropology and the practical theory of science. We shall go on to show how little it is able to provide foundations for psychology, or to assist us in pure logic and the theory of knowledge.

[1] My negative criticism, in this chapter, of one main tendency in Avenarius's philosophy, does not mean that I do not deeply respect him as a thinker torn all too early from the labours of science, and that I do not likewise respect the solid seriousness of his scientific works.

§53 The teleological character of the principle of Mach and Avenarius and the scientific meaning of an 'economy of thought' (Denkökonomik)

However we may express our principle, it is a principle of evolution or adaptation: its concern is to conceive science as the most purposive (economical, power-saving) adaptation of thought to the varied fields of phenomena.

Avenarius, in the preface to his Habilitationsschrift (*Philosophy as thought about the world according to the Principle of Least Action. Prolegomena to a Critique of Pure Experience* (Leipzig, 1876), p. iii *f*.), expresses his principle as follows: 'The change imposed by the mind on its presentations when new impressions enter, is always the least possible.' Immediately afterwards he says:

Since the mind is subject to the conditions of organic existence and its purposive demands, the principle cited becomes a *principle of development*. The mind uses only as much energy as it needs to use in an apperception, and, where there are many possible apperceptions, prefers that one which achieves more with the same expenditure of energy. In favourable circumstances, the mind even prefers a temporary spurt of effort, to a momentary reduction of energy, with which, however, a lesser effectiveness or duration of effect would be connected, a temporary spurt which promises so many more, and so much longer enduring, effective advantages.

The increase in abstraction, due to Avenarius's introduction of the notion of 'apperception', with all its sweeping vagueness and emptiness, is dearly bought. Mach rightly gives a central position to a fact which in Avenarius seems the outcome of tortuous and generally dubious deductions: the fact that science achieves as complete an orientation as possible in each relevant empirical field, and also the most economical of possible adjustments of thought to such a field. He is further not fond, and quite rightly, of speaking of a principle, but simply of the 'economical character' of scientific research, of the 'thought-economies' achieved by concepts, formulae, theories, methods etc.

We have not therefore to do, in the case before us, with a principle in the sense of a rational theory, with an exact law capable of functioning as the ground for a rational explanation (as the laws of pure mathematics or of mathematical physics *can* function), but with one of those valuable *teleological viewpoints*, which are of great use in the biological sciences in general, and which may all be attached to the general notion of development.

The relation to self-preservation and preservation of the species is obvious. Animal actions are determined by presentations and judgements, and if these were insufficiently adapted to the course of events, if past experience could not be put to use, if novelties could not be anticipated, means and ends not properly adjusted – at least on an average, in the life-situations of the individuals concerned, and in relation to threats of injury and advantageous utilities – their self-preservation would not be possible. A creature resembling man, but who only experienced sense-contents, who formed no associative and no imaginative habits, and who accordingly lacked all capacity to *interpret sense-contents objectively*, to perceive external things and events, to anticipate them through custom, or reconstitute them in memory, and who could not rely on average success in all these acts of experience – how could such a creature survive? Even Hume spoke in this connection of 'a sort of pre-established harmony between the course of nature and the sequence of our ideas' (*An Enquiry concerning Human Understanding*, Sect. v, part II), and the modern theory of development has prompted further pursuit of this viewpoint, as well as detailed investigation of the relevant teleologies of our mental constitution. It will without doubt be a point of view as fruitful for psychological biology as it has long been for physical biology.

This viewpoint not only presides over the sphere of 'blind' thinking, but also over the sphere of logical, of scientific thinking. Man's superiority lies in his intelligence. He is not solely a being who brings perception and experience to bear on external situations: he also thinks, employs concepts, to overcome the narrow limits of his intuition. Through conceptual knowledge he penetrates to rigorous causal laws, which permit him to foresee the course of future phenomena, to reconstruct the course of past phenomena, to calculate the possible reactions of environing things in advance, and to dominate them practically, and all this to a vastly greater extent, and with vastly more confidence, than would otherwise be possible. *Science d'où prévoyance, prévoyance d'où action*, as Comte tellingly remarks. Whatever misery the one-sidedly overstrained yearning to know may bring to the individual thinker, and that not seldom, the fruits, the treasures of science ultimately accrue to the whole of humanity.

In what we have said the 'economy of thought' has not as yet been mentioned. This notion, however, crops up as soon as we go into the question of what the notion of adaptation involves. A creature obviously will have a more purposive constitution, be better adapted to its living conditions, the more rapidly it can perform the acts needed for, or favourable to, its own mainten-ance, and the less energy it expends on such performance. It will become more quickly ready for, and more successful in avoiding the injuries, or pursuing the advantages, that occur with a certain average frequency in a given sphere: it will also pile up a larger stock of superfluous power to avoid new injuries or compass new advantages. We are of course only dealing here with vague, roughly coordinated, roughly assessable relations: they are none the less such as can be talked of with sufficient definiteness, and can, at least in certain fields, be instructively, if sketchily, weighed.

This is certainly true of the field of mental performances. Having recognized them as promoting survival, one can treat them from an economic standpoint, and can test men's actual performances from a teleological angle. One can also, so to speak, *a priori*, show certain excellences to be demanded by an economy of thought, and then show them to be realized in the forms and manners of our thought-procedures, whether in general, or in advanced minds, or in the methods of scientific research. We have here, in any case, a field of extensive, rewarding, instructive investigations. The field of mind is a sub-field of biology, and accordingly has room, not merely for abstract psychological researches, aimed, like physical researches, at elementary laws, but also for concrete, psychological investigations, and, in particular, for teleological ones. The latter make up *mental* anthropology as the necessary counterpart of physical anthropology; they deal with man in the living human community, as well as in the wider community of all life on earth.

§54 *Closer treatment of the justified ends of an 'economy of thought', in the sphere, mainly, of purely deductive methodology. Its relation to a logical technology*

The standpoint of a 'thought-economy', applied especially to the sphere of science, may achieve important results: it may throw clear light on the anthropological grounds of varying methods of research. Many of the most fruitful and characteristic methods of the most advanced sciences, only achieve satisfactory intelligibility if we look to the peculiarities of our mental constitution. As Mach excellently remarks on this point: 'To do mathematics without achieving clearness in this regard, is often to have the disagreeable impression that one's paper and pencil are cleverer than oneself.'[1]

The following points merit consideration. Men's intellectual powers are severely limited, and there is, in particular, a narrow sphere within which complex, abstract notions can be fully understood: there is also a vast effort involved in the mere understanding of genuine complexities of this sort. We are also similarly restricted in our genuine grasp of the sense of even moderately complex propositional combinations, and even more restricted in our power to grasp and genuinely carry out deductions of even moderate complexity. The sphere in which active research originally moves in full comprehension, and operating with the thoughts themselves, is *a fortiori* a small one. When all these facts are considered, it is quite astonishing that the more comprehensive rational theories and sciences should have been developed at all. It is, e.g., a most serious problem how mathematical disciplines are possible, disciplines not conducted in terms of relatively simple thoughts, but in which veritably towering thought-piles, and thought-combinations intertwined in a thousand ways, are moved about with the most sovereign freedom, and are spawned in ever increasing intricacy by our researches.

All this is due to art and method. They overcome the defects of our mental constitution, and permit an indirect achievement by way of symbolic processes from which the intuitive element, as well as all true understanding and inner evidence are absent, but which are rendered secure because a *general* proof of the efficiency of the method has been once and for all guaranteed. All the arts which belong here, and which are generally had in mind when there is talk of 'method' in a certain pointed sense, have the character of devices which economize thought. They arise in history, and in the individual case, out of certain natural *processes*

---

[1] E. Mach, *Die Mechanik in ihrer Entwicklung* (1883), p. 460. The passage is worth quoting in full. It goes on: 'Mathematics taught in this manner has barely more educational value than absorption in the Kabbala or in mystic squares. It necessarily breeds a mystical tendency, which on due occasion bears its fruits.'

of thought-economy: the thinker's practical reflection makes him see the advantages of these processes, they are then perfected in full consciousness, and artificially constructed, and they are thus made into more complex but infinitely more efficient pieces of machinery than the natural processes ever were. Following such a path of *insight*, and with constant reference to the peculiarities of our mental constitution,[1] the pioneers of research discover methods which they justify once and for all. When this has been done, such methods can be used without insight, so to say *mechanically*, in each given case: an objectively correct result is assured.

This far-reaching reduction of insight to mechanism in our thought-processes leads to an indirect mastery over those endlessly winding paths of thought that admit of no direct mastery: such a reduction rests on the psychological nature of signitive-symbolic thinking. It plays an immeasurable role in the construction of blind mechanisms, e.g. the rules for the four arithmetical operations, and for higher operations with decimals, where a result emerges, perhaps with the help of logarithmic or geometric functional tables, but without assistance from insight. But it also plays a part in contexts where *insight* guides our researches and our proofs. We might mention here, e.g., the remarkable duplication of all concepts of pure mathematics, and in particular those of arithmetic, so that the original arithmetical signs which at first signify the correlated number-concepts, with which definition has connected them, subsequently function as merely operational signs, whose meaning is wholly determined by external types of operation, each sign counting as a mere something-or-other to which this or that definite thing can be done on paper.[2] These surrogative, operational concepts which turn signs into a kind of counters, preside exclusively over the most extensive fields of arithmetical thought and research. They represent a vast easing of the latter, they take them down from the exhausting heights of abstraction to comfortable, intuitive ways, where imagination,

---

[1] This of course does not mean: 'with the help of *scientific psychology*'.

[2] If, instead of the external forms of operation, one takes, so to say, the internal ones, and understands signs in the sense of 'certain objects of thought', which stand in 'certain' relations, permit of 'certain' combinations, so that, in the corresponding *formal* sense, the laws of operation and relation hold for them, e.g. $a+b = b+a$ etc. – a new set of concepts emerges. These are the concepts which lead to the 'formal' generalization of our original disciplines, which will be immediately discussed in the text above.

guided by insight, can move, within the limits of rules, with freedom and with relative effortlessness, as in regulated games.

One should point, in this connection, to the revolutionary thought-economy which occurs in the purely mathematical disciplines, when genuine thought is replaced by surrogative, signitive thinking, an economy which leads imperceptibly to formal generalizations of our original thought-trains, and even of our sciences. In this manner, almost without specially directed mental labour, deductive disciplines arise having an infinitely enlarged horizon. Out of arithmetic, the original theory of numbers and numerical magnitudes, a generalized, formal arithmetic arises in more or less spontaneous fashion: in this numbers and magnitudes no longer count as basic concepts, but merely as chance objects of application. Fully conscious reflection now takes over, and the pure theory of manifolds emerges as a further extension. In its form this covers all possible deductive systems: the form-system of formal arithmetic is merely one of its special instances. (See under this head some points in chapter XI, §§69, 70.)

To analyse these and like types of method, and fully to clarify their achievement, is perhaps the most beautiful and least developed field in the theory of science, the extremely important, instructive theory of deductive method (of mathematical method in the widest sense). We do not of course get to do this through mere generalities, through vague talk of the surrogative function of signs, of mechanisms which save energy etc.: deep-going analyses are everywhere needed. Each typically different method must be genuinely investigated, and its economic achievement actually shown and precisely explained.

Once the meaning of the task here set us has been clearly grasped, the problems of an economy of thought in pre-scientific or extra-scientific thinking also acquire new light and a new form. Survival requires a certain adaptation to external nature, it demands, we said, the capacity to judge things more or less rightly, to foresee the course of events, to assess causal consequences correctly etc. Real knowledge of all this is achieved first, if at all, in science. But how can we in practice judge and infer without the insight which only science, the possession of so few, can offer? The practical needs of pre-scientific life are subserved by many highly complex, efficient procedures – one need only think of the decimal system of numbers. If they are not discovered by insight, but naturally developed, one must ponder the question of their possibility, as to how the operation of blind mechanism can coincide in outcome with the demands of insight.

Considerations such as those indicated above show us the way. To throw light on the teleology of pre-scientific or extra-scientific procedures, one must first carefully analyse the combinations of presentations and judgements in question, and the dispositions at work: one must establish the actual facts, the psychological mechanism of the thought-procedure in question. The economy of thought achieved is made plain when we show our procedure to be one whose results can, in logically perspicuous fashion, be indirectly proved to accord with the truth (whether of necessity, or with a certain, not too small, probability). If the natural origin of the machinery which economizes thought is not to remain a miracle – or, what is the same, a product of a peculiar, creative act of divine intelligence – we shall have to start with a careful analysis of the naturally dominant circumstances and motives of the ordinary man's ideas (perhaps of a savage's or animal's ideas), and show on this basis how a procedure which has had such success could and must have issued spontaneously out of purely natural causes.[1]

In this manner, the idea of an economy of thought, which to me seems well-justified and fruitful, has been given some definiteness and clarity: we have given an outline of the problem that it must solve, and the main paths that it must enter upon. Its *relation to logic*, in the practical sense of a technology of knowledge, is immediately understandable. It plainly yields an important foundation for such a technology, it gives essential aids towards constituting the Idea of technical methods of human knowledge, towards useful specifications of such methods, and to the deduction of rules for their assessment and discovery.

§55 *The meaninglessness of an economy of thought for pure logic and epistemology, and its relation to psychology*

To the extent that these thoughts coincide with those of R. Avenarius and E. Mach, we have no differences: I gladly agree

---

[1] No example throws more light on the essence of the briefly indicated problems here posed than the natural number-series. Because I thought it so instructive, I treated it *in extenso* in chapter xii of my *Philosophie der Arithmetik* (1891), to illustrate the manner in which I thought such investigations should be conducted.

with them. I am genuinely convinced, in particular, that we owe a vast amount of logical illumination to the historical-methodological labours of E. Mach, and that this is the case where one cannot altogether (or altogether cannot) agree with his conclusions. E. Mach, unfortunately, does not seem to me to have tackled the most fruitful problems of the economy of thought, the problems I tried to formulate above in a somewhat brief but quite sufficient fashion. His failure to do this is, in any case, partly due to the epistemological misinterpretations that he thought of as necessary foundations for his investigations. Mach's writings have, however, had an immense influence in respect of these very misinterpretations. This is the side of his thought that he shares with Avenarius, in respect of which I must here oppose him.

Mach's doctrine of an economy of thought, like Avenarius's doctrine of least action, relates, as we saw, to certain biological facts: ultimately we are dealing with a branch of the theory of evolution. This fact makes plain why such researches throw light on practical epistemology, on the methodology of scientific research, but not at all on pure epistemology, and especially not on the ideal laws of pure logic. *Per contra*, the writings of the school of Mach and Avenarius, seem to aim at an epistemology rooted in an economy of thought. Against such a conception, or such a use of the economy of thought, we must train the whole arsenal of objections which we above opposed to psychologism and relativism. Attempts to found epistemology on an economy of thought ultimately reduce to attempts to found it on psychology: we need not here repeat, nor specially apply, our arguments. Cornelius increases the plain incongruities of his case by endeavouring to derive elementary psychological laws from a teleological principle of mental anthropology, which itself presupposes and is derived from these facts. He also tries, through the instrumentality of psychology, to provide an epistemological foundation for philosophy. This so-called principle, I must further remark, is not at all an ultimate, explanatory, rational principle, but a mere assemblage, a mass of facts regarding adaptation, facts ideally in need of an ultimate reduction to elementary facts and laws, whether we are able to provide such or not.

To underpin psychology with teleological principles as its

'basic laws', principles devised to explain our varied mental functions, does not promise much for the progress of the science. No doubt it is instructive to point out the teleological significance of our mental functions, and of our more important mental structures, to show in detail, therefore, how and why the actually formed combinations of our mental elements have the utilitarian relation to survival that we expect *a priori*. But to treat the descriptively given facts as 'necessary consequences' of such principles, so as to seem to be giving a real explanation of these facts, and that particularly in contexts whose main aim is to lay bare the last foundations of psychology, all this can only breed confusion.

A psychological or epistemological law concerned with an *endeavour* to achieve as much as *possible* in this or that respect, is a chimera. In the pure sphere of fact, there is no maximum possibility, in the sphere of law no endeavour. What happens in each case, as psychological matter of fact, is quite definite: there is so much of it and no more.

The factual element in the principle of economy reduces to the fact that there are such things as presentations, judgements and other thought-experiences, which are further connected with feelings that, in the form of pleasure, promote certain directions of thought-formation, in the form of pain, discourage them. One can then assert, with rough generality, the existence of a progressive formation of presentations and judgements which lead first to the formation of single experiences (*Erfahrungen*) out of originally senseless elements, and then to the combination of such experiences into a *single, more or less orderly, unity of experience*. Psychological laws determine the emergence, out of our first roughly agreeing mental collocations, of the presentation of the *single* world common to everyone, and of an empirically blind belief in its existence. One should, however, note that this world is not the same for everyone, but only so 'on the whole'; it is the same only to an extent which affords a sufficient practical guarantee for our common presentations and actions. It is not the same for the ordinary man and the scientific research-worker: for the former it is a system merely approximate in its regularity, and shot through with countless accidents, whereas for the latter it is a nature ruled throughout by absolutely strict law.

It is plainly an undertaking of great scientific import to show up the psychological ways and means through which the idea of a world as an object of experience, an idea sufficient for the needs of practical life and for survival, should have been developed and established, and, following this, to show up the psychological ways and means through which an objectively adequate Idea of a unified experience should have grown up in the minds of scientific research-workers, the Idea of a unified experience governed by strict laws, and embracing an ever enriched scientific content. This whole investigation is, however, irrelevant to epistemology. It can only have a highly indirect use for the latter, in assisting us to criticize epistemological prejudices, in whose case psychological motives really count. The question is not how experience, whether naïve or scientific, arises, but what must be its content if it is to have objective validity: we must ask on what ideal elements and laws such objective validity of knowledge of the real is founded – more generally, on what any knowledge is founded – and how the performance involved in knowledge should be properly understood. We are, in other words, *not* interested in the origins and changes of our world-presentation, but in the objective right which the world-presentation of science claims as against any other world-presentation, which leads it to call *its* world the objectively true one. Psychology looks for perspicuous explanations of the formation of world-presentations. World-science (the sum total of the different sciences of the real) wishes to know perspicuously what obtains in reality, what makes up the true, the actual world. Epistemology, however, wishes to grasp perspicuously, from an objectively ideal standpoint, in what the possibility of perspicuous knowledge of the real consists, the possibility of science and of knowledge in general.

§56 *Continuation. The* ὕστερον πρότερον *involved in any foundation of pure logic on an economy of thought*

We seem, in the case of the principle of economy, to be dealing with an epistemological or a psychological principle: this appearance mainly stems from confusion between the factually given and the logically ideal, the former being tacitly substituted for the latter. We *perspicuously* see it to be the supreme goal, the ideally justified drift of all explanation which transcends mere description, that it should arrange facts which are in themselves 'blind' (facts at first found in a conceptually delimited field) under laws which are as general as possible, and that it should in this sense bring them together with the maximum possible rationality. This 'maximization' of the work of 'bringing together' is here quite clear: it is the ideal of a pervasive, all-embracing rationality. If all matters of fact obey laws, there must be some minimum set of laws, of the highest generality and maximum deductive independence, from which all other laws can, by mere deduction, be derived. These 'basic laws' are, accordingly, laws of supreme coverage and efficacy, whose knowledge yields the absolute maximum of insight in some field, which permits the explanation of all that is in any way explicable in that field – idealizing the matter, we here assume that there are no limits to our power to deduce and subsume. In this manner the axioms of geometry are basic laws explaining and covering all the facts of space: through them every general spatial truth (i.e. every geometrical truth) achieves a self-evident reduction to its final explanatory grounds.

This goal or principle of maximum rationality we recognize with insight to be the supreme goal of the rational sciences. It is self-evident that it would be better for us to know laws more general than those which, at a given time, we already possess, for such laws would lead us back to grounds deeper and more embracing. Plainly, however, our principle is no mere biological principle, or principle of thought-economy: it is a purely *ideal* principle, an eminently *normative* one. It accordingly permits no resolution or reinterpretation into facts of our mental life, or the life of human society. To identify the drift towards maximum possible rationality with a drift towards biological adaptation, or to derive it from the latter, to saddle it in addition with the function of a basic mental force – all this is a mass of confusions only paralleled by the psychologistic misreadings of the laws of logic, and their conception as laws of nature. To say that our mental life is in fact swayed by this principle is to run counter to obvious truth. Our actual thinking does not in fact conform to its ideals – as if ideals were some sort of natural forces.

The *ideal* drift of logical thinking is as such towards rationality. The thought-economist (*sit venia verbo*) turns it into a dominant *real* drift of human thought, bases it on the vague principle of power-saving, and ultimately on adaptation, and imagines that he has cleared up the norm that we *should* think rationally, has explained the objective sense and worth of rational science in general. Certainly one is justified in talking of an economy in thinking, of an economy of thought in the 'embrace' of facts by general propositions, of subordinate generalizations by higher ones, and the like. One is, however, only justified in that one compares one's actual thought with a perspicuously recognized ideal norm, which is accordingly πρότερον τῇ φύσει. The ideal validity of this norm is *presupposed* by all meaningful *talk* of an economy of thinking; it is not therefore a possible explanatory outcome of a theory of such economy. We *measure* our empirical by our ideal thinking, and we then say that the former to some extent runs as if guided by insight into these ideal principles. We are accordingly right in speaking of a natural teleology of our mental organization, according to which our presentations and judgements proceed 'on the whole' (i.e. proceed sufficiently for the average advantage of living) as if they were logically governed. With the exception of the few cases of truly perspicuous thinking, thought bears in itself no hall-mark of logical validity, it is not intrinsically perspicuous, nor purposively, if indirectly, steered by prior insight. As a matter of fact, thought achieves a certain show of rationality, to an extent which allows us 'thought-economists', reflecting on the ways of our empirical thinking, to prove perspicuously that such ways must lead to results that – roughly and on an average – coincide with those of strict logic. We have in fact discussed the matter above.

The ὕστερον πρότερον is therefore unmasked. Before all economizing of thought, we must already know our ideal, we must know what science ideally aims at, what law-governed connections, what basic laws and derived laws etc., ideally are and do, before we can discuss and assess the thought-economical function of knowing them. Certainly we have vague notions of these Ideas before we explore them scientifically, and so we can talk of economizing thought even before a science of pure logic is constructed. But the essential fact is not changed thereby: pure logic is in itself prior to all such thought-economics, and it remains absurd to base the former on the latter.

One last point. Naturally all scientific grasp and explanation proceeds on psychological laws, in the sense of a thought-economics. It is, however, an error to think that one can therefore play down the distinction between logical and natural thought, that one can treat scientific activity as a mere 'continuation' of natural, blind activity. One may, though it is not quite unobjectionable, talk of 'natural' as well as logical 'theories'. But one must not forget that a logical theory in no sense does the same thing as a natural one, or only does this in a 'higher' manner. It has not the same aim: or rather, *it* has an aim, which we for the first time import into the natural theory. We measure, as shown above, certain natural thought-processes (by which we here mean processes lacking insight) by comparing them to logical theories properly so called, and we call such thought-processes natural theories, since they have certain psychological fruits which are just as they would be if they were really theories, the logical products of perspicuous thought. Our nomenclature, however, leads us into the error of attributing the essential traits of actual theories to such natural ones, to the 'seeing' of authentic theory, as it were, in the latter. These analogues of theories may, as mental processes, be very similar to actual theories, but they remain basically different. A logical theory is a theory on account of the ideal, necessary connection that dominates it, while what is here called a natural theory is a mere course of chance presentations or convictions, not tied together by insight, without binding power, but which has for the most part a utility in practice, just as if it had a theoretical basis.

The errors of this trend toward thought-economics, are due in the end to the fact, that those who go with it, like all psychologistic thinkers, have an interest in knowledge which stops short at the empirical side of science. They fail in a certain manner to see the wood for the mere trees. They concern themselves with science as a biological phenomenon, and do not see that they are touching upon the epistemological problem of science as ideally unified, objective truth. The epistemology of the past, which still reckoned the ideal among its problems, seems to them in error. It can only be made a worthy object of scientific concern for them in one fashion: by showing it to have had, *relatively* speaking, the function of economizing thought at a more profound level of philosophical thinking. But the more that it becomes a philosophical fashion to judge the main drifts of epistemology in this manner, the more must research protest against it, and the more necessary it is to discuss the basic points of dispute in as many-sided a manner as possible. We must, in particular, go as deep as we can into the basically different thought-trends in the spheres of the ideal and the real, thereby opening the way for that perspicuous clarification which is the presupposition for a final foundation of philosophy. The present work is a small contribution towards this end.

CHAPTER TEN

End of our Critical Treatments

§57 *Queries regarding readily formed misunderstandings of our logical endeavours*

OUR investigations up to this point have been predominantly critical. We have, we think, established the untenability of any form of empiricistic or psychologistic logic, whatever its character. Logic in the sense of a methodology of science has its main foundations outside of psychology. The idea of a 'pure logic', a theoretical science independent of everything empirical, and hence also of psychology, a science which first renders possible a technology of scientific knowledge which logic in the theoretico-practical sense is, must be admitted as sound, and the indispensable task of its independent construction must be tackled seriously. May we content ourselves with these results, and may we hope to see them recognized as results? The logic of our time, so sure of its success, so much worked upon by such important thinkers, and so widely recognized, will not readily be admitted to be treading vain paths of futile endeavour.[1] Idealistic criticism may

---

[1] O. Külpe in his *Einleitung in die Philosophie* (1897), p. 44, says of logic that it is 'not only, without doubt, one of the best-developed philosophical disciplines, but also one of the surest and most complete'. This may be true, but in view of my own estimate of logic's scientific certainty and completeness, I must also regard it as a sign of the abysmal state of the *scientific* philosophy of our day. To this I would add the question: Could one not gradually make an end to this sorry state of things, if all scientific energies of thought were devoted to solving the clearly formulable problems, soluble with almost exact certainty, no matter how limited, banal and perhaps even trivial these seem in themselves? Pure logic and epistemology are here quite plainly in the forefront of our concern. Here there is abundance of exact work to be attacked with certainty and finished once for all: one need only get to grips with it. The 'exact sciences' (among which one would one day like to reckon the disciplines in question) plainly owe their whole greatness to this modesty which prefers smallest things, and, to adapt a well-known phrase, 'concentrates its whole power on the smallest point'. Beginnings small from the point of view of the whole, but which are certain, repeatedly prove in such sciences to be springboards for immense advances. This attitude certainly operates in all recent philosophy, but, as

awaken displeasure where problems of principle are discussed, but a mere glance at the proud array of important works from Mill to Erdmann and Lipps, will be enough to re-establish most people's shaken confidence. It will be said that there must be *some* way of resolving the arguments and bringing them into harmony with the content of our flourishing science; if this is not so, one may be dealing with a merely epistemological trans-valuation of that science, which, even if important, will not have the revolutionary result of destroying its essential content. At most it will be a question of conceiving many things more precisely, of suitably limiting some careless statements, or altering the order of one's investigations. There is perhaps something really to be said for keeping a few propositions of pure logic together in their purity, and separating them off from the empirical-psychological statements of logical technology. Such reflections will satisfy many who feel the force of our idealistic arguments, without having the courage to draw the necessary conclusions.

The radical transformation which logic, in the sense of our conception, must necessarily undergo, might further encounter mistrust and antipathy, since it might readily appear, superficially regarded, to be a case of pure reaction. That this is *not* our intention, that our reattachment to the justified trends of older philosophies does not aim at the restoration of traditional logic, should surely have emerged from a close study of the content of

I have learnt to see, mainly in the wrong direction. The best energies of science are directed to psychology, i.e. psychology as an explanatory natural science, which is no more, and no differently interesting to philosophy than are the sciences of physical events. This, however, is not allowed, and great advances are spoken of in finding psychological bases for philosophical disciplines, and not least in the case of logic. A quite widely diffused view of things is, as I imagine, expressed in Elsenhans's recent dictum: 'If contemporary logic has increased its success in grappling with logical problems, it above all owes such success to its psychological immersion in its subject' (*Zeitschr. f. Psychologie*, vol. 109 (1896), p. 203). I should probably have said exactly the same before beginning my present investigations, or before realizing the insoluble difficulties in which I was plunged by a psychologistic view of the philosophy of mathematics. Now, however, having the best reasons to see the error of such a view, I can rejoice and take the liveliest interest in the otherwise very promising development of scientific psychology, but not as one who, expects *philosophical* enlightenment from it. I must, however, add, to guard against mis-understanding, that I sharply distinguish empirical psychology from the phenom-enology (taken as a pure theory of the essences of experiences) that underlies it (as epistemology underlies it in a wholly different manner). This will become clear in the actual Investigations which follow these Prolegomena.

our analyses. We can scarcely hope, however, that such indications will overcome all mistrust, and will guard against the misreading of our intentions.

§ 58 *Our links with great thinkers of the past and, in the*
first place, with Kant

That we are in a position to appeal *to the authority of great thinkers* like Kant, Herbart and Lotze, and, before these, to Leibniz, will not help us. It may even help to strengthen mistrust against us.

We are led back, in the most general terms to Kant's distinction between pure and applied logic. We may indeed approve of his most notable utterances on this point, but only with suitable provisos. We shall naturally not accept Kant's confusing, mythic concepts of understanding and reason, by which he sets such store, and which he uses in such questionable demarcations, as being, in a proper sense, faculties of the soul. Understanding or reason, as the dispositions of a certain normal thought-attitude, presuppose pure logic – which defines normality – in their concept: if we therefore have serious recourse to them, we shall be no wiser than if, in like case, we try to explain the art of dancing by the dancing faculty, i.e. the faculty of dancing artfully, the art of painting by the painting faculty etc. We rather take the terms 'understanding' and 'reason' as merely indicating a direction to the 'form of thinking' and its ideal laws, which logic, as opposed to an empirical psychology of knowledge, must follow. After such reservations, interpretations, closer qualifications, we accordingly feel close to Kant's doctrine.

Must such an agreement not have the effect of compromising our concept of logic? Pure logic, which in truth is alone science, ought, according to Kant, to be 'brief and dry', 'as is required by the scholastic exposition of a theory of the elements of the understanding' (*Cr. of Pure Reason*, Introduction to Tr. Logic, I). Everyone is familiar with Kant's lectures, published by Jäsche, and knows to what a questionable extent they fulfil this characteristic demand. Shall this unutterably defective logic be the model we should strive to imitate? No one will look kindly on the thought of pushing science back to the standpoint of the Aristotelian-Scholastic logic, which seems what Kant's treatment amounts to, since he himself says that logic has had the character of a closed science since the time of Aristotle. A scholastic elaboration of syllogistics, prefaced by some solemnly pronounced conceptual definitions, is surely no inspiring programme.

To this we should of course reply that the fact that we feel ourselves more akin to Kant's conception of logic than to that of, say, Mill or Sigwart, does not mean that we approve of its complete content, nor of the particular manner in which Kant has worked out his idea of a pure logic. We agree with Kant in his main drift, though we do not find that he clearly espied the essence of his intended discipline, nor set it forth in accordance with its adequate content.

§59 *Links with Herbart and Lotze*

We are closer to Herbart than to Kant, particularly so because he sharply stresses one cardinal point, and makes explicit use of it in distinguishing pure logic from psychology. This is indeed the crucial point which decides the matter: *the objectivity of the 'concept', of the presentation in the sense of pure logic*. 'Everything thought of', Herbart says in, e.g., his main work on psychology (*Psychologie als Wissenschaft*, II, 120) 'is, qualitatively treated, a concept in the sense of logic.' In this connection

> nothing relates to the thinking subject, to which concepts can only be attributed in a psychological sense, whereas the concept of Man, of Triangle etc., is no one's property. Each concept in its logical meaning is in fact only *once present*, which could not be the case, if the number of concepts increased with the number of subjects conceiving them, or even with the number of distinct acts of thinking through which, psychologically speaking, a concept is produced and brought forth.

'The entia of the traditional philosophers, even those of Wolff', we read on in the same paragraph,

> are merely concepts in the logical sense ... the old proposition *essentiae rerum sunt immutabiles* belongs here. It merely means that *concepts are wholly timeless things*, which is true of them in all their logical relationships, in consequence of which the scientific propositions and syllogisms that they form are and remain true for the ancients as for us – and in heaven as on earth. But concepts in this sense, in which they are a common knowledge for all men and epochs, are nothing psychological ... Psychologically a concept is

a presentation which has the logically understood concept as its *praesentatum*: it is that through which the latter (the thing to be presented) really is presented. In this sense everyone certainly has his *own* concepts: Archimedes investigated his own concept of a circle, and Newton likewise his own. These were two concepts in the sense of psychology, though logically there was only one concept for all mathematicians.

Similar statements are made in Section 2 of his *Lehrbuch zur Einleitung in die Philosophie* (§34, p. 77). The very first sentence runs: 'All our thoughts can be dealt with from two sides, as activities of mind and as regards *what* is thought through them. In the latter respect we call them *concepts*. This word, meaning *what is conceived*, enjoins abstraction from the manner in which we receive, produce or reproduce thoughts.' In §35 Herbart denies that two concepts can be exactly alike, 'for they would then not differ in respect of *what* is thought by them, and not therefore as concepts at all. As against this, the thinking of one and the same concept can be often repeated, produced and recalled on very different occasions, performed by countless rational beings, without thereby making the concept many'. He warns us in a note 'to keep in mind that concepts are neither *real objects nor real acts of thinking*. The second error is still alive: many accordingly make of logic a natural history of the understanding, and think they recognize in logic the understanding's innate laws and forms of thought, thereby corrupting psychology'. 'One can, if need be, prove by a complete induction', he remarks in another passage,

> that not one of all the doctrines which belong indisputably to logic, from the oppositions and subordinations of concepts to syllogistic sorites, presupposes anything psychological. The whole of pure logic has to do with *relations of what is thought*, of the content of our presentations (though not specifically with this content itself): nowhere does it deal with the activity of thinking, or with the psychological or metaphysical possibility of such thinking. Applied logic, like applied ethics, first requires psychological knowledge, in so far as the character of the material must be discussed that one desires to shape to the prescriptions given (*Psychol. als Wiss.* §119).

In this regard, we find many instructive and important pronouncements which modern logic has rather pushed aside than seriously considered. Our link-up with Herbart's authority must not, however, be misunderstood. It does not at all mean a return to the idea and mode of treatment of logic which Herbart envisaged, and which his worthy pupil Drobisch so eminently carried out. Herbart certainly had great merits, particularly in the respect mentioned above, his emphasis on the ideality of the concept. Even his formation of the concept deserves praise, whether one agrees with his terminology or not. On the other hand, however, Herbart seems to me never to have risen above quite isolated, immature suggestions; many misguided but, alas, very influential thoughts, thoroughly distorted his best intentions.

It was a pity that Herbart failed to notice the fundamental ambiguity of expressions like 'content', 'what is presented', 'what is thought of': on one hand, they stand for the ideal, self-same meaning-content of the corresponding expressions, on the other hand, for the varying presented objects. Herbart, as far as I can see, never said the one thing that could clear up the concept of a concept: that a concept or presentation in the logical sense is nothing but the self-identical meaning of the corresponding expressions.

Herbart's basic mistake was more important: he located what is essential to the ideality of the logical concept in its *normality*, thus shifting the sense of true, genuine ideality, of unified meaning, into the dispersed multiplicity of experiences. The fundamental sense of ideality, which puts an unbridgeable gulf between ideal and real, is thereby lost, and the notion of normality which is substituted for it, confuses the basic conceptions of logic. (Cf. on this point the study which concerns the unity of the Species in the present work.) Closely connected with this error is Herbart's belief that he has found a saving formula when he opposes *logic as the morals of thought* to psychology as the natural history of the understanding (*Lehrbuch der Psychologie*, § 180). Of the pure, theoretic science which underlies such 'morals' (and likewise underlies 'morals' in the ordinary sense) he has no idea, and still less of the extent and natural boundaries of this science, and of its intimate unity with pure mathematics. In this respect therefore, Herbart's logic deserves the reproach of poverty, just as do the logics of Kant and Aristotle and the schoolmen, superior as in other respects it shows itself in virtue of its practice of independent, exact research within its narrow circle. Linked up with this fundamental mistake, is the error of Herbart's theory of knowledge: it shows a complete inability to recognize the apparently profound problem of the harmony of the subjective course of logical thinking with the real course of external actuality, for what it is, and for what we shall later show it to be: a pseudo-problem bred by unclarity.

All this is true of the logicians in Herbart's sphere of influence, and especially of Lotze, who took up many of Herbart's suggestions, thought them out penetratingly, and carried them further with originality. We owe him a great deal, but regrettably find that even his fine approaches are brought to nought by his Herbartian confusion between specific and normative ideality. His great logical work, rich as it is in original thoughts, all worthy of a great thinker, hereby becomes a jarring mixture of psychologism and pure logic.[1]

§60 *Links with Leibniz*

Leibniz was mentioned above as one of the great philosophers to whom our present conception of logic looks back. Our relation to him is relatively of the closest. Herbart's logical opinions, likewise, are only closer to ours than Kant's, to the extent that Herbart, as against Kant, revived Leibnizian ideas. But Herbart proved himself incapable even of an approximate exhaustion of all the valuable material to be found in Leibniz. He lags far behind the conceptions of the mighty thinker, for whom mathematics and logic form a single science. These conceptions stir a particular sympathy in us, and deserve a few words.

The driving motive which set modern philosophy going, the Idea of the completion and transformation of the sciences, inspired Leibniz too to work unremittingly on a reformed logic. More penetrating than his predecessors, he did not heap scorn on scholastic logic as empty, formal rubbish, but saw in it a valuable step towards the true logic, which could truly help thought despite its incompleteness. (See, e.g. Leibniz's elaborate defence of traditional logic, although it is 'hardly a shadow' of logic as 'he would wish it', in his letter to Wagner, *Opera Philosophica*, Erdmann, 418 *ff*.) The development of this logic into a *discipline of mathematical form and strictness, into a universal mathematic in the highest and most comprehensive sense* is the goal towards which his efforts are continually devoted.

[1] In edition 1 I promised to deal with Lotze's epistemology in an Appendix to volume II of this work. This was not printed, owing to lack of space.

I here follow the indications in *Nouveaux Essais*, LIV, chapter XVII, cf. e.g. §4, *Opera philosophica*, Erdmann, 395ᵃ, where the doctrine of syllogistic forms, extended into a quite general doctrine of *argumens en forme*, is called 'une espèce de mathématique universelle, dont l'importance n'est pas assez connue'. 'Il faut savoir', he says there,

> que par les *argumens en forme* je n'entends pas seulement cette manière scolastique d'argumenter, dont on se sert dans les collèges, maid tout raisonnement qui conclut par la force de la forme, et où l'on n'a besoin de suppléer aucun article; de sorte qu'un *sorites*, un autre tissu de syllogisme, qui évite la répétition, même un compte bien dressé, un calcul d'algèbre, une analyse des infinitésimales me seront à peu près des argumens en forme, puisque leur forme de raisonner a été prédémontrée, en sorte qu'on est sûr de ne s'y point tromper.

The sphere of the *mathématique universelle* here conceived would also be very much wider than that of the logical calculus to whose construction Leibniz devoted great pains, without quite reaching its boundaries. Leibniz ought rightly to have included in this universal mathematics the whole *mathesis universalis* in the usual qualitative sense (which constitutes the *narrowest* of Leibniz's concepts of *mathesis universalis*), especially since he had repeatedly called pure mathematical arguments *argumenta in forma* even in other contexts. The *Ars combinatoria, seu Speciosa generalis, seu doctrina de formis abstracta* (cf. the mathematical writings in Pertz's edition, vol. VIII, pp. 24, 49 *ff.*, 54, 159, 205 *ff.*) should also likewise have been included in universal mathematics: it forms the fundamental part of *mathesis universalis* in a wider sense (though not in the above widest sense), while *mathesis universalis* is distinguished from logic as a subordinate territory. Leibniz defines his *Ars combinatoria* (Pertz, VII, p. 61), which is of particular interest to us, as 'doctrina de formulis seu ordinis, similitudinis, relationis, etc. expressionibus in universum'. It is here opposed as 'scientia generalis de qualitate' to the 'scientia generalis de quantitate', which is universal mathematics in the ordinary sense. Compare with this the valuable passage in Gerhardt's edition of Leibniz's philosophical writings, vol. VII, p. 279 *f.*:

> Ars combinatoria speciatim mihi illa est scientia (quae etiam generaliter characteristica sive speciosa dici posset) in qua tractatur de rerum formis sive formulis in universum, hoc est *de qualitate* in genere, sive de simili et dissimili, prout aliae atque aliae formulae ex ipso *a*, *b*,

c etc. (sive quantitates sive aliud quoddam repraesentent) inter se combinatis oriuntur, et distinguitur ab algebra quae agit de formulis ad quantitatem applicatis, sive de aequali et inaequali. Igitur Algebra subordinatur Combinatoriae, eiusque regulis continue utitur, quae tamen longe generaliores sunt, nec in Algebra tantum sed in arte deciphratoria, in variis ludorum generibus, in ipse geometria lineariter ad veterum morem tractata, denique in omnibus ubi similitudinis ratio habetur locum habent.

The intuitions of Leibniz, which speed forth so far beyond their time, seem sharply defined and highly admirable to a modern acquainted with 'formal' mathematics and mathematical logic. This applies also, I must expressly note, to Leibniz's fragments on *scientia generalis* or the *calculus ratiocinator*, in which Trendelenburg's elegant but superficial criticism could pick out so little that was of use (*Historische Beiträge zur Philosophie*, vol. iii).

Leibniz likewise points, in repeated, express pronouncements, to the need to widen logic so as to include a mathematical theory of probabilities. He demands of mathematicians an analysis of the problems which lie hidden in games of chance, and expects great resultant advances in empirical thinking, and the logical criticism of it.[1] Leibniz, in short, had intuitions of genius: he foresaw the most splendid gains which logic has had to register since the time of Aristotle, the theory of probabilities and mathematical analyses of (syllogistic and non-syllogistic) arguments. The latter first matured in the second half of the nineteenth century. Through his *Combinatoria* he is also the intellectual father of the pure theory of manifolds, a discipline close to pure logic and in fact intimately one with it (cf. below §§69–70).

In all this Leibniz bases himself on the same Idea of pure logic as we here support. Nothing is further from him than to think that the essential foundations of a fruitful art of knowledge could be found in psychology. They are for him altogether *a priori*. They constitute a discipline mathematical in form, which as such, just like, e.g. pure arithmetic, immediately includes a vocation for the practical regulation of knowledge.[2]

---

[1] Cf. *Nouveaux Essais*, Bk. iv, ch. xvi, §5, *Opp. phil.*, *Erd.*, p. 388 *f.*; Bk. iv, ch. i, §14, *op. cit.* p. 343. Cf. also the fragments on *scientia generalis*, *op. cit.* pp. 84–5 etc.

[2] Leibniz, e.g. makes *mathesis universalis* in the narrowest sense coincide with the *logica mathematicorum*, (Pertz, *op. cit.* vol. vii, p. 54), which he also called *logica mathematica* (*op. cit.* p. 50): both are *Ars judicandi atque inveniendi circa quantitates.* This of course can be extended to *mathesis universalis* in the wider and widest sense.

§61 *Need for special investigations to provide an epistemological justification and partial realization of the Idea of pure logic*

The authority of Leibniz must, however, count even less for us than that of Kant or Herbart, since he could not give to his great intentions the weight of completed achievements. He belongs to a past age, beyond which modern science feels that it has travelled a long way. Authorities do not in fact carry much weight as opposed to the broad advance of a science supposedly rich and secure in its results. Their influence must be less, in so far as they lack a sufficiently clarified, positively elaborated concept of the discipline in question. Clearly, if we do not want to stick half way, and to run the risk that our critical reflections may be barren, we must take up the task of *constructing the Idea of pure logic on a sufficiently broad basis*. Only in a series of meaty individual treatments, which will provide a more precise idea of the content and character of the essential logical researches, and which will work out the notion of logic more definitely, can one remove the prejudice which sees logic as an insignificant field of more or less trivial statements. As against this, we shall see that our discipline extends far and wide, not merely in respect of its content of systematic theories, but above all in regard to the difficult and important investigations needed for its philosophical foundation and assessment.

But even the putative triviality of the field of purely logical truths, would in itself be no argument for its treatment as a mere aid towards a logical technology. The interests of pure theory require us to treat what constitutes a unified whole of theory in a theoretically closed manner, and not as a mere aid towards external ends. Our investigations so far have, we hope, made plain that a correct grasp of the essence of pure logic, and of its unique position in relation to all other sciences, is one of the most important questions in the whole of epistemology. If this is plain, it is likewise of vital interest to this fundamental philosophical science, that pure logic should be fully expounded in purity and independence. Epistemology must, of course, not be taken to be a discipline following upon or coinciding with metaphysics, but one which precedes metaphysics, as it precedes psychology and all other disciplines.

Appendix

References to F. A. Lange and B. Bolzano

Wide as is the gulf which divides my logic from F. A. Lange's, I am in agreement with him, and regard him as having done the discipline a service, in that, in a period when pure logic was mainly despised, he definitely stood out for the view that 'science may expect important advances from attempts at a separate treatment of the purely formal elements of logic' (*Logische Studien*, p. 1). Our agreement extends further: in the most general features it also applies to the Idea of the discipline, which Lange could not indeed bring to essential clarity. He has good grounds for regarding the hiving off of pure logic as the hiving off of the doctrines which he calls 'the apodeictic element in logic', i.e. 'the doctrines which, like mathematical theorems, can be developed in an absolutely cogent manner'. His next remarks are well worth remembering:

> The mere fact of the *presence of cogent truths* is so important, that every trace of such truths must be carefully followed up. To omit such an investigation on account of the small value of formal logic, or its inadequacy as a theory of human thought, would have to be rejected from this point of view as a confusion of theoretical with practical aims. Such an objection would be as if a chemist refused to analyse a compound because in its compounded state it was very valuable, whereas its single constituents were unlikely to have any value (*op. cit.* p. 7 *f.*).

He is just as right in another passage: 'Formal logic as an apodeictic science, has a value totally independent of its validity: every system of truths which hold *a priori*, deserves the highest respect' (*op. cit.* p. 127).

While Lange warmly supported the Idea of a purely formal logic, he had no notion that this Idea had already been realized to a relatively high degree. I am of course not referring to the many expositions of formal logic, which flourished especially in the schools of Kant and Herbart, and which did so little to live up to their own claims. I am referring to Bernhard Bolzano's *Wissenschaftslehre*, published in 1837, a work which, in its treatment of the logical 'theory of elements', far surpasses everything that world-literature has to offer in the way of a systematic sketch of logic. Bolzano did not, of course, expressly discuss or support any independent demarcation of pure logic in our sense, but he provided one *de facto* in the first two volumes of his work, in his discussions of what underlay a *Wissenschaftslehre* or theory of science in the sense of his conception; he did so with such purity and scientific strictness, and with such a rich store of original, scientifically confirmed and ever fruitful thoughts, that we must count him as one of the greatest logicians of all time. He must be placed historically in fairly close proximity to Leibniz, with whom he shares important thoughts and fundamental conceptions, and to whom he is also philosophically akin in other respects. Even he, however, did not quite exhaust the rich inspiration of Leibniz's logical intuitions, especially not in regard to mathematical syllogistics and to *mathesis universalis*. Too few of Leibniz's posthumous writings were, however, known at the time, and there was no 'formal' mathematics or theory of manifolds to provide a key to their understanding.

In each line of his wonderful book, Bolzano shows himself to be an acute mathematician, who lets the same spirit of scientific strictness rule in logic which he himself first introduced into the theoretical treatment of the basic concepts and propositions of mathematical analysis, which thereby acquired a new foundation. For this the history of mathematics has *not* forgotten to grant him a famous place. Of the ambiguous profundity of that systematic philosophy, which rather aimed at thinking out world-conceptions and a world-wisdom, and which hindered the progress of scientific philosophy so badly by its unholy blend of discordant intentions, Bolzano – the contemporary of Hegel – shows no trace. His thought-patterns are of mathematical straight-forwardness and plainness, but also of mathematical clearness and strictness. Only when one has gone more deeply into the sense and aim of these patterns throughout the whole discipline, does one find what great mental work and achievement lie hidden behind plain statements and formularized expositions. To philosophers bred in the prejudices, in the thought- and speech-habits of the idealistic schools – not all of us have completely outgrown such influences – such a scientific approach readily seems shallow and void of ideas, as well as ponderous and pedantic. Logic as a science must, however, be built upon Bolzano's work, and must learn from him its need for mathematical acuteness in distinctions, for mathematical exactness in theories. It will then reach a new standpoint for judging the mathematicizing theories of logic, which mathematicians, quite unperturbed by philosophic scorn, are so successfully constructing. These theories altogether conform to the spirit of Bolzano's logic, though Bolzano had not an inkling of them. It will at least be impossible for a future historian of logic to be so wrong as the otherwise thorough Ueberweg, who treats a work of the rank of the *Wissenschaftslehre* on a level with – Knigge's *Logic for Females* (*Logik für Frauenzimmer*).[1]

Much as Bolzano's achievement is 'cast in one piece', it cannot be regarded (as such a deeply honest thinker would be the first to admit) as in any way final. To mention only one point, one particularly feels his defects in epistemological directions. There are either no investigations, or else only quite insufficient ones, which give genuine philosophical intelligibility to logical thought-achievements, and so provide a philosophical estimate of logic as a discipline. Such questions can be evaded by a thinker who, like a mathematician, is building theories upon theories, without having to bother himself about questions of underlying principle. They cannot be evaded by someone who undertakes to make clear, to those who either fail to see or to admit a discipline's validity, or who mix up essential tasks with quite heterogeneous ones, what the inherent justification of such a discipline really is, and what the nature of its tasks and objects may be. Our comparison of these present *Logical Investigations* with Bolzano's work is meant to make clear, not that our *Investigations* are in any sense mere commentaries upon, or critically improved expositions of, Bolzano's thought-patterns, but that they have been crucially stimulated by Bolzano (as also by Lotze).

[1] Ueberweg can find as much to mention about both of them: their titles. Some day men will regard an historical treatment of logic, oriented, like Ueberweg's, to the 'great philosophy', an extraordinary anomaly.

CHAPTER ELEVEN

The Idea of Pure Logic

WISHING to gain a provisional image, sketched with a few characteristic touches, of the goal aimed at by the individual discussions which follow these Prolegomena, we shall now try to bring conceptual clarity to that Idea of Pure Logic, for which our critical discussions up to this point have more or less prepared us.

§62 The unity of science. The interconnection of things and the interconnection of truths

Science is, in the first place a unified item in anthropology: it is a unity of acts of thinking, of thought-dispositions, as well as of certain external arrangements pertinent thereto. What makes this unified whole anthropological, and what especially makes it psychological, are not here our concern. We are rather interested in what makes science science, which is certainly not its psychology, nor any real context into which acts of thought are fitted, but a certain objective or ideal interconnection which gives these acts a unitary objective relevance, and, in such unitary relevance, an ideal validity.

More definiteness and clearness are, however, needed at this point. Two meanings can be attached to this objective interconnection which ideally pervades scientific thought, and which gives 'unity' to such thought, and so to science as such: it can be understood as an *interconnection of the things* to which our thought-experiences (actual or possible) are intentionally directed, or, on the other hand, as an *interconnection of truths*, in which this unity of things comes to count objectively as being what it is. These two things are given together *a priori*, and are mutually inseparable. Nothing can be without being thus or thus determined, and that it is, and that it is thus and thus determined, is the self-subsistent truth which is the necessary correlate of the self-subsistent being. What holds of single truths, or single states of affairs, plainly also holds of interconnections of truths or of states of affairs. This self-evident inseparability is not, however, identity. In these truths or interconnections of truths the actual existence of things and of interconnections of things finds expression. But the interconnections of truths differ from the interconnections of things, which are 'truly' in the former; this at once appears in the fact that truths which hold of truths do not coincide with truths that hold of the things posited in such truths.

To forestall misunderstandings, I must expressly emphasize the fact that I use the words 'objectivity', 'object', 'thing' etc., always in the widest sense, in accordance, therefore, with my preferred sense of the term 'knowledge'. An object of knowledge may as readily be what is real as what is ideal, a thing or an event or a species of a mathematical relation, a case of being or of what ought to be. This applies automatically to expressions like 'unified objectivity', 'interconnection of things' etc.

Both sorts of unity are given to us, and can only by abstraction be thought apart, in judgement or, more precisely, in *knowledge* – the unity of objectivity, on the one hand, and of truth, on the other. The expression 'knowledge' is wide enough to cover both simple acts of knowing, as well as logically unified interconnections of knowledge, however complicated: either of these, considered as a whole, is a cognitive act. If now we perform an act of cognition, or, as I prefer to express it, live in one, we are 'concerned with the object' that it, in its cognitive fashion, means and postulates. If this act is one of knowing in the strictest sense, i.e. if our judgement is inwardly evident, then its object is *given* in primal fashion (*originär*). The state of affairs comes before us, not merely putatively, but as actually before our eyes, and in it the object itself, *as* the object that it is, i.e. just as it is intended in this act of knowing and not otherwise, as bearer of such and such properties, as the term of such relations etc. It is not merely putatively, but actually thus, and *as* actually thus it is given to our knowledge, which means that it is not merely thought (judged) but known to be such. Otherwise put, its being thus is a truth actually realized, individualized in the experience of the inwardly evident judgement. If we reflect on this individualization, we perform an ideational abstraction, and the truth itself, instead of our former object, becomes our apprehended object. We hereby apprehend the truth as the ideal correlate of the transient subjective act of knowledge, as standing opposed in its unity to the unlimited multitude of possible acts of knowing, and of knowing individuals.

To the interconnections of knowledge there ideally correspond interconnections of truths. Suitably understood, these are not merely complexes *of* truths, but complex truths, which therefore themselves in their totality fall under the concept of truth. There also the *sciences* belong, the word understood objectively in the sense of unified truth. In the general correlation which subsists between truth and objectivity, there is a unitary objectivity which corresponds to the unity of truth in one and the same science: this is the unity of the *scientific field*. In relation to this, all the singular truths of the same science *belong together in their subject-matter*, an expression which, as we shall see later, seems to be here used in a wider sense than usual (cf. the end of §64).

§63 *Continuation. The unity of theory*

We may now ask what constitutes the *unity of a science*, and therewith the unity of its field. For not every putting of truths together in a single association of truths, which might remain an entirely external one, constitutes a science. To a science, as we said in our first chapter,[1] a certain unified interconnection of demonstration pertains. This too, however, is not enough: it points to demonstration, to proof as something essentially pertaining to the Idea of Science, but fails to say what sort of unity of proof constitutes a science.

To reach clearness, we begin by making certain general pronouncements.

Scientific knowledge is, as such, *grounded knowledge*. To know the ground of anything means to see the necessity of its being so and so. Necessity as an objective predicate of a truth (which is then called a necessary truth) is tantamount to the law-governed validity of the state of affairs in question. To see *a state of affairs*

---

[1] Cf. §6. We were there no doubt concerned under the rubric of 'science', with a narrower concept, that of theoretical explanatory abstract science. This, however, makes no essential difference, especially in view of the eminent position of the abstract sciences, that we shall be discussing immediately below.

as a matter of law is to see *its truth as necessarily obtaining,* and to have knowledge of the *ground of the state of affairs* or of its truth: all these are equivalent expressions.[1] A natural equivocation, of course, leads us to call every general truth that itself utters a law, a necessary truth. Corresponding to our first defined sense, it would have been better to call it the explanatory ground of a law, from which a class of necessary truths follows.

Truths divide into *individual* and *general* truths. The former contain (whether explicitly or implicitly) assertions regarding the actual existence of individual singulars, whereas the latter are completely free from this, and only permit us to infer (purely from concepts) the *possible* existence of what is individual.

Individual truths are as such *contingent.* If in their case one speaks of a grounded explanation, one is concerned with a proof of their necessity under certain presupposed *circumstances.* If the interconnection of one fact with others is one of law, then its existence, resting on the laws which govern interconnections of the sort in question, and on the assumption of the pertinent circumstances, is determined as a *necessary existence.*

If we are not dealing with the proof of a factual, but of a *general* truth (which again has the character of a law in respect of its possible application to facts falling under it) we are referred to certain general laws, which, by way of specialization (not individualization) and deductive consequence yield the proposition to be proved. The proof of general laws necessarily leads to certain laws which in their essence, i.e. intrinsically, and not merely subjectively or anthropologically, are not further proveable. These are called *basic laws.* The systematic unity of the ideally closed sum total of laws resting on *one* basic legality (*Gesetzlichkeit*) as their final ground, and arising out of it through systematic deduction, is the *unity of a systematically complete theory.* This basic legality may here either consist of one basic law or a conjunction of *homogeneous* basic laws.

We possess theories in this strict sense in universal arithmetic, in geometry, in analytical mechanics, in mathematical astronomy etc. Our concept of theory is usually a relative one, i.e. a theory

---

[1] We are therefore not concerned with a subjective psychological character of the judgement in question, e.g. a feeling of necessitation, etc. How ideal objects, and with them ideal predicates of such objects, stand to our subjective acts has been more or less indicated in §39. More in the following Investigations.

is relative to a multiplicity of single items that it governs, for which it provides the explanatory grounds. Universal arithmetic gives us an explanatory theory for numerical and concrete number-propositions, analytical mechanics for mechanical facts, mathematical astronomy for the facts of gravitation etc. The possibility of taking on the function of explanation is an obvious consequence of the essence of a theory in our absolute sense. In a looser sense, we mean by a theory a deductive system in which the last grounds are not basic laws in the strict sense of the word, but, as genuine grounds, take us closer to these. In the gradations of a closed theory, a theory in this relaxed sense forms a step.

We also note the following difference: every explanatory interconnection is deductive, but not every deductive interconnection is explanatory. All grounds are premisses, but not all premisses are grounds. Every deduction is indeed necessary, i.e. it obeys laws: but that its conclusions follow *according* to laws (the laws of inference) does not mean that they follow *from* laws which in a pregnant sense serve to 'ground' them. One tends, indeed, to call every premiss, and especially a universal one, a 'ground' for the consequences which flow from it, a noteworthy equivocation.

§64 *The essential and extra-essential principles that give science
unity. Abstract, concrete and normative sciences*

We are now in a position to answer the question raised above: What makes truths belong together in a *single science*, what constitutes their unity of 'subject-matter'?

The principle of unity may be of two sorts, essential and extra-essential.

The truths of a science are *essentially* one if their connection rests on what above all makes a science a science: a science is, as we know, grounded knowledge, i.e. explanation or proof (in the pointed sense). *Essential unity among the truths of a single science is unity of explanation.* But all explanation points to a theory, and has its goal in the knowledge of the basic laws, the principles of explanation. *Unity* of explanation means, therefore, *theoretical* unity, which means, on what was said above, homogeneous unity of legal base, and, lastly, *homogeneous unity of explanatory principles.*

The sciences whose field is determined by the standpoint of theory, of unity of principle, which embrace in ideal closure all possible facts and general items whose principles of explanation have a single legal base, are called, not very suitably, *abstract sciences*. The best name for them would really be *theoretical* sciences. This expression is, however, used in opposition to practical and normative sciences, and we too have used it above in this sense. Following a suggestion of J. von Kries,[1] one could say, almost as characteristically, that these sciences are *nomological*, in so far as their unifying principle, as well as their essential aim of research, is a law. The name 'explanatory science' which we have used from time to time, will also do, provided it is used to stress the unity reached by explanation, rather than explanation itself.

There are, in the second place, *external* standpoints which range truths into *one* science: the nearest to hand is the *unity of the thing* in a more literal sense. One connects all the truths whose content relates *to one and the same individual object, or to one and the same empirical genus*. This is the case in regard to the *concrete*, or, to use von Kries's term, the *ontological sciences*, such as geography, history, astronomy, natural history, anatomy etc. The truths of geography are united by their relation to the earth, the truths of meteorology concern, even more restrictedly, the weather-phenomena of the earth etc.

These sciences are also often called 'descriptive', and this name is allowable, since the unity of description is fixed by the empirical unity of the object or the class, and it is this descriptive unity which, in the sciences here involved, determines the science's unity. But the word should of course not be so understood as if descriptive sciences aimed at mere description, which would contradict our guiding concept of science.

Since it is possible that explanation which is directed towards empirical unities, leads to widely divergent, or quite heterogeneous theories and theoretical sciences, we rightly call the unity of the concrete science an 'extra-essential' one.

It is at any rate clear that the abstract or nomological sciences are the genuine, basic sciences, from whose theoretical stock the

---

[1] J. von Kries, *Die Prinzipien der Wahrscheinlichkeitsrechnung* (1886), pp. 85 f. and *Vierteljahrschrift für wiss. Philosophie*, xvi (1892), p. 255. Von Kries is, however, drawing a distinction among judgements, not, as here, among sciences, when he uses the terms 'nomological' and 'ontological'.

concrete sciences must derive all that theoretical element by which they are made sciences. Quite understandably, it is enough if the concrete sciences attach the objects they describe to the lower rungs of law in the nomological sciences, and at best indicate the main direction of ascending explanation. For the reduction to principles, and the general build-up of explanatory theories, is the proper field of the nomological sciences; it already exists in such sciences, where fully developed, in the most universal form and as a finished achievement. We are of course not pronouncing on the relative worth of the two sorts of sciences; our interest in theory is not our only interest, nor the sole determinant of value. Aesthetic, ethical, and, in a wider sense, practical interests can attach to what is individual, and impart the highest value to its detailed description and explanation. When, however, our purely theoretical interest sets the tone, the single individual and the empirical connection do not count intrinsically, or they count only as a methodological point of passage in the construction of a general theory. The theoretical natural scientist, or the natural scientist in the context of purely theoretic, mathematicizing discussion, sees the earth and stars quite differently from the geographer and the astronomer. They are to him *per se* indifferent and count merely as examples of gravitating masses in general.

We must finally make mention of *yet another extra-essential principle* of scientific unity: the principle which grows out of a unitary evaluative interest, which is therefore objectively determined by a unitary basic value (or by a unitary basic norm) as has been fully discussed in chapter II, §14. This constitutes 'mutual belongingness' as regards subject-matter among the truths in the normative sciences, or the unity of the field in question. Talk of 'mutual belongingness as regards subject-matter' is most naturally taken to mean a belongingness grounded in things, in subject-matters themselves. Here only a unity in terms of theoretical law or of the concrete thing will be relevant, and our conception will place normative unity over against unity of subject-matter in a single opposition.

As appears from our previous discussion, normative sciences depend on theoretical sciences – above all on sciences theoretical in the narrowest sense of being nomological – so that we can again say that they derive the theoretical element, which alone renders them scientific, from those theoretical sciences.

§65 *The question as to the ideal conditions of the possibility of science or of theory in general. A. The question as it relates to actual knowledge*

We now raise an important question as to the 'conditions of the possibility of science in general'. Since the essential aim of scientific knowledge can only be achieved through theory, in the strict sense of the nomological sciences, we replace our question by a question as to the *conditions of the possibility of theory in general*. A theory as such consists of truths, and its form of connection is a deductive one. To answer our question is therefore also to answer the more general question as to the conditions of the possibility of *truth in general*, and again of *deductive unity* in general. The historical echoes in the form of our question are of course intentional. We are plainly concerned with a quite necessary generalization of the question as to the 'conditions of the possibility of experience' (*Erfahrung*). The unity of an experience is for Kant the unity of objective legality: it falls, therefore, under the concept of theoretical unity.

The sense of our question needs, however, to be more precisely fixed. It might very well be at first understood in the *subjective* sense, in which case it would be better expressed as a question as to the conditions of the possibility of *theoretical knowledge* in general, or, more generally, of inference in general or knowledge in general, and in the case of any *possible* human being. Such conditions are in part *real*, in part *ideal*. We shall ignore the former, the psychological conditions. Naturally the possibility of knowledge in a psychological regard embraces all the causal conditions on which our thinking depends. *Ideal* conditions for the possibility of knowledge may, as said before,[1] be of two sorts. They are either

---

[1] Cf. above §32. Above, when I pinned down the pointed notion of scepticism, there was no place for so subtle a distinction, and I merely opposed the noetic conditions of *theoretical knowledge* to the objectively logical conditions of *theory itself*. But here, where all relevant relationships must be brought to complete clearness, it seems proper to treat the logical conditions, in the first place, as being conditions of *knowledge* as well, and then only to give them a direct relation to *objective theory* itself. This of course has no effect on anything essential to our conception, which rather achieves a clearer unfolding. The like holds in regard to the inclusion in our scope of the empirical, subjective conditions of knowledge together with the noetic, purely logical ones. We are profited in all this by our treatment of logical self-evidence: see above, §50. Self-evidence is indeed nothing other than the character of knowledge as such.

noetic conditions which have their grounds, *a priori*, in the Idea of Knowledge as such, without any regard to the empirical peculiarity of human knowledge as psychologically conditioned, or they are purely *logical* conditions, i.e. they are grounded purely in the 'content' of our knowledge. It is evident *a priori*, as regards the former, that thinking subjects must be in general able to perform, e.g., all the sorts of acts in which theoretical knowledge is made real. We must, in particular, as thinking beings, be able to see propositions as truths, and to see truths as consequences of other truths, and again to see laws as such, to see laws as explanatory grounds, and to see them as ultimate principles etc. But it is also, on the other hand, inwardly evident that truths are what they are, and that, in particular, laws, grounds, principles are what they are, whether we have insight into them or not. Since they do not hold in so far as we have insight into them, but we can only have insight into them in so far as they hold, they must be regarded as objective or ideal conditions of the possibility of our knowledge of them. *A priori* laws, accordingly, relating to truth as such, to deduction as such and to theory as such (i.e. to the universal essence of these ideal unities) must be characterized as laws which express the conditions for knowledge in general, or for deductive and theoretical knowledge in general, conditions which have their 'pure' foundation is the 'content' of knowledge.

Plainly we are here concerned with *a priori* conditions of knowledge, which can be discussed and investigated apart from all relation to the thinking subject and to the Idea of Subjectivity in science. The laws in question have a meaning-content which is quite free from such a relation, they do not talk, even in ideal fashion, of knowing, judging, inferring, representing, proving etc., but of truth, concept, proposition, syllogism, ground and consequent etc., as we fully said above (§47). Obviously these laws may undergo self-evident transformations through which they acquire an express relation to knowledge and the knowing subject, and now themselves pronounce on real possibilities of knowledge. Here as elsewhere, *a priori* assertions regarding ideal possibilities arise through the transferred application of ideal relationships (expressed in purely general propositions) to empirical instances (cf. the arithmetical example in §23 above).

The ideal conditions of knowledge which we have called 'noetic' as opposed to those which are logically objective, are, basically, no more than such modifications of the insights, the laws which pertain to the pure content of knowledge, as render them fruitful for the criticism of knowledge, and, by further modifications, for practical, logical normativity. For the *normative* modifications of the laws of pure logic, which we spoke of above, also come in here.

§66 *B. The question as it relates to the content of knowledge*

Our treatment has shown that questions as to the ideal conditions of the possibility of *knowledge* in general, and of theoretical knowledge in particular, ultimately lead us back to certain *laws*, whose roots are to be found purely in the content of knowledge, or of the categorial concepts that it falls under, and which are so abstract that they contain no reference to knowledge as an act of a knowing subject. These laws (or the categorial concepts which enter into them) are what are to be understood as constituting the conditions of the possibility of *theory* in general, in the objectively ideal sense. For it is possible to raise questions as to the conditions of possibility, not only in regard to theoretical knowledge, as we have so far done, but also in regard to its *content*, i.e. we can raise them directly in regard to theory itself. We then understand by 'theory', let us again stress, a certain *ideal content* of possible knowledge, just as in the case of 'truth', 'law' etc. There is a single truth, which corresponds to the multitude of individual acts of knowledge having the same content, which is just their ideally identical content. In like manner, the ideally identical content of a theory corresponds to the multitude of individual knowledge-combinations, in each of which – whether occurring now or then, in these subjects or in those – the *same* theory comes to be known. It is accordingly not *made up of acts* but of purely *ideal* elements, of truths, and that in purely ideal forms, those of *ground and consequent.*

If we now directly relate our question as to conditions of possibility, to theory in the objective sense and to theory in general, such a possibility can only have the sense which applies to other objects of pure conception. From such objects, we are led back to concepts, and 'possibility' means no more than the 'obtaining' (*Geltung*) or rather essentiality (*Wesenhaftigkeit*) of the concepts in question. This is what is often called the 'reality' as opposed to the 'imaginariness' of concepts, which latter could better be called 'essencelessness'. In such a sense, one speaks of real definitions which guarantee the possibility, the 'obtaining', the reality of the defined concept, and again of the opposition between real and imaginary numbers, geometrical figures etc. Talk of possibility in regard to concepts becomes equivocal through a transfer. What is in an authentic sense possible is the existence of objects falling under the relevant concepts, a possibility guaranteed *a priori* through knowledge of conceptual essence, which flashes upon us, e.g., as the result of such an object's being intuitively presented. The essentiality of the concept is then likewise spoken of as a possibility in a transferred sense.

In this connection, questions as to the *possibility* of a theory as such, and as to the conditions on which such possibility depends, gain an easily grasped sense. The possibility or essentiality of a theory in general is assured by our perspicuous knowledge of some definite theory. The wider question will however be: What are the universal, law-governed conditions of this possibility of theory in general? *What therefore constitutes the ideal essence of theory as such*? What are the primitive 'possibilities' out of which the possibility of theory is constituted, or, what is the same, what are the *primitive essential concepts* out of which the concept of theory, itself an essential concept, is constituted? And further: What are the pure laws which, rooted in these concepts, impart unity to all theory as such, laws which pertain to the form of theory as such, and which determine, in *a priori* fashion, the possible (essential) modifications or species of theory?

If these ideal concepts or laws delimit the possibility of theory in general, if, in other words, they express what essentially pertains to the Idea of Theory, it immediately follows that each putative theory only is a theory to the extent to which it accords with these concepts or laws. The logical justification of a concept, i.e. of its ideal possibility, is achieved by going back to its intuitive or deducible essence. Logical justification of a given theory as such, i.e. justification in virtue of its pure form, demands that we go back to the essence of its form, and so to the *concepts and laws which are ideal constituents of theory in general* (the 'conditions of its possibility'), which regulate, in *a priori*, deductive fashion, all specialization of the Idea of Theory in its possible kinds. Things are here as they are in the wider field of deduction, e.g. in the case of simple syllogisms. Though they may be intrinsically illuminated by insight, they none the less receive their final, deepest justification by recourse to the formal, syllogistic law which imparts insight into the *a priori* ground of syllogistic interconnection. The same holds in the case of any deduction, however complicated, and especially in the case of a theory. In perspicuous, theoretical thought we gain insight into the grounds of some state of affairs explained: but the deeper-going insight into the essence of the theoretical linkage which itself constitutes the theoretical content of such thought, and the *a priori* laws on which such thought-achievement depends, are first reached when we track down the form, the law, and the interweavings of theory, at the quite different level of knowledge to which they belong.

To point to profounder insights and justifications, serves to bring out the supreme value of the theoretical investigations which help to solve our suggested problem. We are dealing with *systematic theories which have their roots in the essence of theory*, with an *a priori, theoretical, nomological science which deals with the ideal essence of science as such*, and which accordingly has parts relating to systematic theories whose empirical, anthropological aspect it excludes. In a profound sense, we are dealing with the theory of theory, with the science of the sciences. Its achievement in enriching our knowledge must, of course, be kept separate from its problems themselves, and from the proper content of their solution.

§67 *The tasks of pure logic. First: the fixing of the pure categories of meaning, the pure categories of objects and their law-governed combinations*

Having provisionally fixed the Idea of the *a priori* discipline whose deeper understanding will be the goal of our efforts, we may now summarize the tasks that we shall assign to it. Three sets of tasks must be distinguished.

We must, *first* of all, lay down the more important concepts, in particular all the *primitive* concepts which 'make possible' the interconnected web of knowledge as seen objectively, and particularly the web of theory. We must also clarify these concepts scientifically. We are, in other words, concerned with the concepts which constitute the Idea of unified theory, or with the concepts which are connected with these through ideal laws. Into such a constitution second-order concepts, i.e. concepts of concepts and of other ideal unities, naturally enter. A given theory is a certain deductive combination of given propositions which are themselves certain sorts of combinations of given concepts. The Idea of the pertinent 'form' of the theory arises if we substitute variables for these given elements, whereby concepts of concepts and of other Ideas, replace straightforward concepts. Here belong the concepts: Concept, Proposition, Truth etc.

The concepts of the *elementary connective forms* naturally play a constitutive role here, those connective forms, in particular, which are quite generally constitutive of the deductive unity of propositions, e.g. the conjunctive, disjunctive, hypothetical linkage of propositions to form new propositions. Such a role is also played by the forms of connection of inferior elements of meaning into one simple proposition, which in their turn lead to the varied subject-forms, predicate-forms, forms of conjunctive and disjunctive connection, plural forms etc. Fixed laws govern the gradual complications through which an unending multiplicity of ever new forms emerges out of our primitive set. These *laws of complication* make possible a sweeping oversight of the concepts derivable from the primitive concepts and forms; these naturally belong, together with this sweeping oversight itself, in the field of research dealt with here. (Cf. Investigation IV in vol. II.)

In close connection with the concepts so far mentioned, i.e. the categories of meaning, and married to them by ideal laws, are other correlative concepts such as Object, State of Affairs, Unity, Plurality, Number, Relation, Connection etc. These are the pure, the formal *objective categories*. These too must be taken into account. In both cases we are dealing with nothing but concepts, whose notion makes clear that they are independent of the particularity of any material of knowledge, and under which all the concepts, propositions and states of affairs that specially appear in thought, must be ordered. They arise therefore solely in relation to our varying thought-functions: their concrete basis is solely to be found in possible acts of thought, as such, or in the correlates which can be grasped in these. (See §62 above and Investigation VI, §44 in vol. II.)

All these concepts must now be pinned down, their 'origin' must in each case be investigated. Not that psychological questions as to the origin of the conceptual presentations or presentational dispositions here in question, have the slightest interest for our discipline. This is not what we are enquiring into: we are concerned with a *phenomenological origin* or – if we prefer to rule out unsuitable talk of origins, only bred in confusion – we are concerned with *insight into the essence* of the concepts involved, looking methodologically to the fixation of unambiguous, sharply distinct verbal meanings. We can achieve such an end only by *intuitive representation* of the essence in adequate Ideation, or, in the case of complicated concepts, through knowledge of the essentiality of the elementary concepts present in them, and of the concepts of their forms of combination.

All these are seemingly trivial, preparatory tasks. To a large extent they are necessarily clothed in the form of discussions of terminology, and readily seem to the layman to be barren, pettifogging word-exercises. But as long as concepts are not distinguished and made clear to ideational intuition, by going back to their essence, further effort is hopeless. In no field of knowledge is equivocation more fatal, in none have confused concepts so hindered the progress of knowledge, or so impeded the insight into its true aims, as in the field of pure logic. The critical analyses of these Prolegomena have everywhere shown this.

It is impossible to overestimate the importance of this first group of problems; it is doubtful whether they do not in fact involve the greatest difficulties in the whole discipline.

§68 *Secondly: the laws and theories which have their grounds in these categories*

Our *second* group of problems lies in the search for the *laws* grounded in the two above classes of categorial concepts, which do not merely concern possible forms of complication and transformation of the theoretical items they involve (see Investigation IV), but rather the *objective validity* of the formal structures which thus arise: on the one hand, the truth or falsity of *meanings* as such, purely on the basis of their categorial formal structure, on the other hand (in relation to their *objective* correlates), the being and not being of objects as such, of states of affairs as such, again on the basis of their pure, categorial form. These laws, which concern meanings and objects as such, with the widest universality conceivable, the universality of logical categories, are in themselves theories. (See Investigation 1, §29.) We have, on the *one* side, the side of meaning, theories of inference, e.g. syllogistics, which is however only one such theory. On the other side, the side of the correlates, we have the pure theory of pluralities, which has its roots in the concepts of a plurality, the pure theory of numbers, which has its roots in the concept of a number – each an independently rounded-off theory. All the laws here belonging lead to a limited number of primitive or basic laws, which have their immediate roots in our categorial concepts. They must, in virtue of their homogeneity, serve to base an all-comprehensive theory, which will contain the separate theories just mentioned, as relatively closed elements in itself.

We are here concerned with the territory of those laws, which in formal universality span all possible meanings and objects, under which every particular theory or science is ranged, which it must obey if it is to be valid. Not that every such theory presupposes every such law as the ground of its possibility and validity. The ideal completeness of the categorial theories and laws in question, rather yields the all-comprehensive fund from which each particular valid theory derives the ideal grounds of essential being appropriate to its form. These are the laws to which it conforms, and through which, as a theory validated by its form, it can be ultimately justified. In so far as theory is an all-embracing unity built out of single, interwoven truths, it is plain that the laws governing the concept of truth, as well as the laws governing the possibility of single combinations of this or that form, will be included in the delimited territory. In spite of, or rather on account of, the fact that theory is the narrower notion, the task of exploring the conditions of its possibility, comprehends more content than the corresponding task in the case of truth in general, and in the case of the primitive forms of propositional combinations (cf. above, §65).

§69 *Thirdly: the theory of the possible forms of theories or the pure theory of manifolds*

When all these investigations have been concluded, we shall have done justice to the Idea of a science of the conditions of the possibility of theory in general. We see at once, however, that this science points beyond itself to a completing science, which deals *a priori* with the *essential sorts (forms) of theories and the relevant laws of relation*. The Idea therefore arises, all of this being taken together, of a more comprehensive science of theory in general. In its fundamental part, the essential concepts and laws which pertain constitutively to the Idea of Theory will be investigated. It will then go over to differentiating this Idea, and investigating *possible theories* in *a priori* fashion, rather than the possibility of theory in general.

The tasks mentioned have been carried out to a sufficient extent, and it is possible to construct, out of purely categorial concepts, many definite concepts of possible theories or pure 'forms' of theories, whose essential status has been deduced from laws. These distinct forms are not mutually unrelated. There will be a definite, ordered procedure which will enable us to construct the possible forms of theories, to survey their legal connections, and to pass from one to another by varying their basic determining factors etc. There will be universal propositions, if not for the forms of theory generally, then at least for forms of theory belonging to defined classes, which will govern the legal connection, the transformation and the mutual interchange of these forms.

The propositions that must here be affirmed will plainly be of a different content and character from the basic propositions and theorems of theories of the second group, from, e.g., syllogistic or arithmetical laws. It is, however, clear from the start that the deduction of such propositions (for there can be no true basic laws in this case) must have their entire basis in the previously mentioned theories.

This is a last, highest goal for a theoretical science of theory in general. It is also not indifferent from the point of view of the practical side of knowledge. To fit a theory into its formal class may rather be of the greatest methodological importance. For, with the extension of the deductive, theoretical sphere, the liveliness and freedom of theoretical research also increases: there is increased richness and fruitfulness of method. The solution of problems raised within a theoretical discipline, or one of its theories, can at times derive the most effective methodical help from recourse to the categorial type or (what is the same) to the form of the theory, and perhaps also by going over to a more comprehensive form or class of forms and to its laws.

§70 *Elucidation of the Idea of a pure theory of manifolds*

These indications will perhaps seem somewhat obscure. That we are not here dealing with vague fantasies, but with conceptions definite in their content, is shown by 'formal mathematics' in a most entirely general sense, or by the 'theory of manifolds', the fine flower of modern mathematics. The theory is in fact none other than the partial realization, correlatively transformed, of the ideal just sketched: this is not to say, of course, that mathematicians themselves, guided and likewise limited by interests which concern the field of number and magnitude, have correctly discerned the ideal essence of the new discipline, or have risen to the height of abstraction of an all-comprehensive theory. The *objective correlate* of the concept of a possible theory, definite only in respect of form, is *the concept of a possible field of knowledge over which a theory of this form will preside*. Such a field is, however, known in mathematical circles as a *manifold*. It is accordingly a field which is uniquely and solely determined by falling under a theory of such a form, whose objects are such as to permit of *certain* associations which fall under *certain* basic laws of this or that *determinate* form (here the only determining feature). The objects remain quite indefinite as regards their matter, to indicate which the mathematician prefers to speak of them as 'thought-objects'. They are not determined directly as individual or specific singulars, nor indirectly by way of their material species or genera, but solely by the *form* of the connections attributed to them. These connections are therefore as little determined in content as are their objects, only their form is determined, and determined through the forms of the elementary laws which are assumed to hold of them. These laws then, as they determine a *field* and its *form*, likewise determine the theory to be constructed, or, more correctly, *the theory's form*. In the theory of manifolds, e.g. '+' is not the sign for numerical addition, but for any connection for which laws of the form $a+b = b+a$ etc., hold. The manifold is determined by the fact that its thought-objects permit of these 'operations' (and of others whose compatibility with these can be shown *a priori*).

The *most general Idea of a Theory of Manifolds* is to be a science which definitely works out the form of the essential types of possible theories or fields of theory, and investigates their legal relations with one another. All actual theories are then specializations or singularizations of corresponding forms of theory, just as all theoretically worked-over fields of knowledge are *individual* manifolds. If the formal theory in question is actually worked out in the theory of manifolds, then all deductive theoretical work in constructing all actual theories of the same form has been done.

This is a point of view of the highest methodological importance, without which there can be no talk of understanding the method of mathematics. Not less important than such a going back to pure form, is the closely related ranging of each such form in more comprehensive forms or classes of forms. That we here have a central item in the wonderful, methodological art of mathematics, becomes plain if we look, not merely at the theories of manifolds which arose from generalizations of geometric theory and its forms, but at the first, simplest case of this sort, the extension of the field of real numbers (i.e. of the corresponding form of theory, the 'formal theory of real numbers') into the formal, two-dimensional field of ordinary complex numbers. In this concept we indeed have the key to the only possible solution of the problem that has not as yet been cleared up: how, e.g., in the field of numbers impossible (essenceless) concepts can be methodically treated like real ones. This is not, however, the place to discuss this more closely.

When I spoke above of theories of manifolds which arose out of generalizations of geometric theory, I was of course referring to the theory of *n*-dimensional manifolds, whether Euclidean or non-Euclidean, to Grassmann's theory of extensions, and, among others, to the related theories of a W. Rowan Hamilton, which can be readily purged of anything geometric. Lie's theory of transformation-groups and G. Cantor's investigations into numbers and manifolds also belong here.

The manner in which variation of curvature makes the various sorts of space-like manifolds pass into one another, gives the philosopher who has familiarized himself with the elements of the Riemannian–Helmholtzian theory a certain picture of the manner of the mutual legal connection among pure forms of theory of determinately distinct types. It would be easy to show that a knowledge of the true intention of such theories, as pure categorial forms of theory, would banish all metaphysical fog and all mysticism from the mathematical investigations in question. If we use the term 'space' of the familiar type of order of the world of phenomena, talk of 'spaces' for which, e.g. the axiom of parallels does not hold, is naturally senseless. It is just as senseless to speak of differing geometries, when 'geometry' names the science of the space of the world of phenomena. But if we mean by 'space' the categorial form of world-space, and, correlatively, by 'geometry' the categorial theoretic form of geometry in the ordinary sense, then space falls under a genus, which we can bound by laws, of pure, categorially determinate manifolds, in regard to which it is natural to speak of 'space' in a yet more extended sense. Just so, geometric theory falls under a corresponding genus of theoretically interrelated theory-forms determined in purely categorial fashion, which in a correspondingly extended sense can be called 'geometries' of these 'spatial' manifolds. At any rate, the theory of n-dimensional spaces forms a theoretically closed piece of the theory of theory in the sense above defined. The theory of a Euclidean manifold of three dimensions is an ultimate ideal singular in this legally interconnected series of *a priori*, purely categorial theoretic forms (formal deductive systems). This manifold itself is related to 'our' space, i.e. space in the ordinary sense, as its pure categorial form, the ideal genus of which the latter represents so to say an individual singular rather than a specific difference. Another fine example is the theory of complex number-systems, within which the theory of 'ordinary' complex numbers is a single item, a last specific difference. In relation to such theories, the arithmetics of number, of ordinal number, of magnitude, of quantité dirigée etc., are more or less like mere individual singulars. To each a formal generic Idea corresponds, a theory of absolute integers, of real numbers, of ordinary complex numbers etc., in whose case 'number' is to be taken in a generalized, formal sense.

§71 *Division of labour. The achievement of the mathematicians and that of the philosophers*

These therefore are the problems that we range in the field of pure or formal logic in the above defined sense: we thereby give this field its widest possible extension compatible with the Idea sketched by us of a science of theory in general. A considerable part of the theories which belong here has been developed as 'pure analysis' or, better, as *formal* mathematics, and is worked on by mathematicians together with other disciplines not in the full sense pure (i.e. formal), such as geometry (as the science of 'our' space), analytical mechanics etc. The nature of the case really demands a thoroughgoing *division of labour* here. The construction of theories, the strict, methodical solution of all formal problems, will always remain the home domain of the mathematician. Peculiar methods and set-ups of research are here presupposed, and are essentially the same in all pure theories. Even the elaboration of syllogistic theory, long enthroned in the very home territories of philosophy and thought to be completed long ago, has recently been taken over by mathematicians, in whose hands it has received undreamt of developments. Theories of new types of inference, ignored or misunderstood by the traditional logic, have at the same time been discovered and worked out with true mathematical elegance. No one can debar mathematicians from staking claims to all that can be treated in terms of mathematical form and method. Only if one is ignorant of the modern science of mathematics, particularly of formal mathematics, and measures it by the standards of Euclid or Adam Riese, can one remain stuck in the common prejudice that the essence of mathematics lies in number and quantity. It is not the mathematician, but the philosopher, who oversteps his legitimate sphere when he attacks 'mathematicizing' theories of logic, and refuses to hand over his temporary foster-children to their natural parents. The scorn with which philosophical logicians like to speak of mathematical theories of inference, does not alter the fact that the mathematical form of treatment is in their case (as in the case of all strictly developed theories in the proper sense of this word) the only scientific one, the only one that offers us systematic closure and completeness, and a survey of all possible questions together with the possible forms of their answers.

If the development of all true theories falls in the mathematician's field, what is left over for philosophers? Here we must note that the mathematician is not really the pure theoretician, but only the ingenious technician, the constructor, as it were, who, looking merely to formal interconnections, builds up his theory like a technical work of art. As the practical mechanic constructs machines without needing to have ultimate insight into the essence of nature and its laws, so the mathematician constructs theories of numbers, quantities, syllogisms, manifolds, without ultimate insight into the essence of theory in general, and that of the concepts and laws which are its conditions. The like holds of all 'special sciences': what is πρότερον τῇ φύσει is not at all what is πρότερον πρὸς ἡμᾶς. It is not, fortunately, essential insight which makes science, in the common, practically most fruitful sense, possible, but scientific instinct and method. For this very reason the ingenious, methodical work of the special sciences, more concerned with practical results and mastery than with essential insight, is in need of a continuous 'epistemological' reflection which only the philosopher can provide, which allows only the interest of pure theory to dominate, and helps it to claim its rights. Philosophical investigation has quite other ends, and therefore presupposes quite other methods and capacities. It does not seek to meddle in the work of the specialist, but to achieve insight in regard to the sense and essence of his achievements as regards method and manner. The philosopher is not content with the fact that we find our way about in the world, that we have legal formulae which enable us to predict the future course of things, or to reconstruct its past course: he wants to clarify the essence of a thing, an event, a cause, an effect, of space, of time etc., as well as that wonderful affinity which this essence has with the essence of thought, which enables it to be thought, with the essence of knowledge, which makes it knowable, with meanings which make it capable of being meant etc. And if science constructs theories in the systematic despatch of its problems, the philosopher enquires into the essence of theory and what makes theory as such possible etc. Philosophical research so supplements the scientific achievements of the natural scientist and of the mathematician, as for the first time to perfect pure, genuine, theoretical knowledge. The *ars inventiva* of the special investigator and the philosopher's critique of knowledge, are mutually complementary scientific activities, through which complete theoretical insight, comprehending all relations of essence, first comes into being.

The following individual investigations preparatory to the philosophical side of our discipline, will further elucidate what the mathematician will not, and cannot do, but what must nevertheless be done.

§72 Broadening of the Idea of pure logic. The pure theory
of probability as a pure theory of empirical knowledge

The concept of pure logic so far developed covers a theoretically closed circle of problems, essentially related to the Idea of Theory. To the extent that no science is possible without grounded explanation, i.e. without theory, pure logic covers the ideal conditions of the possibility of *science in general in the most general manner*. It must, however, be noted that logic so regarded does not include, as a special case, the ideal conditions of *empirical science in general*. To enquire into these conditions is of course a more restricted enquiry: empirical science is *also* science, and naturally falls, in regard to its theories, under the laws of the sphere delimited above. But ideal laws do not determine the unity of the empirical sciences merely in the form of the laws of deductive unity, since empirical science cannot be reduced merely to its theories. Theoretical optics, i.e. the mathematical theory of optics, does not exhaust the science of optics: mathematical mechanics is not the whole of mechanics etc. The whole complex apparatus of knowledge-processes in which the theories of the empirical sciences arise, and are frequently modified in the course of scientific progress, is certainly not merely subject to empirical, but also to ideal laws.

All theory in the empirical sciences is merely putative theory. It explains by means of basic laws which are not for our insight certain, but which are only for this insight probable. The theories themselves only have perspicuous probability; they are provisional, not final theories. The same is in a manner true of the *facts* which require explanation in theory. We start with such facts, they are taken as given; all that we want is to 'explain' them. But when we rise to the explanatory hypotheses and, after deduction, verification and perhaps repeated modification, accept them as probable laws, the facts themselves do not remain quite unchanged; they too change as the process of knowledge progresses. The added knowledge due to hypotheses that have proved workable, enables us to press ever deeper into the 'true essence' of real being: we progressively correct our conceptions, more or less tainted with inconsistencies, of phenomenal things. Facts are originally 'given' to us only in the sense of being perceived (and likewise in the sense of being remembered). In perception things and events themselves putatively confront us, seen and grasped, so to say, without intervening partition. And what we see before us, we utter in judgements of perception: these are the immediate 'given facts' of science. But, as knowledge progresses, the actual factual content that we concede to perceptual appearances gets altered. The intuitively given things – the things with 'secondary qualities' – come to count as 'mere appearances'. To determine the true element in them at a given time, or, in other words, to determine the empirical object of knowledge *objectively*, we need a method adjusted to the sense of this objectivity, and a field of scientifically known laws to be gained and steadily extended by this method.

All the scientific procedures of the objective sciences of fact are governed, as Descartes and Leibniz saw, not by psychological contingency, but by an *ideal* norm. We claim that, at any time, there is only *one* correct attitude in the assessment of the laws which are to explain, and in the fixing of the true facts, and that this is the case at each step in science. When a probable law or theory is rendered untenable by an increment of new empirical instances, we do not conclude that the scientific grounding of this theory must have been mistaken. In the field of our previous experience the previous theory was the 'only right' one, in the field of extended knowledge the theory that we now must try to establish is the 'only right' one, the one that must be justified by correct empirical consideration. We perhaps judge, conversely, that an empirical theory has been wrongly established, even if it becomes plain, in another objectively right way, that it is the only suitable theory in the given state of empirical knowledge. From this we must conclude that there must be *ideal elements and laws even in the field of empirical thinking, in the sphere of probabilities.* In these the *possibility* of empirical science in general, of the probable knowledge of the real, has its *a priori* basis. This sphere of pure laws does not relate to the Idea of Theory or to the more general Idea of Truth, but to the Idea of the Empirical Unity of Explanation, the Idea of Probability. This yields us a second great foundation for logical technology, which is included in the field of pure logic in a sense to which *corresponding width must be given.*

In the following individual Investigations we limit ourselves to the narrower field, which also comes *first* in the essential arrangement of our subject-matter.

Introduction

*§ 1 The necessity of phenomenological investigations as a
preliminary to the epistemological criticism and clarification
of pure logic*

THE necessity that we should begin logic with linguistic discussions has often been acknowledged from the standpoint of a logical technology. 'Language', we read in Mill, 'is evidently one of the principal instruments or helps of thought; and any imperfection in the instrument, or in the mode of employing it, is confessedly liable, still more than in almost any other art, to confuse and impede the process, and destroy all ground of confidence in the result. For a mind not previously versed in the meaning and right use of the various kinds of words, to attempt the study of methods of philosophizing, would be as if some one should attempt to become an astronomical observer, having never learnt to adjust the focal distance of his optical instruments so as to see distinctly.'[1] A deeper ground for this necessity of beginning logic with linguistic analysis is, however, seen by Mill in the fact that it would not otherwise be possible to investigate the meaning of propositions, a matter which stands 'at the threshold' of logical science itself.

This last remark of our distinguished thinker indicates a point of view regulative for *pure* logic, and, be it noted, for *pure* logic treated as a *philosophical* discipline. I assume accordingly that no one will think it enough to develop pure logic merely in the manner of our mathematical disciplines, as a growing system of propositions having a naïvely factual validity, without also striving to be philosophically clear in regard to these same propositions, without, that is, gaining insight into the essence of the modes of cognition which come into play in their utterance and in the ideal possibility of applying such propositions, together

---

[1] *Logic*, Book I, ch. I, § I.

with all such conferments of sense and objective validities as are essentially constituted therein. Linguistic discussions are certainly among the philosophically indispensable preparations for the building of pure logic: only by their aid can the true *objects* of logical research – and, following thereon, the essential species and differentiae of such objects – be refined to a clarity that excludes all misunderstanding. We are not here concerned with grammatical discussions, empirically conceived and related to some historically given language: we are concerned with discussions of a most general sort which cover the wider sphere of an objective *theory of knowledge* and, closely linked with this last, the *pure phenomenology of the experiences of thinking and knowing*. This phenomenology, like the more inclusive *pure phenomenology of experiences in general*, has, as its exclusive concern, experiences intuitively seizable and analysable in the pure generality of their essence, not experiences empirically perceived and treated as real facts, as experiences of human or animal experients in the phenomenal world that we posit as an empirical fact. This phenomenology must bring to pure expression, must *describe* in terms of their essential concepts and their governing formulae of essence, the essences which directly make themselves known in intuition, and the connections which have their roots purely in such essences. Each such statement of essence is an *a priori* statement in the highest sense of the word. This sphere we must explore in preparation for the epistemological criticism and clarification of pure logic: our investigations will therefore all move within it.

Pure phenomenology represents a field of neutral researches, in which several sciences have their roots. It is, on the one hand, an ancillary to *psychology* conceived as an *empirical science*. Proceeding in purely intuitive fashion, it analyses and describes in their essential generality – in the specific guise of a phenomenology of thought and knowledge – the experiences of presentation, judgement and knowledge, experiences which, treated as classes of real events in the natural context of zoological reality, receive a scientific probing at the hands of empirical psychology. Phenomenology, on the other hand, lays bare the 'sources' from which the basic concepts and ideal laws of *pure* logic 'flow', and back to which they must once more be traced, so as to give them all the 'clearness and distinctness' needed for an understanding, and for an epistemological critique, of pure logic. The epistemological or phenomenological groundwork of pure logic involves very hard, but also surpassingly important researches. To revert to what we set forth as the tasks of pure logic in the first volume of these *Investigations*, we have taken it upon us to give firm clarity to notions and laws on which the objective meaning and theoretical unity of all knowledge is dependent.[1]

§2 *Elucidation of the aims of such investigations*

All theoretical research, though by no means solely conducted in acts of verbal expression or complete statement, none the less terminates in such statement. Only in this form can truth, and in particular the truth of theory, become an abiding possession of science, a documented, ever available treasure for knowledge and advancing research. Whatever the connection of thought with speech may be, whether or not the appearance of our final judgements in the form of verbal pronouncements has a necessary grounding in essence, it is at least plain that judgements stemming from higher intellectual regions, and in particular from the regions of science, could barely arise without verbal expression.

The objects which pure logic seeks to examine are, in the first instance, therefore given to it in grammatical clothing. Or, more precisely, they come before us embedded in concrete mental states which further function either as the *meaning-intention* or *meaning-fulfilment* of certain verbal expressions – in the latter case intuitively illustrating, or intuitively providing evidence for, our meaning – and forming a *phenomenological unity* with such expressions.

In these complex phenomenological unities the logician must pick out the components that interest him, the characters of the acts, first of all, in which logical presentation, judgement and knowledge are consummated: he must pursue the descriptive analysis of such act-types to the extent that this helps the progress of his properly logical tasks. We cannot straightway leap, from the fact that theory 'realizes' itself in certain mental states, and has instances in them, to the seemingly obvious truth that such mental states must count as the primary object of our logical researches. The pure logician is not primarily or properly interested in the psychological judgement, the concrete mental

[1] See the final chapter of the Prolegomena, §§66–7 in particular.

phenomenon, but in the logical judgement, the identical asserted meaning, which is one over against manifold, descriptively quite different, judgement-experiences.[1] There is naturally, in the singular experiences which correspond to this ideal unity, a certain pervasive common feature, but since the concern of the pure logician is not with the concrete instance, but with its corresponding Idea, its abstractly apprehended universal, he has, it would seem, no reason to leave the field of abstraction, nor to make concrete experiences the theme of his probing interest, instead of Ideas.

Even if phenomenological analysis of concrete thought-experiences does not fall within the true home-ground of pure logic, it none the less is indispensable to the advance of purely logical research. For all that is logical must be given in fully concrete fashion, if, as an object of research, it is to be made our own, and if we are to be able to bring to self-evidence the *a priori* laws which have their roots in it. What is logical is first given us in imperfect shape: the concept as a more or less wavering meaning, the law, built out of concepts, as a more or less wavering assertion. We do not therefore lack logical insights, but grasp the pure law with self-evidence, and see how it has its base in the pure forms of thought. Such self-evidence depends, however, on the verbal meanings which come alive in the actual passing of the judgement regarding the law. Unnoticed equivocation may permit the subsequent substitution of other concepts beneath our words, and an appeal on behalf of an altered propositional meaning may quite readily, but wrongly, be made on the self-evidence previously experienced. It is also possible, conversely, that a misinterpretation based on equivocation may distort the sense of the propositions of pure logic (perhaps turning them into empirical, psychological propositions), and may tempt us to abandon previously experienced self-evidence and the unique significance of all that belongs to pure logic.

It is not therefore enough that the Ideas of logic, and the pure laws set up with them, should be given in such a manner. Our great task is now *to bring the Ideas of logic, the logical concepts and laws, to epistemological clarity and definiteness.*

Here *phenomenological analysis* must begin. Logical concepts, as valid thought-unities, must have their origin in intuition: they

[1] Cf. §11 of Investigation 1.

must arise out of an ideational intuition founded on certain experiences, and must admit of indefinite reconfirmation, and of recognition of their self-identity, on the reperformance of such abstraction. Otherwise put: we can absolutely not rest content with 'mere words', i.e. with a merely symbolic understanding of words', such as we first have when we reflect on the sense of the laws for 'concepts', 'judgements', 'truths' etc. (together with their manifold specifications) which are set up in pure logic. Meanings inspired only by remote, confused, inauthentic intuitions – if by any intuitions at all – are not enough: we must go back to the 'things themselves'. We desire to render self-evident in fully-fledged intuitions that what is here given in actually performed abstractions is what the word-meanings in our expression of the law really and truly stand for. In the practice of cognition we strive to arouse dispositions in ourselves which will keep our meanings unshakably the same, which will measure them sufficiently often against the mark set by reproducible intuitions or by an intuitive carrying out of our abstraction. Intuitive illustration of the shifting meanings which attach to the same term in differing propositional contexts likewise convinces us of the fact of equivocation: it becomes evident to us that what a word means in this or that case has its fulfilment in essentially different intuitive 'moments' or patterns, or in essentially different general notions. By distinguishing among concepts confounded by us, and by suitably modifying our terminology, we then likewise achieve a desired 'clearness and distinctness' for our logical propositions.

The phenomenology of the logical experiences aims at giving us a sufficiently wide descriptive (though not empirically-psychological) understanding of these mental states and their indwelling sense, as will enable us to give fixed meanings to all the fundamental concepts of logic. Such meanings will be clarified both by going back to the analytically explored connections between meaning-intentions and meaning-fulfilments, and also by making their possible function in cognition intelligible and certain. They will be such meanings, in short, as the interest of pure logic itself requires, as well as the interest, above all, of epistemological insight into the essence of this discipline. Fundamental logical and noetic concepts have, up to this time, been quite imperfectly clarified: countless equivocations beset them, some so pernicious, so hard to track down, and to keep consistently separate, that they yield the main ground for the very backward state of pure logic and theory of knowledge.

We must of course admit that many conceptual differentiations and circumscriptions of the sphere of pure logic can become evident to the natural attitude without phenomenological analysis. The relevant logical acts are carried out and adequately fitted to their fulfilling intuitions, though there is no reflection on the phenomenological situation itself. What is most completely evident can, however, be confused with something else, what it apprehends can be misconstrued, its assured directives can be rejected. Clarifying researches are especially needed to explain our by no means chance inclination to slip unwittingly from an objective to a psychological attitude, and to mix up two bodies of data distinguishable in principle however much they may be essentially related, and to be deceived by psychological misconstructions and misinterpretations of the objects of logic. Such clarifications can, by their nature, only be achieved within a phenomenological theory of the essences of our thought- and knowledge-experiences, with continuous regard to the things essentially meant by, and so belonging to the latter (in the precise manners in which those things are *as such* 'shown forth', 'represented' etc.). Psychologism can only be radically overcome by a pure phenomenology, a science infinitely removed from psychology as the empirical science of the mental attributes and states of animal realities. In our sphere, too, the sphere of pure logic, such a phenomenology alone offers us all the necessary conditions for a finally satisfactory establishment of the totality of basic distinctions and insights. It alone frees us from the strong temptation, at first inevitable, since rooted in grounds of essence, to turn the logically objective into the psychological.

The above mentioned motives for phenomenological analysis have an obvious and essential connection with those which spring from *basic questions of epistemology*. For if these questions are taken in the *widest* generality, i.e. in the 'formal' generality which abstracts from all matter of knowledge – they form part of a range of questions involved in the full clarification of the Idea of pure logic. We have, on the one hand, the fact that all thought and knowledge have as their aim *objects* or *states of affairs*, which they putatively 'hit' in the sense that the 'intrinsic being' of these objects and states is supposedly shown forth, and made an identifiable item, in a multitude of actual or possible meanings, or acts of thought. We have, further, the fact that all thought is ensouled by a thought-form which is subject to ideal laws, laws circumscribing the objectivity or ideality of knowledge in general. These facts, I maintain, eternally provoke questions like: How are we to understand the fact that the intrinsic being of objectivity becomes 'presented', 'apprehended' in knowledge, and so ends up by becoming subjective? What does it mean to say that the object has 'intrinsic being', and is 'given' in knowledge? How can the ideality of the universal *qua* concept or law enter the flux of real mental states and become an epistemic possession of the thinking person? What does the *adaequatio rei et intellectus* mean in various cases of knowledge, according as what we apprehend and know, is individual or universal, a fact or a law etc.? These and similar questions can, it is plain, not be separated from the above-mentioned questions regarding the clarification of pure logic, since the task of clarifying such logical Ideas as Concept and Object, Truth and Proposition, Fact and Law etc., inevitably leads on to these same questions. We should in any case have to tackle them so that the essence of the clarification aimed at in phenomenological analyses should not itself be left obscure.

§3 *The difficulties of pure phenomenological analysis*

The difficulties of clearing up the basic concepts of logic are a natural consequence of the extraordinary difficulties of strict phenomenological analysis. These are in the main the same whether our immanent analysis aims at the *pure* essence of experiences (all empirical facticity and individuation being excluded) or treats experiences from an empirical, psychological standpoint. Psychologists usually discuss such difficulties when they consider introspection as a source of our detailed psychological knowledge, not properly however, but in order to draw a false antithesis between introspection and 'outer' perception. The source of all such difficulties lies in the unnatural direction of intuition and thought which phenomenological analysis requires. Instead of becoming lost in the performance of acts built intricately on one another, and instead of (as it were) naïvely positing the existence of the objects intended in their sense and then going

on to characterize them, or of assuming such objects hypothetically, of drawing conclusions from all this etc., we must rather
practise 'reflection', i.e. make these acts themselves, and their
immanent meaning-content, our objects. When objects are
intuited, thought of, theoretically pondered on, and thereby given
to us as actualities in certain ontic modalities, we must direct our
theoretical interest away from such objects, not posit them as
realities as they appear or hold in the intentions of our acts. These
acts, contrariwise, though hitherto not objective, must now be
made objects of apprehension and of theoretical assertion. We
must deal with them in new acts of intuition and thinking, we
must analyse and describe them in their essence, we must make
them objects of empirical or ideational thought. Here we have a
direction of thought running counter to deeply ingrained habits
which have been steadily strengthened since the dawn of mental
development. Hence the well-nigh ineradicable tendency to slip
out of a phenomenological thought-stance into one that is
straightforwardly objective, or to substitute for mental acts, or
for the 'appearances' or 'meanings' immanent in them, characters
which, in a naïve performance of such acts, were attributed to
their objects. Hence, too, the tendency to treat whole classes of
genuinely subsistent objects, e.g. Ideas – since these may be
evidently given to us in ideating intuitions – as phenomenological
constituents of presentations *of* them.

A much discussed difficulty – one which seems to threaten in
principle all possible immanent description of mental acts or
indeed all phenomenological treatment of essences – lies in the
fact that when we pass over from naïvely performed acts to an
attitude of reflection, or when we perform acts proper to such
reflection, our former acts necessarily undergo change. How can
we rightly assess the nature and extent of such change? How
indeed can we know anything whatever about it, whether as a
fact or as a necessity of essence?

In addition to this difficulty of reaching firm results, capable
of being self-evidently reidentified on many occasions, we have
the further difficulty of *stating such results*, of *communicating them to
others*. Completely self-evident truths of essence, established by
the most exact analysis, must be expounded by way of expressions
whose rich variety does not compensate for the fact that they only
fit familiar natural objects, while the experiences in which such

objects become constituted for consciousness, can be directly referred to only by way of a few highly ambiguous words such as 'sensation' 'perception', 'presentation' etc. One has, further, to employ expressions which stand for what is intentional in such acts, for the object to which they are directed, since it is, in fact, impossible to describe referential acts without using expressions which recur to the things to which such acts refer. One then readily forgets that such subsidiarily described objectivity, which is necessarily introduced into almost all phenomenological description, has undergone a change of sense, in virtue of which it now belongs to the sphere of phenomenology.

If we ignore such difficulties, others emerge concerned with the persuasive communication of our resultant insights to others. These insights can be tested and confirmed only by persons well-trained in the ability to engage in pure description in the unnatural attitude of reflection, trained in short to allow phenomenological relations to work upon them *in full purity*. Such purity means that we must keep out the falsifying intrusion of all assertions based on the naïve acceptance and assessment of objects, whose existence has been posited in the acts now receiving phenomenological treatment. It likewise prohibits any other going beyond whatever is essential and proper to such acts, any application to them of naturalistic interpretations and assertions. It forbids us, i.e., to set them up as psychological realities (even in an indefinitely general or exemplary fashion), as the states of 'mind-endowed beings' of any sort whatsoever. The capacity for such researches is not readily come by, nor can it be achieved or replaced by, e.g., the most elaborate of trainings in experimental psychology.

Serious as are the difficulties standing in the way of a pure phenomenology in general, and of the phenomenology of the logical experiences in particular, they are by no means such as to make the whole attempt to overcome them appear hopeless. Resolute cooperation among a generation of research-workers, conscious of their goal and dedicated to the main issue, would, I think, suffice to decide the most important questions in the field, those concerned with its basic constitution. Here we have a field of *attainable* discoveries, fundamentally involved in the possibility of a *scientific* philosophy. Such discoveries have indeed nothing dazzling about them: they lack any obviously useful relation to practice or to the fulfilment of higher emotional needs. They also lack any imposing apparatus of experimental methodology, through which experimental psychology has gained so much credit and has built up such a rich force of cooperative workers.

§4 *It is essential to keep in mind the grammatical side of our logical experiences*

Analytic phenomenology, needed by the logician in his preparatory laying of foundations, is concerned, among other things, with 'presentations' and with them primarily; it is, more precisely, concerned with those presentations to which *expression* has been given. In the complex objects of its study, its primary interest attaches to the experiences lying behind 'mere expressions', experiences which perform roles either of meaning-intention or of meaning-fulfilment. It cannot, however, quite ignore the sensuous-linguistic side of its complex objects (the element of 'mere expression' in them) nor the way in which this element is associated with the meaning that 'ensouls' it. Everyone knows how readily and how unnoticeably an analysis of meaning can be led astray by grammatical analysis. Since the direct analysis of meaning is, however, difficult, we may welcome each aid, however imperfect, that indirectly anticipates its results, but grammatical analysis is even more important in virtue of the errors its use promotes when it replaces a *true analysis of meaning*, than for any positive aid. Rough reflection on our thoughts and their verbal expression, conducted by us without special schooling, and often needed for the practical ends of thinking, suffice to indicate a certain parallelism between thinking and speaking. We all know that words mean something, and that, generally speaking, different words express different meanings. If we could regard such a correspondence as perfect, and as given *a priori*, and as one particularly in which the essential categories of meaning had perfect mirror-images in the categories of grammar, a phenomenology of linguistic forms would include a phenomenology of the meaning-experiences (experiences of thinking, judging etc.) and meaning-analysis would, so to speak, coincide with grammatical analysis.

Deep reflection is not, however, needed to show that a parallelism satisfying such far-reaching demands has as little foundation in grounds of essence as it obtains in fact. *Grammatically relevant distinctions of meaning* are at times *essential*, at times *contingent*, according as the practical aims of speech dictate peculiar forms for essential or contingent differences of meaning. (The latter are merely such as have a frequent occurrence in human intercourse.)

It is well-known, however, that differentiation of expressions does not merely depend on differences of meaning. I need point only to 'shades' of meaning, or to aesthetic tendencies which fight against any bare uniformity of expression, or against discord in speech-sound or rhythm, and so demand an abundant store of available synonyms.

The rough concomitances among verbal and thought-differences, and particularly among *forms* of words and thoughts, makes us naturally tend to seek logical distinctions behind expressed grammatical distinctions. It is, therefore, *an important matter for logic that the relation between expression and meaning should be made analytically clear*. We should perceive clearly that, in order to decide whether a distinction should, in a given case, count as logical or merely grammatical, we must go back from *vague* acts of meaning to the correspondingly clear, articulate ones, acts saturated with the fulness of exemplary intuition in which their meaning is fulfilled.

It is not enough to have the common knowledge, easily garnered from suitable examples, that grammatical differences need not coincide with logical ones. The common knowledge that such distinctions do not always go hand in hand – that languages, in other words, express material differences of meaning, widely used in communication, in forms as pervasive as the fundamental logical differences having their *a priori* roots in the general essence of meanings – such common knowledge may open the way to a dangerous radicalism. The field of logical forms may be unduly restricted. A wide range of logically significant forms may be cast forth as merely grammatical: only a few may be kept, such as suffice to leave some content to traditional syllogizing. Brentano's attempted reform of formal logic, valuable as it no doubt still is, plainly suffered from this exaggeration. Only a complete clearing-up of the essential phenomenological relations between expression and meaning, or between meaning-intention and meaning-fulfilment, can give us a firm middle stance, and can enable us to give the requisite clearness to the relations between grammatical and meaning-analysis.

§ 5 *Statement of the main aims of the following analytical investigations*

We accordingly pass to a series of analytic investigations which will clear up the constitutive Ideas of a pure or formal logic, investigations which relate in the first place to the pure theory of logical forms. Starting with the empirical connection between meaning-experiences and expressions, we must try to find out what our variously ambiguous talk about 'expressing' or 'meaning' really amounts to. We must try to see what essential phenomenological or logical distinctions apply *a priori* to expressions, and how we may in essence describe, and may place in pure categories, the experiences – to deal first with the phenomenological side of expressions – that have an *a priori* fitness for the meaning-function. We must find out how the 'presenting' and 'judging' achieved in such experiences stand to their corresponding 'intuition', how they are 'illustrated', or perhaps 'confirmed' or 'fulfilled', in the latter, or rendered 'evident' by it etc. It is not hard to see that investigations of such matters must precede all clarifications of the basic concepts and categories of logic. Among our introductory investigations we shall have to raise fundamental questions as to the acts, or, alternatively, the ideal meanings, which in logic pass under the name of 'presentations' (*Vorstellungen*). It is important to clarify and prise apart the many concepts that the word 'presentation' has covered, concepts in which the psychological, the epistemological and the logical are utterly confused. Similar analyses deal with the concept of *judgement* in the sense in which logic is concerned with it. So-called 'judgement-theory' neglects this task: it is in the main, in respect of its essential problems, a theory of presentation. We are naturally not interested in a psychological theory, but in a phenomenology of presentation- and judgement-experiences as delimited by our epistemological interests.

As we probe the essence of the expressive experiences, we must also dig more deeply into their *intentional subject-matter*, their objective intention's ideal sense, i.e. into the unity of its meaning and the unity of its object. We must, above all, dwell upon the enigmatic double sense or manner, the two-sided context, in which the same experience has a 'content', and the manner in which in addition to its real (*reell*) and proper content, an ideal, intentional content must and can dwell in it.

Here also belong questions relating to the 'object-directedness' or 'objectlessness' of logical acts, to the sense of the distinction between intentional and true objects, to the clarification of the Idea of truth in relation to the Idea of judgemental self-evidence, to the clarification of the remaining, closely connected logical and noetic categories. These investigations in part cover the same ground as those dealing with the constitution of logical forms, to the extent, of course, that we settle questions as to the acceptance or rejection of putative logical forms, or doubts as to their logical or merely grammatical distinctness from forms already recognized, in the course of our clarification of form-giving, categorial concepts.

We have thus vaguely indicated the range of problems to which the ensuing investigations will be oriented. These investigations make no claim to be exhaustive. Their aim is not to provide a logical system, but to do the initial spadework for a philosophical logic which will derive clearness from basic phenomenological sources. The paths taken by such an analytic investigation will also naturally differ from those suitable to a final, systematic, logically ordered statement of established truth.

§6 *Additional Notes*

Note 1 Our investigations will often inevitably take us beyond the narrow phenomenological sphere whose study is really required for giving direct evidence to the Ideas of logic. This sphere is itself not given to us initially, but becomes delimited in the course of our investigation. We are, in particular, forced beyond this sphere of research when we prise apart the many confused concepts obscurely confounded in our understanding of logical terms, and when we find which of them are truly logical.

Note 2 To lay down the phenomenological foundations of logic involves the difficulty that we must, in our exposition, make use of all the concepts we are trying to clarify. This coincides with a certain wholly irremoveable defect which affects the systematic course of our basic phenomenological and epistemological investigations. If a type of thought requires prior clarification, we should not make uncritical use of its terms or concepts in that clarification itself. But one should not expect that one should only be required to analyse such concepts critically, when the actual interconnection of one's logical materials has led up to them. Or, put differently, systematic clarification, whether in pure logic or any other discipline, would in itself seem to require a stepwise following out of the ordering of things, of the systematic interconnection in the science to be clarified. Our investigation can, however, only proceed securely, if it repeatedly breaks with such systematic sequence, if it removes conceptual obscurities which threaten the course of investigation *before* the natural sequence of subject-matters can lead up to such concepts. We search, as it were, in zig-zag fashion, a metaphor all the more apt since the close interdependence of our various epistemological concepts leads us back again and again to our original analyses, where the new confirms the old, and the old the new.

Note 3 If *our* sense of phenomenology has been grasped, and if it has not been given the current interpretation of an ordinary 'descriptive psychology', a part of natural science, then an objection, otherwise justifiable, will fall to the ground, an objection to the effect that all theory of knowledge, conceived as a systematic phenomenological clarification of knowledge, is built upon psychology. On this interpretation pure logic, treated by us as an epistemologically clarified, *philosophical* discipline, must in the end likewise rest upon psychology, if only upon its preliminary descriptive researches into intentional experiences. Why then so much heated resistance to psychologism?

We naturally reply that if psychology is given its old meaning, phenomenology is not descriptive psychology: its peculiar 'pure' description, its contemplation of pure essences on a basis of exemplary individual intuitions of experiences (often freely *imagined* ones), and its descriptive fixation of the contemplated essences into pure concepts, is no empirical, scientific description. It rather excludes the natural performance of all empirical (naturalistic) apperceptions and positings. Statements of descriptive psychology regarding 'perceptions', 'judgements', 'feelings', 'volitions' etc., use such names to refer to the real states of animal organisms in a real natural order, just as descriptive statements concerning physical states deal with happenings in a nature not imagined but real. All general statements have here a character of empirical generality: they hold for *this* nature. Phenomenology, however, does not discuss states of animal organisms (not even as belonging to a possible nature as such), but perceptions, judgements, feelings *as such*, and what pertains to them *a priori* with unlimited generality, as *pure* instances of *pure* species, of what may be seen through a purely intuitive apprehension of essence, whether generic or specific. Pure arithmetic likewise speaks of numbers, and pure geometry of spatial shapes, employing pure intuitions in their ideational universality. Not psychology, therefore, but phenomenology, underlies all clarifications in pure logic (and in all forms of rational criticism). Phenomenology has, however, a very different function as the necessary basis for every psychology that could with justification and in strictness be called scientific, just as pure mathematics, e.g. pure geometry and dynamics, is the necessary foundation for all exact natural science (any theory of empirical things in nature with their empirical forms, movements etc.). Our essential insights into perceptions, volitions and other forms of experience will naturally hold also of the corresponding empirical states of animal organisms, as geometrical insights hold of spatial figures in nature.

Translator's Additional Note 4 The above Note 3 is a typical account of what Husserl had come to mean by 'phenomenology' by the time that the Second Edition of the *Logical Investigations* was published in 1913. It replaces the following Note, which indicates what he meant by the term when the First Edition was published in 1901:

> Phenomenology is descriptive psychology. Epistemological criticism is therefore in essence psychology, or at least only capable of being built on a psychological basis. Pure logic therefore also rests on psychology – what then is the point of the whole battle against psychologism?
> The necessity of *this* sort of psychological foundation of pure logic, i.e. a strictly descriptive one, cannot lead us into error regarding the mutual independence of the two sciences, logic and psychology. For pure description is merely a preparatory step towards theory, not theory itself. One and the same sphere of pure description can accordingly serve to prepare for very different theoretical sciences. It is *not the full science of psychology that serves as a foundation*

for pure logic, but certain classes of descriptions which are the step preparatory to the theoretical researches of psychology. These in so far as they describe the empirical objects whose genetic connections the science wishes to pursue, also form the substrate for those fundamental abstractions in which logic seizes the essence of its ideal objects and connections with inward evidence. Since it is epistemologically of unique importance that we should separate the purely descriptive examination of the knowledge-experience, disembarrassed of all theoretical psychological interests, from the truly psychological researches directed to empirical explanation and origins, it will be good if we rather speak of 'phenomenology' than of descriptive psychology. It also recommends itself for the further reason that the expression 'descriptive psychology', as it occurs in the talk of many scientists, means the sphere of scientific psychological investigation, which is marked off by a methodological preference for inner experience and by an abstraction from all psychophysical explanation.

§7 *'Freedom from presuppositions' as a principle in*
epistemological investigations

An epistemological investigation that can seriously claim to be scientific must, it has often been emphasized, satisfy the *principle of freedom from presuppositions*. This principle, we think, only seeks to express the strict exclusion of all statements not permitting of a comprehensive *phenomenological* realization. Every epistemological investigation that we carry out must have its pure foundation in phenomenology. The 'theory' that it aspires to, is no more than a thinking over, a coming to an evident understanding of, thinking and knowing as such, in their pure generic essence, of the specifications and forms that they essentially have, of the immanent structures that their objective relations involve, of the meaning of 'validity', 'justification', 'mediate' and 'immediate evidence', and their opposites, as applied to such structures, of the parallel specifications of such Ideas in relation to varying regions of possible objects of knowledge, of the clarified sense and role of the formal and material 'laws of thought' seen in their *a priori* structural connections with the knowing consciousness etc. If such a 'thinking over' of the meaning of knowledge is itself to yield, not mere opinion, but the evident knowledge it strictly demands, it must be a pure intuition of essences, exemplarily performed on an actual *given* basis of experiences of thinking and knowing. That acts of thought at times refer to transcendent, even to non-existent and impossible objects, is not to the case. For such direction to objects, such presentation and meaning of what is not really (*reell*) part of the phenomenological make-up of our experiences, is a descriptive feature of the experiences in question, whose sense it should be possible to fix and clarify by considering the experiences themselves. In no other way would it be possible.

We must keep apart from the pure theory of knowledge questions concerning the justifiability of accepting 'mental' and 'physical' realities which transcend consciousness, questions whether the statements of scientists regarding them are to be given a serious or unserious sense, questions whether it is justifiable or sensible to oppose a second, even more emphatically 'transcendent' world, to the phenomenal nature with which science is correlated, and other similar questions. The question as to the existence and nature of 'the external world' is a metaphysical question. The theory of knowledge, in generally clearing up the ideal essence and valid sense of cognitive thought, will of course deal with general questions regarding the possibility and manner of a knowledge or rational surmise about 'real' objective things, things in principle transcending the experiences which know them, and regarding the norms which the true sense of such a knowledge requires: it will not enter upon the empirically oriented question as to whether we as men really can arrive at such knowledge from the data we actually have, nor will it attempt to realize such knowledge. On our view, theory of knowledge, properly described, is no theory. It is not science in the pointed sense of an explanatorily unified theoretical whole. *Theoretical explanation* means an ever increased rendering intelligible of singular facts through general laws, and an ever increased rendering intelligible of general laws through some fundamental law. In the realm of facts, our task is to know that what happens under given groups of circumstances, happens *necessarily*, i.e. according to *natural laws*. In the realm of the *a priori* our task is to understand the *necessity* of specific, lower-level relationships in terms of comprehensive general necessities, and ultimately in terms of those most primitive, universal relational *laws* that we call axioms. The theory of knowledge has nothing to explain in this theoretical sense, it neither constructs deductive theories nor falls under any. This is clear enough if we consider the most general, the so-to-say formal theory of knowledge that came before us in our *Prolegomena* as the philosophical completion of pure mathematics conceived in absolute width as including all *a priori*, categorial knowledge in the form of systematic theories. This theory of theories goes together with, and is illuminated by, a formal theory of knowledge which precedes all empirical theory, which precedes, therefore, all empirical knowledge of the real, all physical science on the one hand, and all psychology on the other, and of course all metaphysics. Its aim is not to *explain* knowledge in the psychological or psychophysical sense as a *factual* occurrence in objective nature, but to *shed light* on the *Idea* of knowledge in its constitutive elements and laws. It does not try to follow up the real connections of coexistence and succession with which actual acts of knowledge are interwoven, but to understand the *ideal* sense of the *specific* connections in which the objectivity of knowledge may be documented. It endeavours to raise to clearness the pure forms and laws of knowledge by tracing knowledge back to an adequate fulfilment in intuition. This 'clearing up' takes place in the framework of a phenomenology of knowledge, a phenomenology oriented, as we saw, to the essential structures of pure experiences and to the structures of sense (*Sinnbestände*) that belong to these. From the beginning, as at all later stages, its scientific statements involve not the slightest reference to real existence: no metaphysical, scientific and, above all, no psychological assertions can therefore occur among its premisses.

A purely phenomenological 'theory' of knowledge naturally has an application to all naturally developed, and (in a good sense) 'naïve' sciences, which it transforms into 'philosophical' sciences. It transforms them, in other words, into sciences which provide us with clarified, assured knowledge in every sense in which it is possible to desire the latter. As regards the sciences of 'reality', such epistemological clarification can as much be regarded as a 'scientific' as a 'metaphysical' evaluation.

The investigations which follow aspire solely to such freedom from metaphysical, scientific and psychological presuppositions. No harm will of course be done by occasional side-references which remain without effect on the content and character of one's analyses, nor by the many expository devices addressed to one's public, whose existence (like one's own) is not therefore presupposed by the content of one's investigations. Nor does one exceed one's prescribed limits if one starts, e.g., from existent languages and discusses the merely communicative meaning of their many forms of expression, and so on. It is easily seen that the sense and the epistemological worth of the following analyses does not depend on the fact that there really are languages, and that men really make use of them in their mutual dealings, or that there really are such things as men and a nature, and that they do not merely exist in imagined, possible fashion.

The real premisses of our putative results must lie in propositions satisfying the requirement that what they assert permits of an *adequate phenomenological justification*, a fulfilment through *evidence* in the strictest sense. Such propositions must not, further, ever be adduced in some other sense than that in which they have been intuitively established.

INVESTIGATION I

Expression and Meaning

CHAPTER ONE

Essential Distinctions

---

§1 *An ambiguity in the term 'sign'*

THE terms 'expression' and 'sign' are often treated as synonyms, but it will not be amiss to point out that they do not always coincide in application in common usage. Every sign is a sign for something, but not every sign has 'meaning', a 'sense' that the sign 'expresses'. In many cases it is not even true that a sign 'stands for' that of which we may say it is a sign. And even where this can be said, one has to observe that 'standing for' will not count as the 'meaning' which characterizes the expression. For signs in the sense of indications (notes, marks etc.) *do not express* anything, unless they happen to fulfil a significant as well as an indicative function. If, as one unwillingly does, one limits oneself to expressions employed in living discourse, the notion of an indication seems to apply more widely than that of an expression, but this does not mean that its content is the genus of which an expression is the species. To mean is *not a particular way of being a sign in the sense of indicating something*. It has a narrower application only because meaning – in communicative speech – is always bound up with such an indicative relation, and this in its turn leads to a wider concept, since meaning is also capable of occurring without such a connection. *Expressions* function meaningfully even in *isolated mental life, where they no longer serve to indicate anything*. The two notions of sign do not therefore really stand in the relation of more extensive genus to narrower species.

The whole matter requires more thorough discussion.

§2 *The essence of indication*

Of the two concepts connected with the word 'sign', we shall first deal with that of an *indication*. The relation that here obtains we shall call the *indicative relation*. In this sense a brand is the sign of a slave, a flag the sign of a nation. Here all marks belong, as characteristic qualities suited to help us in recognizing the objects to which they attach.

But the concept of an indication extends more widely than that of a mark. We say the Martian canals are signs of the existence of intelligent beings on Mars, that fossil vertebrae are signs of the existence of prediluvian animals etc. Signs to aid memory, such as the much-used knot in a handkerchief, memorials etc., also have their place here. If suitable things, events or their properties are deliberately produced to serve as such indications, one calls them 'signs' whether they exercise this function or not. Only in the case of indications deliberately and artificially brought about, does one speak of standing for, and that both in respect of the action which produces the marking (the branding or chalking etc.), and in the sense of the indication itself, i.e. taken in its relation to the object it stands for or that it is to signify.

These distinctions and others like them do not deprive the concept of indication of its essential unity. A thing is only properly an indication if and where it in fact serves to indicate something to some thinking being. If we wish to seize the pervasively common element here present we must refer back to such cases of 'live' functioning. In these we discover as a common circumstance the fact that certain objects or states of affairs *of whose reality someone has actual knowledge* indicate to him *the reality of certain other objects or states of affairs*, in the sense that *his belief in the reality of the one is experienced* (though not at all evidently) *as motivating a belief or surmise in the reality of the other*. This relation of 'motivation' represents a *descriptive unity* among our acts of judgement in which indicating and indicated states of affairs become constituted for the thinker. This descriptive unity is not to be conceived as a mere form-quality founded upon our acts of judgement, for it is in their unity that the essence of indication lies. More lucidly put: the 'motivational' unity of our acts of judgement has itself the character of a unity of judgement; before it as a whole an objective correlate, a unitary state of affairs, parades itself, is meant in such a judgement, appears to be in and for that judgement. Plainly such a state of affairs amounts to just this: that certain things *may* or *must* exist, *since* other things have been given. This 'since', taken as expressing an objective connection, is the objective correlate of 'motivation' taken as a descriptively peculiar way of combining acts of judgement into a single act of judgement.

§3 *Two senses of 'demonstration' (Hinweis und Beweis)*

We have sketched the phenomenological situation so generally that what we have said applies as much to the 'demonstration' of genuine inference and proof, as to the 'demonstration' of indication. These two notions should, however, be kept apart. Their distinctness has already been suggested by our stress on the *lack of insight* in indications. In cases where the existence of one state of affairs is evidently inferred from that of another, we do not in fact speak of the latter as an indication or sign of the former, and, conversely, we only speak of demonstration in the strict logical sense in the case of an inference which is or could be informed by insight. Much, no doubt, that is propounded as demonstrative or, in the simplest case, as syllogistically cogent, is devoid of insight and may even be false. But to propound it is at least to make the claim that a relation of consequence could be seen to hold. This is bound up with the fact that there is an objective syllogism or proof, or an objective relationship between ground and consequent, which corresponds to our subjective acts of inferring and proving. These ideal unities are not the experiences of judging in question, but their ideal 'contents', the propositions they involve. The premisses prove the conclusion no matter who may affirm the premisses and the conclusion, or the unity that both form. An ideal rule is here revealed which extends its sway beyond the judgements here and now united by 'motivation'; in supra-empirical generality it comprehends as such all judgements having a like content, all judgements, even, having a like form. Such regularity makes itself subjectively known to us when we conduct proofs with insight, while the precise rule is made known to us through ideative reflection on the contents of the judgements experienced together in the actual context of 'motivation', in the actual inference and proof. These contents are the propositions involved.

In the case of an indication there is no question of all this. Here insight and (to put the matter objectively) knowledge regarding the ideal connections among the contents of the judgements concerned, is quite excluded. When one says that the state of affairs A indicates the state of affairs B, that the existence of the one points to that of the other, one may confidently be expecting to find B true, but one's mode of speech implies no objectively necessary connections between A and B, nothing into which one could have insight. The contents of one's judgements are not here related as premisses are to a conclusion. At times no doubt we do speak of 'indications' even in cases where there is an objective relation of entailment (a mediate one, in fact). A mathematician may make use (so he says) of the fact that an algebraic equation is of uneven order as a sign that it has at least one real root. To be more exact, we are here only concerned with the possibility that someone who fails to carry out and see the cogency of the relevant thought-chain, may make use of a statement about an equation's uneven order as an immediate, blind motive for asserting the equation to have some necessarily connected property which he needs for his mathematical purposes. In such situations, where certain states of affairs readily serve to indicate others which are, in themselves, their consequences, they do not function in thought as logical grounds of the latter, but work through connections which previous actual demonstration, or blind learning on authority, has established among our convictions, whether as actual mental states or as dispositions for such. Nothing is of course altered in all this by the possible presence of an accompanying merely habitual knowledge of an objectively present rational connection.

If an indication (or the connection of 'motivation' in which such a soi-disant objective relation makes its appearance) is without essential relation to a necessary connection, the question arises whether it may not claim to be essentially related to a connection of probability. Where one thing indicates another, where belief in the one's existence furnishes one with an empirical motive or ground – not necessary but contingent – for belief in the existence of the other, must the motivating belief not furnish a *ground of probability* for the belief it motivates? This is not the place for a close discussion of this pressing question. We need only observe that the question may correctly be answered in the affirmative in so far as such empirical 'motivations' all fall under an ideal jurisdiction in virtue of which they may be spoken of as 'justified' or 'unjustified', or, objectively expressed, in which they may be spoken of as real, i.e. valid, motivations which lead to a probability or perhaps to an empirical certainty, or *per contra*, as merely apparent, i.e. invalid, motivations, which do not lead to such a probability. One may, e.g., cite the controversy as to whether volcanic phenomena do or do not indicate that the earth's interior is molten, and so on. One thing is sure, that to talk of an indication is not to presuppose a definite relation to considerations of probability. Usually such talk relates not to mere surmises but to assured judgements. The ideal jurisdiction to which we have here accorded authority must first demand, therefore, that we should scale down our confident judgements to modest surmises.

I shall here observe, further, that we cannot avoid talking about 'motivation' in a general sense which covers strict demonstration as much as empirical indication. Here in fact we have a quite undeniable phenomenological affinity, obvious enough to register itself in ordinary discourse. We commonly speak of reasoning and inference, not merely in the sense of logic, but in a sense connected with empirical indications. This affinity plainly extends more widely: it covers the field of emotional, and, in particular, of volitional phenomena, to which talk of 'motives' was at first alone confined. Here too 'because' has a part to play, covering as wide a linguistic territory as does the most general sense of 'motivation'. I cannot therefore approve of Meinong's censure of Brentano's terminology, which I have here adopted.[1] But I entirely agree with him that in perceiving something as 'motivated' we are not at all perceiving it as caused.

§4 *Digression on the associative origin of indication*

The mental facts in which the notion of indication has its 'origin', i.e. in which it can be abstractively apprehended, belong to the wider group of facts which fall under the historical rubric of the 'association of ideas'. Under this rubric we do not merely have those facts which concern the 'accompaniment' and 'reactivation' of ideas stated in the laws of association, but the further facts in which association operates creatively, and produces peculiar descriptive characters and forms of unity.[2] Association does not

[1] A. V. Meinong, *Göttinger gel. Anz.* (1892), p. 446.
[2] To use personification and to talk of association as 'creating' something, and to employ other similar figurative expressions in common use, is too convenient to

merely restore contents to consciousness, and then leave it to them to combine with the contents there present, as the essence or generic nature of either may necessarily prescribe. It cannot indeed disturb such unified patterns as depend solely on our mental contents, e.g. the unity of visual contents in the visual field. But it can create additional phenomenological characters and unities which do not have their necessary, law-determined ground in the experienced contents themselves, nor in the generic forms of their abstract aspects.[1] If *A* summons *B* into consciousness, we are not merely simultaneously or successively conscious of both *A* and *B*, but we usually *feel* their connection forcing itself upon us, a connection in which the one points to the other and seems to belong to it. To turn mere coexistence into mutual pertinence, or, more precisely, to build cases of the former into intentional unities of things which seem mutually pertinent, is the constant result of associative functioning. All unity of experience, all empirical unity, whether of a thing, an event or of the order and relation of things, becomes a phenomenal unity through the felt mutual belongingness of the sides and parts that can be made to stand out as units in the apparent object before us. That one thing points to another, in definite arrangement and connection, is itself apparent to us. The single item itself, in these various forward and backward references, is no mere experienced content, but an apparent object (or part, property etc., of the same) that appears only in so far as experience (*Erfahrung*) endows contents with a new phenomenological *character*, so that they no longer count separately, but help to present an object different from themselves. In this field of facts the fact of indication also has its place, in virtue whereof an object or state of affairs not merely recalls another, and so points to it, but also provides evidence for the latter, fosters the presumption that it likewise exists, and makes us immediately feel this in the manner described above.

be abandoned. Important as a scientifically exact but circumlocutory description of the relevant facts may be, ready understanding absolutely requires that we talk figuratively wherever ultimate exactness is not needed.

[1] I talk above of 'experienced contents', not of meant, apparent objects or events. Everything that really helps to constitute the individual, 'experiencing' consciousness is an experienced content. What it perceives, remembers, inwardly presents etc., is a meant or intentional object. This point will be further discussed in Investigation v.

§ 5 *Expressions as meaningful signs. Setting aside of a sense of 'expression' not relevant for our purpose*

From indicative signs we distinguish *meaningful* signs, i.e. *expressions*. We thereby employ the term 'expression' restrictively: we exclude much that ordinary speech would call an 'expression' from its range of application. There are other cases in which we have thus to do violence to usage, where concepts for which only ambiguous terms exist call for a fixed terminology. We shall lay down, for provisional intelligibility, that each instance or part of *speech*, as also each sign that is essentially of the same sort, shall count as an expression, whether or not such speech is actually uttered, or addressed with communicative intent to any persons or not. Such a definition excludes facial expression and the various gestures which involuntarily accompany speech without communicative intent, or those in which a man's mental states achieve understandable 'expression' for his environment, without the added help of speech. Such 'utterances' are not expressions in the sense in which a case of speech is an expression, they are not phenomenally one with the experiences made manifest in them in the consciousness of the man who manifests them, as is the case with speech. In such manifestations one man communicates nothing to another: their utterance involves no intent to put certain 'thoughts' on record expressively, whether for the man himself, in his solitary state, or for others. Such 'expressions', in short, have properly speaking, *no meaning*. It is not to the point that another person may interpret our involuntary manifestations, e.g. our 'expressive movements', and that he may thereby become deeply acquainted with our inner thoughts and emotions. They 'mean' something to him in so far as he interprets them, but even for him they are without meaning in the special sense in which verbal signs have meaning: they only mean in the sense of indicating.

In the treatment which follows these distinctions must be raised to complete conceptual clarity.

§6 *Questions as to the phenomenological and intentional distinctions which pertain to expressions as such*

It is usual to distinguish two things in regard to every expression:
1. The expression physically regarded (the sensible sign, the articulate sound-complex, the written sign on paper etc.);
2. A certain sequence of mental states, associatively linked with the expression, which make it be the expression of something. These mental states are generally called the 'sense' or the 'meaning' of the expression, this being taken to be in accord with what these words ordinarily mean. But we shall see this notion to be mistaken, and that a mere distinction between physical signs and sense-giving experiences is by no means enough, and not at all enough for logical purposes.

The points here made have long been observed in the special case of names. We distinguish, in the case of each name, between what it 'shows forth' (i.e. mental states) and what it means. And again between what it means (the sense or 'content' of its naming presentation) and what it names (the object of that presentation). We shall need similar distinctions in the case of all expression, and shall have to explore their nature precisely. Such distinctions have led to our distinction between the notions of 'expression' and 'indication', which is not in conflict with the fact that an expression in living speech also functions as an indication, a point soon to come up for discussion. To these distinctions other important ones will be added which will concern the relations between meaning and the intuition which illustrates meaning and on occasion renders it evident. Only by paying heed to these relations, can the concept of meaning be clearly delimited, and can the fundamental opposition between the symbolic and the epistemological function of meanings be worked out.

§7 *Expressions as they function in communication*

Expressions were originally framed to fulfil a communicative function: let us, accordingly, first study expressions in this function, so that we may be able to work out their essential logical distinctions. The articulate sound-complex, the written sign etc., first becomes a spoken word or communicative bit of speech, when a speaker produces it with the intention of 'expressing himself about something' through its means; he must endow it with a sense in certain acts of mind, a sense he desires to share with his auditors. Such sharing becomes a possibility if the auditor also understands the speaker's intention. He does this inasmuch as he takes the speaker to be a person, who is not merely uttering sounds but *speaking to him*, who is accompanying those sounds with certain sense-giving acts, which the sounds reveal to the hearer, or whose sense they seek to communicate to him. What first makes mental commerce possible, and turns connected speech into discourse, lies in the correlation among the corresponding physical and mental experiences of communicating persons which is effected by the physical side of speech. Speaking and hearing, intimation of mental states through speaking and reception thereof in hearing, are mutually correlated.

If one surveys these interconnections, one sees at once that all expressions in *communicative* speech function as *indications*. They serve the hearer as signs of the 'thoughts' of the speaker, i.e. of his sense-giving inner experiences, as well as of the other inner experiences which are part of his communicative intention. This function of verbal expressions we shall call their *intimating function*. The content of such intimation consists in the inner experiences intimated. The sense of the predicate 'intimated' can be understood more narrowly or more widely. The *narrower* sense we may restrict to *acts which impart sense*, while the *wider* sense will cover *all* acts that a hearer may introject into a speaker on the basis of what he says (possibly because he tells us of such acts). If, e.g., we state a wish, our judgement concerning that wish is what we intimate in the narrower sense of the word, whereas the wish itself is intimated in the wider sense. The same holds of an ordinary statement of perception, which the hearer forthwith takes to belong to some actual perception. The act of perception is there intimated in the wider sense, the judgement built upon it in the narrower sense. We at once see that ordinary speech permits us to call an experience which is intimated an experience which is *expressed*.

To understand an intimation is not to have conceptual knowledge of it, not to judge in the sense of asserting anything about it: it consists simply in the fact that the hearer *intuitively* takes the speaker to be a person who is expressing this or that, or as we certainly can say, *perceives* him as such. When I listen to someone,

I perceive him as a speaker, I hear him recounting, demonstrating, doubting, wishing etc. The hearer perceives the intimation in the same sense in which he perceives the intimating person – even though the mental phenomena which make him a person cannot fall, for what they are, in the intuitive grasp of another. Common speech credits us with percepts even of other people's inner experiences; we 'see' their anger, their pain etc. Such talk is quite correct, as long as, e.g., we allow outward bodily things likewise to count as perceived, and as long as, in general, the notion of perception is not restricted to the adequate, the strictly intuitive percept. If the essential mark of perception lies in the intuitive persuasion that a thing or event is itself before us for our grasping – such a persuasion is possible, and in the main mass of cases actual, without verbalized, conceptual apprehension – then the receipt of such an intimation is the mere perceiving of it. The essential distinction just touched on is of course present here. The hearer perceives the speaker as manifesting certain inner experiences, and to that extent he also perceives these experiences themselves: he does not, however, himself experience them, he has not an 'inner' but an 'outer' percept of them. Here we have the big difference between the real grasp of what is in adequate intuition, and the putative grasp of what is on a basis of inadequate, though intuitive, presentation. In the former case we have to do with an experienced, in the latter case with a presumed being, to which no truth corresponds at all. Mutual understanding demands a certain correlation among the mental acts mutually unfolded in intimation and in the receipt of such intimation, but not at all their exact resemblance.

§8 *Expressions in solitary life*

So far we have considered expressions as used in communication, which last depends essentially on the fact that they operate indicatively. But expressions also play a great part in uncommunicated, interior mental life. This change in function plainly has nothing to do with whatever makes an expression an expression. Expressions continue to have meanings as they had before, and the same meanings as in dialogue. A word only ceases to be a word when our interest stops at its sensory contour, when it becomes a mere sound-pattern. But when we live in the understanding of a word, it expresses something and the same thing, whether we address it to anyone or not.

It seems clear, therefore, that an expression's meaning, and whatever else pertains to it essentially, cannot coincide with its feats of intimation. Or shall we say that, even in solitary mental life, one still uses expressions to intimate something, though not to a second person? Shall one say that in soliloquy one speaks to oneself, and employs words as signs, i.e. as indications, of one's own inner experiences? I cannot think such a view acceptable. Words function as signs here as they do everywhere else: everywhere they can be said to point to something. But if we reflect on the relation of expression to meaning, and to this end break up our complex, intimately unified experience of the sense-filled expression, into the two factors of word and sense, the word comes before us as intrinsically indifferent, whereas the sense seems the thing aimed at by the verbal sign and meant by its means: the expression seems to direct interest away from itself towards its sense, and to point to the latter. But this pointing is not an indication in the sense previously discussed. The existence of the sign neither 'motivates' the existence of the meaning, nor, properly expressed, our belief in the meaning's existence. What we are to use as an indication, must be perceived by us as existent. This holds also of expressions used in communication, but not for expressions used in soliloquy, where we are in general content with imagined rather than with actual words. In imagination a spoken or printed word floats before us, though in reality it has no existence. We should not, however, confuse imaginative presentations, and the image-contents they rest on, with their imagined objects. The imagined verbal sound, or the imagined printed word, does not exist, only its imaginative presentation does so. The difference is the difference between imagined centaurs and the imagination of such beings. The word's non-existence neither disturbs nor interests us, since it leaves the word's expressive function unaffected. Where it *does* make a difference is where intimation is linked with meaning. Here thought must not be merely expressed as meaning, but must be communicated and intimated. We can only do the latter where we actually speak and hear.

One of course speaks, in a certain sense, even in soliloquy, and it is certainly possible to think of oneself as speaking, and even as speaking to oneself, as, e.g., when someone says to himself: 'You have gone wrong, you can't go on like that.' But in the genuine sense of communication, there is no speech in such cases, nor does one tell oneself anything: one merely conceives of oneself as speaking and communicating. In a monologue words can perform no function of indicating the existence of mental acts, since such indication would there be quite purposeless. For the acts in question are themselves experienced by us at that very moment.

§9 *Phenomenological distinctions between the phenomena of physical expression and the sense-giving and sense-fulfilling act*

If we now turn from experiences specially concerned with intimation, and consider expressions in respect of distinctions that pertain to them equally whether they occur in dialogue or soliloquy, two things seem to be left over: the expressions themselves, and what they express as their meaning or sense. Several relations are, however, intertwined at this point, and talk about 'meaning', or about 'what is expressed', is correspondingly ambiguous. If we seek a foothold in pure description, the concrete phenomenon of the sense-informed expression breaks up, on the one hand, into the *physical phenomenon* forming the physical side of the expression, and, on the other hand, into the *acts* which give it *meaning* and possibly also *intuitive fulness*, in which its relation to an expressed object is constituted. In virtue of such acts, the expression is more than a merely sounded word. It *means* something, and in so far as it means something, it relates to what is objective. This objective somewhat can either be actually present through accompanying intuitions, or may at least appear in representation, e.g. in a mental image, and where this happens the relation to an object is realized. Alternatively this need not occur: the expression functions significantly, it remains more than mere sound of words, but it lacks any basic intuition that will give it its object. The relation of expression to object is now unrealized as being confined to a mere meaning-intention. A *name*, e.g., names its object whatever the circumstances, in so far as it *means* that object. But if the object is not intuitively before one, and so not before one as a named or meant object, mere meaning is all there is to it. If the originally *empty* meaning-intention is now fulfilled, the relation to an object is realized, the naming becomes an actual, conscious relation between name and object named.

Let us take our stand on this fundamental distinction between meaning-intentions void of intuition and those which are intuitively fulfilled: if we leave aside the sensuous acts in which the expression, *qua* mere sound of words, makes its appearance, we shall have to distinguish between two acts or sets of acts. We shall, on the one hand, have acts essential to the expression if it is to be an expression at all, i.e. a verbal sound infused with sense. These acts we shall call the *meaning-conferring acts* or the *meaning-intentions*. But we shall, on the other hand, have acts, not essential to the expression as such, which stand to it in the logically basic relation of *fulfilling* (confirming, illustrating) it more or less adequately, and so actualizing its relation to its object. These acts, which become fused with the meaning-conferring acts in the unity of knowledge or fulfilment, we call the *meaning-fulfilling* acts. The briefer expression 'meaning-fulfilment' can only be used in cases where there is no risk of the ready confusion with the *whole* experience in which a meaning-intention finds fulfilment in its correlated intuition. In the realized relation of the expression to its objective correlate,[1] the sense-informed expression becomes one with the act of meaning-fulfilment. The sounded word is first made one with the meaning-intention, and this in its turn is made one (as intentions in general are made one with their fulfilments) with its corresponding meaning-fulfilment. The word 'expression' is normally understood – wherever, that is, we do not speak of a 'mere' expression – as the *sense-informed* expression. One should not, therefore, properly say (as one often does) that an expression *expresses its meaning* (its intention). One might more properly adopt the alternative way of speaking according to which the *fulfilling act* appears as *the act expressed by the complete expression*: we may, e.g., say, that a statement 'gives expression' to an act of perceiving or imagining. We need not here point out that both meaning-conferring and meaning-fulfilling acts have a part to play in intimation in the case of communicative discourse. The former in fact constitute the inmost core of intimation. To

---

[1] I often make use of the vaguer expression 'objective correlate' (*Gegenständlichkeit*) since we are here never limited to objects in the narrower sense, but have also to do with states of affairs, properties, and non-independent forms etc., whether real or categorial.

make them known to the hearer is the prime aim of our communicative intention, for only in so far as the hearer attributes them to the speaker will he understand the latter.

§ 10 *The phenomenological unity of these acts*

The above distinguished acts involving the expression's appearance, on the one hand, and the meaning-intention and possible meaning-fulfilment, on the other, do not constitute a mere aggregate of simultaneously given items in consciousness. They rather form an intimately fused unity of peculiar character. Everyone's personal experience bears witness to the differing weight of the two constituents, which reflects the asymmetry of the relation between an expression and the object which (through its meaning) it expresses or names. Both are 'lived through', the presentation of the word and the sense-giving act: but, while we experience the former, we do not live *in* such a presentation at all, but solely in enacting its sense, its meaning. And in so far as we do this, and yield ourselves to enacting the meaning-intention and its further fulfilment, our whole interest centres upon the object intended in our intention, and named by its means. (These two ways of speaking have in fact the same meaning.) The function of a word (or rather of an intuitive word-presentation) is to awaken a sense-conferring act in ourselves, to point to what is intended, or perhaps given intuitive fulfilment in this act, and to guide our interest exclusively in this direction.

Such pointing is not to be described as the mere objective fact of a regular diversion of interest from one thing to another. The fact that two presented objects *A* and *B* are so linked by some secret psychological coordination that the presentation of *A* regularly arouses the presentation of *B*, and that interest is thereby shifted from *A* to *B* – such a fact does not make *A* the expression of the presentation of *B*. To be an expression is rather a descriptive aspect of the *experienced unity* of sign and thing signified.

What is involved in the descriptive difference between the physical sign-phenomenon and the meaning-intention which makes it into an expression, becomes most clear when we turn our attention to the sign *qua* sign, e.g. to the printed word as such. If we do this, we have an external percept (or external intuitive idea) just like any other, whose object loses its verbal character.

If this object again functions as a word, its presentation is wholly altered in character. The word (*qua* external singular) remains intuitively present, maintains its appearance, but we no longer intend it, it no longer properly is the object of our 'mental activity'. Our interest, our intention, our thought – mere synonyms if taken in sufficiently wide senses – point exclusively to the thing meant in the sense-giving act. This means, phenomenologically speaking, that the intuitive presentation, in which the physical world-phenomenon is constituted, undergoes an essential phenomenal modification when its object begins to count as an *expression*. While what constitutes the object's appearing remains unchanged, the intentional character of the experience alters. There is constituted (without need of a fulfilling or illustrative intuition) an act of meaning which finds support in the verbal presentation's intuitive content, but which differs in essence from the intuitive intention directed upon the word itself. With this act, the new acts or act-complexes that we call 'fulfilling' acts or act-complexes are often peculiarly blended, acts whose object coincides with the object meant in the meaning, or named through this meaning.

In our next chapter we shall have to conduct additional researches into the question as to whether the 'meaning-intention', which on our view characteristically marks off an expression from empty 'sound of words' consists in the mere association of mental imagery of the intended object with the sounded words, or at least necessarily involves such an act of fancy, or whether, on the other hand, mental imagery lies outside of the essence of an expression, and rather performs a fulfilling role, even if only of a partial, indirect or provisional character. In order not to blur the main outlines of our thought, we shall not here enter more deeply into phenomenological questions. In this whole investigation, we need only do as much phenomenology as is required to establish essential, primary distinctions.

The provisional description so far given will have shown how complex is the correct description of a phenomenological situation. Such complexity appears inevitable once we clearly see that all objects and relations among objects only are what they are for us, through acts of thought essentially different from them, in which they become present to us, in which they stand before us as unitary items that we *mean*. Where not the phenomenological, but the naïvely objective interest dominates, where we live in intentional acts without reflecting upon them, all talk of course becomes plain sailing and clear and devoid of circumlocution. One then, in our case, simply speaks of 'expression' and of 'what is expressed', of name and thing named, of the steering of attention from one to the other etc. But where the phenomenological interest dominates, we endure the hardship of having to describe phenomenological relationships which we may have experienced on countless occasions, but of which we were not normally conscious as objects, and we have also to do our describing with expressions framed to deal with objects whose appearance lies in the sphere of our normal interests.

§ 11 *The ideal distinctions between (1) expression and meaning as ideal unities*

We have so far considered 'the well-understood expression' as a concrete experience. Instead of considering its two types of factor, the phenomenal expression and the sense-conferring or sense-fulfilling experience, we wish to consider what is, in a certain fashion, given 'in' these: the expression itself, its sense and its objective correlate. We turn therefore from the real relation of acts to the ideal relation of their objects or contents. A subjective treatment yields to one that is objective. The ideality of the relationship between expression and meaning is at once plain in regard to both its sides, inasmuch as, when we ask for the meaning of an expression, e.g. 'quadratic remainder', we are naturally not referring to the sound-pattern uttered here and now, the vanishing noise that can never recur identically: we mean the expression *in specie*. 'Quadratic remainder' is the same expression by whomsoever uttered. The same holds of talk about the expression's meaning, which naturally does not refer to some meaning-conferring experience.

Every example shows that an essential distinction must here be drawn.

If I sincerely say – we shall always presume sincerity – 'The three perpendiculars of a triangle intersect in a point', this is of course based on the fact that I judge so. If someone hears me and understands my assertion, he likewise knows this fact; he 'apperceives' me as someone who judges thus. But is the judging here *intimated* the meaning of my assertion, is it what my assertion asserts, and in that sense expresses? Plainly not. It would hardly occur to anyone, if asked as to the sense or meaning of my assertion, to revert to my judgement as an inner experience. Everyone would rather reply by saying: What this assertion asserts is *the same* whoever may assert it, and on whatever occasion or in whatever circumstances he may assert it, and what it asserts is precisely this, *that the three perpendiculars of a triangle intersect in a point*, no more and no less. One therefore repeats what is in essence 'the same' assertion, and one repeats it because it is the one, uniquely adequate way of expressing the same thing, i.e. its meaning. In this selfsame meaning, of whose identity we are conscious whenever we repeat the statement, nothing at all about judging or about one who judges is discoverable. We thought we were sure that a state of affairs held or obtained objectively, and what we were sure of we expressed by way of a declarative sentence. The state of affairs is what it is whether we assert that it obtains or not. It is intrinsically an item, a unity, which is capable of so obtaining or holding. But such an obtaining is what appeared before us, and we set it forth as it appeared before us: we said 'So the matter is'. Naturally we could not have done this, we could not have made the assertion, if the matter had not so appeared before us, if, in other words, we had not so judged. This forms part of an assertion as a psychological fact, it is involved in its intimation. But only in such intimation; for while what is intimated consists in inner experiences, what we assert in the judgement involves nothing subjective. My act of judging is a transient experience: it arises and passes away. But what my assertion asserts, the content *that the three perpendiculars of a triangle intersect in a point*, neither arises nor passes away. It is an identity in the strict sense, one and the same geometrical truth.

It is the same in the case of all assertions, even if what they assert is false and absurd. Even in such cases we distinguish their ideal content from the transient acts or affirming and asserting it: it is the meaning of the assertion, a unity in plurality. We continue to recognize its identity of intention in evident acts of reflection: we do not arbitrarily attribute it to our assertions, but discover it in them.

If 'possibility' or 'truth' is lacking, an assertion's intention can only be carried out symbolically: it cannot derive any 'fulness' from intuition or from the categorial functions performed on the latter, in which 'fulness' its value for knowledge consists. It then lacks, as one says, a 'true', a 'genuine' meaning. Later we shall look more closely into this distinction between intending and fulfilling meaning. To characterize the various acts in which the relevant ideal unities are constituted, and to throw light on the essence of their actual 'coincidence' in knowledge, will call for difficult, comprehensive studies. It is plain, however, that each assertion, whether representing an exercise of knowledge or not – whether or not, i.e., it fulfils or can fulfil its intention in corresponding intuitions, and the formative acts involved in these – involves a thought, in which thought, as its unified specific character, its meaning is constituted.

It is this ideal unity men have in mind when they say that 'the' judgement is the meaning of 'the' declarative sentence. Only the fundamental ambiguity of the word 'judgement' at once tends to confuse the evidently grasped ideal unity with the real act of judging, to confuse what the assertion intimates with what it asserts.

What we have here said of complete assertions readily applies also to actual or possible parts of assertions. If I judge *If the sum of the angles in a triangle does not equal two right angles, the axiom of parallels does not hold*, the hypothetical antecedent is no assertion, for I do not say that such an inequation holds. None the less it says something, and what it says is once more quite different from what it intimates. What it says is not my mental act of hypothetical presumption, though I must of course have performed this in order to speak sincerely as I do. But it is rather the case that, when this subjective act is intimated, something objective and ideal is brought to expression: the hypothesis whose conceptual content can appear as the same intentional unity in many possible thought-experiences, and which evidently stands before us in its unity and identity in the objectively-ideal treatment characteristic of all thinking.

The same holds of the other parts of our statements, even of such as do not have the form of propositions.

§12 *Continuation: the objective correlate of an expression*

Talk of *what an expression expresses* has, in the discussion so far, several essentially different meanings. It relates, *on the one hand*, to intimation in general, and especially in that connection to sense-giving acts, at times also to sense-fulfilling acts (if these are present at all). In an assertion, e.g., we express our judgement (we intimate it), but we also express percepts and other sense-fulfilling acts which illustrate our assertion's meaning. *On the other hand*, such talk relates to the 'contents' of such acts, and primarily to the meanings, which are often enough said to be 'expressed'.

It is doubtful whether the examples analysed, in our last section, would suffice even to lend provisional intelligibility to the notion of meaning, if one could not forthwith introduce a new sense of 'expression' for purposes of comparison. The terms 'meaning', 'content', 'state of affairs' and all similar terms harbour such powerful equivocations that our intention, even if expressed most carefully, still can promote misunderstanding. The third sense of 'being expressed', which we must now discuss, concerns the *objective correlate* meant by a meaning and expressed by its means.

Each expression not merely says something, but says it *of* something: it not only has a meaning, but refers to certain *objects*. This relation sometimes holds in the plural for one and the same expression. But the object never coincides with the meaning. Both, of course, only pertain to an expression in virtue of the mental acts which give it sense. And, if we distinguish between 'content' and object in respect of such 'presentations', one's distinction means the same as the distinction between what is meant or said, on the one hand, and what is spoken of, by means of the expression, on the other.

The necessity of distinguishing between meaning (content) and object becomes clear when a comparison of examples shows us that several expressions may have the same meaning but different objects, and again that they may have different meanings but the same object. There is of course also the possibility of their differing in both respects and agreeing in both. The last occurs in the cases of synonymous expressions, e.g. the corresponding expressions in different languages which mean and name the same thing ('London', 'Londres'; 'zwei', 'deux', 'duo' etc.).

Names offer the plainest examples of the separation of meaning from the relation to objects, this relation being in their case usually spoken of as 'naming'. Two names can differ in meaning but can name the same object, e.g. 'the victor at Jena' – 'the vanquished at Waterloo'; 'the equilateral triangle' – 'the equi-angular triangle'. The meaning expressed in our pairs of names is plainly different, though the same object is meant in each case. The same applies to names whose indefiniteness gives them an 'extension'. The expressions 'an equilateral triangle' and 'an equiangular triangle' have the same objective reference, the same range of possible application.

It can happen, conversely, that two expressions have the same meaning but a different objective reference. The expression 'a horse' has the same meaning in whatever context it occurs. But if on one occasion we say 'Bucephalus is a horse', and on another 'That cart-horse is a horse', there has been a plain change in our sense-giving presentation in passing from the one statement to the other. The expression 'a horse' employs the same meaning to present Bucephalus on one occasion and the cart-horse on the other. It is thus with all general names, i.e. names with an 'extension'. 'One' is a name whose meaning never differs, but one should not, for that reason, identify the various 'ones' which occur in a sum: they all mean the same, but they differ in objective reference.

The case of proper names is different, whether they name individual or general objects. A word like 'Socrates' can only name different things by meaning different things, i.e. by becoming *equivocal*. Wherever the word has *one* meaning, it also names *one* object. The same holds of expressions like 'the number two', 'redness' etc. We therefore distinguish equivocal names that have *many meanings* from general or class-names that have *many values*.

The same holds of other types of expression, though in their case talk of objective reference involves certain difficulties in virtue of its manifoldness. If we consider, e.g., statements of the form '*S* is *P*' we generally regard the subject of the statement as the object about which the statement is made. Another view is, however, possible, which treats the *whole* state of affairs which corresponds to the statement as an analogue of the object a name names, and distinguishes this from the object's meaning. If this is done one can quote as examples pairs of sentences such as '*a* is bigger than *b*' – '*b* is smaller than *a*', which plainly say different things. They are not merely grammatically but also 'cogitatively' different, i.e. different in meaning-content. But they express the same state of affairs: the same 'matter' is predicatively apprehended and asserted in two different ways. Whether we define talk of the 'object' of a statement in one sense or the other – each has its own claims – statements are in either case possible which differ in meaning while referring to the same object.

§13 *Connection between meaning and objective reference*

Our examples entitle us to regard the distinction between an expression's meaning and its power to direct itself as a name to this or that objective correlate – and of course the distinction between meaning and object itself – as well-established. It is clear for the rest that the sides to be distinguished in each expression are closely connected: an expression only refers to an objective correlate *because* it means something, it can be rightly said to signify or name the object *through* its meaning. An act of meaning is the determinate manner in which we refer to our object of the moment, though this mode of significant reference and the meaning itself can change while the objective reference remains fixed.

A more profound phenomenological clarification of this relation can be reached only by research into the way expressions and their meaning-intentions function in knowledge. This would show that talk about *two distinguishable sides* to each expression, should not be taken seriously, that the essence of an expression lies solely in its meaning. But the same intuition (as we shall show later) can offer fulfilment of different expressions: it can be categorially apprehended in varying ways and synthetically linked with other intuitions. Expressions and their meaning-intentions do not take their measure, in contexts of thought and knowledge, from mere intuition – I mean phenomena of external or internal sensibility – but from the varying intellectual forms through which intuited objects first become intelligibly determined, mutually related objects. And so expressions, even when they function outside of knowledge, must, as symbolic intentions, point to categorially *formed* unities. Different meanings may therefore pertain to the same intuitions regarded in differing categorial fashion, and may therefore also pertain to the same object. But where a whole range of objects corresponds to a single meaning, this meaning's own essence must be *indeterminate*: it must permit a sphere of possible fulfilment.

These indications may suffice for the moment. They must guard in advance against the error of seriously thinking that sense-giving acts have two distinct sides, one which gives them their meaning, while the other gives them their determinate direction to objects.[1]

§ 14 *Content as object, content as fulfilling sense and content as sense or meaning simpliciter*

Relational talk of 'intimation', 'meaning' and 'object' belongs *essentially* to every expression. Every expression intimates something, means something and names or otherwise designates something. In each case, talk of 'expression' is equivocal. As said above, relation to an actually given objective correlate, which fulfils the meaning-intention, is *not* essential to an expression. If this last important case is also taken into consideration, we note that there are two things that can be said to be expressed in the realized relation to the object. We have, on the one hand, the *object itself*, and the object as meant in this or that manner. On the other hand, and more properly, we have the object's ideal correlate in the acts of meaning-fulfilment which constitute it, *the fulfilling sense*. Wherever the meaning-intention is fulfilled in a corresponding intuition, i.e. wherever the expression actually serves to name a given object, there the object is constituted as one 'given' in certain acts, and, to the extent that our expression really measures up to the intuitive data, as given *in the same manner* in which the expression *means* it. In this unity of coincidence between meaning and meaning-fulfilment, the essence of the meaning-fulfilment corresponds with, and is correlative, to the essence of meaning: the essence of the meaning-fulfilment is the *fulfilling* sense of the expression, or, as one may also call it, the sense expressed by the expression. One says, e.g., that a statement of perception expresses a perception, but also that it expresses the *content* of a perception. We distinguish, in a perceptual statement, as in every statement, between *content* and *object*; by the 'content' we understand the self-identical meaning that the hearer can grasp even if he is not a percipient. We must draw the same distinction in the case of fulfilling acts, in the case,

---

[1] Cf. with this Twardowski's assumption of a 'presentative activity moving in two directions' in his work *Zur Lehre vom Inhalt und Gegenstand der Vorstellungen* (Vienna 1894), p. 14.

therefore, of perceptions and their categorial formations. Through these acts the objective correlate of our act of meaning stands before us intuitively as the very object we mean. We must, I say, distinguish again, in such fulfilling acts, between their *content*, the meaning-element, as it were, in the categorially formed percept, and the *object* perceived. In the unity of fulfilment, the fulfilling content coincides with the intending content, so that, in our experience of this unity of coincidence, the object, at once intended and 'given', stands before us, not as two objects, but as *one* alone. The ideal conception of the act which *confers meaning* yields us the Idea of the *intending meaning*, just as the ideal conception of the correlative essence of the act which *fulfils* meaning, yields the *fulfilling meaning*, likewise *qua* Idea. This is the *identical content* which, in perception, pertains to the totality of possible acts of perception which intended the same object perceptually, and intend it actually as the same object. This content is therefore the ideal correlate of this *single* object, which may, for the rest, be completely imaginary.

The manifold ambiguities in talk about what an expression expresses, or about an *expressed content*, may therefore be so ordered that one distinguishes between a content in a *subjective*, and a content in an *objective* sense. In the latter respect we must distinguish between:

The content as intending sense, or as sense, *meaning simpliciter*, the content as fulfilling sense, and
the content as object.

§15 *The equivocations in talk of meaning and meaninglessness connected with these distinctions*

The application of the terms 'meaning' and 'sense', not merely to the content of the meaning-intention inseparable from the expression, but also to the content of the meaning-fulfilment, engenders a most unwelcome ambiguity. It is clear from previous indications, where we dealt with the fact of fulfilment, that the acts on either side, in which intending and fulfilling sense are constituted, need not be the same. What tempts us to transfer the same terms from intention to fulfilment, is the peculiar way in which the unity of fulfilment is a unity of identification or coincidence: the equivocation which one hoped a modifying adjective might render innocuous, can scarcely be avoided. We shall continue, of course, to understand by 'meaning' *simpliciter* the meaning which, as the identical element in our intention, is essential to the expressions as such.

'Meaning' is further used by us as synonymous with 'sense'. It is agreeable to have parallel, interchangeable terms in the case of this concept, particularly since the sense of the term 'meaning' is itself to be investigated. A further consideration is our ingrained tendency to use the two words as synonymous, a circumstance which makes it seem rather a dubious step if their meanings are differentiated, and if (as G. Frege has proposed)[1] we use one for meaning in our sense, and the other for the objects expressed. To this we may add that both terms are exposed to the same equivocations, which we distinguished above in connection with the term 'expression', and to many more besides, and that this is so both in scientific and in ordinary speech. Logical clarity is much impaired by the manner in which the sense or meaning of an expression is, often in the same thought-sequence, now looked upon as the acts intimated by it, now as its ideal sense, now as the objective correlate that it expresses. Since fixed terminological landmarks are lacking, the concepts themselves run confusedly into one another.

Fundamental confusions arise from these facts. General and equivocal names are, e.g., repeatedly lumped together, since both can be predicatively referred to a plurality of objects. Lacking fixed concepts, men did not know how to distinguish the *multiple senses* of the equivocal names from the *multiple values* of the general ones. Here we also meet with the frequent unclearness as to the true essence of the difference between collective and general names. For, where collective meanings are fulfilled, we intuit a plurality of items: fulfilment is articulated into a plurality of individual intuitions, and so, if intention and fulfilment are not kept apart, it may well seem that the collective expression in question has many meanings.

It is more important for us to set forth precisely the most detrimental equivocations in talk which concerns *meaning* and *sense*, on the one hand, or *meaningless* or *senseless* expressions, on the other. If we separate the blurred concepts, the following list emerges:

1. It is part of the notion of an expression to have a meaning:

[1] G. Frege, *Über Sinn und Bedeutung, Zeitschr. f. Philos. u. philos. Kritik*, vol. 100, p. 25.

this precisely differentiates an expression from the other signs mentioned above. A meaningless expression is, therefore, properly speaking, no expression at all: it is at best something that claims or seems to be an expression, though, more closely considered, it is not one at all. Here belong articulate, word-like sound-patterns such as 'Abracadabra', and also combinations of genuine expressions to which no unified meaning corresponds, though their outer form seems to pretend to such a meaning, e.g. 'Green is or'.

2. In meaning, a relation to an object is constituted. To use an expression significantly, and to refer expressively to an object (to form a presentation of it), are one and the same. It makes no difference whether the object exists or is fictitious or even impossible. But if one gives a very rigorous interpretation to the proposition that an expression, in so far as it has meaning, relates to an object, i.e. in a sense which involves the existence of the object, then an expression has *meaning* when an object corresponding to it exists, and it is *meaningless* when no such object exists. Meanings are often spoken of as signifying the *objects* meant, a usage that can scarcely be maintained consistently, as it springs from a confusion with the genuine concept of meaning.

3. If the meaning is identified with the objective correlate of an expression, a name like 'golden mountain' is meaningless. Here men generally distinguish objectlessness from meaninglessness. As opposed to this, men tend to use the word 'senseless' of expressions infected with contradiction and obvious incompatibilities, e.g. 'round square', or to deny them meaning by some equivalent phrase. Sigwart[1], e.g., says that a self-contradictory formula such as 'square circle' expresses no concept we can think, but that it uses words to set up an insoluble task. The existential proposition 'There is no square circle', on his view denies the possibility of connecting a concept with these words, and by a concept he expressly wants us to understand (if we get him right) the 'general meaning of a word', which is just what we mean by it. Erdmann[2] has similar opinions in regard to the instance 'A square circle is frivolous'. We should, in consistency, have to apply the word 'senseless', not merely to expressions immediately absurd, but to those whose absurdity is mediate, i.e. the countless

---

[1] *Die Impersonalien*, p. 62.
[2] *Logik*, I, p. 233.

expressions shown by mathematicians, in lengthy indirect demonstrations, to be objectless *a priori*. We should likewise have to deny that concepts like *regular decahedron* etc., are concepts at all.

Marty raises the following objection to the thinkers just mentioned. 'If the words are senseless, how could we understand the question as to whether such things exist, so as to answer it negatively? Even to reject such an existence, we must, it is plain, somehow form a presentation of such contradictory material'[1] . . . 'If such absurdities are called senseless, this can only mean that they have no rational sense'.[2] These objections are clinching, in so far as these thinkers' statements suggest that they are confusing the true meaninglessness mentioned above under 1, with another quite different meaninglessness, i.e. *the* a priori *impossibility of a fulfilling sense*. An expression has meaning in this sense if a possible fulfilment, i.e. the possibility of a unified intuitive illustration, corresponds to its intention. This possibility is plainly meant ideally. It concerns no contingent acts of expression or fulfilment, but their ideal contents: meaning as an ideal unity, here to be called 'intending meaning', on the one hand, and fulfilling meaning, standing to it in a certain relation of precise adequacy, on the other. We apprehend this ideal relation by ideative abstraction based on an act of unified fulfilment. In the contrary case we apprehend the real impossibility of meaning-fulfilment through an experience of the incompatibility of the partial meanings in the intended unity of fulfilment.

The phenomenological clarification of these relationships calls for long, difficult analyses, as will appear in a later investigation.

4. If we ask what an expression means, we naturally recur to cases where it actually contributes to knowledge, or, what is the same, where its meaning-intention is intuitively fulfilled. In this manner the 'notional presentation', i.e. the meaning-intention, gains clarity, it shows itself up as 'correct', as 'really' capable of execution. The draft it makes on intuition is as it were cashed. Since in the unity of fulfilment the act of intention coincides with the fulfilling act, and fuses with it in the most intimate fashion – if indeed there is any difference left over here at all – it readily seems as if the expression first got its meaning here, as if it drew meaning

---

[1] A. Marty, 'Über subjektlose Sätze und das Verhältnis der Grammatik zur Logik und Psychologie', Art. VI, *Vierteljahrschrift f. wiss. Phil.* XIX, 80 f.

[2] Ibid. p. 81 note. Cf. Art. V, Vol. XVIII, p. 464.

from the act of fulfilment. The tendency therefore arises to treat the *fulfilling intuitions* – categorially formative acts are here in general passed over – as meanings. But fulfilment is often imperfect – we shall have to devote closer study to all such possibilities – and expressions often go with remotely relevant, only partially illustrative intuitions, if with any at all. Since the phenomenological differences of these cases have not been closely considered, men have come to locate the significance of expressions, even of such as could make no claim to adequate fulfilment, in accompaniments of intuitive imagery. This naturally led to a total denial of meaning to absurd expressions.

The new concept of meaning therefore originates in a confusion of meaning with fulfilling intuition. On this conception, an expression has meaning if and only if its intention – we should say its 'meaning-intention' – is in fact fulfilled, even if only in a partial, distant and improper manner. The understanding of the expression must be given life through certain 'ideas of meaning' (it is commonly said), i.e. by certain *illustrative* images.

The final refutation of highly attractive, opposed notions is an important task which requires lengthy discussions. These we shall postpone to the next chapter, and here go on enumerating different concepts of meaning.

§16 *Continuation: meaning and connotation*

Another equivocation in our talk about meaninglessness was introduced by John Stuart Mill, and again rests on a new, fifth concept of meaning. He locates the essence of the meaning of names in their connotation, and therefore treats non-connotative names as meaningless. (Sometimes he says, more carefully but less clearly, that they are meaningless in the 'proper' or 'strict' sense.) It is well-known that by 'connotative names' Mill understands such as designate a subject and imply an attribute, by 'non-connotative names' such as designate a subject without (as it is here more clearly put) indicating an attribute as attaching to it.[1] Proper names are non-connotative and so too are names of attributes (e.g. 'whiteness'). Mill compares proper names to the distinctive chalk-marks which the robber, in the well-known tale from the *Arabian Nights*, made on the house.[2] And he goes on to

[1] *Logic*, Book I, ch. 2, §5.   [2] *System of Logic*, Book I, ch. 2, §5.

say: 'When we impose a proper name, we perform an operation in some degree analogous to what the robber intended in chalking the house. We put a mark, not indeed upon the object itself, but upon the idea of the object. A proper name is but an unmeaning mark which we connect in our minds with the idea of the object, in order that whenever the mark meets our eyes or occurs to our thoughts, we may think of that individual object . . . When we predicate of anything its proper name; when we say, pointing to a man, this is Brown or Smith, or pointing to a city, this is York, we do not, merely by so doing, convey to the reader any information about them, except that those are their names . . . It is otherwise when objects are spoken of by connotative names. When we say, "The town is built of marble", we give the hearer what may be entirely new information, and this merely by the signification of the many-worded connotative name "built of marble". Such names . . . are not mere marks, but more, that is to say significant marks; and the connotation is what constitutes their significance.'[1]

If we set our own analyses alongside of these utterances of Mill's, we cannot help seeing that he confuses distinctions that should in principle be kept apart. Above all, he blurs the distinction between indicating and expressing. The chalk-mark of the robber is a mere indication, while a proper name is an expression.

Like every expression a proper name functions as an indication, i.e. in its intimating role. Here there is a real analogy with the robber's chalk-mark. If the robber sees the chalk-mark he knows: This is the house I must rob. If I hear a proper name uttered, the corresponding presentation is aroused in me, and I know: This is the presentation the speaker is framing in his mind, and that he likewise wishes to arouse in mine. A name, however, has an additional expressiveness to which the intimating function is merely auxiliary. A man's presentation is not of primary importance: we are not concerned to direct interest to it but to the *object* it presents, to what it *refers to* and therefore *names*, and to set this before us as such. In a statement it makes its first appearance as the object about which something is asserted, in a wish-sentence as the object about which something is wished etc. Only in order to perform this task will a proper name, like any other

---

[1] Op. cit., Book I, ch. 2, § 5.

name, become an element in complex, unified expressions, in statements, wish-sentences and the like. But in its relation to its *object* the proper name is not an index. This is at once clear when we reflect on the fact that it is of the essence of an index to point to a fact, an existence, whereas the object named need not be taken to exist at all. When Mill extending his analogy, holds a proper name to be associated with the idea of the person it names in essentially the same manner as the chalk-mark is associated with the house, but *at once* adds that the point of the association is that we may *think* of the individual object whenever the sign meets our eye or enters our thought, his addition cracks the analogy wide asunder.

Mill correctly stresses the difference between names that are a means towards 'knowing' an object and names which are not, but neither this distinction, nor the equivalent distinction between connotative and non-connotative names, has anything to do with the distinction between the meaningful and the meaningless. The first-mentioned pair of differences are in fact not merely logically equivalent but identical. The difference is simply one of attributive and non-attributive names: to mediate the 'knowledge' of a thing and to mediate its attributes mean exactly the same. It is, no doubt, important, whether a name means a thing directly or only by way of the attributes that pertain to it. But this is a difference within the unitary genus Expression, just as the very important, parallel difference between nominal meanings (or logical 'presentations') which are attributive and those which are not attributive, is a difference within the unitary genus Meaning.

Mill *after a fashion* 'feels' the difference in question by being at times obliged to speak of a meaning of proper names in a sense contrasting with the 'strict' and 'proper' sense ascribed to the meaning of connotative names. He would have done better had he introduced a wholly new sense of meaning (though not, we may say, one to be recommended). The way, at least, in which the distinguished logician brings in his valuable distinction between connotative and non-connotative names has done much to confuse the quite different distinctions we have here been discussing.

One must note, further, that Mill's distinction between what a name *denotes* and what it *connotes* must not be confused with the merely cognate distinction between what a name *names* and what it *means*. This confusion is greatly aided by Mill's exposition.

How important all these distinctions are, and how little it helps to treat them with superficial contempt as being 'merely grammatical', will be shown in further investigations. These will make plain, we hope, that if one blurs the straightforward distinctions we have proposed, we cannot hope for a trustworthy elaboration of the concepts of Presentation and Judgement, in the sense relevant to logic.

CHAPTER TWO

Towards a Characterization of the Acts which Confer Meaning

§17 *Illustrative mental pictures as putative meanings*

WE have oriented our concept of meaning, or meaning-intention, towards the phenomenological character essential to an expression as such, which distinguishes it descriptively in consciousness from a merely sounded word. Such a character is, on our view, possible, and quite often actual, though the expression does not help us to know anything, does not stand in the loosest, remotest relation to sensualizing intuitions. It is now time to take up our stance towards a widely held, perhaps almost dominant conception, which, as against our own, sees the whole role of the expression, with all its living meaning, in the arousal of certain images which regularly accompany it.

To understand an expression means, on this view, to meet with pertinent mental pictures. Where these are absent, an expression is void of sense. These mental pictures are themselves often said to be the meanings of words, and those who say so, claim to be getting at what ordinary speech means by the 'meaning of an expression'.

It shows the retarded state of descriptive psychology that such speciously obvious doctrines should be entertained, and entertained despite long-standing objections urged against them by unprejudiced thinkers. Verbal expressions are no doubt often accompanied by images, which may stand in an intimate or a distant relation to their meanings, but to treat such accompaniments as necessary conditions for understanding runs counter to the plainest facts. Thereby we know that the meaningfulness of an expression – let alone its very meaning – cannot consist in the existence of such images, and cannot be disturbed by their absence. A comparison of a few casually observed imaginative accompaniments will soon show how vastly they vary while the meanings of words stay constant, and how they often are only very distantly related to the latter, whereas true illustrations, which genuinely carry out or confirm the meaning-intention of our expression, can often only be evoked with difficulty or not at all. Let a man read a work in an abstract field of knowledge, and understand the author's assertions perfectly, and let him then try to see what *more* there is to such reading than the words he understands. The circumstances of observation are most favourable to the view we reject, since an interest in finding images tends psychologically to evoke images, while the tendency to read back the findings of reflection into the original situation, makes us include all new images which stream in during the observation in the psychological content of our expression. Despite these favouring circumstances, the view we oppose, which sees the essence of the meaningful in accompanying imagery, must at least cease to look for introspective confirmation in the sort of case in question. Take, e.g., well-understood algebraical signs, or complete formulae, or verbal propositions such as 'Every algebraical equation of uneven grade has at least one real root', and carry out the needful observations. To report my own findings in the last case: I see an open book which I recognize as Serret's *Algebra*, I see the sensory pattern of an algebraical equation in Teubnerian type, while accompanying the word 'root', I see the familiar $\sqrt{}$. I have however read the sentence very many times and have understood it perfectly, without experiencing the slightest trace of accompanying images that have anything to do with its presented object. The same happens when expressions like 'culture', 'religion', 'science', 'art', 'differential calculus' etc., are intuitively illustrated.

We may further point out that what we have said applies not only to expressions which stand for highly abstract objects, mediated by complex relations, but to names of individual objects, well-known persons, cities, landscapes. A readiness for intuitive representation may be present, but it remains unfulfilled at the moment in question.

§18 *Continuation of the above. Arguments and counter-arguments*

Should someone object that there are highly evanescent images even in such cases, that a mental picture emerges only to disappear forthwith, we reply that the full understanding of words, their complete living sense, persists after such an image has vanished, and cannot therefore consist in its presence.

If the objecter shifts to saying that the mental image has become unobservable, perhaps always was so, but that, whether observable or not, it still exists, and makes continued understanding possible, we need not be in doubt as to our answer. We reply that whether or not such an assumption is necessary or plausible on grounds of genetic psychology, this is not anything that need be gone into here. It is quite irrelevant to our essentially descriptive question. Let us grant that there often are unobservable images. Despite this, however, an expression can quite often be understood, and quite observably so. But surely it is absurd to suppose that an abstract, sense-making aspect of an image should be observable, while the whole complete, concrete image-experience remains unobservable? How does the matter stand, further, in cases where our meaning is absurd? Unobservability can here not depend on the contingent limits of mental capacity, since such an image cannot exist at all: if it could, it would provide us with a self-evident guarantee of the possibility, the semantic consistency, of the thought in question.

It can, of course, be pointed out that we do, after a fashion, illustrate even absurdities, such as a straight line enclosing a space, or triangles the sum of whose angles is greater or less than two right angles. In metageometric treatises there are even drawings of such forms. No one would, however, dream of taking intuitions of this sort as truly illustrating the concepts in question, or of letting them pass as owning such verbal meanings. Only in cases where the image of a thing meant is really adequate to it, are we tempted to seek the sense of our expression in such an image. But if we rule out absurd expressions – which none the less have their sense – are images normally adequate? Even Descartes cited his 'chiliagon' to shed light on his distinction between *imaginatio* and *intellectio*. Our imaginative idea of a chiliagon is no more adequate than are our images of space-enclosing straight lines or intersecting parallels: in both cases we have rough, merely partial illustrations of a thing thought of, not complete exemplifications. We speak of a closed straight line, and draw a closed curve, thereby only illustrating the curvature. In the same fashion we think of a chiliagon, while we imagine any polygon with 'many' sides.

We need not look for recondite geometrical illustrations to prove the inadequacy of illustration even in the case of consistent meanings. It is a well-known fact that no geometrical concept whatsoever can be adequately illustrated. We imagine or draw a stroke, and speak or think of a straight line, and so in the case of all figures. The image everywhere provides only a foothold for *intellectio*. It offers no genuine instance of our intended pattern, only an instance of the sort of sensuous form which is the natural starting-point for geometrical 'idealization'. In these intellectual thought-processes of geometry, the idea of a geometrical figure is constituted, which is then expressed in the fixed meaning of the definitory expression. Actually to perform this intellectual process may be presupposed by our first formation of primitive geometrical expressions and by our application of them in knowledge, but not for their revived understanding and their continued significant use. Elusive sensuous pictures function, however, in a phenomenologically graspable and describable manner, as mere aids to understanding, and not as themselves meanings or carriers of meaning.

Our conception will perhaps be censured for its extreme nominalism, for identifying word and thought. To many it will seem quite absurd that a symbol, a word, a sentence, a formula should be understood, while in our view nothing intuitive is present beyond the mindless sensible body of thought, the sensible stroke on paper etc. But we are far from identifying words and thoughts, as our statements in the previous chapter show. We do not at all think that, where symbols are understood without the aid of accompanying images, the mere symbol alone is present: we think rather that an understanding, a peculiar act-experience relating to the expression, is present, that it shines through the expression, that it lends it meaning and thereby a relation to objects. What distinguishes the mere word, as a sense-complex, from the meaningful word, is something we know full well from our own experience. We can indeed ignore meaning and pay attention only to a word's sensuous character. It may also be the case that some sensible feature first arouses interest on its own account, and that its verbal or other symbolic character is only then noted. The sensuous habit of an object does not change when it assumes the status of a symbol for us, nor, conversely, does it do so when we ignore the meaning of what normally functions as a symbol. No new, independent content is here added to the old: we do not merely have a sum or association of contents of equal status before us. One and the same content has rather altered its psychic habit: we are differently minded in respect of it, it no longer seems a mere sensuous mark on paper, the physical phenomenon counts as an *understood* sign. Living thus understandingly, we perform no act of presentation or judgement directed upon the sign as a sensible object, but another act, quite different in kind, which relates to the thing designated. It is in this sense-giving act-character – which differs entirely according as our interest plays on the sensible sign or the object presented through it, with or without representative imagery – that meaning consists.

§19 *Understanding without intuition*

In the light of our conception it becomes wholly understandable that an expression should be able to function significantly without illustrative intuition. Those who locate the meaning-aspect of symbols in intuition, must find purely symbolic thinking insolubly enigmatic. Speech without intuition must likewise be senseless to them. But truly senseless speech would be no speech at all: it would be like the rattle of machinery. This we of course meet with in the case of verses or prayers learnt by rote and repeated unthinkingly, but not in the cases which here require explanation. Popular comparisons with the squawking of parrots or the cackling of geese, the well-known adage 'Where ideas fail us, words come up at the right moment' and so on, are not, soberly considered, to be taken literally. Expressions such as 'talk without judgement' or 'senseless talk' may and should certainly not be otherwise interpreted than such expressions as 'a heartless', 'brainless', 'empty-headed man' etc. 'Talk without judgement' plainly does not mean talk unbacked by judgements, but talk backed by judgements not based on independent, intelligent consideration. Even 'senselessness', understood as absurdity or nonsense, is significantly constituted: the sense of an absurd expression is such as to refer to what cannot be objectively put together.

The opposite view can now only take refuge in the strained hypothesis of unconscious, unnoticed intuitions. How little this helps becomes plain if we consider what basic intuition achieves in cases where it is noticeably present. In the vast majority of cases it is by no means adequate to our meaning-intention, a fact, which, on our conception, presents no problem. If the meaningful is not to be found in intuition, speech without intuition need not be speech deprived of thought. If intuition lapses, an act like that which otherwise hangs about intuition, and perhaps mediates the knowledge of its object, continues to cling to the sense-given expression. The act in which meaning is effective is therefore present in either case.

§20 *Thought without intuition and the 'surrogative function' of signs*

It should be quite clear that over most of the range both of ordinary, relaxed thought and the strict thought of science, illustrative imagery plays a small part or no part at all, and that we may, in the fullest sense, judge, reason, reflect upon and refute positions, without recourse to more than symbolic presentations. This situation is quite inadequately described if one talks of the 'surrogative function of signs', as if the signs themselves did duty for something, and as if our interest in symbolic thinking were directed to the signs themselves. Signs are in fact not objects of our thought at all, even surrogatively; we rather live entirely in the consciousness of meaning, of understanding, which does not lapse when accompanying imagery does so. One must bear in mind that symbolic thinking is only thinking in virtue of a new, intentional act-character: this distinguishes the meaningful sign from the mere sign, i.e. the sounded word set up as a physical object in our mere presentations of sense. This act-character is a *descriptive* trait in the sign-experience which, stripped of intuition, yet understands the sign.

It will perhaps be objected to our present interpretation of symbolic thinking that it conflicts with quite certain facts involved in the analysis of *arithmetical symbolic thought*, facts that I myself have stressed elsewhere (in my *Philosophy of Arithmetic*). In arithmetical thought mere signs genuinely do duty for concepts.

'The reduction of the theory of things to the theory of signs' (to quote Lambert) is what all calculation achieves. Arithmetical signs are 'so selected and perfected, that the theory, combination, transformation etc. of signs can do what would otherwise have to be done by concepts.'[1]

Looked at more closely, however, it is not signs, in the mere sense of *physical* objects, whose theory, combination etc., would be of the slightest use. Such things would belong to the sphere of physical science and practice, and not to that of arithmetic. The true meaning of the signs in question emerges if we glance at the much favoured comparison of mathematical operations to rule-governed games, e.g. chess. Chessmen are not part of the chess-game as bits of ivory and wood having such and such shapes and colours. Their phenomenal and physical constitution is quite indifferent, and can be varied at will. They become chessmen, counters in the chess-game, through the game's rules which give them their fixed *games-meaning*. And so arithmetical signs have, besides their original meaning, their so-to-say games-meaning, a meaning oriented towards the game of calculation and its well-known rules. If one treats arithmetical signs as mere counters in the rule-sense, to solve the tasks of the reckoning game leads to numerical signs or formulae whose interpretation in their original, truly arithmetical senses also represents the solution of corresponding arithmetical problems.

We do not therefore operate with *meaningless signs* in fields of symbolic-arithmetical thought and calculation. For mere signs, in the sense of *physical* signs bereft of all meaning, do duty for the same signs alive with arithmetical meaning: it is rather that signs taken in a certain *operational or games-sense* do duty for the same signs in full *arithmetical meaningfulness*. A system of natural, and, as it were, unconscious equivocations bears endless fruit, and the much greater mental work which our original array of concepts demanded is eased by 'symbolic' operations employing a parallel array of games-concepts.

Naturally such a procedure must be logically justified and its boundaries reliably fixed: here we were only concerned to remove confusions readily caused by misunderstanding of the nature of such 'merely symbolical' mathematical thought. If one grasps the

---

[1] Lambert, *Neues Organon* (1764), Vol. II, §§23-4, p. 16. (Lambert is not referring expressly to arithmetic.)

sense, set out above, in which the 'mere signs' of arithmetic do duty for arithmetical concepts (or for signs in their full arithmetical meaning) it is clear that talk of the surrogative function of arithmetical signs is irrelevant to our present question, the question whether an expression of thought is or is not possible without an accompaniment of illustrative, instantiating or demonstrative intuitions. Non-intuitive symbolic thought in the sense just mentioned, and symbolical thought in the sense of thought which employs surrogative operational concepts, are two quite different things.

§ 21 *A difficulty regarding our necessary recourse to corresponding intuitions in order to clarify meanings or to know truths resting on them*

One might here ask: If the sense of expressions functioning purely symbolically lies in an act-character which distinguishes the understanding grasp of a verbal sign from the grasp of a sign stripped of meaning, why is it that we have recourse to intuition when we want to establish differences of meaning, to expose ambiguities, or to limit shifts in our meaning-intention?

Again one might ask: Why, if our conception of meaning is right, do we employ corresponding intuitions in order to know purely conceptual truths, i.e. truths known through an analysis of meanings? One can say in general, that in order to be quite clear as to the sense of an expression (or as to the content of a concept) one must construct a corresponding intuition: in this intuition one sees what the expression 'really means'.

But an expression functioning symbolically also means something, and means the same thing as an expression intuitively clarified. Meaning cannot first have been acquired through intuition: otherwise we should have to say that much the greater part of our experience in speaking and reading is merely an external perceiving or imagining of optic and auditory complexes. We need not again stress that this plainly conflicts with the phenomenological data, that we *mean* this or that with our spoken or written signs, and that this meaning is a *descriptive character* of intelligent speech and hearing, even when these are purely symbolic. Our first question is answered by observing that purely symbolic meaning-intentions often do not clearly keep themselves apart, and do not permit of the easy, sure distinctions and identifications which are needed for practically useful judgements, even if these are not self-evident. To recognize differences of meaning such as that between 'moth' and 'elephant', requires no special procedures. But where meanings shade unbrokenly into one another, and unnoticed shifts blur boundaries needed for firm judgement, intuitive illustration naturally promotes lucidity. Where an expression's meaning-intention is fulfilled by divergent, conceptually disparate intuitions, the sharp difference in the direction of fulfilment shows up the cleavage of meaning-intentions.

Answering our second question, we recall that all self-evidence of judgement (all realized knowledge in the strong sense of the word) presupposes meanings that are intuitively fulfilled. Where there is talk of a knowledge 'springing from the analysis of the mere meanings of words', more is meant than these words suggest. The knowledge meant is one whose self-evidence calls only for pure representation of the 'conceptual essences', in which the general word-meanings find their perfect fulfilments: all question as to the existence of objects corresponding to such concepts, or falling under such conceptual essences, is ruled out. But these 'conceptual essences' are not the verbal meanings themselves, so that the phrases 'based purely on the concepts (essences)', and 'springing from a mere analysis of word-meanings', are only by equivocation equivalent. Conceptual essences are rather the fulfilling sense which is 'given' when the word-meanings (i.e. the meaning-intentions of the words) terminate in corresponding, directly intuitive presentations, and in certain cogitative elaborations and formations of the same. Such analysis is not therefore concerned with empty thought-intentions, but with the objects and forms by which they are fulfilled. What it therefore offers us are not mere statements concerning elements or relations of meanings, but evident necessities concerning the *objects* thought of in these meanings, and thought of as thus and thus determined.

These discussions point to a field of phenomenological analyses which we have already repeatedly seen to be unavoidable, analyses which bring self-evidence into the *a priori* relations between meaning and knowing, or between meaning and clarifying intuition. They will therefore also have to bring complete clarity into our concept of meaning, both by distinguishing meaning from *fulfilling* sense, and by investigating the sense of such fulfilment.

§22 *Varying marks of understanding and the 'quality of familiarity'*

Our conception presupposes a certain separation, even if not quite a sharp one, among the act-characters which confer meaning even in cases which lack intuitive illustration. One cannot indeed think that the 'symbolic presentations' which govern the grasp or the significant application of signs, are descriptively equivalent, that they consist in one *undifferentiated* character, the same for all expressions, as if only the sound of the words, the chance sensuous carriers of meaning, made all the difference. Examples of equivocal expressions readily show that we can effect and can recognize sudden changes of meaning, without in the least needing accompanying illustrations. The descriptive difference, here evidently apparent, cannot be the sensuous sign, which remains the same: it must concern the act-character, which is specifically altered. One can likewise point to cases where meaning remains identical while a word changes, in the case, e.g., of mere differences of idiom. Sensuously different signs here count as equivalent (we perhaps even speak of the 'same' word, only occurring in different languages), they at once greet us as the same, even before reproductive fancy can furnish images that illustrate their meaning.

Such examples reveal the untenability of the view, plausible at first, that the note of understanding is no more ultimately than what Riehl[1] called the 'character of familiarity', and what Höffding,[2] not so suitably, called the 'quality of familiarity'.[3] Words not understood are just as capable of coming before us in the form of old acquaintances: well-memorized Greek verses stick in our memories longer than our understanding of their sense, they appear familiar but are no longer understood. The missing grasp often comes in a flash afterwards, possibly some time before mother-tongue translations or other aids come up in

[1] A. Riehl, *Der philosophische Kritizismus*, Vol. II, p. 399.
[2] H. Höffding, 'Uber Wiedererkennen, Assoziation und psychische Aktivität', *Vierteljahrschrift f. wiss. Philos.* Vol. XIII, p. 425.
[3] As against this cf. Volkelt, *Erfahrung und Denken*, p. 362.

memory, and the note of understanding now adds its obvious novelty to the note of familiarity, not altering the content sensuously, yet giving it a new mental character. One may similarly recall the way in which the reading or recitation of familiar poetry, unthinking at first, suddenly becomes charged with understanding. There are countless other examples which make evident the peculiar character of understanding.

§23 *Apperception as connected with expression and with intuitive presentations*

The grasp of understanding,[1] in which the meaning of a word becomes effective, is, in so far as *any* grasp is in a sense an understanding and an interpretation, akin to the divergently carried out 'objective interpretations' in which, by way of an experienced sense-complex, the intuitive presentation, whether percept, imagination, representation etc., of an object, e.g. an external thing, arises. The phenomenological structure of the two sorts of 'grasp' is, however, somewhat different. If we imagine a consciousness prior to all experience, it may very well have the same *sensations* as we have. But it will intuit no things, and no events pertaining to things, it will perceive no trees and no houses, no flight of birds nor any barking of dogs. One is at once tempted to express the situation by saying that its sensations *mean* nothing to such a consciousness, that they do not *count as signs* of the properties of an object, that their combination does not count as a sign of the object itself. They are merely lived through, without an objectifying *interpretation* derived from experience. Here, therefore, we talk of signs and meanings just as we do in the case of expressions and cognate signs.

To simplify comparison by restricting ourselves to the case of perception, the above talk should not be misread as implying that consciousness first looks at its sensations, then turns them into perceptual objects, and then bases an interpretation upon them, which is what really happens when we are objectively conscious of physical objects, e.g. sounded words, which function as signs in the strict sense. Sensations plainly only become presented

---

[1] I am not here restricting the use of the word 'understanding' to the hearer-speaker relation. The soliloquizing thinker 'understands' his words, and this understanding is simply his act of meaning them.

objects in psychological reflection: in naïve, intuitive presentations they may be *components* of our presentative experience, parts of its descriptive content, but are not at all its objects. The perceptual presentation arises in so far as an experienced complex of sensations gets informed by a certain act-character, one of conceiving or meaning. To the extent that this happens, the perceived *object* appears, while the sensational complex is as little perceived as is the act in which the perceived object is as such constituted. Phenomenological analysis teaches us, further, that sense-contents provide, as it were, the analogical building-stuff for the content of the object presented by their means. Hence talk of colours, extensions, intensities etc., as, on the one hand, sensed, and as, on the other hand, perceived or imagined. Examples readily show that what corresponds in the two cases is in no sense the same, but only generically allied. The *uniform* colouring of a sphere as *seen* by us (i.e. perceived, imagined etc.), was never *sensed* by us.

Signs in the sense of expressions rest on a similar 'interpretation', but only in their first conception. In the simpler case where an expression is understood, but is not as yet given life by intuitive illustrations, this first conception makes the *mere sign* appear before us as a physical object, e.g. as a sounded word, given here and now. On this first conception, however, a second is built, which goes entirely beyond the experienced sense-material, which it no longer uses as analogical building-material, to the quite new object of its present meaning. The latter is meant in the act of meaning, but is not presented in sensation. Meaning, the characteristic function of the expressive sign, presupposes the sign whose function it is. Or to talk pure phenomenology: meaning is a variously tinctured act-character, presupposing an act of intuitive presentation as its necessary foundation. In the latter act, the expression becomes constituted as a physical object. It becomes an expression, in the full, proper sense, only through an act founded upon this former act.

What is true in this simplest case of an expression understood and not as yet intuitively illustrated, must also hold in the more complex case where an expression is bound up with a *corresponding* intuition. One and the same expression, significantly used with or without illustrative intuition, cannot derive its meaningfulness from different sorts of act.

It is certainly not easy to analyse the descriptive situation in certain finer gradations and ramifications that have been passed over here. It is extremely hard to achieve a right conception of the part played by illustrative presentations in confirming meaning-intentions or in conferring self-evidence on them, as well as their relation to the characteristic note of understanding or meaning, the experience which lends sense to an expression even in default of intuition. Here we have a broad field for phenomenological analysis, a field not to be by-passed by the logician who wants to bring clarity into the relations between meaning and object, between judgement and truth, between vague opinion and confirmatory evidence. The analysis in question will receive a thoroughgoing treatment later.[1]

---

[1] See Investigation VI.

CHAPTER THREE

Fluctuation in Meaning and the Ideality of Unities of Meaning

§24 *Introduction*

IN our last chapter we dealt with the act of meaning. But among the conclusions of our first chapter was a distinction between the act of meaning, on the one hand, and meaning itself, on the other, the ideal unity as against the multiplicity of possible acts. This distinction, like the others which go along with it – the distinction between expressed content taken in a subjective, and the same taken in an objective sense, and, in the latter respect, the distinction between content as significatum and content as nominatum – are in countless cases undoubtedly clear. This holds of all expressions which occur in the context of an adequately expounded scientific theory. There are, however, cases where the situation is different, which require particular consideration if they are not to plunge all our hard-won distinctions back into confusion. Expressions whose meaning shifts, especially such as are occasional or vague, here raise serious problems. To solve these problems by distinguishing between shifting acts of meaning, on the one hand, and ideal units of meaning, on the other, is the theme of the present chapter.

§25 *Relations of coincidence among the contents of intimation and naming*

Expressions may relate to the contemporary mental state of the person using them as much as they relate to other objects. They accordingly divide into those that also *intimate what they name*, (or what they generally stand for) and those in whose case *named and intimated contents fall asunder*. Instances of the former class are interrogative, optative and imperative sentences, of the latter, statements relating to external things, to one's own past experiences, to mathematical relationships etc. If someone utters the wish 'I should like a glass of water', this serves to indicate to the hearer the speaker's wish, which is also the object of the statement. What is intimated and what is named here coincide in part. I say 'in part', since the intimation obviously goes further. It extends to the judgement expressed in the words 'I should like etc.'. The like naturally holds of statements about the ideas, judgements, and surmises of the speaker which are of the forms 'I imagine that . . .', 'I am of the opinion that . . .', 'I judge that . . .', 'I conjecture that . . .'. A case even of total coincidence seems at first sight possible, in, e.g., the words 'the state of mind intimated by the words I am now uttering', though the interpretation of our example breaks down on closer examination. But intimation and the state of affairs asserted fall quite apart in statements such as '2 × 2 = 4'. This statement does not say what is said by 'I judge that 2 × 2 = 4'. They are not even equivalent statements, since the one can be true when the other is false.

One must of course stress that if the notion of 'intimation' is given the *narrower* sense defined above, the objects named in the above examples are *not* among the experiences they intimate. A man saying something about his contemporary mental state, communicates its presence through a judgement. Only as intimating such a judgement (whose content is that he wishes, hopes etc., this or that) is the man apperceived by the hearer as one who wishes, hopes etc. The meaning of such a statement lies in this judgement, whereas the inner experiences in question are among the objects judged *about*. If we limit intimation in the narrower sense to experiences which carry an expression's meaning, the contents of intimation and naming remain as distinct here as they are generally.

§26 *Essentially occasional and objective expressions*

The expressions which name the momentary content of intimation belong to a wider class of expressions whose meaning varies from case to case. This happens, however, in so peculiar a manner, that one hesitates to speak of 'equivocation' in this case. The same words 'I wish you luck' which express my wish, can serve countless other persons to express wishes having 'the same' content. Not only do the wishes themselves differ from case to case, but the meanings of the wish-utterances do so too. At one time a person A confronts a person B, at another time a person M confronts a person N. If A wishes B 'the same' that M wishes N, the sense of the wish-utterances, which includes the idea of the confronting persons, is plainly different. This ambiguity is, however, quite different from that of the word 'dog' which at one time means a type of animal, and at another a foot or a grate.[1] The class of ambiguous expressions illustrated by this last example are what one usually has in mind when one speaks of 'equivocation'. Ambiguity in such cases does not tend to shake our faith in the ideality and objectivity of meanings. We are free, in fact, to limit our expression to a *single* meaning. The ideal unity of each of the differing meanings will not be affected by their attachment to a common designation. But how do things stand in the case of the other expressions? Can we there still stick to self-identical meaning-unities, elsewhere made clear in their opposition to varying persons and their experiences, when here our meanings must vary *with* such persons and their experiences? Obviously we are here dealing with a case of unavoidable rather than chance ambiguity, one that cannot be removed from our language by an artificial device or convention.

To promote clearness we shall define the following distinction between *essentially subjective and occasional* expressions, on the one hand, and *objective* expressions, on the other. For simplicity's sake we shall deal only with expressions in their normal use.

We shall call an expression *objective* if it pins down (or can pin down) its meaning merely by its manifest, auditory pattern, and can be understood without necessarily directing one's attention to the person uttering it, or to the circumstances of the utterance. An objective expression may be in varying ways equivocal: it may stand in the stated relation to several meanings, so that it depends on the psychological context (on the chance drift of the hearer's thoughts, on the tenor of the talk already in progress and the tendencies it arouses etc.) which of these meanings it arouses and means. It may be that a glance at the speaker and his situation may help all this. But whether or not the word *can* be understood in one or other of such meanings does not depend on this glance as a *sine qua non*.

[1] Husserl's example is of the German word *Hund* meaning both a dog and a truck used in mines.

On the other hand, we call an expression essentially subjective and occasional, or, more briefly, *essentially occasional*, if it belongs to a conceptually unified group of possible meanings, in whose case it is essential to orient actual meaning to the occasion, the speaker and the situation. Only by looking to the actual circumstances of utterance can one definite meaning out of all this mutually connected class be constituted for the hearer. Since we regularly understand such expressions in normal circumstances, the very idea of these circumstances, and of their regular relation to the expression, involves the presence of generally graspable, sufficiently reliable clues to guide the hearer to the meaning intended in the case in question.

Among objective expressions we have, e.g., all expressions in theory, expressions out of which the principles and theorems, the proofs and theories of the 'abstract' sciences are made up. What, e.g., a mathematical expression means, is not in the least affected by the circumstances of our actual use of it. We read and understand it without thinking of a speaker at all. The case is different with expressions which serve the practical needs of ordinary life and with expressions which, in the sciences, prepare the way for theoretical results. I mean by the latter expressions with which the investigator accompanies his own thought, or acquaints others with his considerations and endeavours, with his methodical preparations and his provisional beliefs.

Every expression, in fact, that includes a *personal pronoun* lacks an objective sense. The word 'I' names a different person from case to case, and does so by way of an ever altering meaning. What its meaning is at the moment, can be gleaned only from the living utterance and from the intuitive circumstances which surround it. If we read the word without knowing who wrote it, it is perhaps not meaningless, but is at least estranged from its normal sense. Certainly it strikes us differently from a wanton arabesque: we know it to be a word, and a word with which whoever is speaker designates himself. But the conceptual meaning thus evoked in not what the word 'I' means, otherwise we could simply substitute for it the phrase 'whatever speaker is designating himself'. Such a substitution would lead to expressions, not only unusual, but also divergent in sense, if, e.g., instead of saying 'I am pleased' I said 'Whatever speaker is now designating himself is pleased'. It is the universal *semantic function* of the word 'I' to designate whoever is speaking, but the notion through which we express this function is not the notion immediately constitutive of its meaning.

In solitary speech the meaning of 'I' is essentially realized in the immediate idea of one's own personality, which is also the meaning of the word in communicated speech. Each man has his own I-presentation (and with it his individual notion of I) and this is why the word's meaning differs from person to person. But since each person, in speaking of himself, says 'I', the word has the character of a universally operative indication of this fact. Through such *indication* the hearer achieves understanding of the meaning, he takes the person who confronts him intuitively, not merely as the speaker, but also as the immediate object of this speaker's speech. The word 'I' has not itself directly the power to arouse the specific I-presentation; this becomes fixed in the actual piece of talk. It does not work like the word 'lion' which can arouse the idea of a lion in and by itself. In its case, rather, an indicative function mediates, crying as it were, to the hearer 'Your *vis-à-vis* intends himself'.

We must, however, add something to what has been said. Properly speaking, we should not suppose that the immediate presentation of the speaker sums up the entire meaning of the word 'I'. The word is certainly not to be regarded as an equivocal expression, with meanings to be identified with all possible proper names of persons. Undoubtedly the idea of self-reference, as well as an implied pointing to the individual idea of the speaker, also belong, *after a certain fashion*, to the word's meaning. We shall have to admit that two meanings are here built upon one another in peculiar fashion. The one, relating to the word's general function, is so connected with the word that its indicative function can be exercised once something is actually presented: this indicative function is, in its turn, exercised *for* the other, singular presentation, and, by subsumption, makes the latter's object known as what is here and now meant. The former meaning can be called the *indicating* meaning, the latter the meaning *indicated*.

What is true of personal pronouns is of course also true of demonstratives. If someone says 'this', he does not directly arouse in the hearer the idea of what he means, but in the first place the idea or belief that he means something lying within his intuitive or thought-horizon, something he wishes to point out to the hearer. In the concrete circumstances of speech, this thought is an adequate guide to what is really meant. 'This' read in isolation likewise lacks its proper meaning, and is understood only to the extent that it arouses the notion of its demonstrative function (which we call its indicating meaning). In each case of normal use, its full, actual meaning can only grow out of the prominent presentation of the thing that it makes its object.

We must grant, of course, that a demonstrative often works in a manner that can claim equivalence with an objective use. A 'this' in a mathematical context points to something determined in a conceptually fixed manner, that is understood as meant in this manner, without our needing to regard the actual utterance. A mathematical exposition, after expressly stating a proposition, may go on to say 'This follows from the fact that . . .'. Here the proposition in question could itself have been substituted for the word 'this' without greatly altering the sense; this follows from the exposition's objective sense. One must of course attend to the continuous exposition since, not the intended meaning, but only the thought of an indication, belongs to the demonstrative considered by itself. Mediation by indicating meanings merely promotes brevity and increases mastery over the main drift of one's thought-intentions. The same plainly does not apply in the common case where the demonstrative 'this' and similar forms stand for the house confronting the speaker, for the bird flying up before him etc. Here individual intuition, varied from case to case, must do duty: it is not enough to look back to previously uttered objective thoughts.

In the sphere of essentially occasional expressions one has also the subject-bound determinations 'here', 'there', 'above', 'below', 'now', 'yesterday', 'tomorrow', 'later' etc. 'Here' (to think out a last example) designates the speaker's vaguely bounded spatial environment. To use the word is to refer to one's place on the basis of an intuitive, believing presentation of one's own person and location. This changes from case to case, and changes likewise from person to person, though each can say 'here'. It is again the general function of the word to name the spatial environment of the speaker, so that the genuine meaning of the word is first constituted in the variable presentation of this place. The meaning of 'here' is in part universal and conceptual, inasmuch as it always names a place as such, but to this universal element the direct place-presentation attaches, varying from case to case. In the given circumstances of speech, it acquires heightened intelligibility by subsumption under the conceptual indicating presentation of 'here'.

An essentially indicating character naturally spreads to all expressions which include these and similar presentations as parts: this includes all the manifold speech-forms where the speaker gives normal expression to something concerning himself, or which is thought of in relation to himself. All expressions for percepts, beliefs, doubts, wishes, fears, commands belong here, as well as all combinations involving the *definite article*, in which the latter relates to something individual and merely pinned down by class- or property-concepts. When we Germans speak of *the* Kaiser we of course mean the present German Kaiser. When we ask for *the* lamp in the evening, each man means his own.

Note. Expressions with essentially occasional meaning, as dealt with in this section, do not fit into Paul's useful division of expressions into those of usual and those of occasional meaning. His division is based on the fact 'that the meaning which a word has in each application need not coincide with what usage accords in it in and for itself' (H. Paul, *Prinzipien der Sprachgeschichte*, p. 68). Paul has, however, included our essentially occasional expressions in his treatment, for he says: 'There are some words in occasional use which are essentially framed to designate the concrete, but which none the less lack their own relation to a definite concretum till individual application gives them one. Here belong personal pronouns, possessive and demonstrative adjectives, demonstrative adverbs, also words like "now", "today", "yesterday".'[1] It seems to me that occasional expressions in this sense fall outside of Paul's definitory antithesis. For it pertains to the *usual* sense of this class of expressions, that they owe their determinate meaning to the occasion, and are therefore occasional in a somewhat *different* sense. Expressions of usual meaning (in Paul's sense) can be divided into those usually univocal and those usually equivocal, and the latter into expressions usually varying among definite meanings assignable in advance (such as the casual equivoca 'cock', 'bear' etc.) and those in which this is not so,

---

[1] The restriction to concreta is not essential. Demonstratives, e.g., can also refer to abstracta.

since their meaning is oriented in each case to the individual instance, though the manner of this orientation is a matter of usage.

§27 *Other sorts of fluctuating expressions*

The variation of essentially occasional expressions is heightened by the incompleteness with which they often express the speaker's meaning. The distinction between essentially occasional and objective expressions cuts across many other distinctions standing for new forms of ambiguity, the distinctions, e.g., between complete and incomplete (enthymematic) expressions, between expressions functioning normally and expressions functioning abnormally, between exact and vague expressions. The impersonalia of ordinary speech are good examples as to how apparently firm, objective expressions really vary subjectively in virtue of enthymematic abbreviation. No one would understand the sentence 'There are cakes' as he understands the mathematical sentence 'There are regular solids'. In the first case we do not mean that cakes exist absolutely and in general, but that there are cakes *here* and *now* – for coffee. 'It is raining', likewise, does not have the general meaning that rain is falling, but that it is doing so *now, outside*. What the expression lacks is not merely unspoken, it is not even expressly thought: it certainly belongs, however, to what our speech means. If additions are made, we plainly get expressions that must be called 'essentially occasional' in the sense defined above.

There is an even greater difference between the properly expressed content of speech, i.e. the content picked out and pinned down by the uniform meaning-functions of the words involved, and its meaning on occasions when expressions are so shortened as not to express complete thoughts without the aids given to understanding by the fortuitous occasion, e.g. 'Onward!', 'You!', 'Man alive!', 'But my dear, my dear' etc. Through the common intuitive situation in which both speaker and hearer find themselves, these last can supplement or differentiate mutilated and subjectively indeterminate meanings: the defective expressions thus become understandable.

Among the distinctions relating to ambiguity of expressions, we mentioned those between *exact* and *vague* expressions. Most expressions used in ordinary life, such as 'tree', 'shrub', 'animal', 'plant' etc., are vague, whereas all expressions integral to pure theories and laws are exact. Vague expressions have no single meaning-content, the same in all cases of their application: their meaning is oriented towards types, only partially conceived with clearness and definiteness, types which tend to vary from case to case, perhaps even in a single train of thought. The types, stemming from what are, or from what seem to be, genuinely unified fields, yield a number of concepts, more or less cognate or related, which emerge in turn according to the circumstances of our talk and its varied thought-promptings. These do not permit, for the most part, of definite identifications and distinctions such as might guard against unnoticed confusions among closely connected concepts.

Similar to the haziness of such vague expressions, is the haziness of expressions standing for relatively simple genera and species of phenomenal properties, which shade continuously into one another, whether spatially, temporally, qualitatively or intensively. The typical characters which press in upon us in perception and experience, characters, e.g., of space- and time-pattern, of colour- and tone-pattern etc., lead to significant expressions which, in virtue of the fluid transitions among such types (i.e. among their higher genera) must themselves be fluid. Within certain ranges and limits their application is unhesitant, i.e. in fields where the type appears clearly, where it can be evidently identified and evidently distinguished from remotely unlike characters, e.g. 'signal-red' and 'coal-black', *andante* and *presto*. But these fields have vague borders, and flow over into correlative spheres comprehended in the same genus, and so give rise to transitional regions where application varies and is wholly uncertain.[1]

§28 *Variations in meanings as variations in the act of meaning*

We have become acquainted with various classes of expressions changeable in meaning, which count as subjective and occasional, since chance circumstances of speaking influence their change. To these expressions other expressions stand opposed, which are, in a correspondingly wide sense, objective and fixed, their meaning being normally free from all variation. If we take this freedom

[1] Cf. B. Erdmann, 'Theorie der Typeneinteilungen', *Philos. Monatshefte*, Vol. xxx.

from all variation quite strictly, only exact expressions are ranged on this side, whereas vague expressions and expressions which, for differing reasons, vary with the occasion, stand ranged on the other side.

We have now to consider whether these important facts of fluctuation of meaning are enough to shake our conception of meanings as ideal (i.e. rigorous) unities, or to restrict its generality significantly. Those ambiguous expressions we called *essentially* subjective, in particular, as also our distinction between vague and exact expressions, might make us doubtful on this point. Do meanings *themselves* divide into objective and subjective, into meanings fixed and meanings changeable on occasion? Must we, in other words, so interpret this difference, with seeming obviousness, that it becomes one between meanings that are ideal unities, on the one hand, fixed species untouched by the flux of our subjective picturing and thinking, and such, on the other hand, as live submerged in the flux of subjective mental experiences, and are transitory events, at one time there, and at the next moment not?

We shall have to look on such a notion as invalid. The content meant by the subjective expression, with sense oriented to the occasion, is an ideal unit of meaning in precisely the same sense as the content of a fixed expression. This is shown by the fact that, ideally speaking, each subjective expression is replaceable by an objective expression which will preserve the identity of each momentary meaning-intention.

We shall have to concede that such replacement is not only impracticable, for reasons of complexity, but that it cannot in the vast majority of cases, be carried out at all, will, in fact, never be so capable.

Clearly, in fact, to say that each subjective expression could be replaced by an objective expression, is no more than to assert the *unbounded range of objective reason*. Everything that is, can be known 'in itself'. Its being is a being definite in content, and documented in such and such 'truths in themselves'. What is, has its intrinsically definite properties and relations, and if it has natural, thinglike reality, then it has also its quite definite extension and position in space and time, its quite definite ways of persisting and changing. But what is objectively quite definite, must permit objective determination, and what permits objective determination, must, ideally speaking, permit expression through wholly determinate word-meanings. To being-in-itself correspond truths-in-themselves, and, to these last, fixed, unambiguous assertions. Of course, to be able to say all this actually, would require, not merely the necessary number of well-distinguished *verbal signs*, but a corresponding number of *expressions* having precise meanings – in the strict sense of expressions. We must be able to build up all expressions covering all meanings entering into our theory, and to identify or distinguish such meanings with self-evidence.

We are infinitely removed from this ideal. One need only think of the defective way in which we pin down time- and space-positions, our necessary recourse to relations to previously given individual existents, these last themselves inaccessible to an exact pinning down without making use of expressions having an essentially subjective sense. Strike out the essentially occasional expressions from one's language, try to describe any subjective experience in unambiguous, objectively fixed fashion: such an attempt is always plainly vain.

Plainly therefore, considered as such, meanings do not differ essentially among themselves. Actual word-meanings are variable, often changing in a single spell of thought, by their nature mainly adjusted to the occasion. Rightly seen, however, such change in meanings is really *change in the act of meaning*. In other words, the subjective acts which confer meaning on expressions are variable, and that not merely as individuals, but, more particularly, in respect of the specific characters in which their meaning consists. But the meanings themselves do not alter: this is in fact an absurd manner of speech if we adhere to our view of meanings as ideal unities, whether in the case of equivocal, subjectively defective expressions, or in the case of univocal, objectively fixed ones. This is not merely a view demanded by our ordinary orientation to fixed expressions, and by our talk of meanings which stay the same, whenever anyone uses the same expression; it fits in with the whole guiding aim of our analyses.

§29 *Pure logic and ideal meanings*

Pure logic, wherever it deals with concepts, judgements, and syllogisms, is exclusively concerned with the *ideal* unities that we here call 'meanings'. If we take the trouble to detach the ideal essence of meanings from their psychological and grammatical connections, if we try, further, to clear up their *a priori* relations of adequacy, founded in this essence, to the objective correlates that they mean, we are already within the domain of pure logic.

This is clear from the start if we *first* think of the position logic takes up to the many sciences, the position of nomological science, concerned with the ideal essence of science as such, or, what is the same, the position of nomological science, of scientific thought in general, taken purely in its theoretic content and connection. It is clear, *secondly*, when we note that the theoretic content of a science is no more than the meaning-content of its theoretical statements, disembarrassed of all contingent thinkers and occasions of judgement, and that such statements are given *unity* by the theory's pattern, which in its turn acquires objective validity through the ideally guaranteed adequacy of its unified meaning to the objective correlate meant by it (which is 'given' to us in self-evident knowledge). Undeniably what we call 'meaning' in this sense covers only ideal unities, expressed through manifold expressions, and thought of in manifold act-experiences, but none the less clearly separable from such chance expressions and from such chance experiences of thinking subjects.

If all given theoretic unity is in essence a unity of meaning, and if logic is the science of theoretic unity in general, then logic evidently is the science of meanings as such, of their essential sorts and differences, as also of the ideal laws which rest purely on the latter. Among such essential differences we have those between meanings which have, and meanings which have no objects, between true and false meanings, and, among such laws, we have the pure 'laws of thought', which express the *a priori* connection between the categorial form of meanings and their objectivity or truth.

This notion of logic as a science of meanings is of course at odds with the mode of speech and treatment of the traditional logic, which operates with psychological or psychologically slanted terms such as 'idea', 'judgement', 'affirmation', 'denial', 'presupposition', 'inference' etc., and which thinks it is really only establishing differences of psychology and tracking down psychological laws relating to these. After the critical investigations of our *Prolegomena* we can no more be taken in by all this.

It only shows how far logic still is from a proper understanding of the objects which make up its own true field of research, and how much it has still to learn from the objective sciences, whose essence it none the less claims to make theoretically intelligible.

Where the sciences unfold systematic theories, when they no longer merely communicate the progress of personal research and proof, but set forth the objectively unified, ripe fruit of known truth, there is absolutely no talk of judgements, ideas and other mental acts. The objective researcher of course *defines* his expressions. He says: By '*vis viva*', by 'mass', by an 'integral', by a 'sine' etc., this or that is meant. But he only points thereby to the *objective meaning* of his expressions, he indicates what 'contents' he has in mind, which play their part as constitutive moments in the truths of his field. He is not interested in understanding, but in the concepts, which are for him ideal unities of meaning, and also in the truths, which themselves are made up out of such concepts.

The investigator then propounds propositions, and naturally, in so doing, he asserts or judges. But he has no wish to speak of his own or of anyone else's judgements, but of the correlated *states of affairs*, and when his critical discussions concern propositions, he means by the latter the ideal meanings of statements. He does not say that judgements are true or false, but that propositions are so: his premisses are propositions, and so are his conclusions. Propositions are not constructed out of mental acts of presentation or belief: when not constructed out of other propositions, they ultimately point back to concepts.

Propositions are themselves the elements of *inferences*. Here too there is a distinction between acts of inferring and their unified contents, syllogisms, i.e. the self-identical *meanings* of certain complex statements. The relation of necessary consequence in which the form of an inference consists, is not an empirical-psychological connection among judgements as experiences, but an ideal relation among possible statement-meanings, among propositions. It 'exists' or 'subsists', i.e. it is valid, and such validity is something without essential relation to an empirical thinker. If a natural scientist deduces a machine's working from the laws of the lever, gravitation etc., he no doubt experiences all sorts of subjective acts. What, however, he thinks of, and what he knits together in unity, are concepts and propositions together with their objective relations. An objective unity of meaning, i.e. one adequate to the objectivity which is self-evidently 'given', thereby corresponds to his subjective thought-connections: this is whatever it is, whether anyone realizes this in thought or not. This holds in general. Though the scientific investigator may have no reason to draw express distinctions between words and symbols, on the one hand, and meaningful thought-objects, on the other, he well knows that expressions are contingent, and that the thought, the ideally selfsame meaning, is what is essential. He knows, too, that he does not *make* the objective validity of thoughts and thought-connections, of concepts and truths, as if he were concerned with contingencies of his own or of the general human mind, but that he *sees* them, *discovers* them. He knows that their ideal being does not amount to a psychological 'being in the mind': the authentic objectivity of the true, and of the ideal in general, suspends *all* reality, including such as is subjective. If some scientists at times think differently on this point, they do so, not in their professional scientific settings, but on subsequent reflection. If, with Hume, we may hold that men's true beliefs are better documented by their deeds than by their words, then we may twit such thinkers with not understanding themselves. They pay no unprejudiced heed to what they think in their unreflective enquiries and demonstrations, but are led astray by the supposed authority of logic, with its psychologistic fallacies and subjectively distorted terminology.

All theoretical science consists, in its objective content, of *one* homogeneous stuff: it is an ideal fabric of *meanings*. We can go even further and say that the whole, indefinitely complex web of meanings that we call the theoretical unity of science, falls under the very category that covers all its elements: it is itself a unity of meaning.

If meaning, rather than the act of meaning, concept and proposition, rather than idea and judgement, are what is essential and germane in science, they are necessarily the general object of investigation in the science whose theme is the essence of science. Everything that is logical falls under the two correlated categories of *meaning* and *object*. If we speak in the plural of *logical categories*, we have only to do with the pure species distinguishable *a priori* within the genus of meaning, or with the correlated forms of *categorially considered objectivity*. In such categories the laws formulable in logic have their foundation. We have, on the one hand, such laws as abstract from the ideal relations between meaning-intention and meaning-fulfilment, and so from any possible knowledge-use of meanings, and consider only how meanings can be compounded to form novel meanings (whether 'real' or 'imaginary').[1] We have, on the other hand, *logical laws*, in the more emphatic sense, which consider meanings in respect of their having or not having objects, in respect of their truth or their falsity, their consistency or their absurdity, to the extent that such things are merely determined by the categorial form of such meanings. Corresponding with these latter laws, we have equivalent, correlated *laws for objects in general, objects determined in thought by mere categories*. All valid assertions regarding existence and truth, that are capable of being framed in abstraction from all material of knowledge on a mere foundation of meaning-forms, find their place among such laws.

CHAPTER FOUR

The Phenomenological and Ideal Content of
the Experiences of Meaning

---

§30 *The content of the expressive experience taken in its*
psychological sense and in the sense of a unified meaning

THE essence of meaning is seen by us, not in the meaning-
conferring experience, but in its 'content', the single, self-
identical intentional[1] unity set over against the dispersed multiplicity of actual and possible experiences of speakers and thinkers.
The 'content' of a meaning-experience, in this ideal sense, is not
at all what psychology means by a 'content', i.e. any real part or
side of an experience. If we understand a name – whether standing
for what is individual or general, physical or psychic, existent or
non-existent, possible or impossible – or if we understand a
statement – true in content or false, consistent or absurd, believed
or figmentary – then what either expression 'says' – the meaning
which forms its *logical* content and which, in contexts of pure
logic, is called either an idea or concept, or a judgement or proposition – is nothing which could, in a real sense, count as part
of our act of understanding. This experience naturally has its
psychological components, is a content, consists of contents, in
the ordinary sense of psychology. Here belong primarily all the
sensuous elements of our experience, the appearances of words,
in their purely visual, auditory or motor content, and, in the next
place, the acts of objective reference which locate such words in
space and time. The psychic stuff here involved is well-known to
be vastly manifold, varying greatly from one individual to the
next, and for the same individual from one moment to another,
even in respect of 'one and the same' word. The verbal presenta-

---

[1] The word 'intentional' is so framed as to permit application both to the meaning
and the object of the *intentio*. Intentional unity does not therefore necessarily mean
the intended, the objective unity.

tions which accompany and support my silent thinking sometimes involve picturings of words spoken by my own voice, sometimes of letters written by *me* in shorthand or longhand – all these are individual peculiarities, and belong merely to the psychological content of *my* presentational experience. Among contents in this psychological sense are also many differences in respect of act-character, not always easily seized descriptively, such as the subjective difference which constitutes reference or understanding. If I hear the name 'Bismarck' it makes not the slightest difference to my understanding of the word's unified meaning, whether I imagine the great man in a felt hat or coat, or in a cuirassier's uniform, or whatever pictorial representation I may adopt. It is not even of importance whether *any* imagery serves to illustrate my consciousness of meaning, or to enliven it less directly.

Battling against a seductive notion, we laid it down that the essence of expression lies in a meaning-intention, and not in the more or less perfect, more or less close or remote, illustration that accompanies or fulfils that intention. If, however, such illustrations are present, they will be intimately fused with the meaning-intention. It is therefore understandable that our unified experience of the meaningfully functioning expression should, from case to case, reveal considerable psychological differences even on the meaning side, whereas its meaning remains strictly the same. We have also shown that there is *something* in the correlated acts which really corresponds to such selfsameness of meaning, that what we call a meaning-intention is not an undifferentiated character to which a connection with fulfilling intuitions first imparts an *external* differentiation. Meaning-intentions of intrinsically different character belong rather with differing meanings, or with expressions used with differing meanings, whereas all expressions understood with like sense are clothed with the same meaning-intention as an invariant mental character. Through this character, expressive experiences strongly differing in psychological make-up first become experiences endowed with the same meaning. Fluctuation of meaning here certainly involves restrictions which make no essential difference.

§31 *The act-character of meaning and the ideally unified meaning*

We have opposed what is psychologically common to what is psychologically variable, but we have not thereby hit off the distinction we wanted to clarify: that between the psychological and logical content of our expressions and expressive acts. For the psychological content as much includes what is constant from case to case as what varies with the occasion. It is not, therefore, our doctrine that an act-character which stays the same in all cases, is itself our meaning. What, e.g., the statement 'π is a transcendental number' says, what *we* understand when we read it, and mean when we say it, is no individual feature in our thought-experience, which is merely repeated on many occasions. Such a feature is always individually different from case to case, whereas the sense of the sentence should remain *identical*. If we or others repeat the same sentence with like intention, each of us has his own phenomena, his own words and his own nuances of understanding. Over against this unbounded multiplicity of individual experiences, is the selfsame element expressed in them all, 'selfsame' in the very strictest sense. Multiplication of persons and acts does not multiply propositional meanings; the judgement in the ideal, logical sense remains single.

That we here insist on the strict identity of what is meant, and oppose it to the constant mental character of meaning it, does not spring from our personal fondness for subtle distinctions, but from the firm theoretical belief that so alone can we do justice to a fact fundamental for the understanding of logic. We are not here dealing with a mere hypothesis, justifiable only by explanatory fruitfulness; we are appealing to an immediately graspable truth, following in this the self-evidence which is the final authority in all questions of knowledge. I see that in repeated acts of presentation and judgement I mean, or can mean, the same concept or proposition: I see that, wherever there is talk of the *proposition* or *truth* that π *is a transcendental number*, there is nothing I have less in mind than an individual experience, or a feature of an individual experience of any person. I see that such reflective talk really has as its object what serves as a meaning in straightforward talk. I see lastly that what I mean by the sentence in question or (when I hear it) grasp as its meaning, is the same thing, whether I think and exist or not, and whether or not there are *any* thinking persons and acts. The same holds of all types of meanings, subject-meanings, predicate-meanings, relational and combinatory meanings etc. It holds, above all, in the case of the ideal properties which pertain primarily to meanings. Here belong, to mention a few only of the most important, the predicates *true* and *false*, *possible* and *impossible*, *general* and *singular*, *determinate* and *indeterminate* etc.

The genuine identity that we here assert is none other than the *identity of the species*. As a species, and only as a species, can it embrace in unity (ξυμβάλλειν εἰς ἕν), and as an ideal unity, the dispersed multiplicity of individual singulars. The manifold singulars for the ideal unity Meaning are naturally the corresponding act-moments of meaning, the *meaning-intentions*. Meaning is related to varied acts of meaning – Logical Presentation to presentative acts, Logical Judgement to acts of judging, Logical Syllogism to acts of syllogism – just as Redness *in specie* is to the slips of paper which lie here, and which all 'have' the same redness. Each slip has, in addition to other constitutive aspects (extension, form etc.), its own individual redness, i.e. its instance of this colour-species, though this neither exists in the slip nor anywhere else in the whole world, and particularly not 'in our thought', in so far as this latter is part of the domain of real being, the sphere of temporality.

Meanings constitute, we may say further, a class of concepts in the sense of 'universal objects'. They are not for that reason objects which, though existing nowhere in the world, have being in a τόπος οὐράνιος or in a divine mind, for such metaphysical hypostatization would be absurd. If one has accustomed oneself to understand by 'being' only real being, and by 'objects' only real objects, then talk of universal objects and of their being, may well seem basically wrong; no offence will, however, be given to one who has first used such talk merely to assert the validity of certain judgements, such in fact as concern numbers, propositions, geometrical forms etc., and who now asks whether he is not evidently obliged, here as elsewhere, to affix the label 'genuinely existent object' to the correlate of his judgement's validity, to what it judges about. In sober truth, the seven regular solids, are, logically speaking, seven objects precisely as the seven sages are: the principle of the parallelogram of forces is as much a single object as the city of Paris.[1]

[1] Regarding the question of the essence of universal objects see Investigation II.

§32 *The ideality of meanings is no ideality in the normative sense*

The ideality of meanings is a particular case of the ideality of what is specific in general. It has not the sense of *normative ideality*, as if we were here dealing with an ideal of perfection, an ideal limiting value, over against particular cases which realized it more or less approximately. No doubt the 'logical concept', i.e. the term in the sense of *normative* logic, is an ideal in respect of its meaning. For the demand of the craft of knowledge runs: 'Use words with an absolutely selfsame meaning: exclude all meaning-variations. Distinguish meanings and keep them distinct in declarative thought, and employ sharply distinct sensible signs.'

This prescription relates, however, as it only can relate, to the formation of meaningful terms, to care in the subjective sifting out and expression of one's thoughts. Meanings 'in themselves' are, as we have argued, specific unities, however much the act of meaning may vary: they themselves are not ideals. Ideality in the ordinary, normative sense does not exclude reality. An ideal is a concrete original that may exist, and that may confront one in reality, as when a young artist takes the work of a great master as the ideal that he relives and that he strives after in his own creations. Even where an ideal is not realizable, it is at least an individual in our presentative intention. The ideality of what is specific is, contrariwise, the complete opposite of reality or individuality; it represents no end of possible endeavour, its ideality lies in a 'unity in multiplicity'. Not the species itself, but the individual falling under it, can be a practical ideal.

§33 *The concepts Meaning and Concept (in the sense of Species) do not coincide*

Meanings, we said, constitute a *class* of 'universal objects' or species. Each species, if we wish to speak of it, presupposes a meaning, in which it is presented, and this meaning is itself a species. But the meaning in which an object is thought, and its object, the species itself, are not one and the same. Just as in the sphere of individuals, we distinguish, e.g., between Bismarck himself and presentations of Bismarck, e.g. *Bismarck – the greatest of German statesmen* etc., so also, in the field of species, we distinguish between, e.g., the number 4 itself and the presentations, i.e.

meanings, which have 4 as their object, as, e.g., *the number 4 – the second even number in the number-series* etc. The universality *that* we think of, does not therefore resolve itself into the universality of the meanings *in which* we think of it. Meanings, although as such they are universal objects, fall, *in respect of the objects to which they refer, into individual and specific meanings,* or (to conform to a readily understandable linguistic preference) *into individual and general meanings.* Individual presentations, e.g., are therefore *generalia, qua* unities' of meaning, though their objects are *individualia.*

§34 *In the act of meaning we are not conscious of meaning as an object*

In the actual experience of meaning an individual feature, a singular case of the species (we said) corresponds to the unitary meaning, just as to the specific difference Redness the aspect of red in the object corresponds. If we perform the act and live in it, as it were, we naturally refer to its object and not to its meaning. If, e.g., we make a statement, we judge about the thing it concerns, and not about the statement's meaning, about the judgement in the logical sense. This latter first becomes objective to us in a reflex act of thought, in which we not only look back on the statement just made, but carry out the abstraction (the Ideation) demanded. This logical reflection is not an act that takes place only under exceptional, artificial conditions: it is a normal component of *logical* thinking. What is characteristic of such thought is the context of theory, and the theoretical consideration of the latter, which is carried out in step-by-step reflections on the *contents* of the thought-acts just performed. A very common form of thoughtful pondering may serve as an instance: 'Is *S P*? That could very well be. But from this proposition it would follow that *M* is the case. This cannot be, and so what I first thought possible, *that S is P*, must be false etc.'. The italicized words should be noted, as well as the idealizations they express. *This* proposition, that *S is P*, which is the pervasive theme of discussion, is plainly not the fleeting moment of meaning in the thought-act in which the notion first occurred to us. Logical reflection rather sets in at later stages, and an identical propositional meaning is continuously meant in it, idealized and identified in our unified thought-context, and thought of as one and the same. The same is the case wherever a unified theoretical demonstration is being wound up. We could utter no 'therefore' unless there was also a glance at the meaning-content of the premisses. In judging the premisses, we not merely live in our judgements, but reflect on their contents: only by glancing back at these does the conclusion appear 'motivated'. Thus and only thus can the logical form of the premisses – which of course is not stressed in that universal, conceptual way that finds expression in syllogistic formulae – determine with insight the drawing of the conclusion.

§35 *Meanings 'in themselves' and meanings expressed*

We have so far preferred to speak of meanings which, as the normal, relational sense of the word suggests, are meanings of expressions. There is, however, no intrinsic connection between the ideal unities which in fact operate as meanings, and the signs to which they are tied, i.e. through which they become real in human mental life. We cannot therefore say that all ideal unities of this sort are expressed meanings. Wherever a new concept is formed, we see how a meaning becomes realized that was previously unrealized. As numbers – in the ideal sense that arithmetic presupposes – neither spring forth nor vanish with the act of enumeration, and as the endless number-series thus represents an objectively fixed set of general objects, sharply delimited by an ideal law, which no one can either add to or take away from, so it is with the ideal unities of pure logic, with its concepts, propositions, truths, or in other words, with its meanings. They are an ideally closed set of general objects, to which being thought or being expressed are alike contingent. There are therefore countless meanings which, in the common, relational sense, are merely possible ones, since they are never expressed, and since they can, owing to the limits of man's cognitive powers, never be expressed.

INVESTIGATION II

The Ideal Unity of the Species and Modern Theories of Abstraction

INTRODUCTION

FOLLOWING the discussions of the last investigation, we conceive the ideal unity of a meaning in the light of the act-character of an act of reference; this act's peculiar 'tincture' distinguishes the significant consciousness of a given expression from the significant consciousness of an expression which differs in meaning. This does not of course mean that this act-character is the concrete reality upon whose basis the meaning as Species is constituted for us. The relevant concrete reality is rather the total experience of the understood expression, which is informed by this act-character as its animating 'tincture'. The relation between the meaning and the significant expression (or its 'meaning-tincture') is the same as the relation, e.g., between the Species Red and a red object of intuitive experience (or the 'moment' of red which appears in this object). When we mean Red *in specie*, a red object appears before us, and in this sense we look towards the red object to which we are nevertheless not referring. The aspect of red is at the same time emphasized in this object, and to that extent we can again say that we are looking towards this aspect of red. But we are not referring to this individually definite trait in the object, as we are referring to it when, e.g., we make the phenomenological observation that the aspects of red in the separate portions of the apparent object's surface are themselves separate. While the red object and its emphasized aspect of red appear before us, we are rather 'meaning' the single identical Red, and are meaning it in a novel conscious *manner*, though which precisely the Species, and not the individual, becomes our object. The same would apply also to a meaning in its relation to an expression, and an expression's meaningful orientation, whether this expression relates to a corresponding intuition or not.

Meaning as a Species therefore arises out of the above-mentioned background through *abstraction*, but not through abstraction in that improper sense by which empiricist psychology and epistemology are dominated, a sense which altogether fails to seize what is specific, and whose inability to do so is even counted as a virtue. The issue of abstraction has a twofold relevance to a philosophical laying down of the foundations of pure logic. It is relevant in the first place since among the categorial distinctions of meanings which pure logic must essentially consider, we find a distinction which corresponds to the opposition between individual and universal objects. But it also has, in the second place, a particular relevance, since meanings as such, i.e. meanings in the sense of specific unities, constitute the domain of pure logic, so that to misread the essence of the Species must in each case be to strike at the very essence of logic. It will accordingly not be unsuitable to tackle the problem of abstraction even at this early point in our introductory series of investigations, so as to assure the basic foundations of pure logic and epistemology by defending the intrinsic right of specific (or ideal) objects to be granted objective status alongside of individual (or real) objects. This is the point on which relativistic, empiricistic psychologism differs from idealism, which alone represents the possibility of a self-consistent theory of knowledge.

To talk of 'idealism' is of course not to talk of a metaphysical doctrine, but of a theory of knowledge which recognizes the 'ideal' as a condition for the possibility of objective knowledge in general, and does not 'interpret it away' in psychologistic fashion.

CHAPTER ONE

Universal Objects and the Consciousness
of Universality

§ 1 *We are conscious of universal objects in acts which differ
essentially from those in which we are conscious of individual objects*

OUR own position has been indicated above in a few words; its
justification should require few additional explanations. All that
we maintain – the validity of the distinction between specific and
individual objects, and the difference of the manner in which each
type of objects is present to us, is brought clearly before our
consciousness – has the guarantee of self-evidence. This self-
evidence automatically emerges as soon as the relevant presentations are clarified. We need only refer to cases where individual
or specific presentation are intuitively 'fulfilled', to be utterly
clear as to the sorts of objects 'meant' by such presentations, and
as to what counts as an essential homogeneity or disparity in their
sense. Reflection on both classes of acts simply makes plain
whether or not there are essential differences in the manner in
which they are performed.

In the latter regard comparison shows that the act in which we
mean the Species, is in fact essentially different from the act in
which we mean the individual, whether, in this later case, we
refer to a whole concrete thing, or to an individual piece or
property attaching to it. There are, of course, certain phenomenal
communities in either case. In either case the same concrete thing
makes its appearance, and to the extent that it does so, the same
sense-contents are given and interpreted in an identical manner,
i.e. the same course of actually given sense and image-contents
serves as a basis for the same 'conception' or 'interpretation', in
which the appearance of the *object* with the *properties* presented by
those contents is constituted for us. But the same appearance
sustains different acts in the two cases. In the first case it provides

the presentative basis for an act of *individual* reference, i.e. for an act in which we apply ourselves to the apparent thing itself, and 'mean' this thing or this feature, this part of the thing. In the latter case it provides the presentative basis for an act of conception and reference directed to a Species: i.e. while the thing appears, or rather the feature in the thing, it is not this objective feature, this feature here and now, that we mean. We mean its *content*, its 'Idea'; we mean, not this aspect of red in the house, but Red as such. This act of meaning is plainly an act 'founded' on underlying apprehensions (see Investigation VI, §45); a new mode of apprehension has been built on the intuition of the individual house or of its red aspect, a mode of apprehension constitutive of the intuitive presence of the Idea of Red. And as the character of this mode of apprehension sets the Species before us as a universal object, so too there develop, in intimate connection with such an object, formations like 'red thing' (thing containing an instance of red), 'this case of red' (the red of this house) etc. The primitive relation between Species and Instance emerges: it becomes possible to look over and compare a range of instances, and perhaps to judge with self-evidence: 'In all these cases individual aspects differ, but in each the same Species is realized: this Red is the same as that – specifically treated it is the same colour – and yet again this red differs from that one – i.e. individually treated, it is a different objective individual feature'. This distinction, like all fundamental logical distinctions, is categorial. It pertains to the pure form of possible objects of consciousness as such. (See also Investigation VI, ch. 6 *f*.)

§2 *The indispensability of talk about universal objects*

The excesses of conceptual realism have led men to dispute, not merely the reality, but the objectivity of the Species. This is certainly quite wrong. The question as to whether it is possible or necessary to treat Species as objects can plainly only be answered by going back to the meaning (the significance, the sense) of the names standing for Species, and to the meaning of the assertions claiming to hold for Species. If these names and assertions can be interpreted as making the true objects of our intention individual, if the intention of the nominal and propositional thoughts which give them meaning can be thus understood, then we must yield to our opponents' doctrine. But if this is not so, if the semantic analysis of such experiences, shows that their direct, true intention is plainly not directed upon individual objects, and if in particular their universal relation to a range of individual objects is plainly shown up as merely an indirect pointing to logical connections whose content (sense) will first be unfolded in new thoughts, or which will require new expressions – then our opponents' doctrine is evidently false. Now in fact we cannot at all help distinguishing between *individual* singulars, like the 'things' of experience, and *specific* singulars, like the numbers and manifolds of mathematics, or like the presentations and judgements (the concepts and propositions) of pure logic. *Number* is a concept which, as has often been stressed, has 1, 2, 3 . . . as its subordinate singulars. *A* number is, e.g., the number 2, not any group of two individual objects. If we mean these, even quite indefinitely, we should also say so; our thought will then at least march with our expression.

The difference between individual and specific singulars corresponds to the no less essential difference between individual and specific universals (or between individual and specific universality). These differences at once carry over into the field of judgement, and run through the whole of logic. Singular judgements divide into *individually singular* judgements such as *Socrates is a man*, and *specifically singular* judgements such as *Two is an even number*, or *A Round Square is a nonsensical concept*. Universal judgements divide into *individually* universal judgements such as *All men are mortal*, and *specifically universal* judgements such as *All analytic functions can be differentiated*, or *All propositions of pure logic are* a priori.

These distinctions and others like them are quite irremoveable. We are not merely dealing with abbreviated expressions: we cannot eliminate such differences through any elaboration or circumscription.

Inspection of each instance will, for the rest, yield the conviction that a Species really becomes an object in knowledge, and that judgements of the same logical force are possible in relation to it, as is the case with individual objects. We may choose an instance from the group that concerns us particularly. Logical ideas, unitary meanings as such, are, as we said, ideal objects, whether they present what is universal or what is individual, e.g. *the city of Berlin* as an identical sense which recurs in talk and reference, or the direct idea of the theorem of Pythagoras (whose explicit utterance need not be carried out), or this very idea *the theorem of Pythagoras.*

We, from our point of view, would point out that each such meaning certainly counts as a unit in our thought and that on occasion we pass evident judgements upon it as a unit: it can be compared with other meanings and distinguished from them. It can be an identical subject for numerous predicates, an identical term in numerous relations. It can be summed together with other meanings and can be counted as a unit. As self-identical, it can in its turn serve as the object for many new meanings. All these things are the same in its case as in the case of other objects, e.g. horses, stones, mental acts etc., that are not meanings. A meaning can be treated as self-identical only because it is self-identical. This argument we find unassailable: it applies of course to all specific unities, even to such as are not meanings.

§3 *Must the unity of the Species be regarded as a spurious unity? Identity and exact likeness*

We wish to follow tradition in upholding a strict view of the identity of the Species, in contrast with prevailing doctrines which pin their faith on the wide diffusion of improper uses of 'identity'. Very often we speak of *the same* thing in the case of exactly like things. We speak, e.g., of 'the same cupboard', 'the same dress', 'the same hat' in the case of exactly similar products framed on the same pattern, products, i.e., exactly like one another in such respects as interest us in connection with such things. We speak in this sense of 'the same conviction', 'the same doubt', 'the same question', 'the same wish' etc. etc. Such impropriety of usage is thought likewise to be present in talk of the 'same Species' and, in particular, in talk of the 'same meaning'. We speak of 'the same meaning' ('the same concept', 'the same proposition') in relation to a pervasively like meaning-experience, we speak of 'the same red' (red in general) 'the same blue' etc., in respect to a pervasively like colouring.

Against this argument I object, that an improper use of identity in the case of like things, refers us back, through its very impropriety, to a proper use of the same term, i.e. to an identity. We find in fact that wherever things are 'alike', an identity in the strict and true sense is also present. We cannot predicate exact likeness of two things, without stating the respect in which they are thus alike. Each exact likeness relates to a Species, under which the objects compared, are subsumed: this Species is not, and cannot be, merely 'alike' in the two cases, if the worst of infinite regresses is not to become inevitable. If we specify the respect of our comparison, we point by way of a more general class-term to the range of specific differences among which the one which appears in our compared members is to be found. If two things are 'alike' as regards form, then the Form-Species in question is the identical element, if they are 'alike' as regards colour, the Colour-Species is this element etc. etc. Not every Species has of course an unambiguous verbal expression, and so at times a suitable expression for a 'respect' is lacking, and to state it clearly might be difficult. We none the less keep it in view, and it governs our talk of 'alikeness'. It would of course appear as a total inversion of the true state of things, were one to try to define identity, even in the sensory realm, as being essentially a limiting case of 'alikeness'. Identity is wholly indefinable, whereas 'alikeness' is definable: 'alikeness' is the relation of objects falling under one and the same Species. If one is not allowed to speak of the identity of the Species, of the respect in which there is 'alikeness', talk of 'alikeness' loses its whole basis.

§4 Objections to the reduction of ideal unity to dispersed multiplicity

We now direct attention to another point. Should anyone wish to reduce talk about a single attribute to a subsistence of certain relations of exact likeness, we ask him to consider the difference which comes out in the following opposition. We make a comparison between:

1. Our intention, when we grasp any group of intuitively like objects in unitary fashion, or when we recognize their exact likeness *at a single glance*, or when in single acts of *comparison* we recognize the likeness of one definite object to certain others and ultimately to all objects in the group,[1] and

[1] For more detailed treatment of the intuitive apprehensions of collections see my *Philosophie der Arithmetik* (1891), ch. XI, on the intuitive cognition of likeness, p. 233 in particular.

2. Our intention when, possibly basing ourselves on the same intuitive foundations, we apprehend as an *ideal unity* the attribute which constitutes the respect in which the things are alike or are compared.

It is plain that, in our two cases, the target of our intention, the object meant and named as subject of our assertion, is quite different. However many like objects may float before us in intuition or comparison, they and their 'alikenesses' are certainly not what we mean in our second case. What we mean is the 'universal', the ideal unity, and not these units and pluralities.

The two intentional situations are utterly different, not merely logically, but also psychologically. In the second case no intuition of likeness, not even a comparison, is at all needed. I recognize this paper as paper and as white, and thereby make clear to myself the general sense of the expressions 'paper' and 'white as such', but I need not carry out any intuitions of likeness nor any comparisons. One can say for the rest, no doubt, that these conceptual ideas would never have arisen had like objects never appeared together, nor been intuitively related by their likeness. This psychological fact is, however, totally irrelevant here, where the question weighed concerns what an attribute counts as in knowledge, and what it should count as in the full light of 'evidence'.

It is clear, further and lastly, that when we try to make plain an intention to a Species by somehow presenting singulars as belonging to groups of exact similars, such presented singulars only comprise a few members of such groups, and can never exhaust their total range. One may then well ask what will give unity to this range, what will make it a possible object for awareness and knowledge, if the unity of the Species altogether lapses, and together with it the thought-form of 'allness', which gives the Species a bearing on the whole host of A's represented in our thought, which we refer to through the sense of the expression 'the totality of A's'. To point to the 'same' universally shared moment will of course not help us at all. It is numerically present as often as there are single objects represented within the range of the Species. How can anything unify if it must itself first be unified?

We can also derive no assistance from the objective possibility of recognizing all members of the range to be *like* one another: it cannot give unity to this range for our thought and knowledge.

For, as a possibility, it is nothing for our consciousness, unless we think of it and grasp it. But such a grasp would, on the one hand, presuppose the thought of the unity of the range, and this range would itself also confront us as an ideal unity. Each attempt to transform the being of what is ideal into the possible being of what is real, must obviously suffer shipwreck on the fact that possibilities themselves are ideal objects. Possibilities can as little be found in the real world, as can numbers in general, or triangles in general.

The empiricistic attempt to dispense with Species as objects by having recourse to their extensions can therefore not be carried out. It cannot tell us what gives unity to such extensions. The following objection makes this particularly clear. The conception we are criticizing operates with 'circles of similars', but makes too much light of the difficulty that each object belongs to a plurality of 'circles of similars', and that we must be in a position to say what distinguishes these 'circles of similars' among themselves. It is plain that, in default of a previously given Specific Unity, we cannot avoid a regress *in infinitum*. An object *A* is similar to other objects, to one object in the respect *a*, to another in the respect *b* etc. But such 'respects' do not imply that a Species is there, which effects unity. What then unifies the circle of similars determined, e.g., by Redness, as against the circle determined by Triangularity? The empiricistic conception only says: These are differing similarities. If *A* and *B* are similar in respect of red, and *A* and *C* in respect of triangularity, these similarities must differ *in kind*. But here we again come up against kinds. Similarities are compared, and form genera and species, just as their absolute members do. We should then have to have recourse to similarities of such similarities, and so on *in infinitum*.

§5 *Continuation. The controversy between John Stuart Mill and*
H. Spencer

It has doubtless been felt often enough that psychologistic approaches which splinter specific unities into the multiplicity of their subordinate objects involve some difficulties: men have, however, acquiesced too readily in 'solutions' of such difficulties. It is interesting to observe how J. Stuart Mill, in opposition to his own psychologistic doctrine, wants to keep to talk about the *identity* of attributes, and to justify it against Spencer, who is much more consistent in only wanting to permit talk of *exactly similar* attributes.[1] The sight of different people does not arouse identical sensations in us, but only exactly similar ones: Spencer therefore thinks that the humanity in each such person must be a different attribute. The same should, however, apply, Mill objects, to the humanity of the same man at this moment, and a half-hour later. 'No', he says,

> if every general conception instead of being 'the One in the Many', were considered to be as many different conceptions as there are things to which it is applicable, there would be no such thing as general language. A name would have no general meaning, if 'man' connoted one thing when predicated of John and another though closely resembling thing when predicated of William.[2]

The objection is valid, but it affects Mill's own doctrine no less. For a few lines further on he says: 'The meaning of any general name is some outward or inward phenomenon, consisting in the last resort of feelings; and these feelings, if their continuity is for an instant broken, are no longer the same feelings in the sense of individual identity.' Mill thinks he can easily escape the difficulty he has so sharply emphasized. 'What then,' he asks,

> is the common something which gives a meaning to the general name? Mr Spencer can only say: it is the similarity of the feelings, and I rejoin, the attribute is precisely the similarity. The *names of attributes* are in their ultimate analysis names *for the resemblances of our sensations* (or other feelings). Every general name, whether abstract or concrete, denotes or connotes one or more of these resemblances.[3]

An extraordinary solution. Connotation therefore no longer consists in attributes in the ordinary sense of the word, but in these similarities. What has been achieved by this change-over? Each such similarity does not mean a momentary, individual *feeling* of similarity, but an identical one-in-many; it therefore presupposes what it should explain away. We have not even reduced the number of such inexplicabilities, since a distinct similarity corresponds to each distinct attribute. But to what extent can we even speak of a single similarity, since to each single

---

[1] See Spencer, *Psychology*, II, §294, Note.
[2] Mill, *Logic*, Book II, ch. II, §3, Final note.
[3] *Ibid.*

case of comparison a particular similarity corresponds, so that an indefinite number of similarities pertains to each attribute? This leads to the question discussed above, as to what may underlie the unitary mutual belongingness of all these similarities, a question that need only be raised to show up the wrongness of the relativistic conception.

Mill himself feels how dubious his explanation is, for he makes the following statements:

> It will not, probably, be denied, that if a hundred sensations are undistinguishably alike, their resemblance ought to be spoken of as one resemblance, and not a hundred resemblances that merely *resemble* one another. The *things compared* are *many*, but the something common to all of them must be conceived as *one*, just as the name is conceived as one, though corresponding to numerically different sensations of sound each time it is pronounced.

Remarkable self-deception: as if by laying down a mode of speech we could decide whether a unitary thought-object corresponds to a multitude of acts or not, and as if our talk did not derive its unitary sense from an ideal unity of intention. Certainly there are many compared 'things' and certainly we must conceive what is common to them as one: but this 'must' plainly rests on the fact that this common element *is* one. And if this is true of the similarities, it is true of the undisguised attributes themselves, which must in this respect be essentially kept apart from the 'feelings'. One must therefore cease to speak as if one were doing psychology where concepts are being investigated.

'The question between Mr Spencer and me,' says Mill,

> is merely one of language, for neither of us believes an attribute to be a real thing, possessed of objective existence; we believe it to be a particular mode of naming our sensations, or our expectations of sensation, when looked at in their relation to an external object which excites them. The question raised by Mr Spencer does not, therefore, concern the properties of any really existent thing, but the comparative appropriateness, for philosophical purposes, of two different ways of *using a name*.

We also, of course, do not believe in the *reality* of attributes, but we demand a somewhat keener analysis of what lies behind such 'ways of using a name', and of what establishes the 'appropriateness of names for philosophical purposes'. Mill fails to see that the unitary sense of a name, and of every expression, is a Specific Unity, and we merely push the problem back a stage when we reduce the Unity of the Species to the unity of a verbal meaning.

§6 *Transition to the following chapters*

We have, in our last treatment, been forced to react critically to conceptions opposed to ours. In this we encountered a line of thought common to all forms of empiricistic theories of abstraction, however much they may otherwise differ in content. It seems necessary, however, to grant greater play to such criticism, so as to draw more profit from our conception of the essence of universal objects and universal presentations, in analysing and testing the various main types of modern theories of abstraction. Critically to point out errors in other thinkers' views will provide an opportunity to round off and complete our own conception, and at the same time to test its reliability.

The empiricistic 'theory[1] of abstraction', like most parts of modern epistemological theory, suffers from the mixture of two essentially different scientific interests, one concerned with the psychological *explanation of experiences*, the other with the 'logical' *classification* of their *thought-content* or *sense*, and the criticism of their possible achievement as acts of knowing. In the former regard we seek to establish empirical bonds tying the thought-experiences in question to other facts in the flux of real happenings, facts responsible for them causally, or on which they exert effects. In the latter regard we are intent upon the 'origin of the concepts' which pertain to our words: we seek to clarify their 'true meaning' or significance through plainly establishing their intention in the sense of their *fulfilments*, which are first realized when suitable intuitions are adduced. To study the essence of these phenomenological connections is to lay bare the indispensable foundation for an epistemological clarification of the 'possibility' of knowledge. It is also, in our case, to give essential clearness to the possibility of making valid assertions regarding universal objects (or regarding individual objects *as* objects of corresponding universal concepts) and, in connection therewith, to set forth in self-evident fashion the correct sense in which a

---

[1] It is not suitable to speak of a theory when, as the following treatments will show, there is nothing at all to be theoretically treated, i.e. to be explained.

universal counts as an 'entity', and an individual as a thing ranged under universal predicates. If a theory of abstraction is to have an epistemological function, if it is to clarify knowledge, it must set forth the immediate descriptive situation in which a Species comes to consciousness, it must through this clarify the sense of names of attributes, and thence go on to resolve perspicuously the many misinterpretations that the essence of the Species has suffered. It will go astray from the start if it loses itself in empirical-psychological analyses of the abstractive process and its cause and effects, and if, rapidly dismissing the descriptive content of the abstractive consciousness, it directs its main concern to unconscious dispositions and hypothetical associative linkages. What generally happens in such cases is that the essential immanent content of the consciousness of universality, which could have been classified properly without more ado, goes disregarded and unmentioned.

And, even if a theory of abstraction aims at the field of what is immanently discoverable in all true (and therefore intuitive) abstraction, and steers clear of the misguided confusion between essential (i.e. epistemologically clarifying) and empirical (i.e. psychologically explanatory) analysis, it will still go astray from the start if it falls into the other confusion (strongly suggested by ambiguous talk of 'general representation') between *phenomenological* and *objective* analysis. What our acts of meaning merely assign to their objects, will be assigned to these acts themselves as their real (*reelles*) constituent. Here the regulative field of consciousness and its immanent essence are again covertly abandoned, and all given over to confusion.

The following analyses will show that our sketchy characterization fits the most influential modern theories of abstraction, and that these really go astray for reasons that we have just summarily stated.

CHAPTER TWO

The Psychological Hypostatization
of the Universal

---

§7 *The metaphysical and psychological hypostatization of the*
universal. Nominalism

TWO misunderstandings have dominated the development of
doctrines concerning universal objects:

First: the metaphysical hypostatization of the universal, the
assumption that the Species really exists *externally* to thought.

Secondly: the *psychological hypostatization* of the universal,
the assumption that the Species really exists *in* thought.

The older nominalism, whether of an extreme or a conceptualistic type, attacked the first misunderstanding, the misunderstanding which underlies Platonic realism (in the sense in which
this is traditionally conceived). To combat the second misunderstanding, especially in the form of Locke's abstract ideas, has
inspired the development of the modern theory of abstraction
since Berkeley's time, and has given it its definite trend towards
extreme nominalism (which is now usually called 'nominalism'
simpliciter, and opposed to conceptualism). It was thought needful,
to avoid the absurdities of Locke's abstract ideas, altogether to
reject universal objects as peculiar thought-unities, and universal
presentations as peculiar acts of thought. Ignoring the difference
between universal intuitions on the one hand – among which not
only such abstract ideas, but the general images of traditional
logic belong – and universal meanings on the other, men rejected
'conceptual presentations', with their peculiar presentative intentions, if not in word, then at least in the sense of these words, and
replaced them by individual presentations merely functioning in
an extraordinary manner.

Nominalism therefore adds itself, as a third misunderstanding,
to our previous two: in various forms it seeks to transform

what is universal in object and act of thought, into what is individual.

These misunderstandings, in so far as they are still of actual interest, must be gone through in order. It lies in the nature of our subject-matter, as our discussions up to this point have made plain, that we cannot separate vexed issues regarding the essence of universal objects from issues regarding the essence of universal presentations. It is vain to seek to make out a persuasive case validating talk about universal objects, if one does not also remove doubts as to how such objects can be presented, and if one does not further refute theories apparently proving, by scientific psychological analysis, that only individual presentations exist, that only individual objects therefore can be, and ever have been brought to consciousness, and that talk about universal objects can only be understood as fictitious or as gravely improper.

We may leave aside, as long disposed of, the misunderstandings of Platonic realism. But the thought-motives pressing towards a psychologizing realism are obviously still operative, as appears particularly in the manner in which Locke tends to be criticized. We must go deeper into such motives in this chapter.

§8 *A deceptive line of thought*

The following line of thought might be opposed to our conception, not so much out of serious conviction, as in order to give an apagogic proof of the untenability of talk about Species as universal objects:

If Species are nothing real (*reales*), and if they are also nothing in thought, then they are nothing at all. How can we talk about something if it does not at least exist *in our thought*? The being of the ideal is therefore obviously a being in consciousness; the name 'content of consciousness' rightly applies to it. As opposed to this, real being (*reales Sein*) is no mere being in consciousness, or being-a-content: it is self-existence, transcendent being, being outside of consciousness.

We do not wish to lose ourselves in the erring paths of such a metaphysics. For us what is 'in' consciousness counts as real (*real*) just as much as what is 'outside' of it. What is real (*real*) is the individual with all its constituents: it is something here and now. For us temporality is a sufficient mark of reality. Real being and temporal being may not be identical notions, but they coincide in extension. We do not, of course, suppose that psychical experiences are in a metaphysical sense 'things'. But even they belong to a thinglike unity, if the traditional metaphysical conviction is right in holding that all temporal existents must be things, or must help to constitute things. Should we wish, however, to keep all metaphysics out, we may simply define 'reality' in terms of temporality. For the only point of importance is to oppose it to the timeless 'being' of the ideal.

It is further clear that the universal, as often as we speak of it, is a thing thought of by us: it is not therefore a thought-content in the sense of a real (*realen*)[1] constituent in our thought-experiences, and likewise not a thought-content in the sense of an intension, but is rather an object that we think of. Is it not obvious that an object, even when real (*real*) and truly existent, cannot be conceived as a real part of the act which thinks it? And isn't even the fictitious and the absurd, whenever we speak of it, something we think of?

It is naturally not our intention to put the *being of what is ideal* on a level with the *being-thought-of which characterizes the fictitious or the nonsensical*.[2] The latter does not exist at all, and nothing can properly be predicated of it: if we none the less speak of it as having its own, 'merely intentional' mode of being, we see on reflection that this is an improper way of speaking. There are, in fact, merely certain necessary and valid connections among 'objectless ideas', whose analogy with truths governing ideas having objects, has prompted this talk of objects merely presented which do not genuinely exist. Ideal objects, on the other hand, exist genuinely. Evidently there is not merely a good sense in speaking of such objects (e.g. of the number 2, the quality of redness, of the principle of contradiction etc.) and in conceiving them as sustaining predicates: we also have insight into certain categorial truths that relate to such ideal objects. If these truths hold, everything presupposed as an object by their holding must have being. If I see the truth that 4 is an even number, that the predicate of my assertion actually pertains to the ideal object 4,

---

[1] [It would have been possible for Husserl here to have used his other term *reellen*, signifying an actual part, not something intended or meant.]

[2] As against this see B. Erdmann, *Logik*, 1, pp. 81–5, and K. Twardowski, *Zur Lehre vom Inhalt und Gegenstand der Vorstellungen*, p. 106.

then this object cannot be a mere fiction, a mere *façon de parler*, a mere nothing in reality.

This does not exclude the possibility that the sense of this being, and the sense also of this predication, does not coincide exactly with their sense in cases where a real (*reales*) predicate, a *property* is asserted or denied of a real subject. Otherwise put: we do not deny but in fact emphasize, that there is a fundamental categorial split in our unified conception of being (or what is the same, in our conception of an object as such); we take account of this split when we distinguish between ideal being and real being; between being as Species and being as what is individual. The conceptual unity of predication likewise splits into two essentially different sub-species according as we affirm or deny properties of individuals, or affirm or deny general determinations of Species. This difference does not, however, do away with a supreme unity in the concept of an object, nor with the correlated concept of a categorial propositional unity. In either case something (a predicate) pertains or does not pertain to an object (a subject), and the sense of this most universal pertinence, together with the laws governing it, also determines the most universal sense of being, or of an object, as such; exactly as the more special sense of generic predication, with its governing laws, determines (or presupposes) the sense of an ideal object. If everything which has being is rightly recognized as having being, and as having such and such a being, in virtue of the evidence with which, in thought, we apprehend it as being, then without doubt we may not reject the self-justifying claims of ideal being. No interpretative skill in the world can in fact eliminate ideal objects from our speech and our thought.

§9 *Locke's doctrine of abstract ideas*

The psychological hypostatization of the universal in Locke's philosophy had, as we saw, an extraordinary historical influence. It grew out of the following line of thought:

In actual reality nothing like a universal exists; only individual things, arranged into genera and species by their exact or less exact resemblances, have real existence. If we remain within the sphere of what is immediately given and experienced, in the sphere of 'ideas' in Locke's sense, phenomenal things are complexes of 'simple ideas', in which the same simple ideas, the same phenomenal attributes, recur simply or in groups. Things now receive names, and not merely proper names, but for the most part common names; the fact that many things can be unambiguously named by one and the same universal name, shows that a universal sense or 'idea' must correspond to such a name.

If we consider how the general name applies to the objects of the pertinent class, it becomes plain that it does so because one and the same attribute (or complex of attributes) is common to all these objects. The univocality of the universal name extends only as far as objects are named by way of this and no other attribute (or *idea* of an attribute).

The universal thought carried out in such universal meanings therefore presupposes that we have the *power of abstraction*, i.e. the power to separate off partial ideas, ideas of such attributes, from the phenomenal things given to us as complexes of attributes, and to associate them with words of which they are the general meanings. The possibility and actuality of such separation is guaranteed by the fact that each universal name has its own meaning, conveys an attributive idea exclusively bound up with itself; as also by the fact that we can at will pick out any attributes and make them the specific meanings of new general names.

The formation of 'abstract' or 'universal ideas', those 'creations' and 'artefacts' of the word, is indeed not without difficulty: they

> do not so easily offer themselves as we are apt to imagine. For example: does it not require some pains and skill to form the general idea of a triangle (which is yet none of the most abstract, comprehensive and difficult) for it must be neither oblique, nor rectangle, neither equilateral, equicrural nor scalenon, but all and none of these at once. In effect, it is something imperfect, that cannot exist, an idea wherein some parts of several different and inconsistent ideas are put together. It is true, the mind in this imperfect state has need of such ideas, and makes all the haste to them it can, for the conveniency of communication and enlargement of knowledge ... But yet one has reason to suspect such ideas are marks of our imperfection.[1]

---

[1] Locke's *Essay*, IV, vii.

§10 *Criticism*

In this line of thought several fundamental errors are intertwined. The basic defect of Locke's theory of knowledge, and of the English theory of knowledge in general, its unclear concept of 'idea', is very plainly revealed in its consequences. We note the following points:

1. An 'idea' is defined as any object of interior perception: 'Whatever the mind perceives in itself, or is the immediate object of perception, thought or understanding, that I call idea.'[1] By a ready extension – perception need not actually follow – every *possible* object of interior perception, and finally every content in the immanent-psycholological sense, is ranged under the rubric of 'idea'.

2. 'Idea' also has for Locke the narrower sense of *presentation*, in the sense which marks out a very restricted class of experiences, i.e. intentional experiences. Each idea is an idea of *something*, it presents something.

3. Locke confuses presentation with what is as such presented, appearance with what appears, the act or act-phenomenon, as a really immanent element in the stream of consciousness, with the object intended. The apparent object therefore becomes an idea, its attributes partial ideas.

4. The confusion mentioned in 3 is connected with the fact that Locke confounds the attributes pertaining to the object with the immanent contents constituting the sensuous kernel of the presentative act, the *sensations* on which the interpretative act puts an objective interpretation, or by way of which it putatively perceives, or otherwise envisages, the object's attributes.

5. Under the rubric of 'general idea', properties as specific attributes, and properties as objective aspects, are confused.

6. It is of great significance, lastly, that Locke altogether fails to distinguish between an idea in the sense of an intuitive presentation (a phenomenon, a floating image), and an idea in the sense of a significant reference. This latter likewise can be interpreted either as a meaning-intention or as a meaning-fulfilment, for these two also are never separated by Locke.

These confusions (still rampant in contemporary epistemology)

---

[1] *Essay*, II, viii. Cf. the second Epistle to the Bishop of Worcester 'he that thinks must have some immediate object of his mind in thinking, i.e. must have *ideas*'.

gave Locke's doctrine of abstract general ideas an air of obviousness which could impose on its author. Objects of intuitive
presentation, animals, trees etc., conceived as they appear to us,
and not as being the patterns of 'primary qualities' and 'powers'
which real things are for Locke – these certainly are not the
things which appear in our intuitive presentation – cannot be
allowed by us to be complexes of 'ideas', and therefore themselves 'ideas'. They are not objects of possible 'interior perception', as if they constituted a complex phenomenological content
in consciousness, in which they could be picked out as real data.

We should not be led astray by the fact that we make an
equivocal use of the same words to refer to the sensuously
apparent determinations of things, and to the presentative aspects
of our percepts, and that we at one time speak of 'colour',
'smoothness', 'shape' etc., in the sense of objective properties,
and at another time in the sense of sensations. An opposition of
principle divides the two. Sensations, animated by interpretations,
present objective determinations in corresponding percepts of
things, but they are not themselves these objective determinations. The apparent object, as it appears in the appearance,
transcends this appearance as a phenomenon. We may be led by
certain reasons to distinguish apparent determinations into merely
apparent and genuine ones, perhaps as in the sense of the traditional distinction between secondary and primary qualities. The
subjectivity of the secondary qualities can never amount to the
nonsensical assertion that they are real constituents of phenomena.
The apparent objects of external intuition are *meant* unities, not
'ideas' or complexes of ideas in the Lockean sense of these terms.
Naming by means of universal names does not, moreover, consist
in picking out particular universal ideas from such complexes of
ideas, and attaching them to words as their 'meanings'. The
naming which, in the true sense of the word, rests on intuition,
may direct itself specially to an isolated attribute, but this self-
direction is an act of meaning in a sense analogous to the sense in
which the self-direction to the concrete object is itself such an
act of meaning. This act of meaning means something *for itself*,
which, in the meaning of the concrete object, is, we may say,
meant *along with* something else. But this does not mean that it
achieves a separation.

We may say generally: what an intention is directed to, is

thereby made the intention's peculiar object. But to say that it is made the intention's peculiar object, and to say that it is made an object separated from all other objects, are two totally different assertions. Properties understood as attributive aspects, are plainly inseparable from their concrete basis. Contents of this sort cannot exist independently, but they can none the less be independently meant. The intention does not separate, but it refers, and what it refers to, it *eo ipso* shuts off to the extent that it means this and nothing else. This holds of every sort of meaning, and one must be clear that not every meaning is an intuitive beholding, and not every intuition an adequate beholding of its object, embracing that object perfectly and exhaustively in itself.

All this does not suffice to decide our question. The single individual objective aspect is not the attribute *in specie*. If the former, the aspect, is meant, the meaning is individual in character, if the Species is meant, the meaning is specific in character. Naturally again the emphasis which the attributive aspect receives, does not mean a separation of the same. Our meaning, in the latter case, certainly in a fashion directs itself to the apparent aspect, but in an essentially new manner; the intuitive foundation being identical, the act-character makes all the difference. Similar differences are observable between the generic idea in the usual sense (e.g. *tree, horse* etc.), and direct presentations of things or concrete realities in general. Everywhere we must distinguish between simple intuitions, whether total or partial, which form our foundation, and the changing act-characters, which, as thoughts, are built on this foundation, without the least change in their sensuous, intuitive basis.

For a closer analysis we should here have to start discussing many more distinctions of acts than we need in criticizing Locke. The intuitively-singular is on one occasion directly meant as *that thing there*, on another occasion as *sustaining a universal*, as subject of an attribute or as individual member of an empirical class, on yet another occasion the *universal itself* is meant, e.g. the Species of an attribute stressed in a partial intuition, or, yet again, such *a species is meant as a sub-species of an ideal genus* etc. One and the same sensuous intuition can on occasion serve as a basis for all these modes of conceiving.

To these differences of genuine thought, in which manifold categorial forms are actually constituted, correspond the *symbolic intentions* of our expressions. As merely asserting and meaning, we can say and mean everything which we perhaps do not actualize at all in the genuine, intuitively fulfilled manner. Our 'thought' is then of a 'merely symbolic', 'non-authentic' sort.

Locke cannot do justice to this phenomenological state of things. The sensuous-intuitive image, through which the significant intention fulfils itself, is taken by Locke, as said above (sixth confusion), for the meaning itself. Our last assertion confirms and explains our objection. For Locke's identification is inept, whether we understand by a 'meaning' the intending or the fulfilling variety. The former lies in an expression as such; its significant intention constitutes a universal presentation in the sense of a universal meaning, and as such it is possible without any actual intuitive foundation. If fulfilment now enters, our discussions show that the sensuous-intuitive image is not the fulfilment of meaning itself, but the mere foundation for this fulfilling act. To the universal thought, merely symbolically realized, i.e. the mere meaning of the universal word, the 'authentically' carried out thought corresponds, which in its turn rests on an act of sensuous intuition, without being identical with the latter.

Now we completely see the deceptive confusions in Locke's train of thought. From the obvious truth that each universal name has its own peculiar universal meaning, he passes on to assert that a *general idea* corresponds to every general name, which idea is for him simply a *separate intuitive presentation* (a separate appearance) of an attribute. This follows necessarily from the fact that he confuses the word's meaning, whose fulfilment tests this appearance, with the appearance itself: the separated meaning (whether intending or fulfilled) of the attribute, becomes a separated intuition of this attribute. Since Locke fails to hold apart an attribute's appearance from the attribute which appears (Confusion 3), and as little holds apart an attributive aspect from an attribute *specifically* understood (Confusion 5), he indeed achieves a *psychological hypostatization of the universal* in his 'general idea', he makes of the universal a real datum in consciousness.[1]

---

[1] It is very remarkable that even Lotze to whose interpretation of Plato's theory of forms we are deeply indebted, fell into the error of psychologically hypostatizing the universal. See the discussions in the *Logic* of 1874, p. 569 *ff.*, especially §316.

§11 *Locke's universal triangle*

These errors avenge themselves in the absurdities into which, in his example of the universal idea of a triangle, they plunge the great thinker. This idea is the idea of *a* triangle which is neither rectangular nor acute-angled etc. So it readily seems, if one first takes the universal idea of the triangle for the universal meaning of the name, and then replaces the latter in consciousness by the separated intuitive presentation, or by the intuited separate existence of the attributive complex in question. Thus we might have an interior image which is triangular and no more, the generic attributes torn adrift from their specific differences, and turned into a psychic reality.

That this conception is not merely false but nonsensical, need scarcely be said. The inseparability of the universal, its incapacity for being made real, holds *a priori*, it is rooted in the essence of the Genus as such. One might perhaps say more impressively, with Locke's example in view, that geometry uses the definition of 'triangle' to prove *a priori* that every triangle is either acute-angled or obtuse-angled or right-angled, etc. It knows no distinction between triangles 'in reality' and triangles 'in idea', i.e., triangles floating as pictures before the mind. What is incompatible *a priori*, is absolutely so, and so also in a picture. The adequate picture of a triangle is itself a triangle. Locke therefore is deceived when he thinks to combine his express recognition of the plain non-existence of a real universal triangle, with its existence in our presentations. He forgets that mental existence is also real existence, and that, when being-presented is opposed to being-real one does not and ought not to point to the opposition between the mental and the extra-mental, but to the opposition between what is presented, in the sense of being merely *meant*, and what is *true*, in the sense of corresponding to such a meaning. To be meant does not, however, mean to have mental reality.

Locke should, above all, have reminded himself that a triangle is something which has triangularity, but that triangularity is not itself something that has triangularity. The universal idea of triangle, as an idea of triangularity, is therefore the idea of what every triangle as such possesses, but it is not therefore itself the idea of *a* triangle. If one calls the general meaning a concept, the attribute itself the *concept's content*, and every subject having this attribute the *concept's object*, one can put the point in the form: It is absurd to treat a concept's content as the same concept's object, or to include a concept's content in its own conceptual extension.[1]

One sees further how Locke piles up his absurdities in not only thinking of the universal triangle as a triangle stripped of all specific differences, but also as a triangle which *unites all such differences together*, and so puts into the content of the concept of triangle the extension of the sub-species which divide it. This is, however, merely a passing lapse in Locke. It is plain at least that difficulties regarding universal meanings give no ground for serious complaints regarding the 'imperfections' of the human mind.

Note: How little the errors of the Lockean doctrine of general ideas have been clarified up to date, is shown among other things by the recent treatment of the doctrine of universal objects, which, following Erdmann, are now accorded a place alongside of individual objects, though not indeed in *our* sense. Thus Twardowski thinks that, what is presented in the universal idea 'is an object[2] specifically peculiar to it' and that this is 'a group of *constituents* which several objects have in common'.[3] The object of the universal idea is 'a part of the object of an idea subordinated to it, which stands in relation of exact likeness to definite parts of the objects of other individual ideas'. The general idea is 'to this extent spurious' that it is held by many to be incapable of an actual carrying-out.

But that there nevertheless are such ideas, must be granted by the man who sees that we can say something about their objects. This we plainly can do. No one can represent a universal triangle *intuitively*, a triangle neither right-angled, nor obtuse-angled nor acute-angled, which is without colour or definite size, but it is as plain that we have an indirect idea of such triangles as that we have indirect ideas of a female stallion[4] or of a steel cannon made of wood etc.

[1] I should not therefore think it correct to say with Meinong (*Humestudien*, 1, 5) that Locke confuses the content and the extension of the concept.

[2] Twardowski, 'Zur Lehre vom Inhalt und Gegenstand der Vorstellingen', p. 109.

[3] Twardowski, loc. cit. p. 105.

[4] *Weisser Rappe*, = white black-horse, in the original.

We read further that 'Plato's ideas are no more than objects of universal ideas. Plato attributes existence to these objects. This we no longer do. The object of the universal idea is represented by us, but does not exist . . .'[1]

Here it is clear that Locke's absurdities are with us again. We certainly have an 'indirect presentation' of 'a universal triangle', for this merely refers to the meaning of that nonsensical expression. But one would not grant that the universal presentation of *the triangle* is this indirect presentation of *a universal* triangle, or that it is the presentation of a triangle concealed in all triangles, but without being acute-angled, obtuse-angled etc. Twardowski is consistent in rejecting the existence of universal objects – he is right in so regarding the absurd objects he has substituted for them. But what is the case in regard to such existential propositions as *There are concepts, There are propositions, There are algebraic numbers* etc. For Twardowski as for us, existence does not mean the same as real *(reale)* existence.

It is also hard to understand how the universal object, which is supposed to be a 'constituent' of the subsumed concrete object, should lack intuitive givenness, and should not rather share in the intuitive quality of this concrete object. If a total content is intuited, all its single traits are intuited together with, and in it, and many are independently noted, 'set in relief', and so made objects of their own proper intuitions. May we no longer say that we see the tree's green colouring in the tree precisely as we see the green tree? The notion of *Green* can indeed not be seen, whether this be the notion in the sense of the meaning of 'green', or the notion in the sense of the attribute green, the Species *Green*. But it is also absurd to treat the concept as a part of the individual object, the 'object of the concept'.

§ 12 *The doctrine of generic images*

The above discussions have made clear without further analysis that the other way of hypostatizing the universal, which has played its part in traditional logic under the rubric of 'generic images', is infected with the same absurdities as Locke's notion and has grown out of similar confusions. The vagueness and elusiveness of generic images in respect of specific differences

---

[1] Twardowski, loc. cit. p. 106.

makes no difference to their concreteness. Vagueness is a definite *feature* of certain contents, it consists in a certain mode of continuity in qualitative transition. And as to elusiveness, it makes no difference to the concreteness of each rapidly changing content. The essence of the matter does not reside in changing contents, but in the unity of an intention directed to constant attributes.

CHAPTER THREE

Abstraction and Attention

---

§13 *Nominalistic theories which regard abstraction as an achievement of attention*

WE now pass on to analyse an influential theory of abstraction, first framed by J. S. Mill in his polemic against Hamilton, according to which abstraction is merely an achievement of attention. There are, it is held, neither general presentations nor general objects, but we may, while forming intuitive presentations of individual concrete things, devote exclusive attention or exclusive interest to various parts and sides of our object. The attribute which neither can actually exist 'in and for itself', i.e. *separately*, nor be represented as such, can be regarded *by itself*, can become the object of an exclusive interest which ignores all associated attributes. The double use of the word 'abstraction', positive in one content and negative in another, thereby becomes understandable.

These main lines of thought are then supplemented by treatments of the associative linkage of general names with the stressed traits of intuited objects, and of the influence which names exert on such traits, whether by arousing them reproductively, or by habitually concentrating attention on them. It is pointed out how they dominate and direct the drift of further association through the content of such stressed attributes, and so promote unity of theme in the course of our thinking. The detailed execution of these thoughts is best taken from the above-mentioned polemic of Mill, who for the rest borrows his notion of abstraction as a function of attention from his conceptualistic opponent Hamilton. We read: 'The formation of a concept, does not consist of separating the attributes which are said to compose it from all other attributes of the same object, and enabling us to conceive those attributes, disjoined from any others. We neither conceive them, nor think them, nor cognize them in any way, as a thing

363

apart, but solely as forming, in combination with numerous other attributes, the idea of an individual object. But, though thinking them only as part of a larger agglomeration, we have the power of fixing our attention on them, to the neglect of the other attributes with which we think them combined. While the concentration of attention actually lasts, if it is sufficiently intense, we may be temporarily unconscious of any of the other attributes, and may really, for a brief interval, have nothing present to our mind but the attributes constituent of the concept. In general, however, the attention is not so completely exclusive as this: it leaves room in consciousness for other elements of the concrete idea: though of these the consciousness is faint, in proportion to the energy of the concentrative effort, and the moment the attention relaxes, if the same concrete idea continues to be contemplated, its other constituents come out into consciousness. General concepts, therefore, we have, properly speaking, none; we have only complex ideas of objects in the concrete: but we are able to attend exclusively to certain parts of the concrete idea: and by that exclusive attention, we enable those parts to determine exclusively the course of our thoughts as subsequently called up by association; and are in a condition to carry on a train of meditation or reasoning relating to those parts only, exactly as if we were able to conceive them separately from the rest.

'What principally enables us to do this is the employment of signs, and particularly the most efficient and familiar kind of signs, viz., Names.'[1]

We read further, in connection with a passage from Hamilton's Lectures:[2]

> The rationale of this is, that when we wish to be able to think of objects in respect of certain of their attributes – to recall no objects but such as are invested with those attributes, and to recall them with our attention directed to those attributes exclusively – we effect this by giving to that combination of attributes, or to the class of objects which possess them, a specific name. We create an artificial association between those attributes and a certain combination of articulate sounds, which guarantees to us that when we hear the sound, or see the written characters corresponding to it, there will be raised in the mind an idea of some object possessing those

[1] J. S. Mill, *An Examination of Sir W. Hamilton's Philosophy*, pp. 393 f.
[2] Loc. cit. p. 394.

attributes, in which idea those attributes alone will be suggested vividly to the mind, our consciousness of the remainder of the concrete idea being faint. As the name has been directly associated only with those attributes, it is as likely, in itself, to recall them in any one concrete combination as in any other. What combination it shall recall in the particular case, depends on recency of experience, accidents of memory, or the influence of other thoughts which have been passing, or are even then passing, through the mind: accordingly, the combination is far from being always the same, and seldom gets itself strongly associated with the name which suggests it; while the association of the name with the attributes that form its conventional signification is constantly becoming stronger. The association of that particular set of attributes with a given word, is what keeps them together in the mind by a stronger tie than that with which they are associated with the remainder of the concrete image. To express the meaning in Sir W. Hamilton's phraseology, this association gives them an unity in our consciousness. It is only when this has been accomplished, that we possess what Sir W. Hamilton terms a concept; and this is the whole of the mental phenomenon involved in the matter. We have a concrete representation, certain of the component elements of which are distinguished by a mark, designating them for special attention; and this attention, in cases of exceptional intensity, excludes all consciousness of the others.

§14 *Objections to any and every form of nominalism. (a) The lack of a descriptive fixation of aims*

We see from the above, and from similar expositions, how, despite great elaboration, no attempt has really been made to pin down what is descriptively given and what demands clarification, and to relate the two to one another. Let us once more run through our own undoubtedly clear, natural train of thought. What we are *given* are certain differences in the field of names: among others, the difference between such names as name what is individual, and such as name what is specific. If we confine ourselves, for the sake of simplicity to direct names ('proper names' in an extended sense of the word), names like 'Socrates' or 'Athens', on the one hand, stand opposed to names like 'Four' (the number-Four as a *single* member of the number-series), '*C*' (the note *C* as *one member* of the musical scale), 'Red' (as the name of *one* colour), on the other. To these names certain meanings correspond, and through these we refer to objects. What these named objects are can, one would imagine, not be in doubt. In the one case it is the person Socrates, the city of Athens, or any other *individual* object, in the other case the Number Four, the note *C*, the colour Red, or any other *ideal* object. What we mean by the significant use of words, what objects we name by them, and what these objects count as when we name them, this no one can dispute with us. It is accordingly *evident* that when I say 'Four' in the generic sense, as, e.g., in the statement 'Four is a prime number relatively to seven', I am meaning the Species *Four*, I have *it* as object before my logical regard, and am passing judgement on it, and not on anything individual. I am not judging about any individual group of four things, nor about any constitutive moment, piece or side of such a group, for each part, *qua* part of what is individual, is itself likewise individual. But to make an object of something, to make it a subject of predications or attributions, merely differs in name from having a presentation of it, and having a presentation in a sense which, while not the only one, is none the less the standard one for logic. We therefore assert with self-evidence: There are 'universal presentations', i.e. presentations of what is specific, just as there are presentations of what is individual.

We spoke of self-evidence, but self-evidence in respect of objective differences of meanings implies that we go beyond the merely symbolic use of expressions and refer ourselves to corresponding intuitions for final correction. Basing ourselves on intuitive presentations, we carry out the fulfilments of meanings corresponding to our merely significant intentions, we realize their 'genuine' purport. If we do this in our present case, some individual group of four units certainly floats pictorially before us, and to that extent underlies our presentation and our judgement. But we do not pass judgement on this group of four, we do not mean *it* in the subject-idea of our above example. Not the pictured group, but the number Four, the Specific Unity is our subject, and it is of *this* that we say that it is prime relatively to Seven. Strictly speaking, this Specific Unity is likewise nothing in, or attached to, the apparent group, for, if it were, it would be something individual, a thing here and now. But our reference, though itself existing now, refers to nothing less than what is now, it refers to Four, the ideal, timeless unity.

Reflecting on our experiences of individual and specific meaning – whether purely intuitive, purely symbolic, or at once a symbolic and a fulfilled significant intention – we must now carry out further phenomenological descriptions. Their task would be to lay bare the relations, fundamental to a clarification of knowledge, which hold between blind (or pure symbolic reference) and intuitive (or authentic) reference, and in the case of the latter to show the varying manner in which individual images function in consciousness, according as we intend what is individual or what is specific. This would enable us, e.g., to answer questions as to how, and in what sense, the universal is brought to subjective awareness in the individual act of thought, and perhaps achieves self-evident givenness, and how it can acquire a connection with the boundless sphere of individual cases ranged under it, of which we can of course form no adequate pictorial presentation.

In Mill's exposition, as in all similar expositions, there is no question of simply recognizing evident data and consequently proceeding on the path we have just sketched. What should have been a fixed point in reflective clarification, is pushed aside unnoticed; the theory therefore misses its target, which it had lost sight of before, or rather never clearly seen. What it tells us may be informative in regard to this or that psychological precondition or component of our intuitively achieved consciousness of universality, or in regard to the psychological role of signs in directing unitary trains of thought etc. etc. This has, however, no immediate relevance to the objective use of universal meanings, and to the undoubted truth enshrined in talk about universal objects (subjects, singulars) and in predications which relate to these; that it has mediate relevance must first be established. Mill's conception, like all empiricistic conceptions, can indeed not appeal to such evident starting-points or goals, since its whole concern is to prove the nullity of what such self-evidence shows to have genuine subsistence, namely universal objects and the universal presentations in which such objects are constituted for consciousness. Expressions such as 'universal object', 'universal presentation' certainly arouse memories of old, burdensome errors. But, however much they may have been historically misinterpreted, they must still have a normal interpretation which justifies them. Empirical psychology cannot teach us this normal meaning: we can learn it only by going back to the self-evident sense of propositions which are built upon general presentations and which relate to general objects as subjects of their predications.

§15 (b) The origin of modern nominalism as an exaggerated reaction to Locke's doctrine of general ideas. The essential character of this nominalism, and of the theory of abstraction in terms of attention

The theory of abstraction held by Mill and his empiricist followers, like the theories of abstraction held by Berkeley and Hume, gets stuck in its attack on the error of 'abstract ideas'. It gets stuck by allowing itself to be misled by the chance circumstance that Locke, in his interpretation of general ideas, hit on his absurd general triangle: it thinks that serious talk of such ideas necessarily demands Locke's absurd interpretation. The fact is overlooked that this error is especially due to the unclarified ambiguity of the word 'idea' (and of the German word *Vorstellung*), and that what is absurd for one concept of 'idea' is possible and justifiable for another. How could this fact be apparent to Locke's opponents, when their notion of an 'idea' remained in the same obscurity that had misled Locke? In consequence of this fact, men fell into that *modern nominalism*, whose essence no longer lies in the rejection of realism, but of what is, properly speaking, conceptualism. Not only did men reject the absurd general ideas of Locke, but also general concepts in the full, true sense of the word, in the sense, that is, that is evidently revealed by an analysis of the objective meaning-content of our thinking as constitutive of the Idea of what is a unity-for-thought (*Denkeinheit*).

Such a view is fostered by wrongly interpreted psychological analyses. We tend naturally to turn our gaze among logical phenomena to whatever has primary intuitive palpability; we are then misled into taking the inner pictures which are found to accompany our names as the meanings of those names. If we become clear, however, that a meaning is merely what we mean, or what we understand by an expression, we cannot maintain such a conception. For if meaning consisted in the intuitive individual presentations which 'illustrate' the sense of general names, the objects of such presentations, precisely as they are intuitively presented, would be just what we meant by those names, and each name would be an equivocal proper name. To cope with such differences, intuitive individual presentations are said to sustain new psychological functions when they occur in association with general *names*: they determine other trains of ideas, they fit otherwise into the course of our thoughts, they influence this course in a different fashion.

All this is quite irrelevant to the phenomenological facts. Here and now, at the very moment that we significantly utter a general name, we mean what is general, and our meaning differs from our meaning when we mean what is individual. This difference must be pinned down *in the descriptive content of the isolated experience*, in the individually and actually performed general assertion. What things are causally connected with such an experience, what psychological consequences may follow from it, all this does not concern us. Such things concern the psychology of abstraction, not its phenomenology.

The nominalistic currents of our time have certainly threatened to change our notion of conceptualism so that the nominalism of John Stuart Mill, avowed by him so decisively, has lately been disputed.[1] We should not, however, see it as the essence of nominalism that, in its attempted clarification of the sense and theoretical achievement of universals, it loses itself in a blind associative play of names as mere verbal noises; its essence lies in the fact that its attempted clarifications overlook the *peculiar consciousness* exemplified in our living sense of the meaning of signs, in our actual understanding of them, in the grasped sense of our assertions, and also exemplified in correlative acts of fulfilment, which yield us the 'true' Idea of the universal, the wholly evident ideation in which the universal 'itself' is given to us. This consciousness means what it means to us, whether or not we know anything about psychology, or about mental antecedents and consequences, associative dispositions, etc. If the nominalist wishes to give an empirical explanation of this consciousness of the universal, as a fact of our human nature, if he wishes to connect it causally with such and such factors, such and such previous experiences, such and such unconscious dispositions, we should not object in principle. We should merely deny the interest, for pure logic and epistemology, of such empirical psychological facts. Instead of this, however, the nominalist says that to differentiate general ideas from individual ones, and to

---

[1] See A. v. Meinong, *Hume-Studien*, I, p. 68.

oppose the former to the latter, is really to talk senselessly. He denies that there is abstraction in the sense of a peculiar consciousness of the universal which lends evidence to general names and meanings: in reality only individual intuitions exist, some with an interplay of conscious and unconscious happenings, which never take us beyond the sphere of what is individual, nor constitute, i.e. bring to awareness and perhaps to self-presentation, any essentially new sort of objectivity.

Each thought-experience, like every mental state, has, empirically treated, its descriptive content, as well as its causal antecedents and consequents; it makes itself felt in the rush of life, and exercises its productive functions. But in the field of *phenomenology* and, above all, in the sphere of *epistemology* – the phenomenological clarification of ideal thought- and knowledge-unities – only essence and sense matter: what we mean when we make assertions, what object is set up for us by our act of meaning as such, in virtue of its sense, what partial meanings enter essentially into the make-up of our act of meaning, what essential forms and differences it exhibits, and so on. What is of interest to epistemology, must be shown up exclusively in the *content* of the *meaning-experiences and the fulfilment-experiences themselves*, and be shown up as essential. If we also find, in the range of whát can be thus evidently shown up, the distinction between universal presentations and individual, intuitive presentations (which we undoubtedly do), then no talk of genetic functions and associations can be relevant to such a distinction, or contribute a jot to its clarification.

It carries the matter no further and fails to remove our objections, if, like Mill, we look on *exclusive attention* to some single attribute (or dependent feature) of the intuited object, as being the act which, in our actual consciousness, in the supposed genetic situation, gives the name its 'generic' meaning. Though recent thinkers, who share Mill's ideas without sharing his extreme empiricist tendencies, may call themselves 'conceptualists', thinking that the interest which turns 'attributes' into objects will also guarantee the existence of general meanings – their doctrine is and remains essentially nominalistic.

Generality remains for them a matter of the associative function of signs, it consists in the psychologically regulated association of 'the same sign' with 'the same' objective feature – or rather with the feature which always recurs in the same determinate form and is at times emphasized by attention. This *generality of a psychological function* is, however, quite removed from the *generality which belongs to the intentional content of the logical experiences themselves,* or which, described objectively and ideally, belongs to our *meanings and our meaning-fulfilments.* This last generality escapes nominalism entirely.

§16 (c) Generality of psychological function and generality as a meaning-form. Different senses of the relation of a universal to an extension

To bring complete clearness to this important distinction between generality of psychological function, and generality as pertaining to a significant content itself, we must pay heed to the differing logical functions of general names and meanings, and in connection therewith to the differing senses of talk of their generality, or of their relation to a range of particulars.

Let us set the following three forms side by side: *an A, all A, A in general,* e.g. *a triangle, all triangles, the triangle,* the last taken as in the sentence 'The triangle is a species of figure'.[1]

The expression 'an *A*' can function predicatively as the predicate of innumerable categorical assertions, and the aggregate of the true, or intrinsically possible assertions of this sort, determines all the possible subjects to which being an *A* either actually pertains, or could without contradiction pertain, in other words the actual or possible 'range' ('extension') of the 'concept' *A*. This universal concept *A*, or the universal predicate 'an *A*', applies to all the objects in this range – we take for the sake of simplicity the range to which it applies truly – i.e., the assertions in the aggregate in question are all true: there are, phenomenologically speaking, as possibilities, self-evident judgements with a corresponding content. This generality belongs, therefore, to the logical function of the predicate; it is not represented in the

---

[1] The word symbolized by the letter '*A*' in such combinations, must count as syncategorematic. The expressions: 'the lion', 'a lion', 'this lion', 'all lions' etc. certainly and evidently have a common element of meaning, but the word can have no independent sense except as occurring in one of these forms. If we are asked whether one of these meanings is not *contained* in all the rest, whether the direct idea of the Species corresponding to *A* does not lie hidden in the other meanings, we must answer 'No'. The Species *A* 'lies hidden' in these meanings, but only potentially and not as a meant object.

individual act, the single case where the meaning *an A* is enacted, or where we mean the corresponding adjectival predicate. It appears in these only as a form of indefiniteness; the word 'A' expresses a form, which evidently pertains to our meaning-intention or our meaning-fulfilment, and is connected with *what* either intends. This form is a wholly irreducible moment; its peculiarity can only be recognized, not explained away by any sort of psychological-genetic treatment. Ideally put: the word 'A' expresses a primitive logical form. The same plainly holds of the formation 'an *A*', which likewise represents a primitive logical structure.

The generality of which we are here speaking, belongs, we say, to the *logical* function of predicates, it consists in the *logical possibility* of propositions of a certain sort. We stress the logical character of this possibility, to show that we are concerned with a possibility that can be seen *a priori* to belong to meanings as Specific Unities, not to psychologically contingent acts. If we see that Red is a universal predicate, one associable with many possible subjects, our meaning no longer relates to something whose existence is in a real (*realen*) sense governed by those natural laws which govern the coming and going of experiences in time. We are not talking of experiences at all, but of the single self-identical predicate Red, and of the possibility of certain sentences, each single in the same sense, in which this same predicate occurs.

If we now pass to the form 'all *A*'s', generality pertains to the form of the act itself. We expressly mean *all A's*, to all such *A*'s our presentation and predication relates in the universal judgement, though perhaps no single *A* is 'itself' 'directly' presented. This idea of a range, is however, no complex of the ideas of the members of this range; so little is this the case, that such individual presentations as perhaps float before us have nothing at all to do with the significant intention to *all A's*. Here also the word 'all' points to a peculiar semantic form: we leave aside the question whether it can be resolved into simpler forms or not.

If we deal finally with the form *the A* (*in specie*), generality again pertains to our significant content itself. Here, however, we encounter a wholly different sort of universality, the universality of the Species, which, while it may have the closest *logical* relations to universality of range, none the less evidently differs from the latter. The forms *the A* and *all A's* – likewise *any A, no matter which* are not the same in meaning: theirs is no mere grammatical difference, determined in the end by mere verbal noise. They are *logically* distinct forms, giving expression to essential differences of meaning. The consciousness of Specific Generality must count as an essentially new mode of 'presentation', as one, namely, that does not merely present individual singulars in a new manner, but makes us aware of a new sort of singulars, i.e. Singular Species. What sort of singulars these are, and how they stand *a priori* to individual singulars, or how they differ from these latter, must of course be gleaned from the logical truths which, grounded in pure forms, govern both sorts of singulars and their mutual *a priori* relations (i.e. their relations of essence or Idea). Here there is no obscurity or possible error as long as one keeps to the straight sense of these truths, or, what is the same, to the straight sense of the meaning-forms in question, whose self-evident interpretations are called truths of logic. Only an erroneous side-slip into psychologistic and metaphysical trains of thought produces obscurity; it creates pseudo-problems and frames pseudo-theories to solve them.

§17 (d) *Application to the critique of nominalism*

If we now look back on the nominalistic theory of abstraction, we see from the above that its main error lies in quite ignoring the irreducible peculiarities of the forms of consciousness (of the forms of our intentions and of their correlative fulfilments). Its defective descriptive analysis makes it blind to the fact that the forms of logic are no more than these forms of significant intention which have themselves been made objects of a consciousness which treats them as unities, and so turns them into Ideal Species. Generality is also to be found among these forms. Nominalism further confuses the various concepts of generality that we have separated above. It one-sidedly prefers the generality which belongs to concepts in their predicative function, as a possibility of associating the same concept predicatively with several subjects. Being blind to the logically ideal character of this possibility, with its roots in semantic form, it puts psychological associations in its place, associations necessarily alien to, even incommensurable with, the predicates and propositions in question. Since it claims to have completely cleared up the nature of general meanings through such psychological analyses, its confusions grossly distort the generality of universal and specific presentations; this generality we saw belonged to the semantic essence of the individual act as such, as an indwelling meaning-form. What belongs phenomenologically to the immanent essence of the individual act, is turned into a psychological play of events, that throw no light, whether as causes or effects, on the individual act in which the entire total consciousness of universality comes alive.

§18 *The doctrine of attention as a generalizing power*

One last critical observation will of course not affect certain recent followers of Mill (or, more remotely, of Berkeley), who recognize a distinct problem in the emergence of the Species as an undifferentiated unity opposed to its manifold cases, and who do not attempt to solve it by having recourse to the generality of associative functioning, or to the general application of the same name and concept to all objects in their range.

Their idea runs as follows:

Abstraction as exclusive concern eo ipso *produces generalization.* The abstracted attribute is *de facto* an element in the appearance of the individual complex of attributes that we call the phenomenal object. But the 'same' attribute, i.e. one fully agreeing with it in content, can occur in countless such complexes. What distinguishes the repetitions of this same attribute from case to case, is uniquely and solely their individualizing association. Abstraction, therefore, as exclusive concern, causes the distinction, the individualization, of what is abstracted to vanish. The reverse side of our concentrated concern is the ignoring of all individualizing aspects, which yields the attribute as what is everywhere one and the same, since it cannot present itself as different to the abstraction performed in each case.

In this conception, it is said, we have all we need for the understanding of general thinking. Here it will be best to let the inspired Bishop of Cloyne speak, since it was he who first inspired the doctrine in question, though his own doctrine also gave influence to other thoughts than are here touched upon. It seems, he thinks, to be a difficulty how we can know any proposition to be true of all particular triangles, except we have first seen it demonstrated of the abstract idea of a triangle which equally agrees to all. For, because a property may be demonstrated to agree to some one particular triangle, it will not thence follow that it equally belongs to any other triangle, which in all respects is not the same with it. For example, having demonstrated that the three angles of an isosceles rectangular triangle are equal to two right ones, I cannot therefore conclude this affection agrees to all other triangles, which have neither a right angle nor two equal sides. It seems therefore that, to be certain this proposition is universally true, we must either make a particular demonstration for every particular triangle, which is impossible, or once for all demonstrate it of the abstract idea of a triangle, in which all the particulars do indifferently partake, and by which they are all equally represented.

To which I answer, that though the idea I have in view whilst I make the demonstration, be, for instance, that of an isosceles rectangular triangle, whose sides are of a determinate length, I may nevertheless be certain it extends to all other rectilinear triangles, of what sort or bigness whatsoever. And that, because neither the right angle, nor the equality, nor the determinate length of the sides, are at all concerned in the demonstration. It is true, the diagram I have in view includes all these particulars, but then there is not the least mention made of them in the proof of the proposition. It is not said, the three angles are equal to two right ones, because one of them is a right angle, or because the sides comprehending it are of the same length. Which sufficiently shows that the right angle might have been oblique, and the sides unequal, and for all that the demonstration have held good. And for this reason it is, that I conclude that to be true of any obliquangular or scalenon which I had demonstrated of a particular right-angled, equicrural triangle; and not because I demonstrated the proposition of the abstract idea of a triangle. And here it must be acknowledged, that a man may consider a figure merely as triangular, without attending to the particular qualities of the angles, or relations of the sides. So far he may abstract: but this will never prove that he can frame an abstract general inconsistent idea of a triangle. In like manner we may consider Peter so far forth as man, or so far forth as animal, without framing the forementioned abstract idea, either of man or of animal, inasmuch as all that is perceived is not considered.[1]

---

[1] Berkeley, *A Treatise concerning the Principles of Human Knowledge*, Introduction XVI.

§ 19 *Objections. (a) Exclusive attention to one attributive aspect*
does not remove its individuality

That we must reject this conception, so attractive at first sight, is
clear when we envisage the aim that a theory of abstraction must
subserve, i.e. the clarification of the difference between general
and individual meanings, the setting forth of its intuitive essence.
We must envisage those intuitive acts in which mere verbal
intentions, symbolic meanings, are intuitively fulfilled, and so
fulfilled that we can see what is 'really meant' by our expressions
and our meanings. Abstraction must here be the act, in which the
consciousness of universality, as fulfilment of the intention of
general names, is achieved. We must bear this in mind. Let us now
consider whether selective attention is capable of the performance
just set forth, and particularly on the assumption so essential to
the theory: that the content which abstractive attention selects is
a *constitutive aspect* of the concrete object of intuition, a property
really present in it.

However attention may be characterized, it is a function which,
in a descriptively peculiar fashion, *prefers* certain objects of
consciousness, and which (apart from certain differences of degree)
only differs from one case to another in virtue of the objects to
which it gives this preference. The theory, therefore, which
identifies abstraction with attention, can see no essential difference
between the meaning of the individual which pertains to the
intention of proper names, and the meaning of the universal
which attaches to the names of attributes. The difference consists
merely in the fact that, in the one case, our mind's eye, as it were,
fixates the whole individual object, in the other case, only the
attribute. We must ask, however, whether the attribute which, in
the sense of the theory, forms a *constituent property of the object*,
must not be as precisely and individually singular as the whole
object. Suppose we concentrate attention on the green of the tree
which stands before us. If this can be done, let us increase our
concentration till we achieve the complete unawareness of
associated aspects which Mill thought possible. Then, it is said,
all graspable points from which individualizing distinction can
be carried out have vanished. If another object with exactly the
same colouring were suddenly substituted, we should see no
difference; the green, which we are exclusively minding, would

for us be one and the same. Suppose all this is so. *Would* this green, however, *really* be the same as the other? Can our forgetfulness or deliberate blindness towards all that is distinctive, alter the fact that what is objectively distinct is still as distinct as before, and that the objective aspect we are heeding is *this* aspect which exists here and now and no other?

We surely cannot doubt that such a difference really exists. Comparison of two concrete, separated phenomena of the same quality, e.g. green, evidently shows that each has *its own* green. The two phenomena have not become fused, they have not the 'same' green in common as something individually identical. The green of the one is rather as much separated from the green of the other, as are the concrete wholes in which these 'greens' are. How else could there be qualitatively patterned unities in which the same quality occurs repeatedly, and what would it mean to speak of the spread of a colour over a whole surface? Each geometrical fragmentation of the surface evidently corresponds to a fragmentation of the unitary colouring, even though, when the colouring is exactly alike, we say, and say rightly, that 'the' colour is the 'same' everywhere.

Our theory therefore does not throw light on the sense of talk about an identically single attribute, about the Species as a unity in multiplicity. Such talk, it is clear, means something different from the objective aspect, the instance of the Species which occurs in the sensuous phenomenon. Assertions significant and true for the instance are false and even nonsensical for the Species. The colouring has its place and its time, it is spread out and has its intensity, it arises and vanishes. Applied to the colour as Species these predicates yield complete nonsense. When a house burns down, all its parts burn down: its individual forms and qualities, its constituent parts and aspects, all are gone. Shall we say that the relevant geometrical, qualitative and other Species have been burnt? Is such talk not the height of absurdity?

To sum up, if the attention-theory of abstraction is correct, if, as it supposes, attention to the whole object, and attention to its parts and aspects, are in essence one and the same act, only distinct in respect of the objects to which this act is directed, then there are no Species for our consciousness, for our knowledge, or for our statements. However we distinguish or shift matters around, consciousness always directs itself to what is individually singular, which is present to it as individually singular. One cannot, however, deny that we speak of Species in a distinct sense, that in countless cases we both mean and give a name, not to the individual, but to its Idea, that we can make assertions having what is ideally one as their subject, just as we can make assertions about what is individually singular. Our theory has therefore missed its target, its aim was to clarify our consciousness of the universal, and it has managed to lose sight of this consciousness in the course of its clarifications.

§20 (b) Refutation of the argument from geometrical thought

How do matters stand in regard to the advantages claimed for the theory as making general thinking understandable? Is Berkeley not right in insisting that, when we prove a proposition relating to all triangles, we have, on any occasion, only one individual triangle in mind, the one in our drawing, and that we only make use of the features that characterize a triangle as a triangle, while ignoring all others? 'We only make use of these features' means that we attend to them only, make them objects of an exclusive attention. We can therefore get along without assuming general ideas.

We can certainly get along without general ideas if by the latter we mean the general ideas of Locke's doctrine. But to avoid this shoal we need not lose ourselves in the false paths of nominalistic theory. We may in essentials approve of Berkeley's account while we reject the interpretation he puts upon it. He confuses the basis of abstraction with what is abstracted, the concrete instance, from which our consciousness of the universals draws intuitive fulness, with the object our thought intends. Berkeley speaks as if geometrical proofs were conducted for the triangle drawn in ink on the paper or in chalk on the blackboard, as if the chance singulars which float before us in general thought, were not mere aids to our thought's intention, but its actual objects. A geometrical procedure that took its lead from the *drawn* figure in Berkeley's sense, might yield astonishing results, but scarcely very happy ones. No geometrical proposition holds for the drawn figure as a physical object, since the latter is not really rectilinear, nor a geometrical figure at all. We can find no ideal geometrical properties in it, as colour is found in an intuited coloured object.

Certainly the mathematician looks at the drawing, which appears to him just as other intuited objects do. In none of his acts of thought, however, does he *refer* to this drawing, nor to any individual feature in it. He refers, if he does not wander, to 'a rectilinear figure as such'. This thought forms the subject-member of his theoretical proof.

What we therefore *attend to*, is neither the concrete object of intuition, nor an 'abstract partial content' (i.e. a non-independent aspect) in the latter; it is an Idea, in the sense of a Specific Unity, an abstractum in the logical sense. In logic and epistemology, therefore, abstraction must not be said to be a mere stress on a partial content, but a peculiar consciousness which, on an intuitive basis, directly apprehends a Specific Unity.

§21 *The difference between attending to a non-independent aspect of an intuited object and attending to the corresponding attribute in specie*

It will not be profitless to explore the difficulties of our contested theory a little further. Our own conception will become clearer when its whole contrast with this theory has been worked out.

Concentrated attention to an attributive moment is looked on as intuitively fulfilling (as yielding the 'true sense') of the general meaning attaching to the name of the corresponding attribute. To mean the Species intuitively, and to perform an act of concentrated attention, are looked on as one and the same. But how do things stand, we may ask, in cases where *we expressly refer to the individual aspect*? What differentiates the two types of case? If we are struck by an individual trait of an object, by its peculiar colouring, e.g., or by its noble form etc., we pay special attention to this trait, and yet have no general presentation. The same question applies to complete concrete things. What is the difference between exclusive attention to the individually apparent statue, and the intuitive grasp of the corresponding Idea, that could be realized in countless real statues?

Our opponents might reply: in individual treatment, individualizing moments enter our sphere of interest, in specific treatment, they are shut out. Our interest is confined to what is general, i.e. to a content which in itself provides no individual distinctions. Instead of pressing our previous objection – whether attention to individuating determinations creates individuality, while in-attention destroys it – we ask rather whether, in individual treatment, we also necessarily *mean* the individuating moments, which it is held must be concurrently noticed? Does an individual proper name also implicitly name individuating determinations, those, e.g., of time and place? Here is my friend Hans and I call him 'Hans'. He is no doubt individually determined, he is always at a particular point in space and time. If these determinations were, however, concurrently meant, the name 'Hans' would change its meaning with every step that my friend takes, on every occasion that I address him by name. Such a thing can scarcely be maintained, nor would one care to take refuge in saying that a proper name is really general. For the peculiar generality in respect of the varied times, positions, situations of the same individual thing differs in form from the specific generality of the thing's attribute or of the generic Idea 'thing in general'.

Often enough, at least, we are indifferent to the here and the now in attending to some part or characteristic trait of an object. We do not therefore consider it *in specie*, as we certainly do not mean to perform an 'abstraction' in the sense of a general presentation.

Perhaps one might here have recourse to the assumption that individuating determinations are *marginally* noticed. This cannot give much help. A great deal is marginally noticed, but is not for that reason really meant. Where the consciousness of the universal is intuitively achieved, as a true and genuine abstraction, the individual object of the underlying intuition certainly has a subsidiary place in consciousness, but is not at all meant. Mill's talk about our unconsciousness of the determinations that we abstract from is a useless, strictly speaking an absurd fiction.[1] In the numerous cases where, looking to some singular intuitive fact, we utter the corresponding generality, the singular element stays before our eyes, we do not suddenly become blind to what is individual in our case; this certainly does not happen when, e.g.,

---

[1] It is easy to see that as a result of this supposed 'unconsciousness' the absurd χωρισμός, of Locke's general idea returns. What is not 'conscious' cannot be a differentia of what is conscious. If exclusive attention to the moment of triangularity was possible, in a manner which made the differentiating characters vanish from consciousness, then the 'conscious', intuitive object would be the triangle as such and no more.

we look at this jasmine in bloom, and inhaling its scent, say 'Jasmine has a heady scent'.

If finally one grasps at a new evasion and admits that the individuating element is not specially picked out like the preferred point of our interest, not even marginally noticed, as are objects lying outside of our main interest, but that it is rather *subsidiarily* noticed (*mitbeachtet*), as being part of our main interest and peculiarly implied in its intention – then the whole ground of the theory is abandoned. For the theory claimed to make do with the mere emphasis of regard towards the concrete given object, or a peculiar feature given in it, and it now ends by postulating a variety of forms of consciousness that it should surely have dispensed with.

§22 *Fundamental deficiencies in the phenomenological analysis of attention*

This leads us at once to the weakest point of the theory; which is to be found in the question 'What is attention?' We are of course not reproaching the theory for failing to offer us a perfected phenomenology and psychology of attention, but for failing to clear up the nature of attention to an extent absolutely required by its aims. It should have ascertained what gives the word 'attention' its unitary sense, in order to see how far its range of application extends, or what the objects in each case are that we can (in a normal sense) claim to attend to. Above all, it should have inquired into the relation of attention to the meaning or reference which gives names and other expressions their significance. The sort of theory of abstraction just disputed, is possible only through the Lockean prejudice according to which the objects to which consciousness in its acts is immediately and properly directed, and the objects, particularly, of attention, must necessarily be mental contents, real occurrences in consciousness. It seems perfectly obvious that an act of consciousness can immediately act only on what is actually (*wirklich*) given in consciousness, i.e. on contents that it *really* (*reell*) includes among its elements. What is outside consciousness can only be the mediate object of a conscious act; and this occurs simply when the immediate content of the act, its primary object, serves as a representation, an image, a sign, of what is beyond consciousness.

Once accustomed to this mode of approach, one readily tries to clear up the objective relations and forms inherent in the intention of acts, by looking predominantly to their present conscious contents as their supposedly immediate objects, and, misled by the seeming intelligibility of talk about representations and signs, entirely ignores the true, supposedly mediate objects of the acts. Unthinkingly one credits to *contents* everything which acts, in their straightforward reference, place in the *object*; its attributes, its colours, forms etc., are forthwith called 'contents' and actually interpreted as contents in the psychological sense, e.g. as sensations.

How far this whole conception is at odds with the plain phenomenological situation, and how thoroughly it has debauched epistemology, we shall yet have many opportunities to observe. Here it may suffice to point out that when, e.g., we have a presentation or judgement about a horse, it is a horse, not our sensations of the moment, that is presented and judged about. Our sensations are only presented and judged about in psychological reflection, whose modes of conception should not be read into the immediate situation. That an appropriate train of sensations or images is *experienced*, and is in this sense conscious, does not and cannot mean that this is the *object* of an act of consciousness, in the sense that a perception, a presentation or a judgement is directed upon it.

This mistaken conception has further had a detrimental effect on the theory of abstraction. Led astray by the seemingly obvious, one takes experienced contents to be the normal objects to which one pays attention. The concrete phenomenal thing is treated as a complex of contents, i.e. of attributes grown together in a single intuitive image. And it is then said of these attributes, taken as experienced mental contents, that their non-independence precludes their separation from the concretely complete image: they can only be noticed in the latter. How could such a theory of abstraction intelligibly account for the formation of abstract ideas of that class of attributive determinations which are indeed perceived, but which by their nature never are adequately perceived, which cannot be given in the form of a mental content? I need only mention three-dimensional spatial shapes, in particular closed surfaces of solids or complete solids, such as the sphere and the cube. And how does the matter stand with the myriads of conceptual presentations, perhaps realized with the help of sensuous intuition, but which no intuitive aspect, even from the sphere of inner sense, instantiates? Here one can certainly not talk of a mere heeding of what is given in (sensuous) intuition, nor of a heeding of experienced contents.

Our own point of view inclines us first to draw a distinction in the sphere of sensuous abstraction – the sphere usually stressed for simplicity's sake – between acts in which an attributive aspect is intuitively 'given', and acts built upon these, which are not mere acts of attention to such an aspect, but rather acts of a new kind, referring in general fashion to the corresponding Species. Whether intuition presents the attributive aspect adequately or inadequately, is beside the point. We should then draw the further distinction between cases of sensuous abstraction, i.e. of an abstraction straightforwardly and perhaps adequately adjusted to sensuous intuition, and cases of non-sensuous or of at most partially sensuous abstraction, i.e. cases where the realized consciousness of the universal is at most only partially built on acts of sensuous intuition, and for the rest on non-sensuous acts, and accordingly related to thought-forms or categories whose nature does not permit of sensuous fulfilment. Suitable examples of the former, are unmixed concepts from outer or inner sense, such as colour, noise, pain, judgement, will, of the latter, concepts such as series, sense, disjunctive member, identity, being etc. etc. This difference will again seriously engage us in future investigations.

§23 Significant talk of attention embraces the whole sphere of thinking and not merely the sphere of intuition

The unitary sense to talk of 'attending' so little calls for 'contents' in the psychological sense (as the objects to which we attend), that it ranges beyond the sphere of intuition, and embraces the whole sphere of thinking. It makes no difference how thought is conducted, whether on an intuitive basis or in pure symbols. If we are theoretically concerned with *the culture of the Renaissance*, with *ancient philosophy*, with *the development of astronomical ideas*, with *elliptical functions*, with *curves of the nth order*, with *laws of algebraic operations* etc., we attend to all these matters. If our judgement is of the form *All A's are B's*, our attention is given to this universal state of affairs, we are concerned with allness, and not with this or that single matter. And so in general. Each thought, or at least each consistent thought, can no doubt become intuitive, to the extent that it is built in a certain fashion on 'corresponding' intuition. But the attention performed on such an intuition, whether of inner or outer sense, does not amount to attention to that intuition's phenomenological content, and just as little to attention to the object apparent in it. The *a certain*, or the *any*, the *all* and the *each*, the *and*, the *or*, the *not*, the *if* and the *then* etc., are not things we can point to in an object of basic sensuous intuition, that can be 'had' sensationally or externally represented or painted. Certain acts naturally correspond to all of them. The words have their meaning; in understanding them we realize certain forms pertaining to our objective intention. But these acts are not the *objects* that we mean: they are the activity of meaning or presenting, which only becomes objective to psychological reflection. The *object* we mean is variously the universal state of affairs *All A's are B's*, or the generic state of affairs *The A (in specie) is a B*, or the indefinitely singular state of affairs *Any A is a B* etc. We do not attend to the individual intuition, which perhaps accompanies our thought-presentations, and on which their evidence is founded: we do not attend to those act-characters which either give our intuition form, or which find their fulfilment in formed intuition. What we attend to are the *objects of our thinking*, the objects and states of affairs seen by thought in this or that manner, which are revealed to our insight when we perform such acts on such a foundation. And an abstraction in which we seize some point of conception or meaning, where we do not merely look to what is individual and intuitive (perceiving it attentively and what not), means no more than that we perform certain thought-acts with insight, acts sometimes of one form and sometimes of another.

The range of the unitary notion of attention is therefore so wide that it doubtless embraces the whole field of intuitive and cogitative *reference* (*Meinens*), the field of presentation (*Vorstellens*) in a well-defined but sufficiently wide sense, which comprehends both intuition and thought. Ultimately it extends as far as the concept: Consciousness of something. To talk distinctively of attention, as of a certain selectivity in the sphere of consciousness, takes account therefore of a certain difference which is not dependent on the species of our mode of consciousness (on the manner of our consciousness). We have certain 'presentations' while not 'concentrating' on their objects, but upon the objects of other presentations.

Attending is thus represented as a straightforward, not further describable *way* in which contents, otherwise lost in the undivided flow of consciousness, achieve separate consciousness, in which they are 'emphasized' or 'discovered' by us. If, in a similar sense, all differences in the manner of presentation are denied, attention is then seen as an illuminating and indicative function operating within *this* field. But all this involves an extreme narrowing of concepts whose wider meanings cannot be eliminated, and to which one must unavoidably have recourse. Dazed by the confusion between object and mental content, one forgets that the objects of which we are 'conscious', are not simply *in* consciousness as in a box, so that they can merely be found in it and snatched at in it; but that they are first *constituted* as being what they are for us, and as what they count as for us, in varying forms of objective intention. One forgets that, from the mere finding of a mental content, i.e. the pure immanent intuition of such a content, up to the external perception and imagination of objects neither found immanently in consciousness, nor capable of being so found, and from these on to the loftiest thought-formations with their manifold categorial forms and appropriately correlated semantic forms, an *essentially* single concept runs continuously: in all cases, whether we *intuit* in perceptual, fancying or remembering fashion, or whether we think in empirical and logico-mathematical forms, an intending, or reference (*Vermeinen*) is present, that *aims* at an object, a consciousness is present that is the consciousness *of* this object. The mere existence of a content in the psychic interplay is, however, not at all this being-meant or being-referred-to. This first arises when this content is 'noticed', such notice being a look directed towards it, a presentation of it. To define the presentation of a content as the mere fact of its being experienced, and in consequence to give the name 'presentations' to all experienced contents, is one of the worst conceptual distortions known to philosophy. It is without doubt responsible for an untold legion of epistemological and psychological errors. If we stick to the intentional concept of presentation, which alone sets a standard for epistemology and logic, we shall be unable to judge that all differences between presentations reduce to differences in their presented 'contents'. It is clear, on the contrary, and particularly in the field of pure logic, that *to each primitive logical form a peculiar 'manner of consciousness', a peculiar 'manner of presentation'*, corresponds. In so far, of course, as *each new mode of intentional reference always in a manner also concerns objects,* i.e. constitutes novel forms with which the object is brought to consciousness, one can no doubt say that all difference in presentation lies in what is presented. One must carefully note, however, that there are *two sorts of differences in the object, in what is presented,* differences of *categorial form* and differences in the '*thing itself*'; this 'thing' can be brought to consciousness *as* the same in a variety of forms. More will be said on these heads in later Investigations.

CHAPTER FOUR

Abstraction and Representation

---

§24 *The general idea as a device for economizing thought*

THERE is an error originating from mediaeval nominalism which likes to represent general concepts and names as *mere devices* in an economy of thinking, devices which will spare us the individual consideration and naming of all individual things. The function of concepts, it is said, is to enable the thinking mind to transcend the limits set it by the unsurveyable multiplicity of individual singulars; their economizations of thinking enable the mind to reach its goal of knowledge indirectly, as it could never have reached it directly. General concepts make it possible for us to treat things in bundles as it were, to make assertions about whole classes of objects at a single 'go'; we can therefore talk about countless objects, instead of conceiving and judging each object 'on its own'.

Locke brings this thought into modern philosophy when he says, e.g., in the last part of Book III, chapter III of his *Essay* . . . 'that men making abstract ideas, and settling them in their minds with names annexed to them, do thereby enable themselves to consider things, and discourse of them as it were in bundles, for the easier and readier improvement and communication of their knowledge; which would advance but slowly were their words and thoughts confined only to particulars.'[1]

This exposition reveals itself as nonsensical if one reflects that, without general meanings, one can make no assertions at all, not even such as are singular, and that one cannot talk of thinking, judging or knowing, in a sense relevant to logic, on a mere foundation of the direct presentations of individuals. The most ideal adaptation of the human mind to the multiplicity of individual

---

[1] Cf. also the end of the quotation in §9 of the present Investigation, p. 354. Among modern philosophers I may mention Rickert, 'Zur Theorie der naturwissenschaftlichen Begriffsbildung', *Vierteljahreschrift für wiss. Philos.* XVIII.

things, the genuine, effortless realization of adequate individual conceptions, would not render thought superfluous. For performances attainable in this manner are not performances of thinking.

Along intuitive pathways, e.g., no laws come to light. A knowledge of laws may very well promote the survival of thinking beings, it may usefully govern the formation of forward looking intuitive presentations, and may be much more useful in this respect than the natural pull of association. But the relation of the function of thought to the preservation of thinking beings, i.e. of human beings, has its place in psychological anthropology, not in the theory of knowledge. What is performed by a law as an ideal unity, its *logical* embrace of innumerable instances in a general propositional meaning, is something that no intuition can perform, not even the universal intuition of a God. For to intuit is plainly not to think. The perfection of thought lies doubtless in intuitive, i.e. in 'authentic' thinking, in that knowledge in which our thought-intention is 'satisfied' (as it were) by passing over into intuition. Even the brief discussions of the previous chapter permit us, however, to speak of a grave misinterpretation of this fact, when intuition – understood in the usual sense of acts of external or internal sense – is regarded as the proper intellectual function, and when the true role of conceptual thought is taken to be its use of indirect devices which economize intuition, and overcome the all too narrow limits of the latter. Certainly we are accustomed to using an all-seeing mind as a logical ideal, but only because we quietly add to its all-seeing capacities, capacities for knowing and thinking all. We imagine this mind as one not merely active in mere intuitions, i.e. in intuitions perhaps adequate but none the less unthinking, but as also casting these intuitions into categorial forms and combining them synthetically, and finding in such formed, combined intuitions the ultimate fulfilment of its thought-intentions, thereby realizing the ideal of all-inclusive knowledge. We shall, therefore have to say: Not mere intuition, but adequate, categorially formed intuitions, completely accommodated to thought, or conversely, thought which draws its evidence from intuition, constitute the goal of true knowledge. The 'economy of thought' only makes sense, and has its rich field within the sphere of thought and knowledge: it is in fact really an economy of knowledge.[1]

[1] Cf. the Prolegomena to Pure Logic, ch. ix.

§25 *Whether general representation can serve as an essential characteristic of our general presentations*

The notion just sketched of general concepts as thought-saving devices is more fully elaborated in the theory of *representation*. There are, it is held, really only intuitive, individual presentations, and in these all thinking is carried on. Need or comfort, however, leads us to substitute certain ideas to do duty for the presentations that we ought properly to have. The ingenious device of a *general representation which relates to a whole class* has the same results as if the proper presentations were present, or results rather in concentrated performances which sum up all the individual results that could ever be reached through actual presentation.

This doctrine, likewise, is naturally refuted by our previous objections. But the thought of representation plays a part, also, in doctrines of abstraction that attach little or no weight to the supposedly valuable thought-economies that such a representative function effects. It may be asked whether the thought of such a representation, freed from all doctrines of thought-economy, might not be of some use in characterizing the essence of general meanings. The word 'representation' has in any case a shifting multiplicity of senses. One could certainly say that the general name, or the individual intuition on which it reposes, serves to 'represent' the class. One must, however, see whether the various meanings of the word are not mutually confusing, and whether its use in a characterization does not promote confusion and definite error rather than clarity.

Our discussions have shown that the mark which distinguishes general presentations – whether we understand by these general meaning-intentions or the corresponding fulfilments of meaning – from intuitive individual presentations, can be no mere difference of psychological function, no mere difference in the part played by certain individual presentations of inner or outer sense in the continuous stream of mental life. We need not, accordingly, pay any further attention to expositions of the theory of representation merely as such a psychological function, and say nothing about the fundamental phenomenological fact, the new modes of consciousness responsible for the whole character of our individual experiences of general expression and thinking. This cardinal point may be touched on here and there in passing:

individual utterances show that the phenomenological facts are not wholly ignored. Such theorists would in most cases reply to our remonstrances that what we emphasize is, likewise, what they think. Naturally the representative function will reveal itself by way of some phenomenally peculiar character. A general presentation is thereby only an individual presentation, but one *tinged in a somewhat distinctive manner*: what is intuitively presented, when tinged in this fashion, counts as a *representative* of a whole class of mutually resembling individuals. Such a concession will not help much, if what is logically and epistemologically most important gets treated as a trivial addition to an individual intuition, making no important difference to the descriptive content of such an experience. The new type of act which animates word and illustrative image with thought, may not be wholly overlooked, but is not thought to require special descriptive interest directed upon itself: superficial talk of 'representation' is treated as quite sufficient. Men do not see that everything that relates to logic is summed up in this, and in similar characters of acts, that wherever we talk logically about 'presentations' and 'judgements' and about their manifold forms, acts of this sort alone determine our concepts. Men do not see that it is the immanent essence of such act-characters that makes them the consciousness of what is general, and that all types of intended generality which are of concern to pure logic, whether in its forms or its laws, only come to be given by way of corresponding forms of such intentional characters. Men also fail to see that while individual intuitions in a certain manner provide the basis for the novel acts of cogitative presentation that we build upon them – whether these be acts of 'symbolic' or of 'authentic' presentation – they themselves, with their own sensuous-intuitive intention, do not enter into the content of our thought at all, so that one simply does not have what talk of representation, in its prevailing sense, implies, the sense upheld by those who defend a theory of such representation.

§ 26 *Continuation. The varying modifications of the consciousness of generality, and the intuitions of sense*

A closer treatment will here be useful. Each new conception which gives to a name or an image a representative character is, we emphasized, a new type of presentative act; in the act of meaning (and not merely the act of general meaning) we achieve what, in relation to mere intuition, whether of 'outer' or 'inner sense', is a new mode of reference, with a sense, and also often with an object, quite different from those of the reference occurring in mere intuition. The content of this new reference varies (as we have already noted by the way)[1]; it undergoes multiple differentiation of its descriptive essence in accordance with the logical function of the general name, with the semantic context in which this name occurs, and which it helps to bring to expression. What is individually intuited is no longer simply referred to as it appears before us: but on one occasion we refer to the species in its ideal unity (the pitch C, the number 3, e.g.), on another, to the class as sum total of the individual items which share in a universal (all tones of this pitch, or, formally, all A's), on yet another, to an unspecified individual of this sort (an A), or coming from this class (one of the A's), and on yet another occasion to this intuited individual, but thought of as exhibiting the attribute (this A over here) etc. Each such modification alters the 'content' or 'sense' of our intention: there is, in other words, at each step, an alteration in our 'presentation' in the logical sense of this word, i.e. in the presented thing *as* it is logically grasped and meant. It does not matter whether our accompanying individual intuition remains constant or varies continually: the logical presentation changes if its meaning (the sense of our expression) changes, and stays the same as long as its meaning does so. We need scarcely stress the fact that the phenomenon which serves as basis for all this may drop out altogether.

The distinction between the cogitative and the sensuous 'conception' is one of essence. It is not like a case where, e.g., we conceive 'the same object' as at one time a wax-figure and at another time (caught in illusion) as a living person, as if two individually-intuitive 'conceptions' were merely being exchanged. Nor should we be led astray by the fact that our presentative intention in the form of a cogitative individual presentation, of a presentation of plurality and one of totality, can likewise be directed to individual items (to one, to several, or to all of a kind). It is indeed evident that the character of the intention, and with it that of the semantic content, differs totally from that of any intuitive (sensuous) presentation. To refer to *an A* is a different

---

[1] Above ch. III, §16.

thing from representing an A in simple intuition without the thought of *an A*, and a different thing again from referring to it in an act of direct meaning and naming, i.e. by way of proper names. The presentation *a man* differs from the presentation *Socrates*, and just so also the presentation *the man Socrates* differs from both of them. The presentation *some A's* is not a series of intuitions of these or those A's, not an act of collection which gathers previously presented individual intuitions together (though such a unification, with its objective correlate the aggregate, is an additional performance transcending the sphere of sensuous intuition). Where such a sum or collection of intuitions underlies our presentation and serves to exemplify it, we are not concerned with the individuals that appear before us, nor with the aggregate they form: what we mean is 'some A's', and this cannot be spied out by an external or even by an internal act of sense. The same naturally holds of other general meaning-forms, of number-forms, e.g., such as 'two' or 'three', or again of an exhaustively universal form such as 'all A's'. We have a presentation of exhaustive universality in the logical sense of this term whenever we understand the expression 'All A's' and apply it significantly. Exhaustive universality is therefore presented by way of a unitary thought; and it can only be brought to consciousness as exhaustive universality in this or in some corresponding 'authentic' form of thinking. For we can only intuit a this or a that. However many individual items we may run through, and however zealously we may collect them, we can at best – if we really have exhausted our concept's range of application – only have presentations of all A's, which would not mean that we had the presentation of *All A's*, that we had really achieved this logical presentation. If, however, we do achieve such a presentation, we may try to intuit its content, and may both hope for and achieve clarification by doing so. One sees, however, that a sensuous-intuitive assembling of the objects presented, in this case the sum total of the A's, cannot bring before us 'what we really meant'. Our thought-intention must rather, in virtue of the demands made by its form and its content, both relate to intuition and also fulfil itself in such intuition, thereby giving rise to a complex act, superior in clarity and insight, yet not dispensing with thought, nor replacing it with a mere picture.

These provisional, more or less superficial indications will have to suffice at this point. We shall have to clear up the distinction between thought and intuition, between presentation of an 'authentic' and a 'non-authentic' sort, by instituting a comprehensive set of analyses in the last Investigation in this book. In the course of these analyses a new notion of intuition will present itself, differing from the usual notion of sensuous intuition.

§ 27 The justifiable sense of general representation

After these discussions we might feel little inclined to be kind to the long-cherished talk of the representative function of general signs and intuitive pictures. This talk is so ambiguous that, especially in its common acceptation, it can contribute nothing toward an elucidatory characterization of the thought which is deployed in general forms.

Generality of presentation (*Vorstellung*) consists, it is held, in generality of representation (*Repräsentation*). If we could interpret the latter as the new modes of consciousness which we build on an intuitive basis, varying modifications in which the consciousness of generality is characterized as consciousness of the Species, consciousness of *all* cases, or as indefinite consciousness of a case or of *cases* etc., all would be in order. Talk of the representative function of an intuitive picture would to this extent be applicable, that the intuitive picture presents only one single individual from the species in question, but serves as *point d'appui* for the conceptual consciousness built upon this, so that through it the intention towards the Species, towards the total objective range of the concept, towards an unspecified individual of the sort in question, comes into being. The intuitive object could then itself be regarded and spoken of as being a representative of the Species, of the class, of the unspecified intended individual etc.

What holds of the illustrative intuitive picture holds also of names which function 'representatively' without illustrative aids. As the consciousness of meaning may be developed on an inadequate intuitive basis, which may be far from exemplifying properly, it may do so also on the basis of a mere name. That the name represents something, means only that its physical manifestation serves to carry the significant intention, in which the conceived object is intended.

Such a conception would exclude nominalism. Thought in its

view no longer reduces to any external manipulation of names and individual ideas, nor to unconscious associative mechanisms which cause individual items to jump up in their places, as numbers jump up from a computer. There exists for it a conceptual presentation which differs descriptively from an intuitive presentation (from a reference directly related to some phenomenal object before us): a reference of a fundamentally new sort, to which the forms *some X* or *some X's*, or *two* or *three*, or *something or other in general*, or *all* etc., essentially pertain. Among these forms is also one in which the *Species* is made to function as a *presented object*, and so as a subject for possible attributions and predications.

§28 *Representation as substitution. Locke and Berkeley*

Talk of general representation was not, however, given the sense expounded above – the only sense it can correctly have, though the name 'representation' does not fit it very well – in the historical treatment of abstraction. It rather meant that *the sign did duty for the thing signified*.

Locke had already made such substitution play an essential role in his doctrine of abstract ideas, and the theory of abstraction held by Berkeley and his successors took this over from Locke. We read, e.g., in Locke:[1]

> It is plain ... that general and universal belong not to the real existence of things; but are the inventions and creatures of the understanding, made by it for its own use, and concern only signs, whether words or ideas. Words are general ... when used for signs of general ideas, and so are applicable indifferently to many particular things: and ideas *are general when they are set up as the representatives of many particular* things ... their general nature being nothing but the capacity they are put into by the understanding, of *signifying or representing many particulars*; for the signification they have is nothing but a relation that by the mind of man is added to them.

Berkeley's lively attacks on Locke's theory of abstraction concern these 'abstract ideas'; but he transfers the representative functions which Locke accords to such ideas to our individual ideas at the moment or to general names in their own right. Let

---

[1] *Essay*, III.iii.11.

me recall the following passages from the Introduction to the
Principles of Human Knowledge:

> Now if we will annex a meaning to our words, and speak only of
> what we can conceive, I believe we shall acknowledge *that an idea*
> *which, considered in itself, is particular*, becomes general *by being made to*
> *represent or stand for all other particular ideas of the same sort.* To make
> this plain by an example, suppose a geometrician is demonstrating
> the method of cutting a line into two equal parts. He draws, for
> instance, a black line of an inch in length, this which in itself is a
> particular line is nevertheless *with regard to its signification general*,
> since, as it is there used, *it represents all particular lines whatsoever*: for
> what is there *demonstrated of it*, is demonstrated of all lines or, in
> other words, of a line in general. And as that particular line becomes
> general, by being *made a sign*, so the *name line* which taken absolutely
> is particular, by being a sign is made general. And as the former
> owes its generality, not to its being the sign of an abstract or general
> line, *but of all particular right lines that may possibly exist*, so the latter
> must be thought to derive its generality from the same cause,
> namely, the various particular lines which it indifferently denotes.[1]

> Universality, so far as I can comprehend, does not consist in the
> absolute, positive nature or conception of anything, but in the rela-
> tion it bears to the particulars signified or represented by it: by
> virtue whereof it is that things, names or notions, being in their
> own nature particular, are rendered universal.[2]

> But it seems that a word becomes general by being made the sign,
> not of an abstract general idea, but of several particular ideas, *any*
> *one of which it indifferently suggests to the mind.* For example, when it is
> said the *change of motion is proportional to the impressed force*, or that
> *whatever has extension is divisible*, these propositions are to be under-
> stood of motion and extension in general, and nevertheless it will
> not follow that they suggest to my thoughts an idea of motion
> without a body moved, or any determinate direction and velocity . . .
> it is only implied that, whatever motion I consider, whether it be

---

[1] Introduction, XII.

[2] 'Things or notions'. 'Things' for Berkeley, as is well-known, are no more than
complexes of 'ideas'. As regards his 'notions', they mean, at least in this place,
presentations relating to mind and its activities, or presentations where objects
'include' such activities as all relations do. These presentations, which Berkeley
separates and radically distinguishes from ideas of sense, and will not allow us to
call 'ideas', are therefore identical with Locke's ideas of reflection. Berkeley's
concept of a 'notion' can for the rest not be given a single exact and clear sense.

swift or slow, perpendicular, horizontal or oblique, or in whatever object, the axiom concerning it holds equally true. As does the other of every particular extension . . .[1]

§29 *Critique of Berkeley's Doctrine of Representation*[2]

Against these contentions the following objections are in place. No acceptable sense can be given to Berkeley's assertion that an individual idea is used to represent all other individual ideas of the same kind, in view of the normal meaning of the word 'represent'. We speak of something representing another where one object takes over performances (or undergoes performances) which another object would otherwise perform (or undergo). Thus the attorney who has been granted full powers represents his clients and carries out their business, the ambassador represents the ruler, the symbolic abbreviation represents the complex algebraical expression etc. We may, however, ask, in our case, whether the individual idea in its momentary life likewise functions representatively, whether it takes over a performance, which another individual idea, or perhaps every individual idea in its class, could properly be called on to perform? This certainly fits in with the plain letter of what Berkeley says, but there can be no question of its being true. Obviously we can only maintain that the performance which our present individual idea carries out *could as well* have been carried out by any other individual idea; each could have served as well as a basis for our abstraction, as an intuitive foundation for our general meaning. The thought of representation first arises from the *reflection* that each individual idea is equivalent in respect of this function, and that when one has been chosen, any other could replace it, and conversely. Wherever a general meaning is carried out intuitively, such a thought is possible, but it is not for that reason actual, above all since it presupposes the general concept that it is designed to replace. Individual ideas are therefore merely possible, not actual, representatives for other similar individual ideas.

But Berkeley takes representation seriously and takes his stand, on the one hand, on the sense of general assertions, on the other hand, on the part played by figures in geometrical proofs. The former applies to the above quotation from paragraph XI of the

[1] Introduction, xv.   [2] Introduction, XI.

Introduction of his *Principles*. If we judge that 'whatever is extended is divisible' we mean that whatever extended thing we may deal with will show itself to be divisible. The general name (or possibly the accompanying individual idea) represents, in conformity with the simple sense of our sentence, every individual extended thing, no matter which – the individual idea in question therefore 'suggests indifferently to the mind' every other individual idea which belongs to the class of extended things.

In all this Berkeley has confused two essentially different things:

1. That the sign (name or individual idea) is a representative of each individual falling within our concept's range, whose presentation Berkeley says that it suggests.

2. That the sign has as its meaning the sense *all A's* or *any A whatsoever*.

In regard to the latter there can be no question of representation in the sense of replacement. One or more A's may be suggested or presented with intuitive fullness, but the individual I look at (without intending to look at it) refers me to no other individual for which it serves as a substitute, let alone to every individual of the same kind. *All A's*, or every A whatsoever, are represented in a wholly different sense: they are *presented in thought*. We achieve the consciousness of *all A's* in a single pulse, in a homogeneous, peculiar act, in an act which has no components directed to all the individual A's, and which can neither be reconstituted nor replaced by a sum or combination of individual acts or individual suggestions. This act refers to each member of its range in virtue of its 'content', in virtue of its ideally seizable sense; it does not do so in a real (*realer*), but in an ideal, i.e. in a logical manner. What we assert of all A's, i.e. what we assert in a unitary sentence of the form '*All A's* are *B's*', obviously holds with *a priori* force of every A that definitely comes before me. An inference from universal to singular can be carried out in each given case, and the predicate B ascribed with logical correctness to A. The universal judgement does not for this reason include the particular judgement in itself, nor the general presentation the individual presentation that falls under it, or it does not do so in a psychologically or phenomenologically 'real' (*reell*) manner, and so not in the fashion of a bundle of 'representations'. The mere infinity of the range of all pure general concepts, i.e. concepts unmixed with empirical assertions of existence, such as Number, Spatial Figure, Colour, Intensity, shows such a misinterpretation to be nonsensical.

§30 Continuation. Berkeley's argument from geometrical demonstrations

Berkeley appeals in the second place to the *instance of the drawn line,* which assists the geometer in his proof. He here allows himself to be misled by his empiricist tendency to give preference to the sensuous individual case (or rather to the sensuous analogon of such an individual case) over genuine objects of thought: this tendency shows itself, here as elsewhere, in his treatment of the sensuous individual case, which lends support to mathematical thought, as the subject of his proof. As if we went through the proof to apply it to the stroke on paper, to the triangle chalked up on the board, and not to the straight line or the triangle 'as such' or 'in general'. This error has already been corrected above;[1] we have shown that the proof is not in reality conducted on behalf of the individual in the drawing, but has from the start a general application. It applies to all straight lines whatever, grasped in a single act of thought. Nothing is changed in all this by the geometer's mode of speech, when he enunciates his proposition generally and perhaps starts his proof with the words: 'Let *AB* be any straight line . . .' This does not at all mean that the proof is in the first instance performed for this single straight line *AB* (or for a particular ideal straight line that it represents), and that this single straight line then functions as representing every other straight line; it only says that *AB* must render presentable, through intuitive symbolism, an instance which then may serve to catch, as intuitively as possible, the thought of *a straight line in general,* which thought constitutes the true, the continuously pervasive theme of our logical context.

How little 'representation' helps to clear up the nature of general thought, appears from the question: What is the position of the general presentations that would have to appear for *the straight line on the paper* in the given proof? The intuitive data which correspond to them are surely not to be taken as objects of our demonstrative thought? For we should otherwise fail to set

[1] Cf. §20, p. 378. Cf. also Locke, *Essay,* IV, 1.9.

up a single proposition: we should have only representative individual ideas, but no thinking. Does anyone think that a conglomeration of such individual items can give rise to a predication? The function of a general name in the predicate certainly differs from its function in the subject, and its function varies, as noted above, according to our logical forms, to the forms of the thought-combinations into which our general meanings are welded, keeping a selfsame semantic nucleus, but varying with their varied syntactical functions (cf. the note to p. 371). How could all these forms, in which the make-up of 'thought' is as such manifest, or in which (to use objective language) the ideal essence of meaning is unfolded *a priori* (as the essence of number is unfolded in the forms of the numbers), how could one hope to cover all these matters by the one blanket phrase of 'representing'?

§31 *The main source of the errors that we have indicated*

One would be going too far were one to reproach Locke and Berkeley for altogether overlooking the descriptive difference between an individual idea, as part of an individual intention, and the same idea as part of a general intention (as serving to found a conceptual consciousness). One is assured, with many turns of phrase, that it is the 'mind' which gives such ideas their representative function, that it is the 'mind' that applies individual appearances as representatives; that all these mental activities are conscious activities, and so fall into the sphere of reflection, would certainly have been admitted by these great thinkers. Their fundamental epistemological errors or obscurities spring from a source that we have already laid bare:[1] in their phenomenological analysis, they stick almost exclusively to the intuitive individual, to the palpable side, as it were, of our thought-experiences, to names and illustrative intuitions, while they are quite unable to do anything with 'act-characters', since these are not at all 'palpable'. They therefore go on in quest of further sensuous details, and of sensuously presentable manipulations of such details, so as to give thought the sort of reality that they favour, and that flatly refuses to show itself in the actual phenomenon. They cannot bring themselves to take acts of thought for what

[1] §15, p. 368.

they show themselves in pure phenomenological examination; they cannot let them count as wholly new 'act-characters', as new modes of consciousness opposed to direct intuition. They cannot see what is quite plain to anyone who approaches the matter unconfused by traditional prejudices, that these 'act-characters' are modes of meaning, modes having this or that significant content, behind which nothing whatever may be looked for that either differs or could differ from meaning, significant reference.

What 'meaning' is, is a matter as immediately given to us as is the nature of colour and sound. It cannot be further defined, it is ultimate in description: whenever we perform or understand an act of expression, it means something to us, we have an actual consciousness of its sense. This understanding, meaning, enactment of sense, is not the hearing of the spoken word nor the experiencing of some contemporaneous image. Just as plainly as phenomenological differences between apparent sounds are self-evidently given to us, so are differences among meanings likewise self-evidently given. This is not of course the last word in the phenomenology of meanings, it is only its beginning. One will have, on the one hand, to pin down the distinction, fundamental for epistemology, between symbolical, 'empty' meanings and meanings having intuitive 'fulfilment', and one will have, on the other hand, to devote study to the essential kinds of meaning and to the modes in which meanings are combined. This is the sphere of actual meaning-analysis. Its problems are solved when we represent to ourselves the acts concerned and the things given in them. Pure phenomenological identification and distinction, combination and separation, as well as generalizing abstraction, will lead us on to the essential species and forms of meaning: one will get down, in other words, to the logically elementary concepts which are merely the idealized forms of primitive semantic differences.

Instead, however, of analysing meanings phenomenologically in order to determine the basic forms of logic, or instead, conversely, of becoming clear that the basic forms of logic are merely the typical characters of our acts and their forms of combination (in the build-up of complex intentions), people engage in *logical analysis in the ordinary sense of the word*, they consider what these meanings objectively intend, and then seek what is thus objectively meant as something really present in the act. One thinks *in* meanings and not *about* meanings: one concerns oneself with states of affairs presented or judged about, not with their presentations and judgements (i.e. not with nominal and propositional meanings). One claims and thinks that one has carried out a descriptive analysis of acts, though the territory of reflection has been long left, and *objective* has been substituted for phenomenological analysis. Even purely logical analysis is objective when it investigates 'what is contained *in our mere concepts or meanings*', i.e. what must be attributed *a priori* to objects, in so far as these are thought of in such forms. The act-analysis of meaning investigates 'what is contained in our meanings' in a totally different sense. Here alone such a mode of expression is appropriate: meanings are reflected upon and made objects of investigation, their real *parts* and *forms* are enquired into, not what is true of their objects. The manner in which Locke arrives at his doctrine of general ideas and, among other things, at his doctrine of representation: the manner, likewise, in which Berkeley applies and defends this doctrine, and especially his approach to the meaning of general propositions – cf. his analyses of the examples quoted on p. 395 from paragraph XI of the *Introduction* to the *Principles* – merely confirm what we have said.

CHAPTER FIVE

Phenomenological Study of Hume's
Theory of Abstraction

§32 *Hume's dependence on Berkeley*

ONE need not nowadays stress the fact that Hume's conception of abstraction is not at all the same as Berkeley's.[1] Nonetheless, the two notions are so closely akin, that it is quite comprehensible that Hume at the start of his exposition in Part I, Section VII of the *Treatise*, should have gone so far as simply to attribute his thesis to Berkeley. 'A great philosopher,' he tells us,

> has disputed the received opinion ... and has asserted that all general ideas are nothing but particular ones annexed to a certain term which gives them a more extensive signification, and makes them recall upon occasion other individuals which are similar to them ... I look upon this to be one of the greatest and most valuable discoveries that has been made of late years in the republic of letters.

This is plainly not quite Berkeley's view, who does not, like Hume, want to attribute to general names the primary power of making individual presentations that accompany them into representations of other individual presentations of the same class. On Berkeley's view, general names may function representatively in isolation from corresponding individual presentations, individual presentations may also function representatively without names, and both may, lastly, occur together, in which case, however, the name has no special advantage in its association with the representative presentation. Nonetheless the main point remains the same; generality consists in representation, and this is expressly conceived by Hume as a 'doing duty' by an individual item before us for other individual items, which, in Berkeley's

[1] Cf. Meinong's *Hume Studien*, I, 36 (218).

402

mode of expression, are mentally 'suggested' by the former, or in Hume's straight phrase, are *recalled to memory*.

Hume is accordingly hit by all our objections to Berkeley, and more severely hit, since in Berkeley the literal treatment of representation, and of the evocation of represented individual presentations, still floats in obscure suspense, whereas in Hume it appears with unveiled sharpness and clearness.

§33 *Hume's critique of abstract ideas and its supposed outcome.* *His ignoring of pivotal phenomenological issues*

The spirit of Berkeley's doctrine therefore lives on, as regards its main features, in Hume. Hume, however, does not merely re-produce this doctrine but extends it further: he tries to elaborate it more exactly and especially to deepen it *psychologically*. In this regard the arguments Hume directs against the doctrine of abstract ideas are not so important as the associationist-psychological discussion that he appends to them. The arguments in question do not go essentially beyond Berkeley's circle of ideas, and are, for one that fixes the aim of the proof correctly, quite irrefragable. The impossibility of abstract ideas *in the sense of Locke's philosophy*, i.e. of abstract images formed by disengaging ideas of properties from concrete images, has certainly been proved. Hume himself sums up his result in the proposition: 'Abstract ideas are therefore in themselves individual, however they may become general in their representation. The image in the mind is only that of a particular object; though the application of it in our reasoning be the same as if it were universal.'[1] *These* propositions could naturally not be proved by Hume's critique which showed abstract images to be impossible, and which tried to conclude from this that, if we nonetheless speak of general ideas, ideas belonging to general names as their meanings or meaning-fulfilments, something must be added to our concrete images to create such generality of meaning. This added element – so the discussion *should* properly have continued – cannot con-sist in new concrete ideas, and therefore not in the ideas of names: a conglomeration of concrete images can do no more than present just those objects whose images it contains. We must not overlook the fact that generality of meaning – whether this be

[1] *Treatise*, I, VII.

generality of meaning-intention or generality of meaning-fulfil-ment – is something *felt* as immanent in *each individual case* where a general name is understood, and is applied to intuition in accord-ance with its sense, and that it is something which, in immediately evident fashion, distinguishes such a case from an individual intuition. It only, therefore, remains to argue that it must be the *manner* of consciousness, the *manner* of our intention, that makes the difference. A new type of reference makes its appearance, in which we neither mean the intuitively apparent object as such, nor the object of our verbal idea, nor that of our accompanying thing-idea, but the quality or form exemplified in the latter, which we understand in general fashion as a unity in the sense of a Species.

Hume, however, remains attached to Berkeley's thought of representation, and externalizes it completely. Instead of looking to the semantic character of meaning-intention and meaning-fulfilment, he loses himself in the genetic connections which give names an associative relation to the objects of a class. He quite fails to mention, and does not see with operative lucidity, that generality evinces itself in our subjective experience, and, as previously stressed, in each single enactment of a general meaning. Still less does he note, that what is here evinced exhibits sharp descriptive differences: that our consciousness of 'generality' at one time takes on a generic character, at another time a character of universal application, or that it becomes otherwise tinged in virtue of this or that 'logical form'.

Modes of consciousness, acts in the sense of *intentional* experi-ences, certainly cause discomfort to a psychology and epistemology of 'ideas', which aims at reducing everything to 'impres-sions' (sensations), and associative concatenations of 'ideas' (images, the enfeebled shadows of 'impressions'). I recall here Hume's vain efforts over *belief*, and how he repeatedly has recourse to treating this character of our acts as an intensity, or as an analogue of intensity, in our ideas. 'Representation', likewise, must in some manner be reduced to something seizable. This is what a genetic-psychological analysis must achieve: it must show how, in our judgements, we come to apply the mere individual image that we experience, '*beyond its own nature*', and '*as if* it were general'.

This last-mentioned turn of speech shows, to an extraordinary extent, the characteristic obscurity of Hume's position. With his 'as if', Hume fundamentally concedes to his great predecessor Locke that his theory of general ideas – *if* such ideas were possible – would achieve its purpose. He does not perceive that Locke's general ideas, as fragments torn from concrete contents, would themselves again be individual singulars, and that the fact that they were inseparable from other similar ideas (whether torn from or immanent in concrete ideas) would not yet endow them with the generality of thought. He does not perceive that peculiar acts, peculiar manners of referring or meaning, are necessary to do all this. Even if we accept Lockean abstracta, we still need the form of thought about 'all' in order to intend an infinite range of individual singulars not really presented. The self-identical unity of the genus was likewise first set up for consciousness by an act of generic thinking, and so on. An objective relation of exact similarity, that exists, yet is not subjectively revealed, will obviously not alter the single similar individual set before consciousness: only *thought* can give this individual a thought-relation to such a circle of similars.

§34 *Reduction of Hume's investigation to two questions*

If we now cast a glance at the content of Hume's psychological analyses, we can express what he hoped to achieve in the two following questions:

1. How does the individual idea come by its representative function? Through what psychological processes does it become capable of functioning as a substitute for other similar ideas, and ultimately for every possible idea of the same class?

2. The same individual idea fits into many circles of similarity, though in each *definite* thought-context it only represents ideas from *one* such circle. What circumstance picks out this circle of representation in a given context, what limits the representative function of the individual idea in this manner and so makes unity of sense possible?

It is clear that these psychological questions retain their good sense if one here drops the guiding concept of representation, and substitutes for it the well-understood, genuine concept of a general presentation as being an act of general meaning or meaning-fulfilment (cf. general intuition in the sense of Investigation VI, §52). That general presentations have emerged genetically out of intuitive, individual ones is generally accepted. But though the consciousness of the universal is repeatedly kindled by individual intuition, and derives clarity and self-evidence from the latter, it is not therefore a direct product of individual intuition. How then did we ever manage to go beyond individual intuition, to mean something quite other than the singular phenomenon before us, a universal instantiated in the latter, and yet not really contained in it? And how did we get all those forms which diversify the objective relations of the universal, and constitute differing logical kinds of presentation? If associative connections are now brought in to explain this, we are at once introduced to dispositional groups of similars and the signs we externally attach to them. This makes the second question a real one, how the circles of similars can maintain their fixed internal coherence, and not be mutually confounded in our thinking.

In this situation we do not contradict ourselves if, on the one hand, we say Hume's treatment of abstraction was an extreme case of error, and yet vindicate for it the glory of having shown the way to a psychological theory of abstraction. It is an extreme case of error from the angle of logic and epistemology, for which it is important that experiences of knowing should be investigated in a purely phenomenological manner, that acts of thought should be treated as what they intrinsically are and contain in themselves, so that we may bring clearness to the fundamental concepts of knowledge. Hume's genetic analyses certainly cannot claim theoretical completeness and finality, since they lack a foundation in an adequate descriptive analysis. This does not, however, mean that they do not contain valuable trains of thought, which could not escape notice and have also had a fruitful effect.

On his complete lack of a strictly descriptive analysis of thinking (or on his substitution of empirical-psychological for epistemological investigations) the further fact depends that Hume likewise imagines that to think of thought as having an economical function in knowledge yields a standpoint from which thought can be epistemologically illuminated. In this regard Hume is the true pupil of Locke and his philosophy. The objections to this point of view have been sufficiently canvassed in a previous section (§24).

§35 *The guiding principle and outcome of Hume's doctrine of abstraction and the main thoughts in which it is worked out*

The *guiding* principle of Hume's psychological exposition is stated in the following words: 'If ideas be particular in their nature, and at the same time finite in number, 'tis only by custom they can become general in their representation, and contain an infinite number of other ideas under them.' Hume's conclusion runs as follows: 'A particular idea becomes general by being annexed to a general term, that is to a term which from a customary conjunction has a relation to many other particular ideas, and readily recalls them in the imagination.'

The main thoughts in which this doctrine is worked out are set forth in the quotation:

> The application of ideas beyond their nature proceeds from our collecting all their possible degrees of quantity and quality in such an imperfect manner as may serve the purposes of life ... When we have found a resemblance among several objects that often occur to us, we apply the same name to all of them, whatever differences we may observe in the degrees of their quantity and quality, and whatever other differences may appear among them. After we have acquired a custom of this kind, the hearing of that name revives the idea of one of these objects, and makes the imagination conceive it with all its particular circumstances and proportions. But as the same word is supposed to have been frequently applied to other individuals, that are different in many respects from that idea which is immediately present to the mind, the word not being able to revive the idea of all these individuals, only touches the soul, if I may be allowed so to speak, and revives that custom which we have acquired by surveying them. They are not really and in fact present to the mind, but only in power: nor do we draw them all out distinctly in the imagination, but keep ourselves in a readiness to survey any of them, as we may be prompted by a present design or necessity. The word raises up an individual idea, along with a certain custom; and that custom produces any other individual one for which we may have occasion. But as the production of all the ideas, to which the name may be applied is in most cases impossible, we abridge that work by a more partial consideration, and find but few inconveniences to arise in our reasoning from that abridgement.[1]

[1] *Treatise*, Book I, §7.

These quotations may serve to recall the gist of Hume's theory with sufficient completeness for our purposes. We need not here proceed to analyse them critically, since genetic problems fall outside the limits of our task.

§36 Hume's doctrine of the distinctio rationis in its moderate and its radical interpretation

Of particular interest for us is Hume's doctrine of the *distinctio rationis*, which also indirectly yields an answer to the second question formulated above. The question is how we are able to distinguish abstract 'moments' from intuitive objects: the former can of course be made into ideas in their own right, i.e. not through an abstraction in the Lockean sense of a separation. How do we rise to a distinction between the *white sphere* we have just intuited and *whiteness* (or sphericity), since 'whiteness' and 'sphericity' cannot count as ideas in the Lockean sense, which are contained in the concrete idea as particular parts separable from it. Berkeley had answered this question by pointing to the emphatic power of attention. Hume here attempts to penetrate further, and provides the following solution:

If we compare a white sphere with a black sphere and on the other hand with a white cube, we notice two differing resemblances. Through repeated comparisons of this sort, objects sort themselves out for us into 'circles of resemblance' and ever strengthening habits teach us to *consider each object 'in different aspects'*, according to the resemblances that permit its placing in different, but definite circles. That in one case we direct our gaze to colour only, does not mean that we have separated colour, but that we accompany what is in fact a unitary and indivisible presentation *'with a kind of reflection, of which custom renders us in a great measure insensible'*. In this obscure consciousness, a white cube perhaps floats before us, and so brings out a resemblance (i.e. that in respect of colour) to which we turn our inner gaze, so that the white sphere we perceive is only given a place in the resemblance-circle of colour. According to the manner of this reflection (or the resemblances that govern it), a different 'moment' in the same intuitive object is noted; or, what is in essence the same, the same intuition serves as a basis for the so-called abstraction of general presentations. With each circle of resemblance a particular name is associatively linked, so that the inner reflection, together with its characteristic 'angle' of treatment, also fixes the general name.

We are not here engaged in psychological research, and it is not therefore for us to set forth critically what is good, and what is also crude, in such a theoretical attempt. Up to a point, however, we must consider it, in view of a paradoxical thought that seems to have inspired Hume's exposition, which modern Humeans have been the first to profess in undisguised crudity. This thought can be expressed as follows:

Characters, inner properties, are not truly immanent in the objects that 'have' them. The distinct, mutually inseparable 'sides' or 'moments' of an intuitive content, e.g. its colour, form etc., that we think we apprehend as being 'there' (*vorhanden*) in it, are not really in it at all. There are rather only one kind of real parts, the parts, namely, that we can also isolate, in other words, the thing's *pieces*. So called abstract part-contents, of which it is said that they can indeed not *be* on their own account, (or be so intuited), but that they can be attended to by themselves, are to some extent a mere fiction *cum fundamento in re*. There is neither colour in a coloured thing, nor form in a thing formed, but there are really only circles of resemblances in which the object in question has its place, and certain *habits* tied to our intuition of it.

Considered more carefully, our doubt certainly is twofold; it is both objective and subjective. Objectively, it concerns the *objects* apparent before us in regard to their intrinsic *properties*, subjectively it concerns the *appearance itself* (taken as immanent experience) in relation to its inner load of sensation and sensuous content in general, i.e. to the contents which receive objectifying 'interpretation' (apperception) in our act of intuition. It is in the 'interpretation' that the appearance of the corresponding objective characters or properties is realized. On the one hand, therefore, we are concerned with the *sphere itself* and its inner properties, e.g. its uniform white colouring: on the other hand we are concerned with the *appearance of the sphere* and the complex of sensations immanent in it, among which is, e.g., the continuously graded sensation of white – the subjective correlate of the objective white which is uniformly apparent in perception. Here as elsewhere, Hume left this difference quite unnoticed; for him appearance and the apparent phenomenon coalesce.

I am not really sure whether I have hit off Hume's own view in the theses formulated above; perhaps he only means, as against the Lockeans, that the concrete object is quite simple in respect of its characters, simple in the sense that *we cannot break it up into such characters*, though these characters as 'corresponding features' still are something really present in individual objects of the same sort. If this interpretation is right, Hume agrees with Berkeley on the matter, and only goes on to give a psychological elucidation of the manner in which the *distinctio rationis* comes into being.

Plainly the problem has a good sense, even if one holds abstract 'moments' to be genuinely immanent. One may ask how individual properties, which can only appear in the most intimate mutual penetration, and never in isolation, can nonetheless become exclusive objects of intuitions or of thought-intentions. What explanation can there be in the former case of that preferential attention which dispenses its favouring notice to differing properties at different times?

§37 *Objections to this doctrine in its radical interpretation*

The objections raised by a moderate interpretation of Hume's statement need not be considered here: psychological interests should not lure us from our cause. We need only say that Hume's thoughts, suitably modified, provide a basis on which a workable theory may very well be built. One need not, above all, take his mythical 'inner reflection' seriously. G. E. Müller (in the dictated notes published by F. Schumann)[1] has worked out the Humean theory more closely, with very great clearness and penetration, and though he himself prefers the radical interpretation, his restatement nonetheless plainly shows the fruitfulness of Hume's germinal suggestions.

Let us now turn to criticism of the radical interpretation of Hume's doctrine. It occupies a central place in our sphere of epistemological interest. The difficulties in which consistent development involves it, are not small.

If the abstract contents which correspond to the absolute properties are themselves simply 'nothing' in concrete intuition, associative and relational contents will even be more absolutely 'nothing' in our intuition of an aggregate with the corresponding

---

[1] F. Schumann, 'Zur Psychologie der Zeitanschauung', *Zeitschrift für Psychologie und Physiologie der Sinnesorgane*, Bd. 7, pp. 107 *ff.*

form of unity. The problem of the *distinctio rationis*, and the principle of its solution, is plainly one and the same for *all* abstract contents. It is therefore the same for relational and associative contents as for absolute contents. One cannot therefore answer questions as to the way in which colour was seemingly found in, or distinguished in (or from) a coloured object, by having recourse to the finding of a similarity between the coloured object and other coloured objects. Since such a finding would, if the explanation is consistently pursued, lead to the finding of a similarity of this similarity with other similarities (in the case or colour, to a group of similar *similarities* such as subsist among coloured objects). The explanatory principle would again have to be applied to this further similarity, and so on.

This argument carries over from abstract *contents*, understood as really experienced (*reell erlebte*) moments in the unity of a concrete intuition, to presentations of properties and modes of composition in 'external' objects. We therefore make use of a distinction which we emphasized against Hume, a distinction between concrete intuition, as the really (*reell*) present appearance or givenness of the object (as experience), and the *object* intuited (perceived, imagined etc.). We must here note that nothing scientifically or metaphysically transcendent should be substituted for this object; by 'the object' we meant the object as it *appears* in *this* intuition, as it *counts* (so to say) *for* this intuition. To the sphere's *appearance* or givenness the apparent *sphere* therefore stands opposed. Just so to the *sensed contents* of the sphere's appearance (moments phenomenologically discoverable by descriptive analysis), the perceived, or imagined parts or sides of the apparent *sphere* stand opposed: to the *sensation* of white, e.g., the sphere's apparent whiteness.

All this having been granted, we may say: Should anyone wish to declare *all* talk of the intuitive presentation of abstract, objective determinations to be senseless, and to maintain that when we think we perceive, e.g., the property of white, we really only perceive, or otherwise present to ourselves, a resemblance between the apparent object and other objects, then such a man has involved himself in an infinite regress, since talk of this presented resemblance calls for a corresponding reinterpretation.

We here at once see the absurdity of the conception we are criticizing in the fact that, in the face of all self-evidence, an object self-evidently different from our intentional object has been substituted for it. The thing comprised in my intuition's intention, the thing I think that I am grasping perceptually or constructing imaginatively, stands by and large above all dispute. I may be deceived as to the existence of the object of perception, but not as to the fact that I do perceive it as determined in this or that way, that my percept's target is not some totally different object, a pine-tree, e.g., instead of a cockchafer. This *self-evidence in characterizing description* (*or in identification and distinction of intentional objects*), has, no doubt, its understandable limits, but it is true and genuine self-evidence. Without it even the far-famed self-evidence of *inner perception* (introspection), with which it is usually confused – wherever, that is, 'inner perception' is understood as the perception of intentional experience – would be wholly useless: when expressive talk begins, and the descriptive distinction of inwardly perceived experiences is carried out, this self-evidence is presupposed, since the distinction and description of intentional experiences without regard to their intentional objects is impossible.[1]

This self-evidence helps us at this point. There is a self-evident difference between intuiting this object's redness and intuiting any relation of resemblance. If the latter intuition is relegated to the unnoticed or the unconscious, one merely adds to one's malaise, since one is sacrificing the self-evidently given intention in favour of what is unobservable.

Our previous discussion runs over into our present discussion of apparent *objects*, to the extent that *contents* become perceived *objects* for reflective phenomenological analysis. Though we would not and should not call the appearance of the sphere (*qua* experience) a thing, nor call its abstract, immanent contents properties or characters, the descriptive situation as regards the points here relevant remains the same. The differences between thing and property are ontological differences, not characters of experience. They correspond to nothing in the phenomenon momentarily given, they are not real moments entering into this phenomenon and discoverable in it. They point rather to combinations of conscious experiences in which they appear conjointly, in which we have experience of them and can pin them down scientifically. Surveying this whole situation, we can appeal to the self-

[1] Cf. the note at the end of this section.

evidence which holds for the distinction of intentional objects in general in the special case of the intentional distinction of interior data. In this limiting case, where the object meant itself belongs to the real content of the experience (taken in its complete concreteness), the self-evidence of 'inner' perception comes into action; we do not merely have a self-evidence as to the difference of our intended data, but self-evidence as to their actual existence. When we direct our analytic interest not so much to the apparent sphere as to the sphere's appearance (*qua* experience), and distinguish parts or sides in *the latter*, while deliberately not noticing what such sensed contents mean, it is not merely self-evident that our colour-content, our total content etc. is perceived, it is also self-evident that it really exists. We may not always be successful in ignoring meaning, nor in carrying the analysis of experienced contents as far as one might wish; broadly and roughly, however, both may be achieved. Just as the self-evident difference of our intentional objects is not shaken by the fact that we may readily deceive ourselves regarding our intentions once we leave the sphere of grosser differences – just as the difference between a cockchafer and a pine-tree (both taken purely as they announce themselves to consciousness, intentional objects of our intentions) has genuine self-evidence – so there is a genuine self-evidence by which we often know that a colour-moment, a sensation, is really *there* in our unitary intuition, that it helps to build up the latter, and that it is quite different from the moment of shape that is likewise present. The situation is not affected by the fact that the separation of these moments, their independent being without inherence or being possessed, is unthinkable.

One does not do justice to this self-evident situation if one says: 'Certain mental events exist in themselves, certain unnoticed arousals of series of similars, which impart a certain character to the absolutely simple concrete things in question, a certain colouring, a Jamesian "fringe".' In the first place such 'fringes' have their reality quite as much as the supposed unconscious events, which are in any case wholly irrelevant for pure phenomenology. In the second place, 'fringes' are mere appendages which may equally well be present or absent. If we therefore identify these supposed 'fringes' with the moments self-evidently noticed in the concrete thing, these 'fringes' would all become mere appendages of a carrier, a carrier quite of the type of the wonderful, featureless 'substance' that no one any longer takes seriously.

The self-evident fact that the sensory moments, the colour-moment, the shape-moment and other immanent determinations, really belong to the unity of intuition, are moments making it up, cannot in any manner be interpreted away. One can no doubt explain them as the results of certain fusions, as products really but unnoticeably embracing their factors, but, however interesting this may be from the psychological standpoint, it does not affect our immediate descriptive findings, which alone have relevance for the clarification of our concepts and acts of knowing. Theoretically to conjure abstract contents, and with them abstract concepts, out of existence, is to try to expose as fictions, what we really presuppose in all insight, whether in our thoughts or our proofs.

Possibly one may defer to hypercritical doubts, and object that a *distinctio rationis* is only given by way of a judgement. On one side stands the absolutely unitary phenomenon, to which our assertion accedes, attributing inner differences to it, which do not prove that the phenomenon really *has* inner differences.

We should reply: obviously where we pass judgement on an experience, two things are present, the experience and our assertion. The assertion, however, may be correct, and it is correct when accompanied by *insight*. If one wants to approve a case as valid where containment is genuinely given and experienced, one can only do so on the basis of self-evidence. If ever self-evidence spoke for such a containment, it certainly does so in the present case. The notion of containment should not be unnecessarily restricted, not restricted, i.e. to the concept of articulation into discrete 'pieces'. If one keeps to this narrower concept the word is rendered inapplicable, but the fact is still clear.

Notes

1. We encountered a line of thought similar to the one just dealt with on a previous occasion.[1] We there dealt with the question whether Species could be treated as objects, whether it was not more correct to say that there are in reality only individual objects, variously ordered according to their similarities. But in our last discussions we were not dealing with Species but with

[1] Cf. ch. 1 of this Investigation.

their instances. There is not merely a denial that one can speak of Red in general as an object of thought, but also that one can speak of an instance of red, of red as a 'moment' of an intuition which occurs here and now. We could not achieve the self-evident consciousness of generality, in which the Species is (as it were) given in person, if the instance, whose intuitive givenness is presupposed in the actual performance of abstraction, were reinterpreted in relativistic fashion. The parallel arguments are therefore essentially connected.

2. I note subsequently that A. von Meinong, in his valuable essay 'Über Gegenstände höherer Ordnung und deren Verhältnis zur inneren Wahrnehmung' (which unfortunately appeared too late to be of assistance to me in these *Logical Investigations*) has devoted some discussion to the relation between the self-evident recognition of immanent objects and inner perception (*Zeitsch. f. Phil. u. Psych. d. S.* Bd. 21, Section 2, p. 205 *ff.*). If I understand him rightly, Meinong makes the former case of self-evidence coincide with that of the inner perception relating *to the existence of the presentation concerned*. In that case he cannot have meant the self-evidence that we meant in the text. That the so-called immanent object is not in a serious sense an object in our presentation (as Twardowski still put it),[1] is naturally my definite opinion too: on the side of the presentation nothing exists but the reference-to-this-object, the significant scope (*Bedeutungsgehalt*), as it were, of the presentation. But the self-evidence of the fact that I mean a pine-tree in my presentation of *pine-tree*, a tree of a sort determined by such and such features, and not possibly a cock-chafer or anything else – is not what can be attributed to a mere percept, even to one relating to the mere experience of presentation. One is here dealing with the self-evidence of assertions, whose complex meaning-intention is fulfilled on a basis of numerous acts, of numerous presentations, and of identifications and differentiations which connect them. Even if we ignore the acts to be found on the intentional side, it is quite impossible to make do with mere acts of inner perception in the case of fulfilment. The inner perception of the acts of identification and differentiation just mentioned is obviously not adequate to account for the self-evident subsistence of identities and differences.

---

[1] In the treatise that I have repeatedly criticized above, but which is nonetheless a most careful and thorough work.

§38 *Transference of our scepticism from abstract part-contents*
to all parts whatsoever

Scepticism in regard to abstract part-contents is paralleled by
possible scepticism in regard to concrete part-contents, i.e.
'pieces'. A homogeneous white surface we take to be a divisible
object; all parts that can be distinguished by us in actual division
are treated as pre-existent parts in the surface. This practice we
carry over to the case of sensation. The contents we actually
experience in dealing with the white surface are bits analogously
related to the total content as the objective bits of the surface are
to the total surface. If it is pointed out that, in the intuitive
presentation of the surface, we 'allow our glance to glide over it',
thereby experiencing a multitude of continuously differing
contents, we are not at a loss. We simply transfer our conception
to each such content.

But how do we know that the content is really composite? If
we imagine divisions in the unbroken white surface, the corresponding sense-content may really exhibit connected parts, but
such imaginative intrusions do not leave our original content
unaltered. The complex, discontinuously fragmented content we
now have is not the same as the original, quite single, inwardly
undivided one. 'The parts, into which one can think such a unity
broken up, are fictitious parts.'[1] Certain activities of imagination
and judgement have been superimposed on an indivisible content
of consciousness, and what the former produce we credit to the
latter.

Doubt grips us further, if we turn to consider a case, at first
unassailed, where the intuitive content already exhibits divisions.
Does our experience in such a case not first offer us a certain
unitary content, that we afterwards say is compounded of parts,
and is our saying this not due to a prior performance of certain
novel operations? We pay attention, it is commonly said, now to
one part, now to another, and now to yet another part of *the*
content. But with each step our experience alters. Our tendency
to confuse sense-contents with perceived or imagined objects,
makes us substitute quite different contents for our original
content at each step. The part we are attending to at the moment
not merely lies in our focus of attention but also, more literally,

[1] F. Schumann, *Z. f. Psych.* Vol. 17, p. 130

in our focus of vision, and so yields sensations differing from those that it yields when remaining in the background. Keeping more strictly to contents, we may say that the content we momentarily pick out is surrounded only by an obscure, wholly chaotic mass, a fringe, a penumbra, or however one may wish to name the unnameable. It is not separated from the latter, but 'inwrought' with it. As one passes from part to part, the situation remains generally the same, though always differing in content: this is the case even when we do not let our glance wander. It would be a crude account of the descriptive situation were one to speak of this or that indirectly seen part (or of the corresponding experiential part) as if it were merely made individually noticeable in an identical unity of content, without suspicion of accompanying changes in the experience itself. Here, as in the case of abstract contents, genetic grounds point to certain connections in past experience which render selective notice possible, and whose effects are also shown in other facts of consciousness. What we see indirectly operates as a sign for anything coming from a sphere of similars bounded by past experience: the emphasis of attention involves, further, an interpretation, and with this, generally a change in content (an 'elaboration in fancy').

But if we object that repeated revival and comparison of experienced contents teaches us that it is right to talk of a division even in the case of such contents, the sceptic may well point to the abiding illusions to which such comparisons are subject, to the confusions between apparent things and experienced contents, between comparisons of objects and comparisons of contents etc.

§39 *The extreme limit of scepticism and its refutation*

If we persist in this sceptical direction, we shall have to doubt whether there are parts of any sort; and in consequence whether there is ever a plurality of concrete contents, since ultimately (if we may still presume to judge the matter) the contents which appear in co-existence and succession are always in a manner unified. Our scepticism would at length be crowned by the assertion: consciousness is something quite unitary, regarding which we can at least not *know*, whether it has partial contents at all, or whether it in any way unfolds itself in simultaneous or temporally successive experiences.

Such a scepticism, it is plain, would render all psychologies impossible.[1] How one must combat it need not be said after our previous explanations. Whatever the flux of immanent phenomena, it does not rule out the possibility of first grasping these phenomena in vague but quite clear concepts (clear because directly formed on an intuitive basis), and then, based on such concepts, of making many decisions, rough in fact but *self-evident*, which are quite enough to render psychological research possible.

As regards the white surface – I am not here referring to the white surface itself, treated as a thing, but to the 'conscious content' – we see very well how it changes, but also how, despite all such changes, it stays alike, even identical. The boundaries added by imagination do not constitute its pieces originally; they merely *bound* them. It is self-evident to us that these pieces really were present in the unity of the content 'white surface'. The content, held without boundaries in an identical intention, coincides with the same content changed only by such imagined boundaries; the two coincide in respect of the outlined parts. The parts were, and always are, in the whole, not however as separated unities in their own right. A certain fluctuation and flux of contents, the uncertainty, even the impossibility, of keeping them just the same, does not destroy the self-evidence of these judgements. Like all *purely* descriptive judgements passed on intuitive data as such in a faithfully 'expressive' manner, they hold within a certain range of variability, with a certain index, therefore, of vagueness.[2] Naturally we only adduce examples where all relationships exhibit *gross* differences, and so really fall within the sphere of the gross self-evidence spoken of above.

Self-evidence is also present if we proceed in the opposite direction, and remove in thought a fragmentation that is actually present. If a surface divides into a white and a red section, then, if there are merely qualitative changes, the identity of the two extended parts is maintained. If we now think of the white of the one, and the red of the other, as shading continuously into one another, both parts now coalesce in an inwardly undivided unity. But however this may come about, the result is evidently not an

---

[1] If I am right, Schumann is drifting towards such a scepticism in his endeavour, praiseworthy in itself, towards maximum strictness and freedom from presuppositions.

[2] Closer investigations are undoubtedly required here.

absolutely simple unity, but a homogeneous one, in which alone all inner separations have been blurred. The parts are self-evidently there, but, though each part has its own quality and every condition of concreteness, it still lacks qualitative discontinuity to set itself off, and with this the character of shutting itself off from the parts which melt into it.

If we make empirical concepts and relations into precise ones, if we frame ideal concepts of extension, surface, qualitative alikeness and continuity etc., we arrive at exact, *a priori* propositions which set forth what is founded on the intentions of such strict concepts. Compared with these, merely descriptive assertions are inexact approximations. Though the vague sphere of singular phenomenal individuality in general, does not fall within the sphere of exact knowledge (which operates merely with ideals), it is none the less not at all excluded from the general sphere of knowledge.

From this we see also the stand we must take up against doubts which go further, and which lead ultimately to the denial of all parts and differences. In individual cases the flux of sense-experiences, or also of specific mental experiences, may very well leave room for doubt: this is not possible in all cases. Where differences are gross, a self-evidence is attainable which renders all doubt unjustifiable.

Appendix

Modern Humeanism

Hume's philosophy, with its richly brilliant psychological analyses, and its systematically applied psychologism in epistemology, corresponds so closely to tendencies dominant in our time, that it could scarcely fail to have a lively influence. One can perhaps even say that Hume has never been more influential than he is now, and one could even apply the name 'modern Humeans' to quite a fair number of contemporary thinkers. Here again one may note that, in this spread of historical influence, the errors have spread as much as, or more than, the good features. Particularly as regards the doctrine of the *distinctio rationis*, recent writings often offer us utterances or explanations which fit in with the radical sense of this doctrine.[1] H. Cornelius has, however, taken up this doctrine in a peculiarly wholehearted, articulate

---

[1] Cf. also, e.g. B. Erdmann, *Logik*, I, p. 80.

manner: his *Psychologie* is an attempt to work out a fully-developed, psychologistic theory of knowledge, in the most extreme manner so far conceived, on the basis of modern psychology. To the extent that his work really is psychology, it contains many highly interesting, stimulating expositions of detail. To the extent, however, that it is epistemology, I think I may say that Cornelius confuses matters pertaining to the *intentional content* of knowledge (to knowledge's ideal sense, to what knowledge means and what is therefore necessarily posited along with it), with matters pertaining to the *intentional object* of knowledge, and both with matters pertaining to the mere *psychological constitution* of the knowledge-experience (perhaps only to mere phenomenal accompaniments of our intention, or to its unconscious, unnoticed genetic grounds). These confusions, I should say, have never been so richly represented in the literature, and have never stamped themselves so strongly on the whole treatment of problems of knowledge, as in the expositions of Cornelius.[1] This is particularly plain in the type of questions which here concern us. In the interests of truth, we shall here linger a little and prove our point by way of a few quotations, partly from the *Psychologie*, partly from a supplementary treatise of our author. To show that a scientific movement has gone astray, nothing is more instructive than to study its consequences as worked out by its adherents, and so to convince oneself that the final theory they think they have gained, has rather involved them in self-evident contradictions.

In regard to the dictated notes of G. E. Müller, of whose content Cornelius wholly approves, he says:[2]

> the distinction of differing features . . . is based . . . on the fact that the contents are gathered into groups according to their similarities, and are named with common names. There is therefore nothing else that *we mean* when we talk of the varying features of a content, than the fact that this content belongs to various such groups of contents, all mentally similar and therefore called by the same name.

[1] Cornelius took over from W. James his attack on 'mosaic-psychology', and his doctrine of 'fringes', but not his epistemological position – James is not a modernizer of Hume's philosophy, as I would say Cornelius is. How little James' genius for observation in the field of the descriptive psychology of presentational experience entails psychologism, can be seen from the present work. For the advance in descriptive analysis that I owe to this distinguished thinker have only facilitated my release from the psychologistic standpoint.

[2] H. Cornelius, 'Uber Gestaltqualitäten', *Zeitschr. f. Psychol. u. Physiol. d. Sinnesorgane*, Vol. 22, p. 103.

Nothing so definite is to be found in Hume: the great thinker would probably have hesitated before accepting *this* proposition. 'What we mean' is surely our sense, and can one say even for an instant that the sense of the proposition 'This tone is faint' is the same as the sense of the proposition. 'This tone belongs to a group (of whatever sort) of similars?' If someone says that, in order to speak of the tone's faintness, one must necessarily imagine tones similar in their faintness, we need not dispute what he says. It may be so. But do we *mean* that the tone belongs to this group, one consisting perhaps of *n* objects? And if the infinitely many similar objects could stand before our eyes as a single group, and actually did so stand, would the sense of our expression be the membership of this group? Naturally the utterances 'A tone is faint' and 'A tone belongs to the sum total of objects alike in their faintness' are semantically equivalent, but equivalence is not identity. If someone says that talk about faintness of tones could arise only if we had noticed similarities among faint tones, and that, further, the memory-traces of such previous experiences are somehow excited when we meaningfully speak of such tones, and that their dispositional after-effects determine the character of our present experience, he may well be right. But what has all this to do with our sense, with what we *mean* by our words? My reference is plainly an immediately given, present experience. How this experience, with its evident content, may have *arisen*; what may be necessarily true of it from the genetic standpoint; what may underlie it physiologically or psychologically, whether in the marginal or the unconscious – all these are interesting themes for enquiry. But it is absurd to seek information about our meaning along such paths. It is an error more or less analogous to the common materialism that seeks to assure us that tones really are air-vibrations, excitations of the acoustic nerve etc. Here, too, theoretical hypotheses which explain the given genetically, are substituted for the given.

That we are not here dealing with a passing looseness of expression on Cornelius' part, is shown by his further statements. We read:

We need hardly say that, on the theory just set forth, this 'common feature' of simple contents cannot be used generally to explain the similarity among these contents – as one is accustomed to reduce the similarity of two carpets to an exact match of colour. *For to assert*

such a match of colour is on the present theory nothing but to assert the
similarity of both contents with other previously known contents.

The one assertion *is* the other (this is stressed by Cornelius), they are therefore the same assertion. It would therefore harmonize with the sense of our statement that the assertion of this colour-match had a different sense for each man, and a different sense at different times. It would depend on the 'otherwise known' contents, and thus on previously experienced contents, which plainly differ from man to man, and from time to time.

When Cornelius adds that the 'meaning of predicates need not appear in the form of separate presentations on each occasion, but can be given in "rudimentary association",' we are not greatly helped: what actual associations cannot do, 'rudimentary' association, brought in as a substitute, cannot do either. Cornelius so darkens facts with theory that he even says[1] that the expression 'abstract content' or 'abstract presentation' are 'abbreviations' for 'presentation of the similarity in a certain respect of one content to others'. *Which* of the various features of a content is spoken of at a time, in which *direction* or *respect* the content is treated, depends on 'which of these differing similarities will be brought to consciousness (will be "inwardly perceived" by us)'.[2]

Cornelius will not permit us to call his conception 'nominalistic'. Yet extreme nominalism has always thought that similarity mediated the relation between a general name and the class it applies to, and for Cornelius, as for such nominalism, general names are in a manner equivocal. Psychological grounds (the theory maintains) limit the application of a name to a class, but the name's meaning consists in particular similarities experienced from moment to moment, and therefore varies from case to case. The ideal unity of the class sets bounds to this multiplicity of meanings, but it does not and cannot create the single meaning of the univocal concept. But how we should know anything of this ideal unity, of *the* group of objects which *one* similarity encompasses, remains, on the theory, mysterious.[3] The content of the theory liquidates its own presupposition.

[1] Loc. cit. p. 108.
[2] Loc. cit. p. 107.
[3] This would seem in essentials to be Meinong's argument (*Zeitsch f. Psych.* vol. 21, p. 235), though his theory also leaves out the ideal consciousness of unity. Only a consideration of the identity of our intention, and of its peculiar form, will make Meinong's objection cogent.

A certain sense that the consciousness of generality also makes itself felt descriptively and demands explanation, shows itself in several passages in Cornelius. We read, e.g., that a predicate-word, in virtue of its origin and meaning, does not stand for this or that individual content, nor for a certain number of particular contents, but rather for something common to all these contents. 'The general idea associated with the predicate, which determines its meaning, is the *memory of the similarity binding all those contents together*, a thing not further describable, but immediately known to internal perception.' Of course the 'thing not further describable but immediately known to internal perception' is the peculiar consciousness of meaning, the *act* of general meaning: but the words certainly manage to describe this indescribable, and, it seems to me, in an incorrect fashion, since they substitute a sense-content for an 'act-character', and a fictitious sense-content at that, one at least that eludes phenomenological scrutiny.

If we do not take this passage quite literally, let us seek closer guidance in Cornelius' exposition of psychology, to see how Cornelius does justice to the meaning-conferring character of acts: this, as the thing really requiring explanation, should be sharply focussed, distinguished in regard to its essential modifications, and set up in these fixed differences to illuminate genetic analysis. Here *two* fundamental confusions may be noted. The first is the confusion of the *objective* fact, that the general name is confined by associative connections to the circle of similarity, with the *subjective* fact, that we mean the universal in the individual act, and so refer ourselves in our intention to the class, or to an indefinite individual as member of that class, or to the unitary species etc. This is the confusion on which extreme nominalism is, as it were, nourished: it alone makes such nominalism possible, with it such nominalism stands and falls. Mixed up with this first confusion, there is a second confusion in Cornelius's *Psychologie* which runs basically different things together, the confusion of the *inexactness* of memory, of the *indistinctness* and fluidity of 'obscurely' reproduced images, with the *character of generality* which characterizes the consciousness of generality as its act-form, or with the *indefiniteness of content* in our intention which makes up the *definite* meaning of the '*indefinite*' article. The following quotations may serve to prove our point:

'The more that similar contents have been experienced, the less will ... their memory images refer back to temporally *definite* contents, and the more will they achieve the character of *general* presentations, and so be able to serve as symbols of any content whatever within definite limits of similarity.'[1] Next to this we put the following passage:

> A word heard for the first time cannot as yet be understood, but as soon as any of the other contents which occurred together with the verbal sound-complex we once heard, is recalled together with it, this word's *first meaning* is given ...[2] Corresponding to the ... inexactitude of recall, the word's meaning will at first likewise be *inexact*. Since the memory presentation associated with the word does not merely serve to symbolize a *completely determined* experience, but *leaves its properties undetermined within certain limits*, the word likewise must be rendered ambiguous through its association with this memory presentation. A later content, conversely, will likewise be in a position to be associated with the word as long as its difference from the content previously bound up with this word, does not go beyond these limits ... When the meaning of a word thus emerges ... an *abstract*, ambiguous symbol is necessarily created, standing equally for a series of different contents alike in a particular respect. The word obtains *conceptual* meaning to the extent that, in virtue of the emergence of its meaning, it serves the individual as a symbol for all contents lying within certain limits in a definite similarity-series.[3]

At the close of the same section we read further:[4]

> We find ... that not only words, but also presentations can be general (and are in fact always general within limits) in the sense in which conceptualism asserts such generality. This generality, however, remains bound within limits fixed by our acquired fineness of discrimination, whereas the generality of the word is in no way limited by the limited generality of the associated image.
>
> That there is no presentation of a triangle in which the properties of the acute-angled and obtuse-angled triangle are united, we can unconditionally grant to Berkeley as against Locke, but that *in every*

[1] *Psychologie als Erfahrungswissenschaft*, p. 58.
[2] Does the circumstance that an α recalls a β, make β the 'meaning' of the 'expression'? If so, the church is the 'meaning' of the presbytery etc.
[3] Following on this, meaning is defined as the range covered by the possible application of a name – in contrast with talk of the 'emergence of meaning' which deals with a sense of words which comes alive in each individual case. But the distinction between meaning as sense, and meaning as naming, is never completely brought out by Cornelius.
[4] Loc. cit. p. 66 *ff.*

presentation of a triangle completely definite relations of sides and angles are presented could be *denied* as definitely. We can as little frame the image of a triangle with a definite, wholly exact proportion of sides, as we are in a position to draw it. The presentation just spoken of is impossible since the differences of form between acute and obtuse-angled triangles are too gross and familiar, for us to be in any possible doubt regarding the corresponding properties in the case of a triangular form. The fully-executed presentation of a completely determinate triangle is also impossible for the reason that our discrimination of triangular forms can never be quite exact – small differences at least are lost in memory.

The confusions noted above at once spring out in the above quotation. A symbol for a single item, which, through our regular confusion of this single item with similar singulars, stands for each member of a range of similars, and can presumably recall each such member, is, on the view of Cornelius, a general symbol. The indifference of the general concept towards such features of its object as do not fall within its content, is further identified with the vagueness of the memory-image. And, in his final passage, Cornelius thinks that he can mediate in the Berkeleyan–Lockean dispute over the general triangle, by substituting for a question about the sensuous presentability of a triangle having conflicting properties (Locke's idea of a triangle), the quite different question as to the possibility of framing a precise mental image of a geometrically definite triangle of given proportions, or of recognizing one so framed as corresponding to our geometrical ideal, and of distinguishing it from others slightly different. In this indefiniteness, taken as vagueness, seems confused with inexactness in the exemplification of an ideal. Cornelius thinks that a sensuous triangle can unite contradictory properties, infinitely many of these in fact: it must only avoid trying to unite large differences, like those between being obtuse-angled and being acute-angled. One would hardly care to accept such a psychologistic rehabilitation of Locke's idea of a triangle, even when confined to such finer differences. We cannot agree to believe something to be psychologically possible if it is logically and geometrically absurd.

CHAPTER SIX

Separation of Varying Concepts of
Abstraction and Abstract

---

§40 *Confusion of concepts of abstraction and abstract concerned
with non-independent part-contents, on the one hand, and Species
on the other*

THE 'attentional' theory of abstraction presupposes, what the
doctrine of the *distinctio rationis* rejects, *that there is a certain
difference in our contents themselves, corresponding to the difference
between abstract and concrete.* On the *distinctio rationis* doctrine there
are only one kind of parts, i.e. 'pieces', parts capable of separation
or of being presented as separated. On the former view, however,
one distinguishes between 'independent' parts (in Stumpf's
terminology), on the one hand, and non-independent 'part-
contents', on the other. Among the latter we count the inner
determinations of a content (exclusive of its 'pieces'), and among
these also the forms of unity discernible in this content (or,
objectively regarded, present in it), through which its parts are
combined to make up the unity of the whole. In relation to this
same distinction, one speaks also of *concrete* and *abstract contents* or
parts of contents.[1]

In the theory of abstraction since Locke, the problem of
abstraction in the sense of an emphatic pointing to 'abstract contents' has
been mixed up with the problem of *abstraction in the sense of
concept-formation.* In regard to the latter, we are concerned to give
a descriptive analysis of the essence of the act in which we are
self-evidently aware of a Species, or to clarify the meaning of
general names by recourse to fulfilling intuitions. From an
empirical, psychological viewpoint, we must try to explore the

---

[1] Investigation III is devoted to closer research into this distinction, with a
necessary extension of the distinction to abstract objects and parts of objects in
general.

corresponding psychological facts in the context of human consciousness, the genetic origin of men's general presentations in the natural process of naïve, unconsidered living or in the artificial process of deliberate, logical concept-formation. The abstract presentations which are *here* in question, are presentations whose intention is to Species and not to non-independent or abstract contents. Should these intentions be intuitively fulfilled, concrete intuitions with (as it were) stressed part-contents will serve as their foundation. The intended Species are not, however, these latter part-contents; however much we may stress the latter in our consciousness of generality, they do not become our intended objects themselves, nor are they objects of separate contemplation. There is, however, a constant confusion, as can be seen from our present critical investigation, between abstract, non-independent moments *in the object*, and the *Species*, or between the corresponding *subjectively experienced* abstract contents and *abstract concepts* (the meanings of certain names), or also between the acts of emphasis or *regarding* of these abstract contents, and the *acts of general presentation*. Locke, e.g., wants abstract ideas to be general meanings, but they are described as features of objects, and psychologized as abstract sense-contents torn from concrete intuitions. The 'attentional' theory likewise points to the possibility of a peculiar notice paid to such abstract contents (without a tearing of them from their context), and thinks that it has thereby shed light on the origin of our general concepts (as meanings). In the same vein some deny the intuitive character of abstract contents,[1] though, as aspects of concrete intuitions, they must be intuited with the latter: this error occurs since men are led astray by the inaccessibility of general concepts to sensuous intuition. If it is absurd to try to paint tones, or to represent colours by smells, or, generally, to represent one heterogeneous content by another, it is doubly absurd to try to represent what is essentially non-sensuous sensuously.

We may say in general that there are differing concepts of abstract and abstraction that call for distinction: our present task is to pursue their distinctions.

---

[1] See, e.g. Höfler–Meinong *Logik*, p. 25. Cf. also my critical remark regarding Twardowski, above p. 360 *f*.

§41 *Separation of concepts grouped about the concept of the non-independent content*

If we adhere to the talk of 'contents' favoured by recent theories of abstraction, we may say:

(*a*) '*Abstract*' contents are *non-independent* contents, '*concrete*' contents are *independent*. We think of this difference as objectively determined, perhaps, as follows: concrete contents are by their nature such as to be capable of existing in and for themselves, whereas abstract contents are only possible in or attached to concrete contents.[1]

It is plain that this talk about *contents* can and must be carried further than it is in the phenomenological sense of real (*reellen*) elements in consciousness. The phenomenal external object which appears, but which is not a real datum of consciousness – at least if one does not falsely interpret the 'intentional' or merely *intended* object, as a real constituent of the experience in which the intention takes place – is as a whole concrete: its immanent determinations, colour, form etc., understood as moments constituting its unity, are abstract. This *objective* distinction between abstract and concrete is the more general, since immanent contents are only a special class of objects (which naturally does not mean of *things*). The difference in question could therefore more suitably be called a difference between abstract and concrete *objects* or parts of objects. If I here still continue to talk of 'contents', I do so as not to give persistent offence to most of my readers. The distinction has arisen in the field of psychology, where intuitive illustration naturally grasps at sensuous examples. Here the interpretation of the word 'object' to mean a thing, is so dominant, that to call a colour or form an object might be felt disturbing or even confusing. We must, however, bear in mind that *talk about contents is not here at all restricted to the sphere of contents of consciousness in any real (reellen) sense, but embraces all individual objects and parts of objects as well*. We do not even restrict ourselves to the sphere of objects which are intuitive to us. The restriction has, rather, an ontological significance: objects are certainly possible, that in fact lie beyond the phenomena accessible to any human consciousness. The distinction, in short, concerns

[1] There will be more about the justification and content of this assertion in the next Investigation.

individual objects as such with unrestricted generality, its true place is in the framework of an *a priori* formal ontology.

(*b*) Taking the objective (ontological) concept of 'abstract contents' as our foundation, we may mean by 'abstraction' the *act* through which an abstract content is distinguished, i.e. through which it is not prised loose, but none the less made the peculiar object of an intuitive presentation directed upon it. It appears in and with the relevant concretum, from which it is abstracted, but it is specially meant, and further not merely meant (as in 'indirect' merely symbolic presentation) but also intuitively given *as* what it is meant as being.

(*c*) Here we must, however, take account of an important difference that has been more than once previously emphasized.[1] If we pay attention to one of the side-surfaces of a cube which appears before us, this surface is the 'abstract content' of our intuitive presentation. But the genuinely *experienced* content, which corresponds to this phenomenal side-surface, itself differs from the latter: it only forms the basis of an 'interpretation', through which, while it is sensed, a side of the cube differing from itself manages to appear. The sensed content is not in this case the object of our intuitive presentation: it first becomes such an object in psychological or phenomenological 'reflection'. Descriptive analysis none the less teaches us that it is not merely contained in the total concrete appearance of the cube, but that it is in a certain fashion set in relief, accented as against all other contents, which in *their* presentation of the side-surface in question do not function representatively. It naturally remains so emphasized, when it becomes *itself the object* of a presentative intuition peculiarly directed to *it*, except that then (in reflection) this intuition is added. This setting-in-relief of the content, which itself is *no act*, but a descriptive peculiarity of the phenomenal side of the acts in which the content becomes the bearer of its own intention, could likewise be called 'abstraction'. We should thus have laid down a totally new concept of abstraction.[2]

(*d*) If one assumes that abstraction is a peculiar act or (in general) a descriptively peculiar experience, responsible for setting the abstract content in relief from its concrete background, or if one sees in the manner of such setting in relief the essence of the

---

[1] Cf. also Investigation vi, §15.
[2] In the strict sense to be laid down in Investigation v, §9 *ff.*

abstract content as such, one comes to yet another concept of the abstract. Its difference as against the concrete, is *not sought in the intrinsic nature of its contents*, but *in the manner in which they are given*. A content is said to be abstract, in so far *as it is abstracted*, concrete in so far as it is *not* abstracted.

It will readily be noted that the tendency to characterize a difference in content by having recourse to acts, stems from a confusion with more advanced concepts of abstract and concrete, in which the essence of the matter certainly lies in the acts.

(*e*) If one understands by abstraction, in the *positive* sense, the *preferential notice paid* to a content, by abstraction in the *negative* sense the *ignoring* of simultaneously given contents, the word loses its exclusive relation to abstract, in the sense of non-independent, contents. Even in the case of concrete contents one speaks, certainly only in a negative sense, of abstraction: one attends, e.g., to such contents 'in abstraction from their background'.

§42 *Separation of the concepts that group themselves about the concept of the Species*

(*a*) One distinguishes abstract and concrete *concepts*: by 'concepts' one understands the *meanings of names*. To this distinction there accordingly corresponds a distinction of names: in a nominalistic logic only this grammatical distinction tends to be drawn. We may very well start with grammar. Names can name individuals, e.g. 'man', 'Socrates', likewise attributes, e.g. 'virtue', 'whiteness', 'similarity'. The former are called 'concrete', the latter 'abstract' names. Predicative expressions corresponding to the latter, e.g. 'virtuous', 'white', 'similar', count as concrete names. More precisely we should have to say that they are concrete when the possible subjects to which they relate are concrete subjects. This is not always the case. Names like 'attribute', 'colour', 'number' etc., relate predicatively to attributes (as specific singulars) and not to individuals, or at least only mediately to individuals, and with an alteration in predicative sense.

Behind this grammatical distinction there is plainly a logical one, the distinction, namely, between *nominal meanings directed to attributes* and *nominal meanings directed to objects in so far as they share in such attributes*. If one follows Herbart in calling all logical presentations (this means, we hold, all nominal meanings) 'concepts', their concepts in this sense divide into abstract and concrete. But if one prefers to talk of concepts in *another* sense, which puts *concept = attribute*, we have a distinction among the meanings which present concepts as such, and which present the objects of concepts. This is a relative distinction in so far as objects of concepts can, in relation to certain new objects, have the character of concepts. This cannot, however, continue *in infinitum*, and we necessarily come at last to the absolute distinction between concepts on the one hand, and those objects of concepts, that can no more function as concepts, on the other. On one side there will therefore be attributes, on the other side objects that 'have' attributes without themselves being attributes. To the distinction of meanings there accordingly corresponds a distinction in the field of objects, the distinction, in other words, between individual and specific (i.e. 'general') objects. General objects and general presentations or meanings, i.e. *direct* presentations of general-objects, are alike called concepts, but equivocally so. The concept of Redness is either Redness itself – as when its manifold objects, i.e. red things, are opposed to this concept – or it is the meaning of the name 'redness'. Both plainly stand in the same relation to one another as do the meaning *Socrates* and Socrates himself. The word 'meaning' is no doubt likewise equivocal, so that men do not hesitate at times to call the object of a presentation a 'meaning', and at times to say the same of its 'content' (the *sense* of its name). To the extent that a meaning is also called a 'concept', the relative talk of concept and object of concept likewise becomes ambiguous. At one time one is dealing with the relation, just now taken as basic, between the attribute (Redness) and the object to which this attribute belongs (the red house), at another time with the totally different relation between the logical presentation (the meaning, e.g., of the word 'redness', or of the proper name 'Thetis') and the presented object (the attribute Redness and the goddess Thetis).

(*b*) The distinction between concrete and abstract presentations can also be interpreted in another fashion: *a presentation can be called concrete* when it directly *presents an individual object*, without the mediation of conceptual (attributive) presentations, abstract in the contrary case. On the one side, in the realm of meanings, we shall then have the *meanings of proper names*, on the other side *all other nominal meanings*.

(*c*) To the above marked off meanings of the word 'abstract', there corresponds a new range of meanings for talk of 'abstraction'. This will include the acts through which abstract 'concepts' arise. Put more precisely, we are dealing with *the acts in which general names achieve their direct relation to specific unities*, and also with the acts which belong with these names in their attributive or predicative function, in which, therefore, forms like *an A, all A, some A, S which is A* etc., are constituted; and lastly with the acts in which the objects apprehended in these manifold forms of thought are self-evidently 'given', with the acts, in other words, in which our conceptual intentions are fulfilled, achieve self-evidence and clarity. Thus we directly apprehend the Specific Unity *Redness* on the basis of a singular intuition of something red. We look to its moment of red, but we perform a peculiar act, whose intention is directed to the 'Idea', the 'universal'. Abstraction in the sense of this act is wholly different from the mere attention to, or emphasis on, the moment of red; to indicate this difference we have repeatedly spoken of *ideational or generalizing abstraction*. This is the act aimed at by traditional talk of 'abstraction': through 'abstraction' in this sense we do not get at individual traits, but at general concepts (direct presentations of attributes as unities for thought). The same talk possibly extends to conceptual presentations of the more complex forms indicated; in the presentation *an A, several A's* etc., there is an abstraction from all other properties. The abstract presentation *A* takes on new 'forms', but acquires no new 'matter'.

International Library of Philosophy & Scientific Method

Editor: Ted Honderich

List of titles, page two

International Library of Psychology Philosophy & Scientific Method

Editor: C K Ogden

List of titles, page six

ROUTLEDGE AND KEGAN PAUL LTD
68 Carter Lane London EC4

International Library of Philosophy and Scientific Method
(*Demy 8vo*)

Allen, R. E. (Ed.)
Studies in Plato's Metaphysics
Contributors: J. L. Ackrill, R. E. Allen, R. S. Bluck, H. F. Cherniss, F. M.
Cornford, R. C. Cross, P. T. Geach, R. Hackforth, W. F. Hicken, A. C. Lloyd,
G. R. Morrow, G. E. L. Owen, G. Ryle, W. G. Runciman, G. Vlastos
464 pp. 1965. (2nd Impression 1967.) 70s.

Armstrong, D. M.
Perception and the Physical World
208 pp. 1961. (3rd Impression 1966.) 25s.

A Materialist Theory of the Mind
376 pp. 1967. (2nd Impression 1969.) 50s.

Bambrough, Renford (Ed.)
New Essays on Plato and Aristotle
Contributors: J. L. Ackrill, G. E. M. Anscombe, Renford Bambrough,
R. M. Hare, D. M. MacKinnon, G. E. L. Owen, G. Ryle, G. Vlastos
184 pp. 1965. (2nd Impression 1967.) 28s.

Barry, Brian
Political Argument
382 pp. 1965. (3rd Impression 1968.) 50s.

Bird, Graham
Kant's Theory of Knowledge:
An Outline of One Central Argument in the *Critique of Pure Reason*
220 pp. 1962. (2nd Impression 1965.) 28s.

Brentano, Franz
The True and the Evident
Edited and narrated by Professor R. Chisholm
218 pp. 1965. 40s.

The Origin of Our Knowledge of Right and Wrong
Edited by Oskar Kraus. English edition edited by Roderick M. Chisholm.
Translated by Roderick M. Chisholm and Elizabeth H. Schneewind
174 pp. 1969. 40s.

Broad, C. D.
Lectures on Physical Research
Incorporating the Perrott Lectures given in Cambridge University in 1959
and 1960
461 pp. 1962. (2nd Impression 1966.) 56s.

Crombie, I. M.
An Examination of Plato's Doctrine
1. Plato on Man and Society
408 pp. 1962. (3rd Impression 1969.) 42s.
II. Plato on Knowledge and Reality
583 pp. 1963. (2nd Impression 1967.) 63s.

International Library of Philosophy and Scientific Method
(*Demy 8vo*)

Day, John Patrick
Inductive Probability
352 pp. 1961. 40s.

Dretske, Fred I.
Seeing and Knowing
270 pp. 1969. 35s.

Ducasse, C. J.
Truth, Knowledge and Causation
263 pp. 1969. 50s.

Edel, Abraham
Method in Ethical Theory
379 pp. 1963. 32s.

Fann, K. T. (Ed.)
Symposium on J. L. Austin
Contributors: A. J. Ayer, Jonathan Bennett, Max Black, Stanley Cavell, Walter Cerf, Roderick M. Chisholm, L. Jonathan Cohen, Roderick Firth, L. W. Forguson, Mats Furberg, Stuart Hampshire, R. J. Hirst, C. G. New, P. H. Nowell-Smith, David Pears, John Searle, Peter Strawson, Irving Thalberg, J. O. Urmson, G. J. Warnock, Jon Wheatly, Alan White
512 pp. 1969.

Flew, Anthony
Hume's Philosophy of Belief
A Study of his First "Inquiry"
269 pp. 1961. (2nd Impression 1966.) 30s.

Fogelin, Robert J.
Evidence and Meaning
Studies in Analytical Philosophy
200 pp. 1967. 25s.

Gale, Richard
The Language of Time
256 pp. 1968. 40s.

Goldman, Lucien
The Hidden God
A Study of Tragic Vision in the *Pensées* of Pascal and the Tragedies of Racine. Translated from the French by Philip Thody
424 pp. 1964. 70s.

Hamlyn, D. W.
Sensation and Perception
A History of the Philosophy of Perception
222 pp. 1961. (3rd Impression 1967.) 25s.

3

2*

International Library of Philosophy and Scientific Method
(Demy 8vo)

Kemp, J.
Reason, Action and Morality
216 pp. 1964. 30s.

Körner, Stephan
Experience and Theory
An Essay in the Philosophy of Science
272 pp. 1966. (2nd Impression 1969.) 45s.

Lazerowitz, Morris
Studies in Metaphilosophy
276 pp. 1964. 35s.

Linsky, Leonard
Referring
152 pp. 1968. 35s.

MacIntosh, J. J., and Coval, S. C. (Ed.)
The Business of Reason
280 pp. 1969. 42s.

Merleau-Ponty, M.
Phenomenology of Perception
Translated from the French by Colin Smith
487 pp. 1962. (4th Impression 1967.) 56s.

Perelman, Chaim
The Idea of Justice and the Problem of Argument
Introduction by H. L. A. Hart. Translated from the French by John Petrie
224 pp. 1963. 28s.

Ross, Alf
Directives, Norms and their Logic
192 pp. 1967. 35s.

Schlesinger, G.
Method in the Physical Sciences
148 pp. 1963. 21s.

Sellars, W. F.
Science, Perception and Reality
374 pp. 1963. (2nd Impression 1966.) 50s.

Shwayder, D. S.
The Stratification of Behaviour
A System of Definitions Propounded and Defended
428 pp. 1965. 56s.

Skolimowski, Henryk
Polish Analytical Philosophy
288 pp. 1967. 40s.

4

International Library of Philosophy and Scientific Method
(*Demy 8vo*)

Smart, J. J. C.
Philosophy and Scientific Realism
168 pp. 1963. (3rd Impression 1967.) 25s.

Smythies, J. R. (Ed.)
Brain and Mind
Contributors: Lord Brain, John Beloff, C. J. Ducasse, Antony Flew, Hartwig
Kuhlenbeck, D. M. MacKay, H. H. Price, Anthony Quinton and J. R. Smythies
288 pp. 1965. 40s.

Science and E.S.P.
Contributors: Gilbert Murray, H. H. Price, Rosalind Heywood, Cyril Burt,
C. D. Broad, Francis Huxley and John Beloff
320 pp. about 40s.

Taylor, Charles
The Explanation of Behaviour
288 pp. 1964. (2nd Impression 1965.) 40s.

Williams, Bernard, and Montefiore, Alan
British Analytical Philosophy
352 pp. 1965. (2nd Impression 1967.) 45s.

Winch, Peter (Ed.)
Studies in the Philosophy of Wittgenstein
Contributors: Hidé Ishiguro, Rush Rhees, D. S. Shwayder, John W. Cook,
L. R. Reinhardt and Anthony Manser
224 pp. 1969.

Wittgenstein, Ludwig
Tractatus Logico-Philosophicus
The German text of the *Logisch-Philosophische Abhandlung* with a new
translation by D. F. Pears and B. F. McGuinness. Introduction by
Bertrand Russell
188 pp. 1961. (3rd Impression 1966.) 21s.

Wright, Georg Henrik Von
Norm and Action
A Logical Enquiry. The Gifford Lectures
232 pp. 1963. (2nd Impression 1964.) 32s.

The Varieties of Goodness
The Gifford Lectures
236 pp. 1963. (3rd Impression 1966.) 28s.

Zinkernagel, Peter
Conditions for Description
Translated from the Danish by Olaf Lindum
272 pp. 1962. 37s. 6d.

International Library of Psychology, Philosophy, and Scientific Method
(Demy 8vo)

PHILOSOPHY

Anton, John Peter
Aristotle's Theory of Contrariety
276 pp. 1957. 25s.

Black, Max
The Nature of Mathematics
A Critical Survey
242 pp. 1933. (5th Impression 1965.) 28s.

Bluck, R. S.
Plato's Phaedo
A Translation with Introduction, Notes and Appendices
226 pp. 1955. 21s.

Broad, C. D.
Five Types of Ethical Theory
322 pp. 1930. (9th Impression 1967.) 30s.

The Mind and Its Place in Nature
694 pp. 1925. (7th Impression 1962.) 70s. See also Lean, Martin

Buchler, Justus (Ed.)
The Philosophy of Peirce
Selected Writings
412 pp. 1940. (3rd Impression 1956.) 35s.

Burtt, E. A.
The Metaphysical Foundations of Modern Physical Science
A Historical and Critical Essay
364 pp. 2nd (revised) edition 1932. (5th Impression 1964.) 35s.

Carnap, Rudolf
The Logical Syntax of Language
Translated from the German by Amethe Smeaton
376 pp. 1937. (7th Impression 1967.) 40s.

Chwistek, Leon
The Limits of Science
Outline of Logic and of the Methodology of the Exact Sciences
With Introduction and Appendix by Helen Charlotte Brodie
414 pp. 2nd edition 1949. 32s.

Cornford, F. M.
Plato's Theory of Knowledge
The Theaetetus and Sophist of Plato
Translated with a running commentary
358 pp. 1935. (7th Impression 1967.) 28s.

6

International Library of Psychology, Philosophy, and Scientific Method
(*Demy 8vo*)

Cornford, F. M. (*continued*)
Plato's Cosmology
The Timaeus of Plato
Translated with a running commentary
402 pp. Frontispiece. 1937. (5th Impression 1966.) 45s.

Plato and Parmenides
Parmenides' *Way of Truth* and Plato's *Parmenides*
Translated with a running commentary
280 pp. 1939. (5th Impression 1964.) 32s.

Crawshay-Williams, Rupert
Methods and Criteria of Reasoning
An Inquiry into the Structure of Controversy
312 pp. 1957. 32s.

Fritz, Charles A.
Bertrand Russell's Construction of the External World
252 pp. 1952. 30s.

Hulme, T. E.
Speculations
Essays on Humanism and the Philosophy of Art
Edited by Herbert Read. Foreword and Frontispiece by Jacob Epstein
296 pp. 2nd edition 1936. (6th Impression 1965.) 40s.

Lazerowitz, Morris
The Structure of Metaphysics
With a Foreword by John Wisdom
262 pp. 1955. (2nd Impression 1963.) 30s.

Lodge, Rupert C.
Plato's Theory of Art
332 pp. 1953. 25s.

Mannheim, Karl
Ideology and Utopia
An Introduction to the Sociology of Knowledge
With a Preface by Louis Wirth. Translated from the German by Louis Wirth and Edward Shils
360 pp. 1954. (2nd Impression 1966.) 30s.

Moore, G. E.
Philosophical Studies
360 pp. 1922. (6th Impression 1965.) 35s. See also Ramsey, F. P.

International Library of Psychology, Philosophy, and Scientific Method
(*Demy 8vo*)

Ogden, C. K., and Richards, I. A.
The Meaning of Meaning
A Study of the Influence of Language upon Thought and of the
Science of Symbolism
With supplementary essays by B. Malinowski and F. G. Crookshank
394 pp. 10th Edition 1949. (6th Impression 1967.) 32s.
See also Bentham, J.

Peirce, Charles, *see* Buchler, J.

Ramsey, Frank Plumpton
The Foundations of Mathematics and other Logical Essays
Edited by R. B. Braithwaite. Preface by G. E. Moore
·318 pp. 1931. (4th Impression 1965.) 35s.

Richards, I. A.
Principles of Literary Criticism
312 pp. 2nd Edition. 1926. (17th Impression 1966.) 30s.

Mencius on the Mind. Experiments in Multiple Definition
190 pp. 1932. (2nd Impression 1964.) 28s.

Russell, Bertrand, *see* Fritz, C. A.; Lange, F. A.; Wittgenstein, L.

Smart, Ninian
Reasons and Faiths
An Investigation of Religious Discourse, Christian and Non-
Christian
230 pp. 1958. (2nd Impression 1965.) 28s.

Vaihinger, H.
The Philosophy of As If
A System of the Theoretical, Practical and Religious Fictions of
Mankind
Translated by C. K. Ogden
428 pp. 2nd edition 1935. (4th Impression 1965.) 45s.

Wittgenstein, Ludwig
Tractatus Logico-Philosophicus
With an Introduction by Bertrand Russell, F.R.S., German text with an
English translation en regard
216 pp. 1922. (9th Impression 1962.) 21s.
For the Pears-McGuinness translation—*see page 5*

Wright, Georg Henrik von
Logical Studies
214 pp. 1957. (2nd Impression 1967.) 28s.

International Library of Psychology, Philosophy, and Scientific Method
(*Demy 8vo*)

Zeller, Eduard
Outlines of the History of Greek Philosophy
Revised by Dr. Wilhelm Nestle. Translated from the German by L. R. Palmer
248 pp. 13th (revised) edition 1931. (5th Impression 1963.) 28s.

PSYCHOLOGY

Adler, Alfred
The Practice and Theory of Individual Psychology
Translated by P. Radin
368 pp. 2nd (revised) edition 1929. (8th Impression 1964.) 30s.

Eng, Helga
The Psychology of Children's Drawings
From the First Stroke to the Coloured Drawing
240 pp. 8 colour plates. 139 figures. 2nd edition 1954. (3rd Impression 1966.) 40s.

Koffka, Kurt
The Growth of the Mind
An Introduction to Child-Psychology
Translated from the German by Robert Morris Ogden
456 pp 16 figures. 2nd edition (revised) 1928. (6th Impression 1965.) 45s.
Principles of Gestalt Psychology
740 pp. 112 figures. 39 tables. 1935. (5th Impression 1962.) 60s.

Malinowski, Bronislaw
Crime and Custom in Savage Society
152 pp. 6 plates. 1926. (8th Impression 1966.) 21s.
Sex and Repression in Savage Society
290 pp. 1927. (4th Impression 1953.) 30s.
See also Ogden, C. K.

Murphy, Gardner
An Historical Introduction to Modern Psychology
488 pp. 5th edition (revised) 1949. (6th Impression 1967.) 40s.

Paget, R.
Human Speech
Some Observations, Experiments, and Conclusions as to the Nature, Origin, Purpose and Possible Improvement of Human Speech
374 pp. 5 plates. 1930. (2nd Impression 1963.) 42s.

Petermann, Bruno
The Gestalt Theory and the Problem of Configuration
Translated from the German by Meyer Fortes
364 pp. 20 figures. 1932. (2nd Impression 1950.) 25s.

International Library of Psychology, Philosophy, and Scientific Method
(*Demy 8vo*)

Piaget, Jean
The Language and Thought of the Child
Preface by E. Claparède. Translated from the French by Marjorie Gabain
220 pp. 3rd edition (revised and enlarged) 1959. (3rd Impression 1966.) 30s.

Judgment and Reasoning in the Child
Translated from the French by Marjorie Warden
276 pp. 1928. (5th Impression 1969.) 30s.

The Child's Conception of the World
Translated from the French by Joan and Andrew Tomlinson
408 pp. 1929. (4th Impression 1964.) 40s.

The Child's Conception of Physical Causality
Translated from the French by Marjorie Gabain
(3rd Impression 1965.) 30s.

The Moral Judgment of the Child
Translated from the French by Marjorie Gabain
438 pp. 1932. (4th Impression 1965.) 35s.

The Psychology of Intelligence
Translated from the French by Malcolm Piercy and D. E. Berlyne
198 pp. 1950. (4th Impression 1964.) 18s.

The Child's Conception of Number
Translated from the French by C. Gattegno and F. M. Hodgson
266 pp. 1952. (3rd Impression 1964.) 25s.

The Origin of Intelligence in the Child
Translated from the French by Margaret Cook
448 pp. 1953. (2nd Impression 1966.) 42s.

The Child's Conception of Geometry
In collaboration with Bärbel Inhelder and Alina Szeminska. Translated from the French by E. A. Lunzer
428 pp. 1960. (2nd Impression 1966.) 45s.

Piaget, Jean, and Inhelder, Bärbel
The Child's Conception of Space
Translated from the French by F. J. Langdon and J. L. Lunzer
512 pp. 29 figures. 1956. (3rd Impression 1967.) 42s.

Roback, A. A.
The Psychology of Character
With a Survey of Personality in General
786 pp. 3rd edition (revised and enlarged 1952.) 50s.

Smythies, J. R.
Analysis of Perception
With a Preface by Sir Russell Brain, Bt.
162 pp. 1956. 21s.

International Library of Psychology, Philosophy, and Scientific Method
(*Demy 8vo*)

van der Hoop, J. H.
Character and the Unconscious
A Critical Exposition of the Psychology of Freud and Jung
Translated from the German by Elizabeth Trevelyan
240 pp. 1923. (2nd Impression 1950.) 20s.

Woodger, J. H.
Biological Principles
508 pp. 1929. (Re-issued with a new Introduction 1966.) 60s.

PRINTED BY HEADLEY BROTHERS LTD 109 KINGSWAY LONDON WC2 AND ASHFORD KENT